JUSTICE IN GLOBAL ECONOMIC GOVERNANCE

Studies in Global Justice and Human Rights
Series Editor: Thom Brooks

This series publishes ground-breaking work on key topics in the area of global justice and human rights including democracy, gender, poverty, the environment, and just war. Books in the series are of broad interest to theorists working in politics, international relations, philosophy, and related disciplines.

Published titles
Retheorising Statelessness
Kelly Staples

Health Inequalities and Global Injustice
Patti Tamara Lenard and Christine Straehle

Rwanda and the Moral Obligation of Humanitarian Intervention
Joshua J. Kassner

Institutions in Global Distributive Justice
András Miklós

Human Rights from Community
Oche Onazi

Immigration Justice
Peter W. Higgins

The Morality of Peacekeeping
Daniel H. Levine

International Development and Human Aid
Paulo Barcelos and Gabriele De Angelis

Global Justice and Climate Governance
Alix Dietzel

Data Justice and the Right to the City
Morgan Currie, Jeremy Knox and Callum McGregor

Human Rights and Community-led Development: Lessons from Tostan
Ben Cislaghi

Justice in Global Economic Governance: Normative and Empirical Perspectives on Promoting Fairer Globalisation
Axel Berger, Clara Brandi and Eszter Kollar

Decolonisation and Postcolonial Migration: Citizenship and Empire
Frank Aragbonfoh Abumere

www.euppublishing.com/series/sgjhr

JUSTICE IN GLOBAL ECONOMIC GOVERNANCE

NORMATIVE AND EMPIRICAL PERSPECTIVES ON PROMOTING FAIRER GLOBALISATION

Edited by Axel Berger,
Clara Brandi and Eszter Kollar

EDINBURGH
University Press

Edinburgh University Press is one of the leading university presses in the UK. Publishing new research in the arts and humanities, EUP connects people and ideas to inspire creative thinking, open new perspectives and shape the world we live in. For more information, visit www.edinburghuniversitypress.com.

Edinburgh University Press Ltd
13 Infirmary Street, Edinburgh EH1 1LT

Typeset in 10.75/12.7 Palatino LT Std by
IDSUK (DataConnection) Ltd, and
Printed and bound in the UK using 100% renewable electricity by
CPI Group (UK) Ltd

A CIP record for this book is available from the British Library

ISBN 978 1 3995 3013 2 (hardback)
ISBN 978 1 3995 3015 6 (webready PDF)
ISBN 978 1 3995 3016 3 (epub)

CONTENTS

FIGURES

ACKNOWLEDGEMENTS

This book brings together scholars from diverse fields, including political philosophy, law, economics, and international relations, to address the pressing issues of justice in global economic governance. Given the multipolarity of the international system and the increasing lack of trust between countries of different income and regional groupings the topic of this book seems even more relevant today than when we started this project. Such an ambitious project would not have been possible without the patience, intellectual openness, and collaboration of all contributing authors involved. Their expertise, dedication, and perseverance have been crucial in bringing this volume to life. We would therefore like to express our deepest gratitude to the contributors to this book. Furthermore, we would like to acknowledge project funding of the German Ministry of Economic Cooperation and Development (BMZ) and the state of North Rhine-Westphalia (NRW). Their support was crucial, among other things, to conduct an original workshop at the German Institute of Development and Sustainability (IDOS) that laid the foundation for this volume. Last but not the least we would like to thank our loved ones for their constant support and patience.

LIST OF CONTRIBUTORS

Sara Amighetti is a Postdoctoral Fellow at the Chair of Political Philosophy of the University of Zurich. She holds a PhD in Political Philosophy from University College London and is interested in applied ethics and social and political philosophy. Her research focuses on equality, migration and the ethics and politics of reparations.

Chris Armstrong is a Professor in Political Theory in the Department of Politics and International Relations, University of Southampton. His current research encompasses a wide range of topics normative political theory, including ocean politics, environmental justice, natural resource allocation, global justice and climate change justice.

Ayelet Banai is Senior Lecturer in Politics at the School of Political Sciences and the Haifa Center for German and European Studies, The University of Haifa. Her research focuses on international political theory, self-determination, identity politics and processes of democratisation.

Armando Barrientos is Emeritus Professor of Poverty and Social Justice at the Global Development Institute at the University of Manchester. His research interests lie at the intersection of welfare programmes, labour markets and the evolution of social welfare institutions in emerging economies.

Elizabeth A. Bennett is the Joseph M. Ha Associate Professor of International Affairs and Director of Political Economy at Lewis & Clark College. She is internationally recognised for her expertise on labour exploitation in globalised supply chains.

Kathrin Berensmann is Project Leader and Senior Researcher at the German Institute for Development and Sustainability (IDOS) in Bonn. Her main areas of specialisation are green finance, debt policy, monetary and exchange rate policy, international financial markets and financial sector development.

Axel Berger is Deputy Director (interim) of the German Institute of Development and Sustainability (IDOS). He investigates the design, impact and diffusion patterns of international trade and investment treaties, with a particular emphasis on emerging and developing economies.

Frank Biermann is a Research Professor of Global Sustainability Governance with the Copernicus Institute of Sustainable Development at Utrecht University. He is a leading international scholar in the field of global institutions and organisations related to sustainability, with a wealth of research on international organisations, the Sustainable Development Goals (SDGs), global justice and the fragmented architecture of global governance.

Andrea Bjorklund is a Full Professor and the L.Yves Fortier Chair in International Arbitration and International Commercial Law at McGill University Faculty of Law. She is a renowned expert in international arbitration and litigation, international trade and international investment.

Clara Brandi is Head of Department at the German Institute of Development and Sustainability (IDOS) and Professor of International Economics and Development Economics at the University of Bonn. Her research focus includes global economic governance with a focus on the intersection of economics and sustainable development.

Madison Cartwright is a Senior Lecturer in International Political Economy and the convenor for the Politics and International Relations undergraduate programme at the University of New South Wales. His research interests encompass the political economy, particularly regarding intellectual property, free trade agreements and the intersection of economics and security.

Defne Gönenç is an Associate Professor and program coordinator at the Department of Political Science and International Relations at the Middle East Technical University, Northern Cyprus Campus. She is also a visiting scholar at Istinye University in Istanbul, Türkiye. Her academic research interests include global environmental politics, climate justice, critical theory, and the political economy of developing countries. (particularly Türkiye, Greece, and India).

Aarti Gupta is Professor of Global Environmental Governance with the Environmental Policy Group, Department of Social Sciences, Wageningen University. Her research focuses on global environmental and climate governance, including questions of transparency and accountability.

Christian von Haldenwang is a Project Leader and Senior Researcher at the German Institute for Development and Sustainability (IDOS) in Bonn,

Germany. His research focuses on taxation, decentralisation & urban governance, digitalisation and legitimacy.

Florian Hett is Professor of Digital Economics at the University of Mainz. His research deals with experimental data science, household finance and behavioural economics with a focus on understanding how individuals behave in digital environments.

Sören Hilbrich is a researcher at the German Institute for Development and Sustainability (IDOS) in Bonn, Germany. His research focuses on sustainability, financial markets, and the political institutions that govern the global economy.

Johannes Himmelreich is an Assistant Professor in the Department of Public Administration and International Affairs at the Maxwell School of Syracuse University. His research delves into the realms of applied ethics and political philosophy.

Aaron James is a Professor of Philosophy at UC Irvine. His scholarly pursuits are centred on ethics and political philosophy.

Prakash Kashwan is an Associate Professor of Environmental Studies at Brandeis University. He holds a PhD in Public Policy from Indiana University. His teaching, research, and scholarship focus on the intersections of environment, development, and socio economic and political dimensions of global environmental and climate change.

Jens van 't Klooster is Assistant Professor for Political Economy at the Department of Political Science of the University of Amsterdam. His research focuses on the governance of financial markets, with a specific focus on how climate change and new macroprudential ideas are reshaping the role of central bankers and banking supervisors.

Eszter Kollar is Associate Professor of Philosophy and Ethics of Economics at the Center for Ethics, Social and Political Philosophy, Institute of Philosophy, KU Leuven. Her research focuses on social and global justice and the intricate interplay between struggles for justice, migration, and economic and social structures.

Sabine Laudage Teles is a tax economist at the Organisation for Economic Co-operation and Development (OECD). Her main areas of specialisation are domestic public resource mobilisation, international corporate taxation and transfer pricing rules.

Annabelle Lever is a Professor of Political Philosophy at Sciences Po, Paris. Her current research focuses on equality and democracy.

Daniele Malerba is a Senior Researcher at the German Institute for Development and Sustainability (IDOS) in Bonn. His main areas of specialisation are poverty, economic and social development, social protection and climate change.

Manjiao Chi is Professor and Founding Director of the Center for International Economic Law and Policy (CIELP), School of Law, University of International Business and Economics (UIBE), China. His research interests encompass international trade and investment law, dispute settlement mechanisms, global development and cooperation law.

Marco Meyer is Junior Research Group Lead on the project 'Culpable Ignorance – Moral Knowledge in Organizations' at the Philosophy Department, University of Hamburg. His research draws on philosophy, economics, psychology and data science to address ethical and political issues.

Darrel Moellendorf is a Professor of International Political Theory at Goethe University Frankfurt. Darrel has many interests in political theory and philosophy, including an egalitarian form of cosmopolitanism in the global justice debates.

Jean-Frédéric Morin is Full Professor at the Political Science Department of Laval University. He investigates how international institutions innovate, interact and evolve.

Archna Negi teaches at the Centre for International Politics, Organization and Disarmament, School of International Studies, Jawaharlal Nehru University, New Delhi, India. Her research interests lie in international law and diplomacy, with a focus on trade, environment and climate change.

Chukwumerije Okereke is a Professor of Global Climate and Environmental Governance and Director of Center for Climate and Development at Alex Ekwueme Federal University Ndufu-Alike, Nigeria. He investigates the combination of policies and institutional arrangements that can contribute to addressing climate change and natural resource depletion in Africa.

Miriam Ronzoni is a Professor of Political Theory at the University of Manchester. Miriam is mainly interested in contemporary normative theory, with a focus on global and international issues.

Jakob Schwab is an independent policy consultant, and an Associate Researcher at the German Institute of Development and Sustainablility (IDOS). His work centres on globalization and development, trade and the environment, intergenerational mobility and digitalisation.

Paola Subacchi is Professor of International Economics and Chair Advisory Board at the Global Policy Institute at Queen Mary, University of London. She is a specialist in the field of international finance and monetary systems.

Kok-Chor Tan is Professor of Philosophy at the University of Pennsylvania. His area of expertise lies in the field of political philosophy, particularly delving into the intricate realms of global justice, nationalism, value plurality, equality and human rights.

Cristian Timmermann is a Research Associate at the Ethics of Medicine Group at the University of Augsburg. His research focuses on theoretical and policy-oriented analysis of issues related to the life sciences, social justice, poverty, meaningful work and public goods.

Juri Viehoff is a philosopher working at the Ethics Institute in the Department of Philosophy and Religious Studies at the University of Utrecht. His research centres on moral and political philosophy and topics at the intersection of political philosophy, political economy and public policy.

Ulrich Volz is Professor of Economics and Director of the Centre for Sustainable Finance at SOAS, University of London and a Senior Researcher at the German Institute of Development and Sustainability (IDOS). His research focuses on international finance, macroeconomics, and sustainable finance.

PREFACE

Axel Berger, Clara Brandi and Ester Kollar

The justice of global economic governance is normatively contested and connected to complex empirical questions. While there are many claims about the fairness and unfairness in ongoing debates about globalisation, a systematic analysis of normative and empirical perspectives on the current global economic order and its reform proposal is still lacking. To address this lacuna, this book brings together leading scholars in political philosophy with empirical analysis by influential scholars in international relations, economics and law. Combining these insights and applying a coherent normative framework, this book investigates the most important areas of global economic governance, including trade, investment, finance, labour and taxes.

This book is important and timely as debates about fairness in globalisation have been gaining ever more prominence in the recent past in light of growing geopolitical tensions, financial crises, the economic implications of wars and pandemics and increasing inequality and societal polarisation. Against this background, the book aims to investigate global economic governance from the perspective of justice. Combining insights from political philosophy, law, economics and political science, the book investigates the most important challenges of global economic governance, including in the areas of trade, investment, finance, labour, taxes, intellectual property rights, digitalisation, natural resources and environmental concerns. The book offers a holistic picture of justice concerns that allows accounting for the interdependencies and multidimensional nature of global economic governance.

For each area, there is one chapter with an empirical focus and one chapter with a normative philosophical focus. Empirical chapters provide a detailed analysis of the status quo in a certain policy area. Normative chapters focus on conceptual analysis and normative principles. Based on their different starting points and conceptual approaches all chapters make concrete proposals on how global governance arrangement could be rendered more just. We thus provide the first comprehensive study of global economic governance based on joint empirical and normative analyses by leading scholars from different disciplinary backgrounds.

The book uses a coherent normative framework and argues that reforms of global economic governance should address three key dimensions of justice, which will be operationalised and discussed in the context of key issue areas:

- Firstly, political justice demands reforms that increase the realisation of democratic values in the decision-making procedures of the institutions of global economic governance.
- Secondly, socioeconomic justice aims to reduce poverty and global economic inequality.
- Thirdly, intergenerational justice increases socioeconomic and/or natural capital (e.g. about exhaustible resources, climate change) that we transmit to future generations.

This joint normative framework for conceptualising justice in global economic governance prepares the ground for the authors of the following chapters of this volume, who investigate the state of play of current governance arrangements in eleven specific issues areas. Three of these twin chapters cover issue areas related to the real economy and assess investment, trade and labour. The following four chapters put the spotlight on the financial dimension of the global economy and discuss the financial governance, sustainable finance, taxes and debt. In light of the increasing digitisation of the world economy twin chapters focus on the justice of digitalisation and the related issue area of intellection property rights. The last chapters tackle two crosscutting themes: questions in the context of natural resources and environmental challenges as well as inequality. In the short epilogue, we offer concluding comments on linking empirical and normative perspectives on justice in global economic governance.

Chapter 1

JUSTICE IN GLOBAL ECONOMIC GOVERNANCE: A CONCEPTUAL AND NORMATIVE FRAMEWORK

Sören Hilbrich and Eszter Kollar

INTRODUCTION

Due to the level of global economic interdependence our world has reached, the question of how the global economy should be governed is of utmost importance. The rules of global economic governance have to balance the often-conflicting interests and claims of the diverse actors who participate in or are affected by the global economy. Economic governance structures are never morally neutral; they have particular collective decision-making procedures and they strongly influence how the benefits of economic cooperation are distributed. This book thus asks a twofold question: what kind of justice concerns do existing economic arrangements raise, and how should they be reformed in order to be more just and fair[1] to all?

This chapter provides a conceptual and normative framework regarding justice in global economic governance. The concept of justice is notoriously contested, and even more so when elevated to the global level and applied to international and transnational relations. The chapter aims to introduce the reader to the concept of justice and provide an overview of some of the key distinctions in the contemporary normative philosophy of social and global justice, with special attention to the issues relevant to global economic governance.

[1] The concepts of justice and fairness are closely related. Fairness seems to be used more often (but not exclusively) with regard to procedural issues, while the concept of justice, as is described in this chapter, concerns procedural and substantive issues. One prominent example of how the relationship between fairness and justice can be conceptualised is given in John Rawls' (1971) *A Theory of Justice*. According to Rawls, the basic structure of society should comply with principles of justice to which free and equal citizens would agree in a hypothetical *fair* situation, the original position. The original position is fair in the sense that a *veil of ignorance* hides certain personal characteristics of the participants, such as their race, gender or natural endowments, and should thereby ensure that the participants decide impartially on principles of justice.

The chapter starts by tackling the conceptual question of what the subject of justice is – that is, of what kind of things can be evaluated in light of justice as just or unjust – and of what status the value of justice has with regard to these things. In addition, the chapter discusses the problem of justice in three crucial dimensions, which provide the backbone of this collection: political justice, socioeconomic justice, and intergenerational justice. *Political justice* is concerned with a) the decision-making procedures of the relevant political institutions that should conform to democratic values such as inclusiveness, deliberation and accountability; and b) fostering the capacities of states' self-determination. *Socioeconomic justice* concerns a) the fair distribution of resource endowments and productive capacities among agents of the global economy, and b) reducing global poverty and socioeconomic inequalities. From an *intergenerational justice* perspective, global economic governance needs reform so that a) our generation transmits a greater capital stock to future generations, for instance, with respect to the preservation of our natural environment; as well as b) reckon with and redress past injustices whose enduring effects obstruct the way of justice. These normative desiderata, formulated at a higher level of generality, set the stage for the authors of this volume to investigate i) how governance arrangements look like today, ii) what kind of domain-specific problems of justice they raise, and iii) how the various governance regimes should be reformed and rendered more just.

SUBJECT, FUNCTION, AND SCOPE OF JUSTICE

First, we can approach the idea of justice by distinguishing it from other related principles of international political morality, such as charity or humanitarian assistance. When we say that something is a matter of justice, what we mean is that something is due to a person or a group, as a matter of right or entitlement, and other agents have an obligation to deliver it. Justice is, in this sense, obligatory in a way that charity is not. Another sense in which justice is obligatory is that it can be legitimately enforced by states. Moreover, as Brian Barry (1982) points out, justice is logically prior to charity, because acts of charity – coming to the aid of another person in need – can only be carried out with resources that are rightfully owned. So first the fundamental question of what rightfully belongs to whom, why, and through which procedure, ought to be settled. 'The function of principles of justice is to establish how entitlements to valuable but scarce resources ought to be assigned among a plurality of agents competing over them' (Valentini, 2013, p. 492).

Justice can be understood as concerning a) the right outcome distribution of a set of relevant goods or b) the design of social institutions.

a) According to outcome conceptions of justice, principles of justice are evaluative standards that pertain to a distributive outcome. A utilitarian approach, for instance, seeks to maximise the welfare or utility of a population. Egalitarianism, as an influential alternative approach, rather emphasises the value of equality. Most egalitarians, though, do not think that the ideal distribution is one of perfect equality. Instead, they seek to equalise goods along some dimensions, while allowing inequalities in the distribution of goods along other dimensions. An example is a view called responsibility-adjusted egalitarianism – more commonly referred to as 'luck egalitarianism'. It holds that when unequal distributions result from responsible choices that people make, such as working more hours vs. having more leisure time, they should not be corrected. Instead, when unequal distributions result from external circumstances or internal conditions for which people are not responsible, such as the resources of the family they are born into or innate abilities, they should be corrected or compensated.

b) By contrast, perhaps the most influential account of justice in modern Western philosophy, John Rawls' 'Justice as Fairness', takes institutions to be the primary subject of justice. His *A Theory of Justice*, starts with the proposition that 'Justice is the first virtue of social institutions' (Rawls, 1971, p. 3). This statement includes two claims: firstly, that principles of justice apply to social institutions, and secondly, that the value of justice somehow has a special role in their normative assessment.

Social institutions are distinct from and are constituted by norms, rules and procedures that shape or constrain individual actions and transactions. Rawls calls the major social institutions of a society, which are its 'political constitution and . . . principal economic and social arrangements' (Rawls 1971, p. 7), the *basic structure* of society. He holds that justice as a moral standard of evaluation should apply to the basic structure, and more specifically to 'the way in which the major social institutions distribute fundamental rights and duties and determine the division of advantages from social cooperation' (Rawls, 1971, p. 7).

There are several good reasons to focus on the normative assessment of political and economic institutions, as the contributions in this volume do. One reason Rawls elaborates has to do with their deep and pervasive effect on shaping people's capacities, aspirations and prospects. Basic institutions channel initial inequalities due to contingencies of birth into overall social (dis)advantages. What is just or unjust according to Rawls is not what kind of cards one is dealt with at birth, but how different social arrangements mitigate or exacerbate their effects on one's life prospects. A conception of justice elaborates and publicly justifies what are the morally acceptable and the morally unacceptable institutional effects (Rawls, 1971; Scheffler, 2010). According to Rawls, what free and equal citizens owe one another is that the normative principles that govern the basic structure could be justified from an impartial perspective, leading to a special concern towards improving the situation of the least advantaged members of society.

Another reason to focus justice on institutions has to do with the need to uphold background justice, namely the background conditions under which people act and interact. A series of transactions among individuals that takes place without deceit or coercion, when viewed in isolation, might appear morally unobjectionable. But it can easily lead to a situation in which some suffer from problematic forms of domination or deprivation. Therefore, we need institutions 'to preserve background justice, and a special conception of justice to define how these institutions need to be set up' (Rawls, 1993, p. 267). Safeguarding the erosion of background justice is one important function of just institutions. However, in some areas of global economic governance where agents are regularly transacting with each other, the problem of justice arises due to the lack of proper institutional constraints in place. It is then a demand for justice to create institutions that can achieve and uphold background justice in contexts where it is lacking (Ronzoni, 2009).

Finally, following Rawls, we concur that justice has a special place as *the* primary and overarching value of social structures. It is not merely a valuable feature of an institution alongside other values. A justice judgement is rather the result of the balancing of different more specific values, such as equality or freedom, in an all-things-considered judgement. Justice adjudicates between more specific values and gives them their proper place (Forst, 2012, p. 7f.; Gosepath, 2004, p. 91f.). For instance, principles of justice determine what forms of equality have to be realised and what freedoms need to be guaranteed. Beyond the societal pursuit of equality, Rawlsian justice places a special focus on individual pursuits and collective self-determination, leaving ample space for the exercise of human freedom and diverse conceptions of the good.

'What kind of justice and for whom?' is the core moral concern underlying a series of important challenges levelled at Rawlsian justice and the liberal paradigm more broadly. These seminal debates have led to a critical rethinking of the subject and boundaries of justice in several important directions. Feminist philosophers pointed out that major societal wrongs, such as the oppression of women, could remain out of sight if justice is restricted to public institutions and the private sphere is shielded from the demands of justice, and argued for extending the subject of justice to families and gender norms (Okin, 1989; 2005). According to Iris Marion Young (2011, chapter 2), the subject of justice should be cast broader than Rawls', including not only certain fundamental institutions and formal rules, but the *social structure* as a whole. Young defines structures as 'the confluence of institutional rules and interactive routines, mobilisation of resources as well as physical structures', which provide 'background conditions for individual actions', and 'provide 'channels' that both enable action and constrain it' (Young, 2006, pp. 111–12). When social structures normalise morally unacceptable values and belief systems, unintentional habitual acts, such as everyday sexism, ableism, or consumerism, accumulate and contribute to conditions of domination and marginalisation (Young, 2006, pp. 94–5).

Another acute criticism by Charles Mills (2015; 2019) decries the exclusion of race and racism from theories of liberal justice, partly due to their focus on ideal theory. Philosophers like Rawls formulate their theories at a high level of abstraction and envision agents and social circumstances in their idealised (or utopian) form, for example, a cooperative society among free and equals. Mills argues that by abstracting from real-world, historically situated complex realities of structures of oppression, theories of distributive justice fail to recognise and account for the deep and pervasive role of race and racism in our colonial political and economic histories and the way its legacies are systematically reproduced in contemporary institutions and societal structures. They therefore fail to guide real-world societies that are unjust and oppressive. Moreover, he argues that liberal theories 'focus on distributive justice, conceals the 'social-systemic reproduction of unfair white advantage'. 'Global white supremacy', as Mills calls it, permeates not only our material world; it also introduces a 'white bias' in the concepts and theories that make sense of them (Mills, 2019, pp. 113–14). Taking seriously racial justice, he argues, requires more than compensating for material disadvantages. It requires 'a conceptual shift from distributive to corrective justice', towards non-ideal theorising that aims to correct past wrongs and repair colonial legacies in the present.

Last but not least, several waves of global justice theories have paved the way for one of the premises of this book, namely that the scope of justice extends beyond state borders and is not limited to co-nationals. The scope of justice has been extended beyond borders on different moral grounds. Many scholars have argued, for instance, that global duties of justice arise due to cross-border interactions and institutional relations that render our actions and decisions morally consequential for the lives of faraway others (Beitz, 1979; Pogge, 2002; James, 2012).

Although the primary subject of this book is the global economy, in line with the structural-institutional orientation of justice, it is not directly concerned with the question of what moral principles should inform the interactions of individuals and enterprises in international business relationships. Instead, it addresses the question of why and how the norms, rules and procedures of global economic governance should be more responsive to the different demands of justice that arise in global economic practices.

Global economic governance includes trans-, inter-, and supranational political institutions that provide governance relevant to the economic sphere and the policies that these institutions enact. In addition, national political institutions and their policies – so far as they concern global economic issues – can also be seen as part of global economic governance.

This book considers three dimensions of justice in global economic governance: the conditions and design of collective decision-making (political justice), the allocation of socioeconomic goods (socioeconomic justice), and responsibilities towards future generations and for past injustice (intergenerational justice). These three dimensions might overlap in some respect, both conceptually and in practice, and might not be so neatly separable in all governance domains. For instance, intergenerational justice can also concern the allocation of socioeconomic goods and require certain collective decision-making procedures. Political and socioeconomic justice may overlap in different areas of economic self-determination.

POLITICAL JUSTICE

The political dimension of justice is concerned with the design of political institutions in global economic governance.[2] It includes questions such as how procedures of collective decision-making should be designed, who is entitled to participate in these procedures, and how decisions should be implemented. Before all of these is the crucial question of competency placement; namely, what decisions should be taken on which level of political decision-making. What governance issues properly belong to states and what issues need to be decided by inter- or transnational political institutions? In a sense, these questions concerning the 'Who decides?' are before the question 'Who gets what goods?' as in political procedures decisions are made about rules that then influence the production and distribution of goods (Fraser, 2009, p. 17).

In the traditional debate on political justice within states it is widely accepted that, to be just, procedures of collective decision-making need to conform to democratic principles. Democracy can be justified instrumentally by the policy outputs it tends to produce. For instance, democratic institutions might be comparatively good at preventing abuses of power by office-holders. Decision-makers in democratic institutions might also be more informed about the interests of the citizens and there might at least be a chance that biases related to the specific backgrounds of decision-makers are addressed because in democratic procedures a variety of different perspectives and sources of information are brought together (Christiano, 2008). For instance, Sen (1999, p. 178ff.) observes that no famine has ever occurred in a democracy with a free press because governments in such systems know if a famine is about to start and have strong incentives to take action to prevent it. Besides these instrumental considerations, there is an intrinsic justification for democracy. In this regard, it has been argued that democracy is necessary to decide on controversial issues while still expressing equal respect for all citizens with their diverse opinions (Christiano, 2008, chapter 3; Valentini, 2013).

2 The political dimension of justice is closely related, though not identical, to political legitimacy. For an investigation of legitimacy in global governance, see Hilbrich (2021, 2024).

Although many of these reasons in favour of democratic decision-making procedures also seem to hold for decision-making in global economic governance institutions, it is more controversial than for domestic institutions whether global economic governance institutions should be democratic and if so, how such institutions could be designed. In this context, the most constructive approach seems to be to strive for global governance institutions that realise the principles and values that underlie democracy to the highest possible degree. As Jonathan Kuyper puts it:

> Instead of treating democracy as an idealised set of institutions that need to be induced beyond the state, we should think about the fundamental principles that democracy demands and strive for them under existing conditions. Such values may include inclusiveness, equality, popular control, transparency, accountability, deliberation, or something else. (Kuyper, 2015, section 3.1)

A somewhat more concrete principle whose implementation can help to realise at least some of the values that Kuyper mentions is the so-called all-affected principle. According to this principle, all those whose interests are affected by a political decision should be able to participate in decision-making – in person or via a representative (Goodin, 2007). Despite its great intuitive appeal, the all-affected principle has been criticised for its potentially radical implications for our existing political institutions. Certainly, this principle could only serve as a general normative ideal – rather than as a concrete practical decision-making rule for every specific decision (Arrhenius, 2018, p. 96ff.). Understood in this way, though, it reveals the fundamental injustice associated with the fact that, for instance, those who suffer from environmental pollution often do not have much voice in policy decisions related to the emergence of this pollution.

The concrete ways of realising the all-affected principle and, more generally, democratic values in global economic governance are feasible depending on the context and nature of the institution in question. Often national governments are meant to act as representatives of their citizens in decision-making in institutions of global economic governance. To improve negotiations between national governments, it has, for instance, been suggested to increase transparency and strengthen the role of legislative bodies (Zürn, 2000). In addition, measures to counter power asymmetries among states can play a constructive role. This concerns formal political inequalities, such as unequal voting rights of states in international organisations like the World Bank or the IMF (Woods, 2001). But also, more informal asymmetries, for instance, related to the differences in resources and access to the expertise of negotiation delegations in institutions such as the WTO (Brandi, 2011), play a crucial role in global governance. Public deliberation and more direct forms of political participation (not mediated by national governments) can be facilitated by hearings with directly affected groups or, more generally, the inclusion of civil society organisations in decision-making procedures (Steffek & Nanz, 2008). In addition, the use of digital technologies might enable innovative forms of direct political participation.

These ways of representing those affected by decisions in global economic governance have shortcomings and limitations. For instance, chains of delegations between citizens and decision-makers get longer if national governments act as representatives of their citizens in the international sphere (Buchanan & Keohane, 2006, p. 412ff.). In addition, governments of autocratic states cannot be seen as proper representatives of their citizens. Engagement with civil society has its limitations as well. Those civil society institutions that have the resources to engage in global politics are often controlled by privileged groups, and civil society institutions usually are, if at all, only subject to relatively weak mechanisms of accountability (Scholte, 2004, p. 230f.; Woods, 2011, p. 98f.). In general, participation via dialogue processes with civil society does not seem to be able to realise political equality to the same extent as more formal channels of participation.

It might thus be called for more ambitious steps of democratisation of global economic governance, such as the establishment of a global democratic assembly. It is controversial, though, whether the conditions under which such an institution could function are currently met in the global sphere (Christiano, 2010) and the chance of realisation of such proposals shortly seems to be low.

However, as stated above, democratic values can be achieved to different degrees. That the sketched potential ways of increasing participation, deliberation and accountability in global economic governance have limitations, does not mean that feasible reforms could not improve the approximation of such values. Reforms, such as the decoupling of voting rights and economic wealth in international organisations, clearly have the potential to increase the justice of the institutions of global economic governance.

Global economic governance can also be a relevant tool for promoting democracy and self-determination (see Ayelet Banai's contribution in this volume) in other sites and levels of decision-making below the global level. For instance, in their current constellation global economic governance regimes lend support to autocratic regimes by allowing governments that hold de facto power over a territory to sell its natural resources or to borrow money in the name of its peoples. The prospect of being able to use these privileges to enrich oneself sets incentives for corrupt politicians and military leaders to seize power. By decoupling natural resource rights and borrowing privileges from de facto rule, and moving rights of self-determination into the hands of the people, global governance could be an important tool for democratisation.

Respecting the 'sovereignty of peoples and nations over their natural wealth and resources' (UN Resolution 1803/XVII) would be one way global economic governance institutions could contribute to bringing about more political justice at the state level (Pogge, 2011, p. 29; Wenar, 2008, 2016).

SOCIOECONOMIC JUSTICE

Socioeconomic justice is about the right allocation of goods among persons. How do we avoid morally objectionable patterns of distribution, for example, if hundreds of millions of people live in extreme poverty while others are incredibly rich? Socioeconomic justice may be achieved using re-distributing goods through resource transfers or by rethinking the global economy from the get-go, and designing its norms and rules so that it yields a more just outcome. According to the second approach, it is important to see that questions of production cannot be separated from questions of distribution. How we organise the production of goods in society has important implications for the distribution that arises (Stanczyk, 2012). Socioeconomic justice, according to this view, starts with the allocation of endowments and productive capacities, such as the distribution of property rights, both material and intellectual (see Chapter 19 by Annabelle Lever and Christian Timmermann in this volume), ensuring the people's right to control the natural resources in their territory (see Chris Armstrong in Chapter 21 of this volume), and so on.

It is hardly controversial that absolute poverty is morally problematic in our world of abundant wealth. The most comprehensive account of poverty arguably builds on the capability approach developed by Amartya Sen (1980). According to this approach, human well-being should be understood in terms of capabilities – that is, real opportunities for valuable doings and beings. Absolute poverty is a lack of basic capabilities, such as the capability to be well-nourished or to escape avoidable diseases. In contrast to conceptions of poverty referring to economic income, the focus is not on means (that is, only instrumentally valuable goods) but on ends. This has several advantages. Ends can often be furthered by different means. For instance, financial resources at the disposal of individuals can allow them to get access to education and health care. However, education and health care can also be provided as public services. The situation of two persons who have the same financial resources but live in places that differ in terms of the public services provided is not the same. Measures of income poverty can only take this into account by taking the detour to place a fictitious monetary value on the public services and goods provided. In contrast, the capability approach directly focuses on valuable ends. This also allows us to explicitly address the question of what means are most suitable to foster specific capabilities. Moreover, the capability approach takes into account differences between individuals that affect their capacity to convert instrumental goods into capabilities. For instance, a person with a walking impairment needs more resources to achieve a similar level of mobility than others, and a pregnant or nursing woman has a higher need for nutrients to be well-nourished.

How global economic governance is related to the existence of absolute poverty and how this relation has to be assessed in light of the value of justice, has been articulated by Thomas Pogge (2005). He argues that developed countries coercively impose a global order on the poor which results in human rights deficits. Pogge uses a thin criterion of basic justice according to which 'an institutional order is unjust if it foreseeably produces a substantial and reasonably avoidable human rights deficit' (Pogge, 2010, p. 195). Responsibility to eradicate global poverty on Pogge's account is a negative duty to refrain from harm. Given that affluent nations hold the power in the global economic order, the duty to reform institutions to better fulfil the human rights of the poor falls to a substantial extent on them.

The key question is, then, whether current global economic governance foreseeably and avoidably produces absolute poverty. According to Pogge, this is the case if two conditions are met. Firstly, there are alternative global governance arrangements for which we have reason to believe that their establishment would result in less poverty. Secondly, the production of absolute poverty by the institutional order is reasonably avoidable in the sense that these alternatives were not associated with excessive costs in other domains. Pogge claims that most of the existing absolute poverty is in this sense attributable to the global order (Pogge, 2005, p. 722). Certainly, he does not want to imply that local factors only play a minor role in the existence of absolute poverty. Most absolute poverty could arguably *also* be eliminated by reforms on other political levels. However, this does not disqualify the important role that global institutional reform can play in poverty eradication.

Within the philosophical debates on global justice, global poverty eradication is often framed as a matter of sufficiency or sufficientarian principle, where the moral concern lies with people 'not having enough'. A further crucial question, however, is whether inequalities above the threshold are matters of justice, and if so, why (Moellendorf, 2009; Beitz, 2001). This leads us to questions concerning the moral ground of our obligations of justice.

Non-relational theorists hold that socioeconomic inequality can matter even among those who do not stand in any social relation with each other. Simon Caney (2005, chapter 4) defends such a non-relational account of distributive justice and argues that it is simply unjust that some people face, through no fault of their own, worse opportunities than others, simply because they are born in a different country. Caney believes that this holds even in the absence of any economic or political interlinkages.

Relational theories, by contrast, assert that claims of distributive justice can only be justified if specific social relations exist, for example, relations of coercion or cooperation.[3] Coercion-based relational accounts of distributive justice build on the observation that coercion is a far-reaching impediment to autonomy. According to the proponents of this account, the constraint of autonomy related to coercion can only be justified if no one can bring forward a reasonable complaint. A coercive system has to be regulated by principles that could not reasonably be rejected by any of the persons subject to it. If certain kinds of socioeconomic inequalities exist, those who are disadvantaged by these inequalities might often have a reasonable complaint. Coercion-based accounts have originally been developed to defend the claim that socioeconomic inequality matters only within states because only states were seen as a coercive system of the right kind (Blake, 2001). However, in the meantime, others have convincingly argued that forms of coercion that are relevant to distributive justice also exist in the global realm. For instance, Eric Cavallero describes the 'integrated international system of property norms' (Cavallero, 2010, p. 19) as coercive in the relevant sense. Laura Valentini argues that this holds for 'the effects of the global economic system as a whole' (Valentini, 2011, p. 198).

Another ground of distributive justice is constituted by the existence of relations of cooperation. If a practice includes a 'social activity [that] produces relative or absolute benefits or burdens that would not exist if the social activity did not take place' (Beitz, 1979, p. 131), the question arises of how these benefits and burdens should be distributed. Principles of justice seem to apply to the rules that determine this distribution. International trading relationships, as obvious examples of cooperative endeavours that extend beyond national borders, generate benefits and burdens that are somehow distributed. These relationships might generate claims of distributive justice of those who participate in these relationships, for instance as part of a global value chain.

From a more holistic perspective, the global economy as a whole could, as Charles Beitz (1979, p. 143ff.) argues,[4] be seen as a cooperative scheme that gives rise to claims of distributive justice. To put it very simply, in Germany only so many cars can be produced because the clothes that the workers in the car industry wear are produced by people elsewhere. In a sense, cars and clothes (and all the other goods) are produced *together* by car workers and sewers (and all the rest of us). The institutional rules that are in the background of business interactions among companies and

[3] Coercion and cooperation are not the only relational grounds of justice that are discussed in the literature. For instance, Sangiovanni (2007) focuses in his account of distributive justice on reciprocity in the provision of public goods. The approach of Risse (2012) to global justice is built on a number of different relational and non-relational grounds, including the subjection to a global order.

[4] However, in later publications, Beitz abandoned this position and affirmed a non-relational account of global distributive justice (Beitz, 1983, p. 595).

individuals taking place in economic markets determine who gets what share of the goods commonly produced.

Socioeconomic inequalities among individuals globally, inequalities among countries, inequalities among individuals within countries that are related to transnational social structures, and also more micro-level inequalities (for instance within enterprises) result as morally problematic depending on the context through which they develop, and the conception of justice one uses. This can hold for social structures that enable highly unequal gains from exploitative trade relationships between specific trading partners (be it individuals or countries) or for structures that cause inequalities among all of the participants of economic or political systems.

INTERGENERATIONAL JUSTICE

A third dimension of justice concerns our responsibilities across time, towards future generations, as well as the duties we have regarding the harms and wrongs inflicted on people in the past.

The importance of justice obligations towards future people depends on the degree of our capacity to influence their living conditions. In light of the magnitude that our interference with the natural environment has reached, intergenerational justice is an important issue today. However, intergenerational justice is not confined to environmental matters; it also concerns, for instance, public debt (see also Chapter 14 by Kathrin Berensmann in this volume), pension schemes or technological innovations. In general, the central question of intergenerational justice to future people can be understood as asking what 'capital' we ought to transmit to our successors (Gosseries, 2008, p. 63).[5] For lack of a better alternative, the term 'capital' is used here although it carries an economic connotation that is problematic in this context. The things we pass on to our successors include economic resources and goods, but also knowledge, technologies, institutions, cultures, and a natural environment. The value of the latter for future generations is certainly not exhausted by their role in economic production and consumption.

The question is not only of what *amount* of capital we owe to future generations but also of whether we are allowed to substitute different forms of capital. For instance, are we allowed to preserve fewer natural resources for future generations if, as compensation, they inherit superior technologies from us? These questions are especially intricate because we know so little about the interests and capabilities of those living in the future. Epistemic

[5] A different strand of the debate on intergenerational justice, which is not further discussed here, concerns proposals to represent future generations in political decision-making, for instance by reserving a number of seats in legislative bodies to representatives of future generations (Ekeli, 2005).

constraints in general can constitute reasons to be cautious with regard to actions that have far-reaching impacts on future generations, especially if these impacts are non-reversible (Jonas, 1979/1984, p. 32f.).

Models developed in economics and climate science often include assumptions about intergenerational justice that are operationalised in terms of a social discount rate. Social discount rates specify how benefits arising in the future are valued in comparison to benefits created today. These rates are used, for instance, in cost-benefit analyses of public investments.

Transnational economic activities determine to a considerable extent what capital will be available to future generations, for instance by causing pollution in production processes in global value chains or by spreading knowledge and fostering technological innovations. Global economic governance, which is supposed to govern these activities, thus has to be assessed from the perspective of intergenerational justice.

Scholars have pursued a number of strategies to approach the question of what capital we should transmit to future generations. This section focuses on approaches that specify either a sufficientarian or a relative standard. Sufficientarian standards are absolute thresholds of capital we are morally obligated to transmit to future generations. The definition of these thresholds could, for instance, refer to the capital that is assumed as essential for the capacity of future generations to satisfy basic needs. The concept of planetary boundaries can be interpreted as specifying a sufficientarian conception for the question of what kind of natural environment we ought to preserve. Rockström et al. (2009) describe nine planetary boundaries, which are, for instance, related to climate change, ocean acidification or biodiversity loss. Not surpassing these planetary boundaries should only 'avoid the risk of deleterious or even catastrophic environmental change at continental to global scales' (Rockström et al., 2009, p. 32) and ensure that humanity remains in a 'safe operating space' (Rockström et al., 2009, p. 32), this approach can be seen as a quite minimal sufficientarian conception.

An alternative to sufficientarian approaches makes use of a comparison of the situation in which our generation lives with the situation of future generations. Thus, these alternative approaches use a relative standard. For instance, we might be obligated to preserve at least as much capital as is necessary for future generations to be able to reach a similar level of well-being (however that is measured) to ours (Barry, 1997). Whether the relative approach or the sufficientarian approach is more demanding depends on the questions of how demanding the threshold defined in a specific sufficientarian conception is, of what level of well-being the living generation enjoys, and of how much value is put in the relative approach to the well-being of future generations.

The current levels of resource use and pollution do not seem to meet the demands of any reasonably plausible sufficientarian or relative approach to intergenerational justice. For instance, the estimations of Rockström et al.

(2023) show that many of the planetary boundaries included in their minimal sufficientarian account have already been surpassed. Thus, in particular, concerning our impact on the natural environment, the current economic order has to be reformed so that future generations will have access to a greater capital stock than they would have access to if the current economic order remained unchanged. Reforms of global economic governance can play a crucial role in realising intergenerational justice in this regard.

Another issue of intergenerational justice concerns past wrongdoings, such as imperial colonial extraction and exploitation, the seizure of indigenous land by settlers, the transatlantic slave trade, and so on. *Historical injustice* is the area of political morality that deals with the question of whether we have an obligation to rectify the unjust past, and if so why and how. We may have obligations to rectify past wrongs for the sake of morally amending the past; as a matter of reparation to the victims who might or might not be still alive. Moreover, past injustices have enduring legacies plaguing contemporary global relations, as widely documented by the postcolonial literature. On this account it is the continuity and the enduring injustice that lives on in our present relations, which matters morally:

> The unjust history that should normatively matter in justice-based considerations is present because it has been reproduced over time through different means, and it still is so. The reproduction of unjust history is pervasive as it shapes the background conditions in which some present wrong occurs and relations between agents are established. (Nuti, 2020, p. 4)

Many aspects of contemporary international affairs, such as relations of political domination in international institutions, or relations of economic domination in the context of trade, liberalisation and structural adjustment, have been traced to imperial colonialism and its interlinkages with racialised capitalism, resulting in a critique of a *neocolonial* global political and economic order (for example Getachew, 2019).

Theories of historical injustice contend that the nature of our moral obligation partly depends on the way we conceive of the nature of the past harm or wrong. Colonialism, in this sense, can be conceived either as an interactional harm or a structural harm. On the interactional account, colonial harms have been committed by the colonising state against the colonised people. It focuses on states as main perpetrators and assigns them responsibility to compensate the victims, for example by restituting land or artefacts, paying reparations or issuing official state apologies. On the structural injustice account, by contrast, it is social structural processes – including habitual actions and normalised institutions, discourses and practices – that are based on morally unacceptable value systems and jointly conspire to produce unjust outcomes. The responsibility to remedy is forward-looking and general; everyone who participates in and habitually reproduces unjust structures has a joint responsibility to remedy them (Young, 2011).

CONCLUSION

To sum up, this chapter distinguishes a political, socioeconomic, and intergenerational dimension of justice and discusses what general directions reforms have to take to render global economic governance more just. As a requirement of political justice, we argued that decision-making procedures of the institutions of global economic governance should realise to a higher degree democratic values such as inclusiveness, deliberation and accountability. Moreover, economic governance regimes should aim, at a minimal negative duty, not to undermine the self-determination interest of peoples, and ideally should be arranged to further and promote it. Socioeconomic justice requires bringing about a broader dispersion of productive assets by, for example, reforming the norms governing existing property rights regimes. Moreover, reforming global economic governance should be morally constrained by the joint demands of poverty eradication and reducing socioeconomic inequality between countries and among persons. Finally, intergenerational justice demands that a reformed global economic governance should take into account and redress the enduring legacies of colonial domination in global economic relations, and bring about an economy that transmits a greater capital stock to future generations, in particular by preserving a reasonably intact natural environment.

Certainly, co-benefits and trade-offs can arise if these goals are pursued simultaneously. For instance, on the one hand, giving economically less privileged groups a stronger voice in political decision-making would certainly be a step toward the democratisation of global economic governance. At the same time, such changes in decision-making can also be instrumentally important for reforms that cause a reduction of poverty and socioeconomic inequalities. On the other hand, for instance, some measures that could be employed to reduce poverty today might have environmental impacts that negatively affect intergenerational justice. To investigate such interlinkages will be left to the following chapters of this volume that discuss specific policy areas of global economic governance because the existence of co-benefits and trade-offs is likely to be highly context-sensitive.

This volume seeks to develop reform proposals that are politically feasible. But how realistic is it that decisive steps in the directions specified above are, in fact, taken? On the one hand, far-reaching reforms in this direction are certainly likely to be met with resistance by influential beneficiaries of the current global economic order. In the way in which global governance is currently structured, such reforms might be hard to achieve against the resistance of, for instance, wealthy states and influential business actors. In addition, obviously, future generations cannot make their own voices heard because they are not here yet to do so. This worsens the chance that their interests are taken seriously enough in the relevant political processes.

On the other hand, though, in one form or another, the international community already politically committed itself to further many of the goals described. The *2030 Agenda for Sustainable Development* includes the goal to 'build effective, accountable, and inclusive institutions at all levels' (SDG 16). This reflects at least partly the demands of political justice. The demand to reduce absolute poverty corresponds to human rights recognised in the *Universal Declaration of Human Rights* from 1948 and the *International Covenant on Economic, Social, and Cultural Rights* from 1966 for more than half a century. SDG 1 of the 2030 Agenda demands to end poverty, SDG 10 to reduce inequality within and among countries. The needs of future generations are prominently mentioned in the preamble of the 2030 Agenda and are closely related to the 'environmental' SDGs 12–15.[6] Furthermore, in the Paris Agreement governments committed themselves to the goal to keep temperature increase in comparison to the pre-industrial levels well below 2 degrees and pursue efforts to limit the increase to 1.5 degrees. Thus, those who advocate for reforms of global economic governance can remind governments that, if such international declarations can be taken seriously, they have already committed themselves to many of the demands of justice formulated in this chapter.

Certainly, the above does not exhaust all aspects that are relevant to the justice of global economic governance. Moreover, the search for ideas of justice that every global citizen has reason to value inevitably raises the problem of pluralism about global justice itself. Understanding the merits of broadly liberal and egalitarian global justice theories while at the same time being aware of and critically engaging with its limitations, we hope is a valuable contribution to a global conversation that must include scholars with a wide variety of backgrounds and perspectives rooted in a diversity of philosophical traditions.

REFERENCES

Arrhenius, G. (2018). The Democratic Boundary Problem Was Reconsidered. *Ethics, Politics & Society, 1*, 89–122.

Barry, B. (1982). Humanity and Justice in Global Perspective. NOMOS: *American Society for Political and Legal Philosophy*, 24, 219–52.

Barry, B. (1997). Sustainability and Intergenerational Justice. *Theoria, 44*(89), 43–64.

Beitz, C. R. (1979). *Political Theory and International Relations*. Princeton University Press.

[6] A number of targets in the 2030 Agenda directly concern global economic governance, for instance the targets 17.10–17.12 on trade. However, the realisation of these targets would hardly lead to sufficient progress with respect to the desiderata for reforms of global economic governance that are identified in this chapter.

Beitz, C. R. (1983). Cosmopolitan Ideals and National Sentiment. *The Journal of Philosophy, 80*(10), 591–600.

Beitz, C. R. (2001). Does Global Inequality Matter? *Metaphilosophy*, 32(1–2), 95–112.

Blake, M. (2001). Distributive Justice, State Coercion, and Autonomy. *Philosophy & Public Affairs, 30*(3), 257–96.

Brandi, C. (2011). The World Trade Organization Is a Subject of Distributive Justice. In M. Ronzoni, A. Banai, & C. Schemmel, (eds.), *The Relationship between Social and Global Justice*. Routledge.

Buchanan, A., & Keohane, R. O. (2006). The Legitimacy of Global Governance Institutions. *Ethics & International Affairs, 20*(4), 405–37.

Caney, S. (2005). *Justice without Borders*. Oxford University Press.

Cavallero, E. (2010). Coercion, Inequality and the International Property Regime. *Journal of Political Philosophy, 18*(1), 16–31.

Christiano, T. (2008). *The Constitution of Equality: Democratic Authority and Its Limits*. Oxford University Press.

Christiano, T. (2010). Democratic Legitimacy and International Institutions. In S. Besson & J. Tasioulas, (eds.), *The Philosophy of International Law*, 119–37. Oxford University Press.

Ekeli, K. S. (2005). Giving a Voice to Posterity: Deliberative Democracy and Representation of Future People. *Journal of Agricultural and Environmental Ethics, 18*(5), 429–50.

Forst, R. (2012). *The Right to Justification: Elements of a Constructivist Theory of Justice*. Columbia University Press.

Forst, R. (2013). Transnational Justice and Democracy: Overcoming Three Dogmas of Political Theory. In E. Erman & S. Näsström, (eds.), *Political Equality in Transnational Democracy*, 41–59. Palgrave Macmillan.

Fraser, N. (2009). *Scales of Justice: Reimagining Political Space in a Globalizing World*. Columbia University Press.

Getachew, Adom. 2019. *Worldmaking after Empire: The Rise and Fall of Self-Determination*. Princeton University Press.

Goodin, R. E. (2007). Enfranchising All Affected Interests, and Its Alternatives. *Philosophy & Public Affairs, 35*(1), 40–68.

Gosepath, S. (2004). *Gleiche Gerechtigkeit: Grundlagen eines liberalen Egalitarismus*. Suhrkamp.

Gosseries, A. (2008). Theories of Intergenerational Justice: A Synopsis. *S.A.P.I.EN.S., 1*(1), 61–71.

Hilbrich, S. (2021). Legitimacy as the Right to Function. *Critical Review of International Social and Political Philosophy*.

Hilbrich, S. (2024). *On Legitimacy in Global Governance. Concept, Criteria, and Application*. Palgrave Macmillan.

James, A. (2012). *Fairness in Practice: A Social Contract for a Global Economy*. Oxford University Press.

Jonas, H. (1979/1984). *The Imperative of Responsibility: In Search of an Ethics for the Technological Age*. University of Chicago Press.

Kuyper, J. (2015). Global Democracy. In E. N. Zalta, (ed.), *The Stanford Encyclopedia of Philosophy*, (Winter 2016 ed.). Metaphysics Research Lab, Stanford University.

Mills, Charles W. 2015. 'Decolonizing Western Political Philosophy'. *New Political Science* 37 (1): 1–24.

Mills, Charles W. 2019. 'Race and Global Justice'. In *Empire, Race and Global Justice*, edited by Duncan Bell, 94–119. Cambridge University Press.

Moellendorf, D. (2009). *Global Inequality Matters*. Palgrave Macmillan.

Nuti, A. (2020). On Structural Injustice, Reconciliation, and Alienation. *Critical Review of International Social and Political Philosophy, 23*(4), 530–7.

Okin, S. M. (2005). 'Forty Acres and a Mule' for Women: Rawls and Feminism. *Politics, Philosophy & Economics*, 4(2), 233–48.
Pogge, T. (2002). *World Poverty and Human Rights: Cosmopolitan Responsibilities and Reforms*. Polity Press.
Pogge, T. (2005). Recognized and Violated by International Law: The Human Rights of the Global Poor. *Leiden Journal of International Law, 18*(04), 717–45.
Pogge, T. (2010). Responses to the Critics. In A. Jaggar, (ed.), *Thomas Pogge and His Critics*, 175–250. Polity Press.
Pogge, T. (2011). Allowing the Poor to Share the Earth. *Journal of Moral Philosophy*, 8(3), 335–52.
Rawls, J. (1971). *A Theory of Justice*. Oxford University Press.
Rawls, J. (1993). *Political Liberalism*. Columbia University Press.
Risse, M. (2012). *On Global Justice*. Princeton University Press.
Rockström, J., Gupta, J., Qin, D., Lade, S. J., Abrams, J. F., Andersen, L. S., & Zhang, X. (2023). Safe and Just Earth System Boundaries. *Nature* 619, 102–11.
Rockström, J., Steffen, W., Noone, K., Persson, Å., Chapin III, F. S., Lambin, E., Schellnhuber, H. J. (2009). Planetary Boundaries: Exploring the Safe Operating Space for Humanity. *Ecology and Society, 14*(2).
Ronzoni, M. (2009). The Global Order: A Case of Background Injustice? A Practice-Dependent Account. *Philosophy & Public Affairs, 37*(3), 229–56.
Sangiovanni, A. (2007). Global Justice, Reciprocity, and the State. *Philosophy & Public Affairs, 35*(1), 3–39.
Scholte, J. A. (2004). Civil Society and Democratically Accountable Global Governance. *Government and Opposition, 39*(2), 211–33.
Sen, A. (1980). Equality of What? In S. McMurrin, (ed.), *Tanner Lectures on Human Values*. Cambridge University Press.
Sen, A. (1999). *Development as Freedom*. Knopf.
Stanczyk, L. (2012). Productive Justice. *Philosophy & Public Affairs, 40*(2), 144–64.
Steffek, J., & Nanz, P. (2008). Emergent Patterns of Civil Society Participation in Global and European Governance. In J. Steffek, C. Kissling, & P. Nanz, (eds.), *Civil Society Participation in European and Global Governance*, 1–29. Palgrave Macmillan.
Valentini, L. (2011). *Justice in a Globalized World: A Normative Framework*. Oxford University Press.
Valentini, L. (2013). Justice, Disagreement and Democracy. *British Journal of Political Science, 43*(1), 177–99.
Wenar, L. (2008). Property Rights and the Resource Curse. *Philosophy & Public Affairs* 36: 2–32.
Wenar, L. (2016). *Blood Oil: Tyrants, Violence, and the Rules That Run the World*. Oxford University Press.
Woods, N. (2001). Making the IMF and the World Bank More Accountable. *International Affairs, 77*(1), 83–100.
Woods, N. (2011). The Impact of the G20 on Global Governance: A History and Prospective. In C. I. Bradford & L. Wonhyuk, (eds.), *Global Leadership in Transition: Making the G20 More Effective and Responsive*, 36–47. Korea Development Institute, Brookings Institution Press.
Young, I. M. (2006). Responsibility and Global Justice: A Social Connection Model. *Social Philosophy and Policy, 23*(1), 102–30.
Young, I. M. (2011). *Responsibility for Justice*. Oxford University Press.
Zürn, M. (2000). Democratic Governance beyond the Nation-State: The EU and Other International Institutions. *European Journal of International Relations, 6*(2), 183–221.

Chapter 2

JUSTICE AND THE GLOBAL INVESTMENT REGIME

Axel Berger, Andrea Bjorklund and Manjiao Chi

INTRODUCTION

Foreign Direct Investment (FDI) is considered a key promoter of economic development, since it provides access to external financing, technology, managerial expertise and jobs. However, FDI is limited to a small number of locations and many low and middle-income countries (LMICs) continue to be excluded from global foreign investment flows. The reasons for this exclusion are manifold and may vary from country to country. A particular policy instrument LMICs have traditionally resorted to in order to attract FDI are international investment agreements (IIAs).[1] LMICs have signed thousands of these agreements since the late 1950s. Not only establishing far-reaching substantive investment protection provisions, they also allow foreign investors to enforce these provisions through investor-state dispute settlement (ISDS) mechanisms. However, it is contested to what extent IIAs lead to more FDI flows or whether they are merely a tool to protect investors' rights while restricting host countries' ability to regulate foreign investments in support of public policy goals.

IIAs have become a debated policy tool and some argue that the global investment regime is facing a legitimacy crisis (Waibel et al., 2010). This chapter aims at making sense of the critique against IIAs. We apply the normative framework of this volume by Hilbrich and Kollar and structure the critique against the global investment regime according to its performance in terms of political, socioeconomic and intergenerational justice considerations. Based on this discussion, the chapter discusses key proposals to reform the global investment regime. The next section provides an overview

[1] We use the term IIA to refer to the overall group of bilateral and regional investment treaties, including bilateral investment treaties (BITs) and preferential trade and investment agreements (PTIAs), which establish rules for the protection, promotion and liberalisation of FDI. The terms BIT and PTIA will only be used to address questions relating specifically to these types of treaties.

of the global investment regime and its main legal instruments. The subsequent section, focusing on the political justice dimension, will investigate the decision-making processes that led to the design of traditional IIAs and current attempts to reform the system. The following section reviews the global investment regime from the perspective of socioeconomic justice and analyses the distributional effects of IIAs. Then, the chapter assesses the global investment regime from an intergenerational perspective and asks to what extent IIAs contribute to (or restrict) the pursuit of sustainable development. The final section concludes and provides an overview of current reform proposals.

THE GLOBAL INVESTMENT REGIME

Before this chapter investigates IIAs based on the three justice dimensions mentioned above, it is necessary to briefly describe the main contours of the global investment regime. In contrast to many other realms of international relations, the global investment regime lacks a central organisation. Rather, the regime can be characterised as a decentralised network of almost 3300 IIAs governing global FDI flows (UNCTAD, 2023). The term IIAs covers a range of different treaties. The most widespread legal instruments still are bilateral investment treaties (BITs), which have been negotiated between two countries based on a limited number of treaty templates put forward by member countries of the Organisation for Economic Co-operation and Development (OECD) often dating back to the era of de-colonisation and the time of import-substitution policies of the 1960s and 1970s. At their core, BITs grant investors from one contracting party substantive rights when investing in the other party's jurisdiction and access to ISDS to challenge potential breaches of these substantive rights. The legal rights established in BITs are reciprocal, meaning that they apply to both parties. However, the investment flows covered are often not reciprocal and BITs are typically signed by a capital-exporting country on the one side and a country that (aspires to) import capital on the other. Typically, BITs include provisions on fair and equitable treatment, indirect expropriation and full protection and security. Besides BITs, another important instrument to govern FDI flows are investment chapters in preferential trade and investment agreements (PTIAs) that are concluded between two or more countries, at times also on a regional level. Beyond investor protection and ISDS provisions typically found in BITs, PTIAs often also cover rules on investment liberalisation opening up markets and sectors for foreign investors. Given the fact that investment rules are negotiated in the broader context of a preferential trade agreement, they often feature also a number of safeguards (e.g. provisions on the right to regulate) or exceptions (e.g. for environmental regulation) which are typically not found in traditional single-purpose BITs.

In addition to the thousands of bilateral and regional IIAs, only a few multilateral investment instruments exist. The World Trade Organization (WTO) Agreement on Trade-Related Investment Measures (TRIMs) governs investment measures, such as local content or other performance requirements, which would restrict trade in goods. The WTO General Agreement on Trade in Services (GATS) covers a number of provisions that are relevant for foreign investments in the service sector such as national treatment, most-favoured nation (MFN) treatment and liberalisation of services FDI. In addition, two-thirds of the WTO's membership concluded the so-called Investment Facilitation for Development (IFD) Agreement in mid-2023 and seek to integrate it as a plurilateral agreement into the WTO legal system. The aforementioned WTO agreements are covered by the WTO's Dispute Settlement Understanding, which only allows states to initiate dispute settlement proceedings against other states. Most IIAs, however, allow foreign investors to bring claims directly against other states.

Attempts to establish a truly multilateral framework for investment failed several times in the post-World War Two period (Van Harten, 2007). The first attempt refers to the unsuccessful inclusion of a comprehensive multilateral investment code in the proposed International Trade Organization (ITO) which never was ratified due to the opposition of the United States Congress. Subsequent unsuccessful efforts to establish multilateral rules for investment included, among others, the proposed Multilateral Agreement on Investment (MAI) in the context of the OECD and the discussion of multilateral investment rules at the 2003 Cancún Ministerial Conference of the WTO. The failure of the ITO represented an important crossroads for the future development of the international economic order. The General Agreement on Tariffs and Trade (GATT), concluded in 1947, provided a multilateral forum to negotiate the liberalisation and regulation of cross-border trade flows and formed the basis for the founding of the WTO in 1995. In contrast, the governance of foreign investment did not take place in a multilateral structure but in a growing web of bilateral treaties.

The first BIT was concluded by Germany and Pakistan in 1959. Shortly thereafter it was mainly West European countries that signed a relatively modest number of treaties often with countries from Africa. The number of new treaties picked up in the 1980s partly because more and more LMICs started to sign BITs. The majority of BITs were signed during the 1990s after the discontinuation of import-substitution policies in many LMICs and the breakdown of the Soviet Union that led to the widespread use of BITs as tools to attract foreign investments. High-income countries saw BITs mainly as tools to protect business interests abroad while also depoliticising investment disputes, whereas LMICs saw BITs as a means to attract more FDI (Bonnitcha et al., 2017) or to promote diplomatic relations among the signatories (Poulsen & Aisbett, 2016).

Between the 1960s and 1990s, IIAs remained largely uncontroversial, mainly because the signing of these treaties was inconsequential. In the first decades of the IIA system ISDS cases were non-existent. A first (known) case was initiated against Sri Lanka in 1987 but it was not until 1993 that a second ISDS case was initiated and that the number of cases started to rise gradually. Perhaps the most consequential ISDS cases were launched on the basis of Chapter 11 of the North American Free Trade Agreement (NAFTA). Previous ISDS cases were mainly initiated against LMICs and transition economies such as Sri Lanka, Democratic Republic of the Congo and Poland. Since the late 1990s not only Mexico was hit by ISDS cases in the context of NAFTA but also Canada and the USA. A number of these cases were perceived as 'frivolous' and caused outcries both in policy-making and civil society circles since the 'alleged breaches of obligations under NAFTA were actually measures taken for public policy purposes, apparently not directly related to foreign investment' (Gagné & Morin 2006, p. 635). Meanwhile over ninety cases were initiated on the basis of the NAFTA Chapter 11 and the total ISDS case-load amounted to more than 1250 at the end of 2022 (UNCTAD, 2023). As a result of the growing number of ISDS cases countries have reformed their model treaties, (re-)negotiated IIAs with more nuanced legal language and more safeguards and even terminated treaties.

THE JUSTICE OF THE GLOBAL INVESTMENT REGIME

Political Justice: Who Decides?

The first angle to assess the justice dimension of the global investment regime is to focus on the question of how democratic decision-making processes function with respect to the negotiation of IIAs and their enforcement. Traditionally, IIAs were negotiated on the basis of a limited number of treaty templates formulated by a select group of actors in high-income countries. During the era of de-colonialisation in particular European investors faced the challenge that their foreign investments were no longer protected by imperial legal regimes. The conceptual basis for the European BIT programme was developed by two corporate representatives in Germany and the UK: Hermann Joseph Abs, then Director General of Deutsche Bank, and Lord Hartley Shawcross, former UK Attorney General and a Director of Shell. The so-called Abs–Shawcross Convention significantly influenced the OECD Draft Convention on the Protection of Foreign Property, which in turn formed the basis for a majority of BITs promoted by European countries to protect their nationals' investments abroad. These rather short treaties nevertheless established far-reaching rules on the protection of foreign investors and later also included ISDS provisions. The USA started in the 1980s to negotiate specific investment treaties. In contrast to the European model, the US BIT programme covered not only investment protection and ISDS provisions but also provisions on the liberalisation of host countries' investment frameworks. In general, it is interesting to note that the negotiation of BITs was mainly driven by small units within government with little lobbying from corporations or public discussion involving parliaments or civil society (Bonnitcha et al., 2017).

LMICs mainly acted as rule-takers accepting the treaty templates that they were presented with in order to attract foreign investment (Poulsen, 2015). Even China, the country with the (second) highest number of BITs, has been heavily influenced by European and North American models in the past four decades. The process of reforming IIAs that was initiated after the number of ISDS cases picked up in the late 1990s was mainly driven by high-income countries. In particular the USA, together with Canada and Mexico in the framework of NAFTA, introduced a number of innovative provisions that aimed at better balancing the protection of foreign investors and pursuit of public policies by host countries (Gagné & Morin, 2006). Only in recent years have LMICs begun to introduce international investment policy reforms. Brazil started to negotiate a new treaty type that focused on the facilitation of investment and cooperative arrangements between the parties. India revised its model BIT in 2016 imposing an obligation of exhausting local remedies before arbitration. There are also the SADC Model BIT and the Nigeria-Morocco BIT, both of which attempt to impose obligations on investors to perform environmental impact assessments.

Beyond the negotiation of IIAs, the enforcement of IIAs is also characterised by peculiar patterns. The international investment regime is special in the sense that the enforcement of substantive IIA provisions lies with private investors that are granted the right to initiate ISDS proceedings against host country governments. Furthermore, the enforcement through ISDS does not comply with standards typically applied to domestic legal systems, in particular with regard to the selection of arbitrators, transparency of proceedings, coherence of jurisprudence and the possibility to appeal.

In sum, in large parts the current system of IIAs, including ISDS mechanisms that allow private investors to sue sovereign host states, was negotiated by a small elite within high-income country governments. As a result, IIAs are often criticised for their one-sided design and enforcement mechanisms. Only in the last couple of years have we seen more extensive public and parliamentary debates – often as a result of high-profile ISDS cases – about IIAs which have led to a substantial rethinking of their key design principles.

Socioeconomic Justice: Who Gets What?

The second angle to discuss the justice of IIAs is to assess their distributional effects. The key bargain underpinning IIAs is that (low and middle-income) host countries provide foreign investors with far-reaching substantive and procedural legal protection in exchange for increased FDI inflows. Two key questions follow from this observation: do we know that IIAs actually increase FDI and to what extent do IIAs (unduly) restrict domestic regulatory space in the pursuit of public policy objectives?

The effects of IIAs on FDI flows have been assessed by using econometric as well as survey methods. Most of the more recent econometric studies tend to find a positive relationship between IIAs and FDI flows. However, there are other econometric studies that find no – or even negative – effects of IIAs on FDI flows (Sauvant & Sachs, 2009). This striking difference may be explained, among other reasons, by varying estimation techniques and the quality of FDI data. Furthermore, most of the econometric studies have treated IIAs as 'black boxes' not accounting for important legal variations in these treaties. Interestingly, studies that have tested for the effects of ISDS clauses found – rather counterintuitively – no significant effect on FDI flows (e.g. Berger et al., 2011). Market-access provisions, on the other hand, have a positive effect on FDI flows when they are integrated in PTIAs, but not, however, when included in BITs (Berger et al., 2013). Another way to assess the impact of IIAs on FDI is to ask investors to what extent they take IIAs into account when deciding where and how much to invest. Yackee (2010) finds that this is rarely the case. In sum, the evidence on whether IIAs have helped to increase FDI remains inconclusive (Bonnitcha et al., 2017).

Since IIA may – or may not – lead to more FDI inflows to LMICs the question whether they constrain policy-makers in adopting policies to promote public policy objectives is a crucial one. But let's first take a step back – why should IIAs restrict the space of policy-makers to adopt certain policies? The key reason is that IIAs include substantive provisions that should prohibit certain policies, for example if a host country government discriminates between different classes of investors or adopts measures that lead to the direct or indirect expropriation of foreign investors without paying compensation. Furthermore, the vast majority of IIAs include ISDS provisions that allow foreign investors to enforce IIA provisions without prior consent of their home country governments. These constraints on host country policy-making, one could argue, are intended by the contracting parties who hoped that this would lead to more predictable investment frameworks and in turn more FDI.

In addition to these (intended) direct effects IIAs may also cause (unintended) indirect effects that lead to overly cautious policy-making or even a freezing of regulatory activity. These effects are often referred to as 'regulatory chill'. IIAs may cause such a chilling effect since policy-makers face uncertainty about the legality of their decisions vis-à-vis the international commitments undertaken in the context of IIAs. This uncertainty, on the one hand, may be a result of overly vague and open-ended substantive IIA provisions. The discussion among legal scholars and practitioners regarding the interpretation of the notion of 'fair and equitable treatment' is a prominent example in this regard. On the other hand, the specific design of the enforcement mechanisms in the international investment regime may be another cause of uncertainty. This system is organised in a decentralised fashion meaning that for every ISDS proceeding a new arbitration tribunal is established which is not bound by precedent. There are some glaring examples of tribunals coming to opposing conclusions about similar or even the same disputes. Furthermore, the international investment regime lacks appeal mechanisms that allow for a checking of the legality of the decisions of arbitration tribunals and thus contribute to more certainty about the interpretation of substantive IIA provisions (Berge & Berger, 2021). As a result, policy-makers may be receptive to the threat of foreign investors to take legal action or may put a policy initiative or regulation on hold while an ISDS proceeding is ongoing.

There indeed exists some anecdotal evidence in favour of the regulatory chill hypothesis. For example, New Zealand put its plain tobacco packaging legislation on hold while high-profile ISDS cases initiated by Philip Morris against Australia and Uruguay were ongoing (Berge & Berger, 2021). In addition, a few case studies have investigated the effects of ISDS cases on domestic regulation. Here, however, no clear picture emerges about the prevalence of the regulatory chill effect (e.g., Van Harten & Scott, 2016; Sattorova, 2018). There are, to date, only two large-N studies that have empirically investigated systemic regulatory chill effects. Both studies find no general effect but show that regulatory chill may occur in specific policy fields, such as tobacco legislation (Moehlecke, 2020), and regulatory action in high-capacity (developed) countries is more likely to be chilled (Berge & Berger, 2020; Moehlecke, 2020). Moreover, ISDS may be used as 'strategic legislation' by investors not with the ultimate goal to win the case but to delay legislation (Pelc, 2017).

To sum up, given the available empirical evidence it seems questionable that the 'grand bargain' (Salacuse & Sullivan, 2005) – of LMICs promising to favourably treat foreign investors by signing IIAs in return for more FDI inflows – holds up. Research on the effects of IIAs on foreign investment remain inconclusive while survey evidence suggests that foreign investors rarely know about IIAs when making investment decisions. Furthermore, there exists at least some evidence that IIAs may lead to delays, changes or abandonment of domestic regulatory activity in view of the potential effects of ISDS proceedings. In short, LMICs do not always get what they have hoped for after entering the international investment regime.

Intergenerational Justice

On a general level, sustainable development may be defined as 'meeting the needs of the present generation without compromising the ability of future generations to meet their own needs' (United Nations General Assembly, 1987). Sustainable development is thus key to foster intergenerational justice. In the context of the international investment regime, therefore, the question arises to what extent IIAs help to promote – or prevent – future generations' sustainable development?

Foreign investments often grant host economies access to capital, technological and managerial know-how as well as higher paying jobs and may, in turn, lead to higher levels of productivity, competitiveness, social upgrading and access to better environmental technologies. At the same time, in view of many market failures, governments may need to regulate foreign investors in order to ensure that they contribute to sustainable development. The previous section, however, has shown that IIAs may not always lead to more FDI and global FDI flows remain concentrated on a smaller number of economies. Beyond the economic and social dimension of sustainable development, the question is whether IIAs can promote the green transformation of economic activities by especially promoting green FDI and by granting exceptions for environmental regulations?

A review of the available literature reveals that while more recently concluded IIAs include more sustainable development-related provisions, the bulk of IIAs largely eschews any reference to environmental or social aspects (Chi, 2018). A survey by the OECD in 2014 of 70 per cent of all IIAs revealed that only 12 per cent of these treaties included a reference to sustainable development (Gordon et al., 2014). Especially the thousands of BITs negotiated in the 1990s and in earlier decades do not include references to the promotion of sustainable development or exceptions for the protection of the environment. This situation changed after the year 2000 due to the increasing focus on the effects of IIAs on sustainable development. The USA and other countries reformed their model treaties and included an ever broader range of sustainability-related provisions such as references to overall sustainability goals in the preamble, references to international environmental or social standards or exceptions. What is notable is that these innovations happened in particular in the context of investment chapters of preferential trade agreements and there is a 'sustainability gap' between PTIAs with investment chapters and BITs (Chi, 2018). These more incremental changes in the context of IIAs offer states more regulatory flexibility and ISDS tribunals more flexibility in their decisions (Bjorklund, 2019).

In a number of ISDS cases, sustainable development-related aspects have been raised. Many ISDS cases have been related to measures or sectors that are of direct relevance to climate action, including environmental, fossil fuel and renewable energy ISDS cases (UNCTAD, 2022). In addition, ISDS cases involving public health, labour rights and other sustainable development aspects have also generated broad attention. As states face growing pressure for taking regulatory measures to achieve sustainable development, it is likely that more ISDS cases involving sustainable development aspects will be initiated.

To sum up, more and more countries are integrating environmental and social provisions in their recent IIAs to better reconcile the goals of attracting FDI and supporting sustainable development. Nevertheless, these changes are rather incremental and large parts of IIAs negotiated before 2000 do not take the sustainable development of host countries sufficiently into account.

REFORM PATHS

It is difficult to find another international regime that is under so much pressure as the international investment regime. Discussions about its goals, design and effects have been going on for at least two decades. On a general level, policy-makers, researchers and civil society representatives are reflecting on the goals of the system (Bjorklund, 2011). Should IIAs be conceived as international instruments to (just) promote FDI or does the quality of FDI matter? What about the responsibility of investors? And how can the system support sustainable development? Many of these questions touch upon important justice dimensions discussed in this chapter. However, while many stakeholders would agree that the systems need to be reformed, the direction and substance of the reform are all but clear.

Against the background of such diverging views on reform of the international investment regime, it is hardly surprising that states react very differently to the deficiencies and at times injustices of the regime. We observe a strong current of changes to the substantive and procedural provisions of IIAs. The IIAs that have been (re-)negotiated today look rather different from those concluded twenty or more years ago. These more recent treaties seem less expansive in the rights of protection granted to foreign investors; they attempt to strike a better balance between the rights and obligations of investors as well as the right to regulate of host states. The ISDS mechanisms of newer treaties include stronger rules on transparency and due process and are often less comprehensive compared to traditional BITs. This piecemeal reform – one treaty at a time – has its weaknesses, of course, since investors often can bypass reformed IIAs and instead use traditional BITs to enforce their rights vis-à-vis host states. It is therefore no surprise that a number of countries such as South Africa, Indonesia and India have terminated most if not all of their existing IIAs to renegotiate them. Other countries have terminated their membership in international arbitration forums such as the International Centre for the Settlement of Investment Disputes (ICSID).

In contrast to this exit option, there are at least two multilateral tracks to reform the international investment regime. The adoption of the so-called Mauritius Convention aims at promoting the transparency of ISDS proceedings, which is deemed helpful in promoting sustainable development in an indirect manner. The ongoing ISDS reform under the auspices of United Commission on International Trade Law (UNCITRAL) aims at improving and reforming the ISDS regime in a comprehensive way. Some of the achievements of the reform to date are beneficial to the pursuit of sustainable development. For instance, the prospective Advisory Centre on International Investment Law and Investor-State Dispute Settlement is expected to play a helpful role in assisting LMICs in dealing with ISDS cases. A second multilateral reform track is taking place in the WTO. Two-thirds of the WTO membership, many of them LMICs, have concluded an IFD Agreement that aims at promoting FDI by improving the efficiency, transparency and predictability of domestic investment laws and institutions (Berger & Chi, 2025). Crucially, the negotiating parties have made clear that traditional elements found in IIAs, that is, provisions on investment protection, liberalisation and ISDS, are excluded from the IFD Agreement. The Agreement also includes a comprehensive development section that should help LMICs to be able to implement the agreement (Berger et al., 2019).

However, given the complex nature of the global investment regime and the diverging interests of its actors, a comprehensive reform, especially one that aims at remedying the justice issues analysed in this chapter, may be a long time coming. A step-by-step approach to reform may therefore be the only viable way forward.

REFERENCES

Berge, T. L., & Berger, A. (2021). Do Investor-State Dispute Settlement Cases Influence Domestic Environmental Regulation? The Role of Respondent State Bureaucratic Capacity. *Journal of International Dispute Settlement 12*(1), 1–41.

Berger, A., Busse, M., Nunnenkamp, P., & Roy, M. (2011). More Stringent BITs, Less Ambiguous Effects on FDI? Not a Bit!. *Economics Letters 112*(3), 270–2.

Berger, A., Busse, M., Nunnenkamp, P., & Roy, M. (2013). Do Trade and Investment Agreements Lead to More FDI? Accounting for Key Provisions inside the Black Box. *International Economics and Economic Policy 10*(2), 247–75.

Berger, A., & Chi, M. (eds.) (2025). *The Making of an International Investment Facilitation Framework. Legal, Political and Economic Perspectives*. Cambridge University Press.

Berger, A., Gsell, S., & Olekseyuk, Z. (2019). *Investment Facilitation for Development: A New Route to Global Investment Governance* (Briefing Paper 5/2019). German Development Institute / Deutsches Institut für Entwicklungspolitik (DIE).

Bjorklund, A. (2011). Improving the International Investment Law and Policy System. In: Alvarez, J. E., & Sauvant, K. P. (eds.), *The Evolving International Investment Regime: Expectations, Realities, Options*, 213–46. Oxford University Press.

Bjorklund, A. (2019). Sustainable Development and International Investment Law. In: Miles, Kate, (ed.), *Research Handbook on International Investment and Environmental Law*, 38–68. Edward Elgar.

Bonnitcha, J., Poulsen, L. N. S., & Waibel, M. (2017). *The Political Economy of the Investment Treaty Regime*. Oxford University Press.

Chi, M. (2018). *Sustainable Development Provisions in Investment Treaties: An Empirical Exploration of the Sustainable Development Provisions in BITs of Asia-Pacific LDCs and*

LLDCs. Bangkok: United Nations Economic and Social Commission for Asia and the Pacific (UNESCAP).
Gagné, G., & Morin, J.-F. (2006). The Evolving American Policy on Investment Protection: Evidence from Recent FTAs and the 2004 Model BIT. *Journal of International Economic Law* 9(2), 357–82.
Gordon, K., Pohl, J., & Bouchard, M. (2014). *Investment Treaty Law, Sustainable Development and Responsible Business Conduct: A Fact Finding Survey*. (OECD Working Papers on International Investment 2014/01). Organisation for Economic Co-operation and Development.
Moehlecke, C. (2020). The Chilling Effect of International Investment Disputes: Limited Challenges to State Sovereignty. *International Studies Quarterly, 64*(1), 1–12.
Pelc, K. J. (2017). What Explains the Low Success Rate of Investor-State Disputes? *International Organization, 71*(3), 559–83.
Poulsen, L. N. S. (2015). *Bounded Rationality and Economic Diplomacy: The Politics of Investment Treaties in Developing Countries*. Cambridge University Press.
Poulsen, L. N. S., & Emma Aisbett (2016). Diplomats Want Treaties: Diplomatic Agendas and Perks in the Investment Regime. *Journal of International Dispute Settlement, 7*(1), 72–91.
Salacuse, J. W., Sullivan, N. P. (2005). Do BITs Really Work? An Evaluation of Bilateral Investment Treaties and Their Grand Bargain. In: Sauvant, K. P., & Sachs, L. (eds), *The Effect of Treaties on Foreign Direct Investment: Bilateral Investment Treaties, Double Taxation Treaties, and Investment Flows*, 109–70. Oxford University Press.
Sattorova, M. (2018). *The Impact of Investment Treaty Law on Host States: Enabling Good Governance?* Hart Publishing.
Sauvant, K. P., & Sachs, L. (eds.) (2009). *The Effect of Treaties on Foreign Direct Investment: Bilateral Investment Treaties, Double Taxation Treaties, and Investment Flows*. Oxford University Press.
UNCTAD (United Nations Conference on Trade and Development) (2022). *Treaty-Based Investor-State Dispute Settlement Cases and Climate Action* (IIA Issue Note 4). New York and Geneva: United Nations Conference on Trade and Development.
UNCTAD (2023). *World Investment Report 2023: Investing in Sustainable Energy for All*. New York and Geneva: United Nations Conference on Trade and Development.
United Nations General Assembly (1987). *Report of the World Commission on Environment and Development: 'Our Common Future'*. United Nations.
Van Harten, G. (2007). *Investment Treaty Arbitration and Public Law*. Oxford University Press.
Van Harten, G., & Scott, D. N. (2016). Investment Treaties and the Internal Vetting of Regulatory Proposals: A Case Study from Canada. *Journal of International Dispute Settlement, 7*(1), 92–116.
Waibel, M., Kaushal, A., Chung, K. H., & Balchin, C. (2010). *The Backlash against Investment Arbitration: Perceptions and Reality*. Kluwer Law International.
Yackee, J. W. (2010). Do Bilateral Investment Treaties Promote Foreign Direct Investment? Some Hints from Alternative Sources of Evidence. *Virginia Journal of International Law, 51*(2), 397–441.

Chapter 3

INTERNATIONAL INVESTMENT LAW AND GLOBAL JUSTICE: TOWARDS A POLITICAL THEORY OF INTERNATIONAL INVESTMENT

Ayelet Banai

INTRODUCTION

International investment law (IIL) governs flows of foreign direct investment (FDI), typically (but not exclusively) from wealthier to poorer countries.[1] IIL consists of two parts: international investment agreements (IIAs) between states, and a system of arbitration, the investor-state dispute settlement (ISDS). According to UNCTAD data, there are currently 2,610 international investment agreements (IIAs) in force. Out of 1332 known treaty-based ISDS cases, 354 are currently pending.[2]

IIL is a uniquely de-centralised field of international law. In investment, there is no equivalent to the World Trade Organization (WTO), with a multilateral treaty, and arbitration bodies. Furthermore, IIL is special in establishing legal relationships between private and public actors. The ISDS is a system of ad hoc tribunals, in which investors – i.e., private companies and corporations – can bring cases against a host government. In the WTO's arbitration system, only a member government can bring a case against another member government for violation of treaty obligations. The power of private actors to sue governments is an important feature of IIL that is often criticised for a built-in bias in favour of investors' interests (Schill, 2010; Berger et al., Chapter 2 in this volume).

IIL is a controversial field in the global economy. For proponents, this is a valuable legal regime 'concerned with preserving the rule of law, addressing invidious discrimination, promoting efficient allocation of resources, and

[1] China and Brazil also negotiate investment agreements to protect their own investors abroad.

[2] UNCTAD *International Investment Navigator* <https://investmentpolicy.unctad.org/international-investment-agreement> accessed: April 30, 2024.

facilitating the access of developing countries to the scarce capital they need for their development' (Suttle, 2022, p. 257). Criticisms, however, describe IIL as a system of exploitation, an essentially unjust regime that enables wealthy and powerful corporations and their home states to increase profits at the expense of developing countries and their peoples (James, 2017; Ratner, 2019; Suttle, 2022). These structural criticisms go beyond 'particular provisions of IIAs, viewing the entire project of IIL as part of a Northern agenda (Ratner, 2017, p. 751). Some describe IIL as coloniality, identifying continuities between historic colonialism and the present (Schneiderman, 2022). Apart from the sweeping objections to IIL, critical voices call for reform, to address 'a growing legitimacy crisis' with 'its institutional processes criticised for failing basic rule of law criteria such as coherence, predictability, neutrality, and accountability' (Garcia et al., 2015, p. 862).

In 2017, The United Nation Commission on International Trade mandated a working group to start deliberations about a possible procedural reform of the ISDS system (Bjorklund, 2023). Beyond formal deliberations, this initiative opened the door to a prolific and diverse discussion, among scholars and activists, including proposals for a general reform of the international investment regimes. What, then, a better IIL should be? This chapter develops insights from *political theory,* with a focus on international investment *and global distributive justice.* I propose two general guidelines for two cardinal principles of global justice: fairness in the distributional effects of the regime, and protection of the principle of self-determination. The principles delineate a broad field of possible reforms that meet them.

This chapter maps the main justice-based criticism of IIL under two categories. First, I briefly present structural and systemic criticisms that consider the core rationale of IIL morally problematic and thus develop radical criticisms of the regime. Challenges to the systemic approaches are then presented. Second, I present three central reform-oriented criticisms – authority to negotiate treaties, public–private institutional challenge, and the policy-space critique. I propose insight from theories of international justice as principles towards justice in IIL. A theoretical insight that emerges from the discussion is the following proposition: *international investment treaties and arbitration procedures should protect from violation of the distributive conditions that follow from states' self-determination*. The final section considers possible institutional applications and concludes.

SYSTEMIC AND STRUCTURAL CRITICISMS OF IIL: INJUSTICE BEYOND REFORM?

Structural and systemic criticisms of IIL describe it as a regime of exploitation, coloniality and as essentially unjust towards host (poorer) countries and their populations. The basic claim is that the core principles of IIL are unjust, not just specific treaty clauses or institutional features. Reflecting on the question of investors' rights, Aaron James compares international investors who seek compensations for their losses through the ISDS system with casino gamblers who would claim compensation from the house after their luck went sour (James, 2017, pp. 205–6). Some of the losses that investors challenge before ISDS tribunals concern regulatory developments in the host states that affect gains – for instance, improved standards of environmental protection and labour conditions. Regulation that protects labour conditions or the environment in investors' destination countries, James argues, should be reasonably expected by investors. The ISDS system that enables investors to challenge such regulations, and seek compensation for loss of gains, is fundamentally unfair (James, 2017, p. 217). Some theories of global egalitarian cosmopolitanism argue or imply that the IIL regime is essentially unjust. Shuk Ying Chan argues that IIL obstructs equality and egalitarian politics. The regime 'contributes to entrenching inequality between and within states' (Chan, 2021, p. 204), because it is beneficial to 'a class of agents, whose interests are reliably opposed to egalitarian economic policy' (Chan, 2021, p. 204).

Cosmopolitan egalitarians who argue for equality of opportunity at the global level are also situated in a systemic opposition to IIL, though they do not tackle this subject matter explicitly. An important line of argument is that the principles of socioeconomic justice developed by John Rawls for a society within one state (Rawls, 1999a) should apply globally among individuals worldwide (Pogge, 2002; Caney, 2005). Firstly, fair equality of opportunity: people with similar talents and motivations should have similar life chances, that is, to reach offices and positions with higher socioeconomic rewards. Secondly, the difference principle: social and economic inequalities 'are to be arranged so that they are . . . to the greatest benefit of the least advantaged . . .' (Rawls, 1999a, p. 266). A moral intuition for global equality of opportunity is that if ethnicity, gender, and social origin are regarding our life chances within our domestic society, then nationality and country of birth are similarly arbitrary indicators regarding our life prospects in the global economy.

On this cosmopolitan account, citizens of poorer countries with restricted access to global socioeconomic opportunities are owed as *a matter of justice* far larger portions of global wealth, resources and opportunities. The core rationale of IIL is in opposition to this account, namely 'that (low and middle income) host countries provide foreign investors with far-reaching substantive and procedural legal protection in exchange for increased FDI inflows' (Berger et al., Chapter 2 in this volume).

Poorer countries abide by these conditions because they need foreign investment for development, and to help meet the basic needs of their citizens. In IIL, then, the structural disadvantages of the global poor are manifest, and the basic rules of the game set against cosmopolitan egalitarian conceptions of justice, which require redistribution of wealth and resources to poorer populations in the world. The global economy deprives the global poor of their fair share of wealth and opportunity. IIL worsens the situation by adding the burdens of duties and obligations as conditions to obtain investment that is *owed* to them and resources that they deserve.[3] Furthermore, some theories focus on the duty to redress past wrongs. A core claim is that beyond the injustice of the current rules, former colonies deserve redress for the lingering effects of past colonialism (Lu, 2011).

Other systemic criticisms describe IIL as a system of exploitation, highlighting the gaps in power and wealth between states that export capital and states in need of foreign investment. IIL enables 'rich (mostly Northern) states can take advantage of poor (mostly Southern) states' (Ratner, 2019, p. 114). Exploitation has three aspects: unequal bargaining power and unequal access to reliable information about the risks and potential gains; asymmetry in the negotiated treaties; the situation of developing countries is worsened by investment under IIL (Ratner, 2019, p. 115). Development under IIL does not benefit the majority of the populations in developing countries and even harms them by deteriorating the environment and increasing the power of local repressive elites. In sum, global inequality skews IIL in favour of investors and against the interests of poorer and weaker states and their citizens (Ratner, 2019, pp. 114–16; Ratner, 2017, p. 751).[4]

David Schneiderman analyses IIL as coloniality, by identifying discursive continuities between historic coloniality and the new forms of legal rule where '. . . the preferences of powerful capital-exporting states continue to determine the content of international law . . .' (2022, p. 19). The analysis does not equate IIL with colonialism, but suggests that IIL did not just inherit disparities of power from the colonial past but contributes to perpetuating it.

The radical-critical horizon sheds light on injustices in IIL, but has important limitations: its factual claims are challenged by empirical evidence. Susan Franck argues that OECD membership of the respondent country does not account for its chances of winning or losing ISDS cases, nor for the sums awarded by the tribunals (Franck, 2011, pp. 73–94). Examples from high-profile ISDS cases are illustrative, but further research is required for an evidence-based answer to the question of distribution of benefits and burdens in IIL (Bonnitcha, 2017; Ratner, 2017; Berge & Berger, 2021; Berger et al., Chapter 2 in this volume). Moreover, the normative questions will persist, even with better empirical evidence. To identify exploitation, we need a prior idea of what is due to the participants, and being denied. It is not enough to show that some receive more than others.

[3] This interpretation of what follows from global cosmopolitan principles of justice to IIL is mine. The authors do not engage with IIL explicitly.

[4] Ratner does not endorse this view. In two important articles (2017; 2019) he maps criticisms of IIL coupled with preliminary reflections from political theory.

The criticisms from global equality of opportunity and historical injustice face a normative challenge. They are controversial among theories of global justice and criticised by practitioners for being too demanding to mobilise for effective action. The second kind of criticism focuses on specific aspects of IIL, and sets out to reform it.

REFORM-ORIENTED CRITICISMS OF IIL AND PRINCIPLES OF INTERNATIONAL JUSTICE

Three core reformist criticisms of IIL that pertain to injustices in the current system are: the *policy-space critique* (Tienhaara, 2011; Garcia et al., 2015; Ratner, 2019, pp. 122–7; Berge & Berger, 2021), *asymmetry in negotiation and treaties* (Garcia et al., 2015; Huaqun, 2014) and the *public–private institutional challenge* (Schill, 2010). I discuss them in two sub-sections: first, international political justice – where the asymmetry and public–private criticisms reside; second, international distributive justice and the policy-space criticism.[5]

Asymmetry, Institutions and International Political Justice

The institutional criticism of IIL focuses on the ISDS system and consists of several aspects (Schill, 2010, pp. 401–3; Ratner, 2017, p. 767), traceable to the fusion of *public and private law*. According to Stefan Schill, criticisms:

> relate to the fact that investment treaty arbitration combines a public law regime under international law with what is essentially a private dispute settlement mechanism that is focused on resolving a specific dispute with no effects on non-parties and does not sufficiently take into account the public interests involved. (Schill, 2010, p. 404)

The problem of asymmetry highlights power gaps between negotiating parties, resulting in treaties that place more risks and burdens on weaker parties (Huaqun, 2014, pp. 300–4; Garcia et al., 2015, pp. 869–71).

For political theory, the public–private fusion and the power asymmetry are problems of *international political justice*. Theories of international justice ask which principles of justice are valid across borders, and should guide international and global institutions, and the dealings of states with one another and with foreigners. We have seen above a global cosmopolitan approach to this set of questions that aspire to institute global equality of

[5] This map of criticisms partly overlaps with Steven Ratner's discussion of these issues (Ratner, 2017; Ratner, 2019). My reflection begins in the political theory of global justice, not within international law. This chapter both complements and offers alternatives to Ratner's important work on this issue.

opportunity among individuals *qua* human beings worldwide. An important alternative approach is *international justice,* which assigns states a special role, and thus argues that domestic and international principles of justice are not identical. There is a normatively relevant quality for the relationship among fellow citizens, and among citizens and their states that originate specific principles of justice, typically more demanding principles, than those that apply internationally and globally. Duties of justice do not lapse at the border; they change (e.g. Blake, 2018).

Theories that focus on coercion and domination shed light on the asymmetry and institutional criticisms. The coercion-based theories build on the proposition that coercion, as a form of limiting freedom, ought to be justified and follow specific procedure – so that individuals are not subjected to the arbitrary will of another. 'Coercion is normatively significant because it involves problematic restrictions of freedom that require justification' (Valentini, 2011, p. 210). Formal state institutions that make and execute laws are a clear example of coercion. Liberal approaches to justice require their justification, for example, through civil and political rights to enable political participation, and principles of fair distribution of socioeconomic benefits and burdens. Laura Valentini argues for an *interactional* account of coercion that applies to international and global institutions and practices that do not coerce us in the narrow formal sense, but nevertheless restrict our freedom in normatively equivalent problematic ways (Valentini, 2011). Domination is the subjection to the will of another. On this view, domination is an aspect of global injustice that goes beyond distributive shares and the manifest exercise of coercive power (Buckinx et al., 2015, pp. 1–3). It is the capacity to interfere with others at will and with impunity (Buckinx et al., 2015).

The asymmetry and institutional criticism of IIL correspond with the coercion and domination-based approaches to global justice. IIL is unjust where it establishes unjustified coercion and relationships of domination. IIL's institutions and practices impact individuals and states pervasively, and, therefore, needs to be structured in ways that mitigate domination and protect from unjustified coercion. There are various ways to translate this general principle into policy recommendations. A central avenue requires that IIL's institutions and procedures should have stronger *public characteristics*: (1) equalising the standing of the negotiating parties beyond formal judicial equality; (2) increasing coherence and transparency in arbitration procedures, and designing mechanisms to consider the most relevant public interests. This possibly points towards a multinational body to provide the technical and procedural conditions for fair negotiations, and for coherence and representation of public interests in arbitration. Important reform proposals that reflect the principles emerging from theories of international political justice are already on the agenda (Berger et al., Chapter 2 in this volume), that is, new model treaties, procedural reforms and capacity building for development countries. The proposal that international investment should develop towards multilateralism, following the path of international trade and the WTO (Garcia et al., 2015; Berger et al., Chapter 2 in this volume) is pertinent for international political justice. The WTO has the *institutional infrastructure* to address concerns about fair negotiation procedures among parties with power differences, and improve coherence and transparency in arbitration. To be sure, there is much criticism in political theory of the WTO system and its injustices (James, 2012; Risse, 2012), which will require further consideration, should the IIL follow the paths of international trade law.

Policy Spaces and International Distributive Justice

International investment law, as recently described by Oisin Suttle, is 'fundamentally an exercise in allocating costs and benefits' (2022, p. 260). IIAs include protections for foreign investors, shaping the distributions of benefits and burdens between foreign investors and the host countries. This is the *distributional core* of IIL: its rules allocate benefits between host country gains (e.g., wages, taxes, improved infrastructure and services) and foreign investors' gains (and possibly their home countries). It allocates the burdens of the investment (risks and harms) between those carried locally and by the foreign investors. Therefore, we ought to address the question of fair allocation of benefits and burdens between investor, host states and possible third parties (Suttle, 2021, p. 260). Furthermore, treaty-based commitments of states to foreign investors pertain to domestic regulation with distributional consequences: wages, labour relations, environmental protection and the interests of future generations (Bonnticha et al., 2017; Berge & Berger, 2021). 'IIL raises distinctive moral questions because of its potentially strong constraints on a state's ability to manage its own economy' (Ratner, 2019, p. 107).

The proposition that IIL evolved in the 1990s and 2000s into a regime that restricts states' capacity to regulate important policy areas is a key criticism (Garcia et al., 2015; Bonnitcha, 2017; Berge & Berger 2021). This can be seen as 'one of the most important issues facing investment law today: whether it can consistently and effectively acknowledge and weigh the countervailing social concerns of host states (Garcia et al., 2015, p. 868). While empirical evidence on the chilling effect is inconclusive and continues to evolve, the theoretical normative questions regarding international influence on domestic policy requires consideration on their own. Which scope of international influence is justified (even desirable) and when is international interference wrongful? Some theories of international distributive justice focus on the relationships between socioeconomic justice within a state and the institutions and practices of the global economy.

A key problem of global justice is that the international economic and political order restricts and undermines states' capacity to establish domestic socioeconomic justice (Ronzoni, 2009; Banai et al., 2011; Ronzoni, 2012). International limitations on state sovereignty are not wrong *as such*, they are even desirable sometimes (e.g., international cooperation to combat climate change). Formulating the distinction between legitimate and unjust restrictions is an important challenge for policy-space criticism.

Theories of international justice enable us to rephrase the policy-space criticisms: *which IIL-based restrictions on states' regulatory capacity violate the principles of international justice?* Theories of international justice offer relevant answers because their concern is not with international influence as such, but with restrictions that obstruct states' capacity to promote socioeconomic justice, and frustrate domestic struggles for it. Some theories of international distributive justice focus on the principles of self-determination and sovereignty, arguing for international conditions that safeguard self-determination – including state's capacity to pursue domestic justice (Rawls, 1999b; Miller, 2007; Ronzoni, 2009; Stilz, 2019; Kollar & Banai, 2021). The international order should safeguard the conditions for self-determination of all peoples (typically represented by states). There is a duty of justice for states and global institutions not to violate these conditions.

John Rawls' *The Law of Peoples* is an influential example of this approach. He describes eight principles of international justice that constitute the freedom and equality of peoples in the international society. The core rights that constitute self-determination are rights of domestic self-government. The right of each people to self-determination originates their core international obligations: to respect the self-government of others and observe international treaties and undertakings they signed. There is also a duty to honour human rights and a duty of assistance, designed to help 'burdened societies' – those in dire political and socioeconomic conditions – to establish basic institutions and fulfil the basic needs of their members (Rawls, 1999b). David Miller's theory of global justice develops principles for 'a world in which nation-states are self-determining, but respect the self-determination of others through obligations of non-interference and in some cases of aid' (Miller, 1995, p. 107). These principles consist in self-government and non-interference as well as the duty to respect human rights worldwide; duties correlative to the *capacity to exercise* self-government – that is, 'the opportunity to achieve self-determination and social justice' (Miller, 2000, p. 177).

These influential theories of global justice are comparatively modest (among sovereignty and self-determination-based theories of international justice) in the international socioeconomic duties that they stipulate, because they support a *sufficiency* principle of global distributive justice. There is a threshold of resources that each state is owed, for the provision of basic needs of its citizens and support for basic public institutions. Relative international inequalities in wealth and power, above the sufficiency line, are not injustice.

This approach has preliminary implications for IIL and policy-space. First, poor countries will be owed special protections in investment treaties – a proviso limiting their exposure to risks. Special protections will be owed to countries during periods of acute political or economic crisis that affect their capacity for self-government (e.g., a civil war and post-war reconstruction). Second, investments that pertain directly to the capacity of the host state to provide basic needs (for example, access to clean water and food), will also require provisions that mitigate risk for the host country. Thirdly, the policy-space critique pertains to the *internal dimension* of self-determination – that is, the idea that citizens should have channels of participation, influence or authorisation of collective decisions taken by their government. In a country with an opulent elite and impoverished populations, it is difficult to claim that such channels operate. It is generally unjustified for international institutions to impose socioeconomic policies on a state, because the external dimension of self-determination protects from interference of this kind. However, international institutions must not entrench domestic inequalities of the kind that undermine internal self-determination. Sovereignty and self-determination-based theories of international distributive justice, which endorse the sufficiency standard provide us with insight on which kinds of policy-space restrictions by IIL are indeed unjust and why.

Consider the case of *Pacific Rim* v *El Salvador* filed in 2009 under the CAFTA treaty, following 'the Government's refusal to issue necessary mining licences for Pacific Rim's El Dorado gold mining project ... due to alleged environmental concerns ...'[6] In 1996 the government of El Salvador issued exploration permits , but in 2001 environmental regulations were adopted with stronger protection standards. Accordingly, the Corporation's application of 2003, for a licence to excavate was denied. The government's environmental concerns included risk of pollution for a major source of clean water in the region. The principles stipulated above, *prima facie* apply in this case, judging it as a case of unjust distribution of risks, given: (a) the socioeconomic circumstances in El Salvador at the time (i.e., high poverty rates, lower HDI[7] scores and burdens of reconstruction after a civil war that ended in 1992, a hurricane in 1998 and an earthquake in 2001); (b) the interruption to the state's capacity to fulfil a basic need of clean water. The case was decided in favour of the state. However, IIL will need to grant solid protection for the state in such cases, to mitigate the risk that it incurs. This can be obtained in the form of a proviso in the investment agreements, or in the procedures of the

[6] ISDS Navigator < https://investmentpolicy.unctad.org/investment-dispute-settlement/country/63/el-salvador> Accessed 30 April 2024.

[7] UN Human Development Index.

arbitration tribunals to direct them towards dismissal of the arbitration claims at the preliminary stages. A state in a modest socioeconomic status should not be threatened with a hefty payment, when acting to fulfil its basic duties towards its citizens, of access to drinking water and an intact environment.

In distinction, consider the 2012 *Vattenfall v Germany* case, under the Energy Charter Treaty (1994) that followed Germany's decision to phase out its nuclear power plants by 2022. The Swedish corporation Vattenfall AB, an operator of nuclear power plants, claimed 5.5 billion US$ in compensation. The case was settled with the corporation receiving 1.7 billion US$.[8] Other operators, German corporations that had no access to ISDS tribunals also received compensation, ranging from 42.5 to 880 million US$. Much as one may think that Germany's decision to phase out nuclear power plants is desirable, the exposure to risks of compensation claims does not *prima facie* violate any of the principles of distributive justice stipulated above. The award of compensation does not burden, in a non-trivial way, Germany's capacity to pursue its commitments to domestic justice, nor does it burden the participation capacity of worse off segments of society.

Another group of theories of international distributive justice that draw on sovereignty and self-determination argue for more demanding principles of global distributive justice. The core claim here is that the sufficiency standard is not enough for the effective protection of states' sovereignty and peoples' self-determination. Miriam Ronzoni argues that theories defending a sufficiency principle endorse 'negative sovereignty' but omit important aspects of sovereignty, namely, positive sovereignty (Ronzoni, 2012). A state exercises *negative sovereignty* when 'it enjoys immunity from external intervention, whether or not it is capable and has the necessary means to use such an immunity to self-assigned ends' (Ronzoni, 2012, p. 577). *Positive sovereignty* is enjoyed by a state when 'it possesses the internal resources to decide which kind of polity it wants to become and acts on it successfully' (Ronzoni, 2012, p. 577). Thus, the protection of sovereignty in a world of economic interdependence requires more than the principles of non-interference and threshold conditions defended by Rawls and Miller. States restrict one another's sovereignty in unjust ways, also when they remain above the sufficiency threshold.

Take the example of tax competition, which 'generates external effects that undermine the de facto sovereignty of states. As a consequence, tax competition tends to exacerbate inequalities of income and wealth both within countries and across borders.' (Dietsch & Rixen, 2015, p. 151) The state's capacity to pursue egalitarian socioeconomic objectives is a challenge for some of the developed and high-income economies too, far above the sufficiency standard. Thus, an international coordination of national tax regimes is required

[8] Jack Ballentyne 'Vattenfall saga at an end', *Global Arbitration Review*, 12.11.2021. < https://globalarbitrationreview.com/vattenfall-saga-end> accessed 30 April 2024.

to protect the state's capacity to pursue domestic socioeconomic justice. The global order, then, is a problem of *global background justice* (Ronzoni, 2009); its institutions and practices should not violate the state's capacity to fulfil its duties of domestic justice. On this view, grave international inequalities potentially hinder states from possessing positive sovereignty, and need to be alleviated when this is the case. Furthermore, it supports closer international coordination in the global economy, to pursue international policies that mitigate rising international and domestic inequalities (Dietsch & Rixen, 2015).

Finally, some self-determination-based theories of global distributive justice also argue for limits on global socioeconomic inequality. The core argument here is that the philosophical foundations of self-determination are rooted in the interests of individuals that it protects, in particular agency-interests of individuals to participate in shaping their social and political environment (Banai & Kollar, 2019). On this view, self-determination of each polity has a 'permissible scope', which is circumscribed not only by the right of other polities for self-determination, but also by a principle of fair global equality of opportunity, that enable better access to life chances, for individuals born in opportunity-poor countries (Kollar & Banai, 2023). Here too relative inequalities, between wealthier and worse off countries matter too, and ought to be mitigated, to fulfil the principle of 'permissible scope' of exercise of self-determination.

In sum, sovereignty and self-determination-based theories of international distributive justice, yield pertinent principles to approach the policy-space criticism of IIL. They provide guidelines for distributive justice in IIL, based on the principle of non-violation of self-determination as interpreted in this theoretical field. *International investment treaties and arbitration procedures should protect from violation of the distributive conditions that follow from states' self-determination.*

CONCLUSION

This chapter explored the contribution of political theory of global and international justice to the current debates and efforts to reform the international investment regime – a reform that aims to address IIL's legitimacy crisis and the changing conditions of the global economy. I explored structural-systemic criticisms from the perspective of global cosmopolitan justice, historic justice and coloniality. On different theoretical grounds, they consider IIL unjust *per se* – IIL emerges as a regime that reflects and entrenches global injustice. I then moved on to reform-oriented criticisms, which are modest in their scope (in comparison to the systemic views) but better designed to obtain a conceptual consensus and mobilise for reform. I then spelled out the policy-space criticism and the insights from theories of international distributive justice, which draw on the principles of sovereignty and self-determination. The pertinent principle that emerged is that *international investment treaties and arbitration procedures should protect from violation of the distributive conditions that follow from states' self-determination.* This principle implies not only that all participating countries meet a sufficiency standard of possessing the basic material and political resources necessary for self-determination, but also that the capacity to pursue policies of domestic socioeconomic justice is not obstructed. The proposition does *not* mean that IIL ought to promote domestic socioeconomic justice; it means that it must not hinder (in non-trivial and morally significant ways) states and populations that struggle for socioeconomic justice in their domestic politics. The principle I propose enables us to draw an important distinction between *permissible influence* of international interaction on domestic politics in the context of foreign investment and *unjust interferences* with policy-making. The general principle opens several avenues for designing concrete reform steps. One possible direction is to establish a standing multilateral court of international investment to act as a constraint on the decentralised IIL system. A standing court will aim neither to replace the ad hoc arbitration tribunals nor to centralise the negotiations, but will act as a guardian of basic rules of justice in international investment, with an authority to review bilateral and multilateral IIAs and TIPs, as well as arbitration judgments and procedures. Finally, an important scholarly challenge is to operationalise, beyond the general guidelines proposed here, the principle of harm to self-determination in unjust international interference in domestic policy-making.

REFERENCES

Banai, A., & Kollar, E. 2019. Reading Bedtime Stories to Compatriots: Reconciling Global Equality of Opportunity and Self-Determination. *Review of International Studies, 45*(3), 367–86.

Banai, A., Ronzoni, M., & Schemmel, C. (eds.) 2011. *Social Justice, Global Dynamics: Theoretical and Empirical Perspectives*. Routledge.

Berge, T. L., & Berger, A. (2021). Do Investor-State Dispute Settlement Cases Influence Domestic Environmental Regulation? The Role of Respondent State Bureaucratic Capacity. *Journal of International Dispute Settlement, 12*(1), 1–41.

Bjorklund, A. K. (2023). The Road(s) Not Taken: The Past, Present, and Future of International Investment Law Reform. *Arbitration International, 39*(4), 455–68.

Blake, M. 2018. Justice across Borders. In Olsaretti, S., (ed.), *The Oxford Handbook of Distributive Justice*, 619–39. Oxford University Press.

Bonnitcha, J. 2017. *Assessing the Impacts of Investment Treaties: Overview of the Evidence*. Winnipeg: International Institute for Sustainable Development.

Buckinx, B., Trejo-Mathys, J., & Waligore, T. (2015). *Domination and Global Political Justice*. Taylor & Francis.

Caney, S., 2005. *Justice beyond Borders: A Global Political Theory*. Oxford University Press.

Chan, S.Y., 2021. On the International Investment Regime: A Critique from Equality. *Politics, Philosophy & Economics, 20*(2), 202–26.

Dietsch, P. and Rixen, T., 2015. Tax Competition and Global Background Justice. *The Journal of Political Philosophy*, 22(2), 150–77.

Eberhardt, P., & Olivet, C. 2016. Profiting from Injustice: Tracing the Rise of Investment Arbitration Industry. *Rethinking Bilateral Investment Treaties, Kavaljit Singh and Burghard Ilge, eds.* Amsterdam: Both Ends. 243–52.

Franck. S. 2011. Considering Recalibration of International Investment Agreements: Empirical Insights. In *The Evolving International Investment Regime: Expectations, Realities, Options*, Jose. E. Alvarez et. al eds. Oxford: Oxford University Press. 73–94.

Garcia, F. J., Ciko, L., Gaurav, A., & Hough, K. 2015. Reforming the International Investment Regime: Lessons from International Trade Law. *Journal of International Economic Law, 18*(4), 861–92.

Huaqun, Z. 2014. Balance, Sustainable Development, and Integration: Innovative Path for BIT Practice. *Journal of International Economic Law, 17*(2), 299–332.

James, A. (2012). *Fairness in Practice*. Oxford University Press.

James, A. (2017). Investor Rights as Nonsense–On Stilts. In Herzog L., (ed.), *Just Financial Markets*, 205–30. Oxford University Press.

Kollar, E., & Banai, A. 2021. Sovereignty and the Value of Self-Determination. In *Sovereignty as Value*, Andre Santos Campos and Susana Cadilha eds. Rowman and Littlefield, pp. 183–97.

Kollar, E., & Banai, A. 2023. The Right to Exclude and the Duty to Include: Self-determination, Equal Opportunity, and Immigration. *Journal of Moral Philosophy, 20*(5-6), 483–511.

Lu, C. (2011). Colonialism as Structural Injustice: Historical Responsibility and Contemporary Redress. *The Journal of Political Philosophy 19*(3), 261–81.

Miller, D., 1995. *On Nationality*. Oxford University Press.

Miller, D., 2000. *Citizenship and National Identity*. Polity Press.

Miller, D. 2007. *National Responsibility and Global Justice*. Oxford University Press.

Ratner, S., 2017. International Investment Law through the Lens of Global Justice. *Journal of International Economic Law, 20*(4), 747–75.

Ratner, S., 2019. Global Investment Rules as a Site for Moral Inquiry. *Journal of Political Philosophy, 27*(1), 107–35.

Rawls, J. 1999a, *A Theory of Justice, revised edition*. Harvard University Press.

Rawls, J. 1999b, *The Law of Peoples*. Harvard University Press.

Pogge, T. W., 2002. *World Poverty and Human Rights*. Polity Press.

Risse, M., 2012. *On Global Justice*. Princeton University Press.

Ronzoni, M. (2009). The Global Order: A Case of Background Injustice? A Practice-Dependent Account. *Philosophy & Public Affairs, 37*(3), 229–56.

Ronzoni, M. (2012). Two Conceptions of State Sovereignty and Their Implications for Global Institutional Design. *Critical Review of International Social and Political Philosophy, 15*(5), 573–91.

Schill, S. W. (2010). Crafting the International Economic Order: The Public Function of Investment Treaty Arbitration and Its Significance for the Role of the Arbitrator. *Leiden Journal of International Law, 23*(2), 401–30.

Schneiderman, D. (2022). *Investment Law's Alibis* (Vol. 168). Cambridge University Press.

Stilz, A. 2019. *Territorial Sovereignty: A Philosophical Exploration*. Oxford University Press.

Suttle, O. (2022). Justice and Authority in Investment Protection. *Law and Development Review, 15*(2), 257–82.

Tienhaara, K. 2011. Regulatory Chill and the Threat of Arbitration: A View from Political Science. In *Evolution in Investment Treaty Law and Arbitration*, Chester Brown, Kate Miles, eds., Cambridge University Press, 606–27.

Valentini, L. (2011). Coercion and Global Justice. *American Political Science Review, 105*(1), 205–20.

Chapter 4

GLOBAL TRADE GOVERNANCE FROM THE PERSPECTIVE OF JUSTICE

Archna Negi

INTRODUCTION

International trade has been described as an engine of economic growth. It is claimed that the drop in global poverty as well as the reduction in income inequality among countries is attributable to the growth of international trade (WEF, 2021, p. 3). The positive linking of trade with welfare is founded on the understanding that trade helps to balance the uneven distribution of resources and goods, allows for a better division of labour, ensures a more efficient use of resources, and expands consumers' freedom of choice. But are aggregate gains from trade adequate grounds for overlooking questions about the *fairness* of the processes and outcomes of international trade?

The governance of global trade encompasses a multitude of institutions operating at multiple levels. At the heart of global trade governance sits the World Trade Organization (WTO). While the *normative* aspects of justice in trade or economic governance are discussed elsewhere (Hilbrich & Kollar, Chapter 1 in this volume), this chapter examines the *empirical* side of global trade governance through the lens of justice-related concerns. It identifies specific examples from the workings of the WTO that relate to three different strands of justice. The next section provides an introductory overview of the existing multilateral system of trade governance as manifested in the WTO. Subsequent sections then address the different justice-related dimensions of the WTO's work. The final section concludes by outlining entry points for reforming multilateral trade governance.

AN OVERVIEW OF THE MULTILATERAL TRADING SYSTEM

The WTO, an intergovernmental organisation set up in 1995, replaced the semi-institutionalised treaty regime of the *General Agreement on Tariffs and Trade* (GATT), which had been established in 1947. At the centre of the organisation are the WTO agreements, which are negotiated by the WTO members and then ratified ratified through their domestic processes. What started with the coming together of twenty-three countries as the GATT has now transformed into a trade organisation of 166 member states, accounting for 98 per cent of global trade, with over twenty countries negotiating membership (WTO, 2025).

The essential functions of the WTO are to limit discriminatory treatment, reduce trade barriers, generate rules for international trade, strengthen transparency and dialogue on trade issues, and adjudicate disputes among its member states. The most important principle of the WTO is that of *non-discrimination*, which implies, among other things, that each WTO member must usually extend the most favourable conditions under which it conducts trade with one member state to all other WTO members as well.

While the GATT had limited coverage of trade in goods, during the Uruguay Round of Trade Negotiations (1986–1994), GATT disciplines were extended to sectors previously not covered (agricultural goods, textiles, and apparel), and new areas of coverage were brought in – in particular, trade in services and intellectual property rights (IPRs). A 'new and improved' dispute settlement system (DSS) was put in place to settle disputes relating to WTO obligations, and a regularised system of reviewing the trade-related policies of member states was institutionalised (Trade Policy Review Mechanism).

In contrast to the Bretton Woods Institutions, the WTO follows a 'one country, one vote' system, with all members of the WTO accorded the same weight in decision-making (WTO, 1994, Article IX). 'Formally, the WTO is the most democratic of all intergovernmental organisations with a global mandate' (UNDP et al., 2003, p. 5). Decision-making in the WTO is done by consensus, and new trade rules are deemed to be agreed upon when no member actively voices disagreement. While this consensus approach means that formally all members have an equal say, key challenges remain. First, the influence of WTO members in the negotiations varies in light of their market size and the size of their permanent representation in Geneva. Second, inequalities in information and research capacities among member states impact negotiating capacity due to the increasing complexity of the negotiations. Third, for most of its history, the GATT/WTO system has been dominated by the USA and other economically powerful countries. Negotiations have traditionally been conducted in concentric circles, beginning with the 'Quadrilateral Group' [Canada, the European Union (EU), Japan, and the USA] negotiating in the infamously exclusionary 'Green Rooms', then extending in a limited way to a few emerging economies, and finally expanding to include the remaining member states. Newly emerging powers, such as China, India and Brazil, working through developing country coalitions, have challenged the traditional hold of the USA and its allies on the most significant negotiations. With consensus-building having shifted to small group discussions that now include China, India and

Brazil (Hopewell, 2016), the traditional 'North-South' divide has converted into an 'insider-outsider' divide, with only a small number of developed and major developing countries being included in crucial negotiations.

The attempt by the WTO to launch the 'Millennium Round' of trade negotiations in the year 2000 failed spectacularly in the face of anti-globalisation protests at its third ministerial meeting held in Seattle in 1999. When the new round of trade talks was finally launched in 2001 in Doha, it was explicitly labelled as a 'development' round, with development at the heart of its concerns (WTO, 2001b). However, negotiations faced multiple obstacles, and the collapse of the Doha Round has become one of the significant failures of the WTO. Another 'major governance failure' (Van den Bossche, 2023, p. 1) of the organisation is the fact that its DSS, which it famously referred to as the 'jewel in its crown', is in a state of disrepair with the dismantling of its two-tier structure. The appeals mechanism of the WTO is no longer functional due to the blocking of appointments to the Appellate Body (Payosova et al., 2018), and panel reports are now being 'appealed into the void', thereby weakening the enforceability of WTO rules.

POLITICAL JUSTICE

The WTO brings together hugely diverse countries. Indeed, the *Marrakesh Agreement Establishing the World Trade Organization* (WTO, 1994) acknowledges this diversity, stating in its preamble that it recognises there are 'needs and concerns at different levels of economic development'. More than three-quarters of all members of the WTO are developing or least-developed countries.

Initiatives such as the 'Generalised System of Preferences' (GSP) are designed to address the special concerns of developing countries. The Aid for Trade initiative, launched in 2005, aims at supporting developing economies in building their trading capacities, improving their infrastructure, and strengthening their capacity to benefit from trading opportunities. Additionally, WTO agreements contain provisions for the 'Special and Differential Treatment' (S&DT) of developing and least-developed countries that translate into special rights (or favourable treatment), allowing for flexibilities, such as exemptions and grace periods, in the implementation of their commitments. The focus of the Doha Development Agenda (DDA) on development was meant to address the special concerns of developing countries. Yet negotiations in the Doha Round brought to light the deeply diverging views among members on specific aspects of the DDA.

While the WTO agreements provide for S&DT for developing countries, the organisation does not define the term 'developing countries' and provides no criteria for qualifying as a 'developing country'. Member states 'self-declare' their development status, constituting a challenge for negotiations. China, for instance, still claims 'developing country' status for itself in the WTO despite being the world's largest trading nation. In 2019, the USA questioned the WTO's approach (WTO General Council, 2019a). The argument put forth by the USA was that the S&DT provisions put the industrialised countries at a disadvantage. Citing statistics to indicate that the world had transformed since the 1990s, the USA argued that 'the economic tides since the creation of the WTO have lifted nearly all boats' and that 'the binary 'North-South' construct does not reflect the development realities . . .' anymore (WTO General Council, 2019a, p. 2). The draft decision circulated by the USA soon thereafter proposed criteria based on which developing countries could be disqualified from availing of S&DT, including (i) membership in the OECD; (ii) membership in the G20; (iii) 'high income' classification by the World Bank; and (iv) a global merchandise trade share greater than 0.5 per cent (WTO General Council, 2019b, pp. 1–2). If these criteria were implemented, more than thirty developing countries, representing more than 50 per cent of the world's population, would no longer qualify automatically for S&D flexibilities (Kwa & Lunenborg, 2019, p. 3). According to Kwa and Lunenborg (2019, p. 1), the US proposal would effectively replace a treaty-based right of the developing countries with an offer of conditional concessions to select developing countries that would deprive them of the choice of the pace at which they can adjust to trade rules.

Several WTO members, including India, justify the self-declaration of 'developing country' status and argue that the development divide between countries 'persists and has widened' (WTO, 2019c, p. 11). The S&DT provisions, therefore, remain relevant, and an attempt to dilute them would deprive developing country members of the right to develop and would be an assault on the premises of inclusiveness, equity and fairness (WTO, 2019c, p. 1). India argues that the self-declaration approach is appropriate and best serves the WTO's objectives, given the capacity asymmetry among different member states (WTO, 2019c, p. 7). While this issue is yet to be resolved, it is clear that the fair handling of its members based on proper recognition of their capacity constraints is a prerequisite for the path towards more political justice in the WTO.

SOCIOECONOMIC JUSTICE

The WTO's claimed goal is 'to improve the welfare of the people of the WTO's members (WTO, 2021a, p. 3). The impact of trade on socioeconomic justice has been reviewed at several levels. Trade is viewed as 'a catalyst for economic growth and development . . .', total exports in 2019 increased to 250 times the 1948 level (WTO, 2021a, p. 4). Studies show that while trade has caused a reduction in income inequality among countries (Dorn et al., 2021), it has also caused 'significant increases in within-country income inequality'

(UNCTAD, 2019, p. 1). An integral determinant of the justness of trade is an inclusive sharing of the benefits accruing from international trade.

Trade, according to the WTO, is a 'key driver of global growth and poverty reduction. An open global economy has created opportunities for hundreds of millions of people to lift themselves out of extreme poverty' (WTO & World Bank, 2018, p. 3). It is equally well established, however, that trade creates both winners and losers, and significant work has highlighted the differential impacts of trade on different income groups and types of workers within countries (Egger & Kreickemeier, 2012; Fajgelbaum & Khandelwal, 2016). In some situations, trade liberalisation can adversely impact labour (when the expanding sector is capital-intensive and the returns to labour decrease). Yet, the WTO does not specifically address labour issues, in deference to the 'social justice' mandate of the International Labour Organization (ILO) (see the chapters on labour, Chapters 6 and 7 in this volume).

Importantly, and more so in the context of the Global South, the implications of trade policy on weaker sections of society need to be understood through the lens of intersectionality, given the discrimination-based divides in society on the lines of race, indigenous identity, gender, religion and national origin (WEF, 2021, pp. 6–8). A large part of the perception of the injustice of the trading system stems from the belief that trade policy is not founded on an understanding of the social inequities embedded within societies and the potential implications of international trade on matters of distributive equality.

INTERGENERATIONAL JUSTICE

Concerns relating to intergenerational equity and justice have been intricately interlinked with the work of the WTO. To what extent does the WTO ensure that global trade does not end up threatening planetary ecological limits? The trade and sustainability interface have played out at the WTO for many decades, taking different turns at different points in time.

The predecessor to the WTO, the GATT, made no direct reference to the 'environment', but it contained certain windows of exception that could be applied for environmental protection. The General Exceptions contained in GATT Article XX allowed exceptions for measures 'necessary for the protection of human, animal, or plant life or health' [Article XX(b)] and 'relating to the conservation of exhaustible natural resources . . .' [Article XX(g)]. These provisions were invoked in several disputes, yet they were never allowed during the GATT years (1947–1994) (Negi, 2005).

The setting up of the WTO, however, appeared to witness a turn to sensitivity towards environmental concerns – a phenomenon referred to in the literature as the 'greening' of the institution. To begin with, the preamble to the *Agreement Establishing the World Trade Organization* made explicit mention of the need to 'protect and preserve the environment' as well as the objective of 'sustainable development' (WTO, 1994). Several disputes – most notably the shrimp-turtle (WTO, 1998) and the asbestos (WTO, 2001a) disputes – were settled through reports that were perceived as favourable to environmental and public health concerns. Although the WTO's environmental jurisprudence has also been highlighted for its 'inconsistencies, uncertainties, and risks' (Trachtman, 2017, p. 308), its engagement with sustainability concerns through its jurisprudence has grown tremendously.

On a parallel track, the WTO has developed several agreements that have implications for sustainability, more particularly the *Agreement on Technical Barriers to Trade* (TBT Agreement) (WTO, 1995a) and the *Agreement on the Application of Sanitary and Phytosanitary Measures* (SPS Agreement) (WTO, 1995b). The TBT Agreement allows countries to use packaging, marking and labelling requirements as technical regulations, while the SPS Agreement allows the use of sanitary and phytosanitary measures to protect human, animal or plant life or health. Both agreements encourage the use of international standards but also permit member states to set the levels of protection they deem appropriate to meet their public health or environmental objectives.

The Doha Ministerial Declaration, adopted in 2001 (at the Fourth Ministerial meeting of the WTO), saw the inclusion of certain environmental issues in the negotiating agenda of the WTO, albeit in a fairly limited manner (WTO, 2001b). More recently, a renewed emphasis on the trade-environment interface was witnessed at the WTO, with fifty-three members launching a process in 2020 'to collaborate, prioritise, and advance discussions on trade and environmental sustainability' (WTO CTE, 2020, p. 2). In 2021, the Trade and Environmental Sustainability Structured Discussions (TESSD) issued a ministerial statement acknowledging 'sustainable development and the protection and preservation of the environment' as 'fundamental goals of the WTO' and recognising the role of international trade policy in supporting environmental objectives and advancing sustainable consumption and production (WTO TESSD, 2021, p. 1). In addition, two other ministerial statements were launched at the WTO on plastic pollution and fossil fuel subsidy reform (WTO IDP, 2021; WTO, 2021b). These initiatives are supported by a wide range of countries around the world, including several emerging economies as well as LDCs and TESSD countries, which now represent more than 85 per cent of world trade.

Over its lifespan, the WTO appears to have more visibly developed a 'green conscience', as is evident in its dispute settlement, negotiations, discussions and initiatives. However, its incorporation of sustainability concerns is clouded by the fact that it still permits many types of environmentally harmful subsidies that contribute directly and indirectly to deforestation, soil pollution, biodiversity loss and the climate crisis, marring its contribution to intergenerational equity.

ENTRY POINTS FOR REFORM AND CONCLUDING THOUGHTS

As discussed above, the functioning of the WTO is deeply entrenched in issues related to global justice. Concerns of fairness – among and within countries and across generations – form the dominant thread that runs through many ongoing discussions relating to the WTO's work. At the same time, trade governance does not function in a vacuum, and locating it within the larger framework of global economic governance is crucial. Aaron James (Chapter 5 in this volume) identifies fragmented rule-making as a problem and a source of unfairness and makes a call for 'greater coherence in how we manage our common economic destiny' by better harmonising the systems of trade, money and finance. Increased coherence could also extend beyond the different realms of global economic governance and should include more robust interlinkages between trade governance and environmental governance (Brandi & Morin, 2023).

While formal provision for such coherence is provided for in Article V of the WTO Agreement, which calls for the WTO to 'make appropriate arrangements for effective cooperation with other intergovernmental organisations that have responsibilities related to those of the WTO' (WTO, 1994, Article V), effective use of this provision is what needs to be invoked. Indeed, the WTO will be well-served to make better use of the second part of the provision in Article V as well, which calls for 'consultation and cooperation with non-governmental organisations'. Cooperation with NGOs is crucial to better address the need for reconciling justice-related issues, such as sustainability and rights, with trade (Hoekman & Kostecki, 2001). However, all efforts at cooperation with other entities will need to be preceded by an emergence of the WTO from its internal crises in terms of rule-making and rule implementation.

One much-discussed and increasingly practised approach aimed at resolving the rule-making crisis through a revived use of the WTO's negotiation function involves greater emphasis being placed on plurilateral agreements (Hoekman & Mavroidis, 2015), that is, agreements that are negotiated within a group of like-minded countries that are willing to take steps towards deeper integration. While this may prove to be a promising approach, as illustrated by the conclusion of the WTO Agreement on Investment Facilitation for Development among 125 member states in 2023, several members, such as India and South Africa, are opposed to this approach as they view it as undercutting the intended multilateral design of the WTO.

For rule implementation, the DSS will need to be brought back on its feet in all its former 'two-tier' glory by reviving the Appellate Body. But until that is achieved, interim suggestions include resorting to arbitration proceedings under Article 25 of the *Dispute Settlement Understanding*, disputing parties reaching ex ante agreements to abstain from appeal, allowing automatic completion of appeals through amendment of the Working Procedures of the Appellate Body, etc. (Payosova et al., 2018, pp. 10–11). More recently, the Multi-Party Interim Appeal Arbitration Arrangement (MPIA) has been set up in April 2020 to arbitrate disputes that would otherwise have been appealed (Pauwelyn, 2023). The Outcome Document of the 12th Ministerial Conference held in 2022 committed to discussions towards a 'fully and well-functioning dispute settlement system . . . accessible to all Members' (WTO, 2022, p. 1).

A properly functioning WTO is particularly important for the less powerful countries, who need the multilateral forum of the WTO to have a voice in trade negotiations, to be able to build coalitions to defend their needs and to be able to mould the reform of the system to suit the interests of justice. The original promise of the WTO to provide 'stability and predictability' in global trade is particularly significant in times ridden with geopolitical tensions. It is worthwhile for the members, including the less powerful economies, to strengthen the possibilities for the WTO to meet this stated objective while simultaneously pursuing the justice-related objectives that are expected of the trading system.

REFERENCES

Brandi, C., & Morin, J.-F. (2023). *Trade and the Environment: Drivers and Effects of Environmental Provisions in Trade Agreements*. Cambridge University Press.

Dorn, F., Fuest, C., & Potrafke, N. (2021). Trade Openness and Income Inequality: New Empirical Evidence. *Economic Inquiry, 60*(1), 202–23.

Egger, H., & Kreickemeier, U. (2012). Fairness, Trade, and Inequality. *Journal of International Economics, 86*(2), 184–96.

Fajgelbaum, P. D., & Khandelwal, A. K. (2016). Measuring the Unequal Gains from Trade. *The Quarterly Journal of Economics, 131*(3), 1113–80.

Hoekman, B. M., & Kostecki, M. M. (2001). 'Legitimacy, Coherence and Governance' in Bernard M. Hoekman and Michel M. Kostecki, *The Political Economy of the World Trading System: The WTO and Beyond*, 2nd edn., 2001, 461–78. Oxford University Press.

Hoekman, B. M. & Mavroidis, P. C. (2015). WTO 'à la carte' or 'menu du jour'? Assessing the Case for More Plurilateral Agreements. *The European Journal of International Law, 26*(2), 319–43.

Hopewell, K. (2016). *Breaking the WTO: How Emerging Powers Disrupted the Neoliberal Project*. Stanford University Press.

Kwa, A., & Lunenborg, P. (2019). Why the US Proposals on Development Will Affect All Developing Countries and Undermine WTO. South Centre Policy Brief, *58*, 1–11.

Negi, A. (2005), WTO and the Environment: An Overview, in J. K. Mittal and K. D. Raju, *World Trade Organization and India: A Critical Study of Its First Decade*, New Era Law Publications, 300–21.

Pauwelyn, J. (2023). The WTO's Multi-Party Interim Appeal Arbitration Arrangement (MPIA): What's New? World Trade Review, 22(5), 693–701.

Payosova, T., Hufbauer, G. C., & Schott, J. J. (2018). The Dispute Settlement Crisis in the World Trade Organization: Causes and Cures. *Policy Briefs PB18-5*, Peterson Institute for International Economics.

Trachtman, J. P. (2017). WTO Trade and Environment Jurisprudence: Avoiding Environmental Catastrophe. *Harvard International Law Journal*, 58(2), 273–309.
UNCTAD (2019), *Trade Policies and Their Impact on Inequalities: Note by the UNCTAD Secretariat*, TD/B/66/4, 6 May 2019.
UNDP, Heinrich Böll Foundation, The Rockefeller Foundation and Wallace Global Fund (2003), *Making Global Trade Work for People*, Earthscan Publications Ltd.
Van den Bossche, P. (2023). Can the WTO Dispute Settlement System Be Revived? Options for Addressing a Major Governance Failure of the World Trade Organization. World Trade Institute, Universität Bern.
WEF (World Economic Forum) (2021), *International Trade and Economic Justice: A Revised Approach*, Community Paper, September 2021.
WTO (1994), *Marrakesh Agreement Establishing the World Trade Organization.*
WTO (1995a), *Agreement on Technical Barriers to Trade* (TBT Agreement).
WTO (1995b), *Agreement on the Application of Sanitary and Phytosanitary Measures* (SPS Agreement).
WTO (1998). United States – Import Prohibition of Certain Shrimp and Shrimp Products. Report of the Appellate Body, WT/DS58/AB/R 12 October 1998 (98-3899).
WTO (2001a). European Communities – Measures Affecting Asbestos and Asbestos-Containing Products. Report of the Appellate Body, WT/DS135/AB/R 12 March 2001 (01-1157).
WTO (2001b), *Ministerial Declaration Adopted on 14 November 2001*, WT/MIN(01)/DEC/1, 20 November 2001.
WTO (2021a), *WTO in Brief.*
WTO (2021b), *Ministerial Statement on Fossil Fuel Subsidies (Revision)*, WT/MIN(21)/9/Rev.1, 14 December 2021.
WTO (2022), *MC 12 Outcome Document Adopted on 17 June 2022*, Ministerial Conference Twelfth Session Geneva, 12–15 June 2022, WT/MIN(22)/24 WT/L/1135, 22 June 2022.
WTO (2025). Members and Observers. https://www.wto.org/english/thewto_e/whatis_e/tif_e/org6_e.htm.
WTO and World Bank (2018), *Trade and Poverty Reduction: New Evidence of Impacts in Developing Countries*, World Trade Organization.
WTO CTE (Committee on Trade and Environment) (2020), *Communication on Trade and Environmental Sustainability*, WT/CTE/W/249, 17 November 2020.
WTO General Council (2019a), *An Undifferentiated WTO: Self-Declared Development Status Risks Institutional Irrelevance: Communication from the United States* WT/GC/W/757, 16 January 2019.
WTO General Council (2019b), *Draft General Council Decision: Procedures to Strengthen the Negotiating Function of the WTO*, WT/GC/W/764, 15 February 2019.
WTO, General Council (2019c), *The Continued Relevance of Special and Differential Treatment in Favour of Developing Members to Promote Development and Ensure Inclusiveness: Communication from China, India, South Africa, The Bolivarian Republic of Venezuela, Lao People's Democratic Republic, Plurinational State of Bolivia, Kenya, Cuba, Central African Republic and Pakistan*, WT/GC/W/765/Rev.2, 4 March 2019.
WTO IDP (Informal Dialogue on Plastic Pollution and Environmentally Sustainable Plastics Trade) (2021), *Ministerial Statement on Plastic Pollution and Environmentally Sustainable Plastics Trade (Revision)*, WT/MIN(21)/8/Rev.2, 10 December 2021.
WTO TESSD (2021), *Ministerial Statement on Trade and Environmental Sustainability*, WT/MIN(21)/6/Rev.1, 3 December 2021.

Chapter 5

FRAGMENTATION AND FAIRNESS IN GLOBAL ECONOMIC GOVERNANCE

Aaron James

INTRODUCTION

We manage the global economy in a fragmented 'non-system system' of policy and rule-making bodies, for trade, finance and money. This chapter explains how fairness might call for a more coherent organisation of decision-making authority. Specifically, it suggests that fairness as 'structural equity' provides a powerful kind of moral reason to improve coherence by taking the following steps: expand the use of existing international money – the Special Drawing Right (SDR); establish a proper central bank to the central banks; and let it run a twenty-first-century version of J. M. Keynes's Clearing Union plan.

The global economy is of obvious importance for our national and global fortunes. And yet, along with state action, we leave its management to a 'non-system system' in which an array of policy and rule-making bodies, for trade, finance and money, run in parallel rather than in a consistent, well-organised mesh. Is this fragmentation in decision-making authority a problem? Might *fairness* call for greater coherence in how we manage our common economic destiny?

TRADE AS A MUTUAL RELIANCE PRACTICE

The basic subject matter of 'international trade' and the 'global economy' can at one level of description appear relatively unified. International trade as we know it can be understood to include all flows of goods, services and capital (physical and financial, private and public) across borders. Since those flows happen in a political world carved into so many sovereign territorial states, we have them at all only because states have decided to open their borders when they legally might have chosen economic autarky instead (as they did during the interwar years, at least to a great extent). They do so, as I have argued in previous work, in a sort of state social practice – a practice of mutual national reliance upon common markets, for the sake of augmenting national incomes (James, 2012; 2014).

Aside from state choices, trade of course also involves an inordinately complicated range of sub-state actors and their relationships. Multinational corporations arrange major supply chains and decide in the first instance where the benefits and burdens of trade fall. Their decisions, made under pressure from consumers and transnational advocacy groups and in negotiation with labour unions, have outsized sway over most specific cross-border economic arrangements. But they do so only against the backdrop of state practice. The state's decision to keep borders open makes such cross-border arrangements possible and legal. By imposing or relaxing tariffs and regulations, including by international agreements, states substantially shape both the terms of market competition among corporations and the field of political contestation, whether in corporate lobbying, NGO advocacy or union organising.

To say trade is a state 'practice' is not to say it is a fair or just or highly cooperative or even fully voluntary practice. To be sure, the era of imperial trade is perhaps better regarded as coordination backed by force, a relationship of domination and duress, subjugation and extraction, rather than a practice of mutual reliance. But, the idea goes, trade relations have evolved since the interwar years, the Second World War, and the era of decolonisation – in which 'Third World' countries officially took back charge of their affairs.

The specific terms of trade still often reflect the superior bargaining power and undue influence of richer countries. Perhaps advocates from and for the Global South are right to suggest that politics often rhymes with imperial history. Yet nearly seventy-five years after its post-war reconstruction at Bretton Woods, the global economy as we have come to know it is in basic form concertedly created, organised and managed by formally sovereign governments with at least some rational connection to presumptively legitimate purposes of peace and general prosperity. Trade now at least aspires to augment the 'wealth of nations' as Adam Smith once imagined it – that is, the wealth of *all* the nations (not just imperial England).

But what sort of fairness issue, if any, could be at stake in trade? Once a general practice of mutual market reliance is established, I argue, the practice itself raises an issue of 'structural equity' about its form and its consequences, for countries and their respective classes (James, 2012; 2014). Fairness in trade is not in the first instance about so many trades or the general prerequisites for fair exchange. It is 'structural', and concerned with 'equity' in how the national income gains from trade are shared, across societies and among their respective classes – including, especially, the low-skilled workers, women and racial minorities who are most likely to be 'losers' from trade.

The global practice of trade must be governed somehow, and a fragmented system of governance may have much going for it. Different governance domains may house their sites of expertise, or rightful political authority. Perhaps, in practice, the various state agents or relevant international bodies charged with regulation might be able and even willing to adjust as the need arises. Perhaps a more coherent division of decision-making authority is not needed or helpful or prone to worse outcomes than fragmentation. Perhaps our existing fractured system of governance promotes the greatest welfare overall, or at least the minimisation of poverty, over generations. Perhaps a modicum of 'fairness' or 'structural equity' is good for soothing resentments and ensuring social stability, but otherwise, nothing for the serious-minded to worry about.

My claim in this discussion is that, whatever other values might be in play, there is at least a general fairness rationale for greater cohesion in global economic governance. Fairness as structural equity itself provides a powerful kind of moral reason to better harmonise the systems of trade, money and finance, in at least a few key respects. Namely, we could expand the use of existing international money – the Special Drawing Right (SDR); establish a proper central bank to the central banks; and let it run a twenty-first-century version of J. M. Keynes's Clearing Union plan.

Fragmentation

Consider three key fissures in global decision-making authority.

First, limited trade governance: traditionally, trade agreements (such as the WTO and bilateral or regional agreements) are limited to 'at the border' issues. When they govern issues 'behind the border', it is only with relatively low, issue-specific (for example, labour, environmental, intellectual property or investment) standards. Negotiators normally punt on key questions about social insurance or other compensation for 'losers' from trade, which are left for domestic management, in fiscal or monetary policy.

Second, segregation of trade and finance: as an administrative matter, we have separately-mandated institutions – the WTO for trade, and the IMF for finance – each working mainly on their own. When the two regimes do intersect – amidst accusations of 'unfair trade' due to central bank 'currency manipulation', for instance – our global strategy is to hope parties to the dispute, advised by the IMF and their domestic central banks, will somehow work things out, at some point, amidst what may be severe consequences for domestic employment and politics.

Third, dollar dominance: instead of relying upon international money for international trade, cross-border exchange proceeds to a large extent in national money, US dollars. Dollars also serve as the world's reserve currency – the money in which most countries save for a rainy day. The US central bank – the Federal Reserve System (that is, 'the Fed') – acts as a de facto global central bank despite its lack of a mandate and established capacity to manage the consequences of its actions for both the United States and its trading partner countries, poorer and richer alike.

Consider each of these fissures in turn.

As for limited trade governance, I will not focus here on trade agreements, except to note one general trend. It turns out that governments are better at freeing trade 'at the border' than improving the social insurance systems needed to manage trade's domestic disruptions. Once left for domestic decisions, governments such as the US government have not bothered or made minimal efforts to address them. We could do things rather differently. Much as labour, environmental, intellectual property, and investment standards are now built in from the start, trade agreements might include provisions aimed at social inclusion (Shaffer, 2019).

Would that make trade agreements too contentious? Not necessarily. The way social inclusion commitments are attained might still vary from country to country. And that may or may not call for controversial tax-and-transfer mechanisms, for instance. In countries such as the USA, the Fed could be empowered to pay basic income payments to Citizen Accounts that every citizen has at the Fed, and specifically direct dollar credits to those who suffer unemployment or diminished wage prospects due to trade. As I have argued with Robert Hocket elsewhere, the Fed could do such 'allocation' as part and parcel of money 'modulation', with new tools for inflation management, all in the more efficient service of its mandated *monetary* objectives (Hockett & James, 2020).

Turning to the segregation of trade and finance, our current arrangements partly reflect the breakdown of the post-war Bretton Woods system, which gave birth to the organs of global economic governance that remain. In the destructive interwar years, governments felt free to engage in the 'beggar my neighbour' devaluation of their currencies, to shape exchange rates and boost their immediate benefits from trade. Competitive currency devaluation was never a great problem under the post-war Bretton Woods system, whose fixed currency exchange rates purposefully took questions of exchange rate 'manipulation' off the table – precisely to avoid the monetary competition of the interwar years. But with the move to 'floating' rates after the end of those monetary controls, exchange rate 'manipulation' became a cause of dispute again, most prominently concerning China's 'artificial' devaluation of the renminbi and trade surplus concerning the USA.[1] As noted already, the WTO and IMF rules for exchange rate intervention are not especially helpful. They were, after all, crafted for a now-defunct system of fixed rates, where

[1] Talk of 'currency manipulation' is often itself closely tied to the neoclassical understanding of money as a 'neutral veil': it assumes a 'real' exchange rate from which manipulation leads the currency to diverge. On freeing ourselves from the image in ways that bear on fairness assessment, see Weber and Shaikh (2020).

manipulation was not possible. They do help contain disputes (Shaffer et al., 2015). But what they permit could be far clearer, especially since the rules themselves mention fairness specifically ('unfair competitive advantage').[2]

What has fallen through the governance cracks here could hardly be less important. It is one important cause of today's smouldering US–China tensions over Chinese currency 'manipulation' – along with the long-term decline of manufacturing and persistent wage stagnation in the USA, the collapse of the US social compact with its working class and the consequent rise of 'democratic backsliding' into authoritarian politics. To be sure, many decades of domestic political negligence in the USA are a big factor as well. But fractured global governance – the bed the USA made for itself over the last seventy or so years – is a crucial backstory.

As for the bed the USA made for itself – and for the world – it was US officials that from the start made the Bretton Woods system more fragmented than it needed to be. 'Dollar dominance' wasn't inevitable; it was imposed or at least allowed at the close of the Second World War during the two weeks of negotiations at Bretton Woods. British negotiator J. M. Keynes had proposed an intergovernmental money – the 'bancor' – to facilitate currency conversion, along with a Clearing Union that would identify and address payment imbalances, making adjustments between one money relative to another to remedy them. But American negotiator Harry Dexter White, awash in America's new prominence and creditor position concerning the world, would have his way.

As a result, along with a modest lender of last resort (the IMF) and development bank (the World Bank), a *national* money and *national* central bank – the dollar and the Fed – would try to serve the needed *global* functions. The 'golden' post-war decades of relative financial calm perhaps went well enough. Yet the subsequent liberalisation of the Bretton Woods monetary and banking controls brought a dramatic increase in the number, size, severity and frequency of currency, banking and sovereign debt crises (Reinhard & Rogoff, 2011, Appendix). While the causes of any crisis are many and complex, key implosions – including the 1990s East Asian Crisis, the 2008 crisis and the Great Recession aftermath – came under the long shadow of White's fateful decision to place the US dollar at the heart of the global economy.

To be sure, there may be more than one way to get the needed jobs done. What is crucial to complement significant goods and services flows is a global financial system that reliably serves at least five regulatory 'functions' (Hockett & James, 2020, Appendix):

[2] IMF Article of Agreement (IV. 1. iii) provides that member countries are obliged to 'avoid manipulating exchange rates or the international monetary system in order to prevent effective balance of payments adjustment or to gain an unfair competitive advantage over other members'.

1. Facilitate currency conversion for cross-border trade;
2. Provide or issue the 'global' currency into which national moneys are converted;
3. Provide emergency liquidity as needed, on a global scale;
4. Administer and oversee the global payments system;
5. Oversee and regulate financial stability, including long-run current account balances, globally accounted for, and thus 'provide adjustments' to one money relative to another, mitigating long-run surpluses;
6. Fund global/international investment (for development and public goods) where domestic investment falls short.

These functions can be fulfilled in different ways, with more or less formality, or more or less global centralisation, at least in principle. We now distribute them across a fragmented set of institutions, including the world's central banks, the International Monetary Fund, the World Bank, and the Bank of International Settlements and Basel Committee. These agencies do coordinate in various formal and informal ways, and central bank cooperation has mainly expanded in the wake of the 2008 crisis when central banks turned to 'macro-prudential' measures and extended currency 'swap lines' – mutual promises of free or cheap foreign money when needed. Even among 'freely convertible' currencies, central banks often intervene, running a 'dirty float', or an upper or lower bound on one currency's rate of exchange for another, to manage long-run current account imbalances.

Given the dollar's special place as the money of account for much of international trade and as the dominant reserve asset by which countries save, the Fed looms large in these informal arrangements. This might be fine, in principle, if the Fed could prove itself a reliable steward of global monetary responsibilities. But, in practice, all central banks tend to be nationally minded and work under parochial mandates, even when their decisions are consequential abroad. While the Fed is already something of a global central bank, de facto, a Fed-centric global 'system' is arguably too ad hoc, or too open to arbitrary policies based on considerations of political power or damage potential to the world economy rather than to the needs of a given domestic public.

For those reasons, and others I will come back to, there's a case to make for new arrangements, specifically, a proper central bank for the central banks – with greater formality, a proper mandate and greater institutional capacity. A new global central bank, as guided by nationally appointed officials, could itself be built atop the IMF, the Bank of International Settlements, and the Basel Committee, which already perform global central banking functions (Hockett, 2013). The Special Drawing Right (SDR), an existing international money issued by the IMF, could be vastly expanded and used widely in international commerce. The global bank would do what national central banks now do to limit volatility and spreads in exchange rates, but with expanded currency swap facilities between SDRs and all national currencies. Compensation for needed adjustments to net creditor or debtor positions could be arranged for countries being asked to make painful adjustments, paid in SDRs, issued by fiat. And, crucially, the bank would perform all these functions with less ad hoc, less parochial, and more formal and transparent procedures. Governments would be less subject to what may seem arbitrary national central bank decisions, and find themselves freer in a more stable, reliable, and less crisis-prone order, better able to shape their national destinies.

Why Fairness?

None of this is yet to say why fairness, per se, counsels in favour of the less fragmented arrangements just outlined. Returning to my general account of fairness in trade, structural equity does offer a general rationale for a less ad hoc, more centralised monetary system.

My general account begins with the claim of social interpretation noted earlier. The global economy is organised by the territorial state system, and, within that basic political order, by a social practice in which different societies choose to rely, mutually, upon common markets, for the sake of augmenting their national incomes (James, 2012). They do so, I presume, for the usual economic reasons: imports free up resources for more productive uses, allowing societies to further refine their divisions of labour and, along with technology flows, improve their standards of living.

Here any state choice to rely on common markets – whether in goods, services, or capital, both physical and financial, including public money – counts as part of the general international practice of trade and a matter for structural equity assessment. Likewise, all decisions that significantly influence such flows can be assessed as fair or unfair according to general principles that apply to the larger trade practice. The familiar array of policy and rule-making bodies – the WTO, World Bank, IMF, the Bank of International Settlements, along with trading states themselves – are our formal ways of governing the larger international practices that make or shape such decisions. So those agencies and their decisions, too, can be assessed as fair or unfair by trade practice's principles.

The same goes for any financial and monetary systems, along with monetary decisions by central banks within them. In a world of economic autarky or very minimal trade, central bank decisions about interest rates, credit and money supply would have only domestic effects. But in a relatively integrated modern economy, monetary policy decisions in one country – especially a country such as the USA – can quickly be of profound moment given the potential for money and trade flows to disrupt a foreign country's own economic and social conditions.

Especially relevant here are domestic decisions about monetary policy that impose externalities for other trading countries via its effect on exchange rates, which in turn shape the relative competitiveness of imports or exports, public and private credit and debt positions, employment, inflation or deflation, and a whole country's prospects. In 2014, for example, fears of the US Fed relaxing the dollar supply had immediate adverse results for developing country exchange rates from India to Brazil to Turkey to South Africa – even as many were still recovering in the wake of the global crisis of 2008. Or in a different kind of case, perhaps an undervalued currency in a developing country such as China cheapens exports with adverse consequences for trade flows and employment in the USA.

When Brazil's finance minister, Guido Mantega, spoke of a 'currency war' in 2011, he argued that Brazil was being hurt by externalities of both kinds. He complained of competitive currency devaluation by Asian central banks but also objected to US 'quantitative easing', which caused the Brazilian real to appreciate against the dollar. In both cases, Brazil's exports arguably became less competitive in advanced world markets, while Brazil itself was flooded with cheap imports, causing job losses and a slowed growth path.

In our current system, such 'monetary externalities' work in part by what might be called the exchange rate channel of influence. The channel of influence itself holds, in part, because of the larger mutual reliance practice being allowed and maintained. The decision to allow that channel of influence to exist, or to have the consequences it has – at least when there are other ways of managing money conversion – is, therefore, something we can assess as fair or unfair by the principles that govern the larger relationship.

As for how to reason about what is required for 'structural equity' in that larger relationship, I draw from T. M. Scanlon's general account of 'what we owe to each other' (Scanlon, 1998). We reason by making pairwise comparisons of the relevant interests or claims of each participating country, and their respective social classes, for or against alternative versions of the market reliance practice (or principles for its regulation). We rank order such 'complaints' or 'objections' by their strength, and the strongest one is the 'reasonable' one. (As an 'ordinal' rather than 'cardinal' ranking, this does not require famously problematic 'interpersonal comparisons', or otherwise any single common 'currency' such as welfare.) We conclude that the practice of trade is structurally inequitable if some party could 'reasonably object' to it in favour of a different version, and structurally equitable when no potential objection to it is stronger or more highly ranked than the objections to the alternatives (that is, it takes a form 'no one could reasonably reject').

More specifically, assuming trade benefits all countries to some extent in the longer run, we can begin with claims to the 'gains from trade', seen as the surplus in national income created specifically by international cooperation, leaving aside national endowments. Treating this as a basic problem of 'fair division', I defend three general principles for dividing trade's surplus, which are as follows (James, 2012).

First, national income gains due to trade (gains over autarky) are to be distributed equally, unless special benefits flow to developing countries (for reasons of 'priority for the worse off', that is, the idea that benefits matter more, in fairness, the worse off people are).

Second, harms due to trade require compensation, for example, by social insurance schemes (where 'harm' is judged by subjunctive-historical or historical baselines).

Third, within trading countries, national income gains are to be distributed equally or otherwise acceptably among members of a given society, once harms are compensated for.

What might these principles require? Each would single out a specific kind of monetary externality as presumptively unfair – unless it is necessary for some other compensating benefits, any of which might (or might not) be present in a given case.

The first principle, for instance, might indict costs imposed by a central bank decision on the overall national income of a trade partner over some suitable time frame (for example, by cutting its export income, increasing unemployment, raising its costs of borrowing, discouraging investment, and/or reducing growth). This would be especially difficult to justify when the cost to national income falls to a less well-off country; unless it can be shown to support an optimal growth trajectory over the longer run.

The second principle, which concerns 'losers' within trading countries, might impugn a way foreign monetary decisions lead to a net worsening in the life prospects of specific social groups, especially the most vulnerable groups, say, by way of consequences for the level or distribution of employment. If the externality causes a significant downturn, perhaps certain groups would have fared better over their whole lives under a much more protected economy.

And under the third principle, which concerns how gains are shared within countries, a foreign monetary decision that differentially affects import and export sectors, with consequences for employment level and wages, might leave some worse off relative to others over time, even if everyone is no worse off overall for trade.

CUTTING THE CHANNEL OF INFLUENCE

In any of these ways, a monetary system that allows the exchange rate channel of influence to exist, or be as significant as it is, might be judged structurally inequitable for its relevant adverse consequences. That is true, at least, provided there is some feasible alternative arrangement that does better in the relevant dimension for parties affected, such that they can reasonably complain of our failure to adopt it instead.

We have already said what one possible alternative might be: a global central bank (see Hockett, 2013). Again, a new global central bank could issue SDRs by fiat. SDRs, instead of dollars, would be the world's reserve currency and the primary money of account for international exchange. But, crucially, with the dollar 'dethroned', Fed decisions about the dollar would not cause monetary externalities as they now do, since countries would neither save nor trade nor borrow nor lend mainly in dollars as they now do. Indeed, no country's domestic monetary decisions would alter the value of its exports or imports in any other national money, at least not directly, since all money would first be exchanged for SDRs.

The rate of exchange between SDRs and all other moneys would be managed as a 'dirty float', with regular adjustments to relative values to prevent and resolve excessive imbalances. Again, the bank might also pay compensation in SDRs to countries or their classes that bear the burden of adjustment, as structural equity (or other) principles require. In a well-run version, these adjustments would be made in a transparent and accountable manner, by relevant rules and principles, rather than in an ad hoc, parochial manner.

Is this necessary? Might our Fed-centric system simply do better as a quasi-global central bank than it now does? Instead of blocking the very channel of adverse influence, could the Fed just better mitigate the pitfalls of a dollar-based system, or even compensate for costs after they are incurred in dollars? It might, and should try, but 'try' here is the operative word. If its noble efforts will not suffice, as they arguably will not, it is better, fairer, to simply block the channel of influence by which harm is done in the first place.

Fed efforts at mitigation and compensation are not likely to be entirely adequate for the systemic reasons already noted. Again, central banks have largely parochial mandates and cultures.[3] While those mandates could be reformed, arguably no national bank can be expected to faithfully compensate for harm abroad. The job is not an entirely fair 'ask' even of the smartest and best-intentioned officials, being mainly beyond their institutional epistemic capacity. Better, and fairer to give the jobs of a global central bank to a global central bank, which is duly empowered to work as it should.

Still, it is important to note that central banks are themselves highly cooperative already. And it is fair to worry that new centralisation might hobble what good cooperation there already is. If treasury officials, who tend to be less expert and more beholden to politically motivated executives, were included in a global central bank's deliberations, would that compromise what good we have in central bank 'independence' and politicise existing monetary cooperation in destructive ways? Would monetary decisions

[3] US Fed meeting transcripts do show concerns over implications of monetary easing internationally, given criticism. http://on.ft.com/1RLAmMl

become more responsive to pressure from politicians seeking to boost their short-term popularity and re-election prospects?

I take it any new moves should affirm and preserve central bank 'independence' from short-term political pressure, consistent with after-the-fact accountability to domestic legislators and the public (Hocket & James, 2020). I also grant that the justifiability of a global central bank, on balance, does depend on how confident we can be that it will be a well-run operation.

I might also note that, while any significant consolidation may be politically unlikely at the moment, it is entirely feasible for public banking options to supplement the existing payment system, now run largely through nominally private banks and their highly regulated interbank cooperatives. With the inspiration of digital ledger technology, many central banks (in Singapore, Sweden, China, India, Mexico and the USA, among others) are already exploring or experimenting with ways of running public money outside of private bank payment systems via central bank digital currencies (CBDCs).

This already promises greater inclusion and equity and draws attention to what central banks are technically capable of. Better still, central banks could attach an interest rate to central bank accounts which they raise or lower to influence saving or spending as needed to hold inflation (for this and other new tools of inflation management, see Hocket and James 2020). For being more 'democratic' and inclusive, monetary policy could be run more efficiently, with everyone enjoying the benefit of sure, free money.

Indeed, if we dare to imagine it, why not then pay a basic income grant to everyone the world over, in every country, in SDR credits, by fiat? Every citizen of every country might receive a regular payment in his or her account at his or her national central bank, backed by a global central bank, which he or she can spend from his or her digital wallet on the computer or cellphone, (automatically) exchanging for the local national money. Each domestic central bank, backed by its global centre, could adjust interest rates on public accounts and manage inflation or deflation as appropriate for domestic macroeconomic conditions given global economic conditions.

We should dare to dream. The fragmented nature of global economic governance is itself a source of structural inequity, and unnecessarily so. Greater coherence may not be politically possible now. But, in time, it might become possible – perhaps precisely for giving people a fairer shake.

REFERENCES

Hockett, R. (2013). Bretton Woods 1.0: A Constructive Retrieval for Sustainable Finance. *NYU Journal of Legislation and Public Policy, 16*, 401.

Hockett, R., & James, A. (2020). *Money from Nothing: Or, Why We Should Stop Worrying about Debt and Learn to Love the Federal Reserve*. Melville House.

James, A. (2012). *Fairness in Practice: A Social Contract for a Global Economy*. Oxford University Press.

James, A. (2014). A Theory of Fairness in Trade. *Moral Philosophy and Politics, 1*(2), 177–200.
Reinhart, C. M. and Rogoff, K. S. (2011). *This Time Is Different: Eight Centuries of Financial Folly*. Princeton University Press.
Scanlon, T. M. (1998). *What We Owe to Each Other*. Harvard University Press.
Scanlon, T. M. (2003). Précis of 'What We Owe to Each Other'. *Philosophy and Phenomenological Research, 66*(1), 159–61.
Shaffer, G. (2019). Retooling Trade Agreements for Social Inclusion. *University of Illinois Law Review, 1*.
Shaffer, G., Waibel, M., & Halliday, T. C. (2015). The (Mis) Alignment of the Trade and Monetary Legal Orders. *Transnational Legal Orders, 187*, 206–7.
Weber, I., & Shaikh, A. (2020). The US–China Trade Imbalance and the Theory of Free Trade: Debunking the Currency Manipulation Argument. In *Capitalism: An Unsustainable Future?*, 102–25. Routledge.

Chapter 6

LABOUR JUSTICE IN THE GLOBAL ECONOMY AND GLOBAL ECONOMIC GOVERNANCE: A BROAD OVERVIEW WITH FOCUS ON THE ILO AND CSR

Elizabeth A. Bennett[1]

INTRODUCTION

This chapter presents an empirical analysis of the relationship between labour and global economic governance. 'Labour' refers to workers, national trade unions, global union federations (GUFs), cooperatives, labour rights defenders and labour-oriented civil society organisations (CSOs) (Birchall 2020). It includes both the formally and informally employed, and makes up about half the world's population (ILO, 2023). The chapter focuses on three types of justice: democratic justice is the inclusion of workers and their organisations in decision-making and accountability; socioeconomic justice refers to decent work, freedom from exploitation, non-discrimination, and living wages; and intergenerational justice is the consideration for impact on future generations. The chapter concludes that labour's share of influence on global economic governance and benefits from a globalised economy are meagre and declining. The relationship between waning power and diminishing profits is mutually reinforcing, creating a negative feedback loop that, over time, amplifies challenges to labour justice.

The chapter begins by arguing that labour's influence on global economic governance has declined (relative to the private sector) over the past three decades. It describes the powerful position of a small number of 'lead firms'[2] and shows how this shift has generated devastating socioeconomic outcomes for labour. Next, the chapter examines labour justice in the context of the International Labour Organization (ILO), the international organisation most

[1] The author would like to acknowledge the invaluable contributions of the editors who provided thoughtful direction and feedback on the chapter; Sawyer Mauk, who offered excellent assistance in reviewing literature, gathering figures, organising research, and preparing the manuscript; and Lewis & Clark College for being a supportive institutional home.

[2] 'Lead firms' refers to multi-national corporations with global supply chains.

responsible for the global governance of labour issues. Finally, the chapter analyses labour justice in the context of corporate social responsibility (CSR), which has emerged as a central feature of non-governmental global economic governance. In closing, the chapter makes clear that although the current system of global economic governance compromises democratic justice, socio-economic justice, and intergenerational justice, labour advocates are advancing myriad innovations and strategies for more just and equitable outcomes.

THE GLOBAL ECONOMY AND GLOBAL ECONOMIC GOVERNANCE

Scholarly accounts of the global history of work make clear that labour relations – the systems that define 'for whom or with whom one works, and under what rules' have long resulted in the exploitation of labour in both the local and global contexts (Hofmeester & van der Linden, 2018, p. 4).

Although several significant shifts occurred in favour of labour justice in the 1800s and early 1900s, these changes neither resolved root challenges of uneven power between workers and employers, nor eliminated widespread labour injustice (Hofmeester & van der Linden, 2018). For instance, the abolishment of chattel slavery was a milestone in preventing workers from being treated as mere property without personal freedom or rights. However, it did not eradicate other forms of slavery, such as debt bondage, human trafficking, and forced labour, which continue to afflict more than 30 million people (Kara, 2017). Likewise, the rise of labour unions brought about improvements in wages and rights for many workers through collective bargaining agreements. However, a significant portion of workers remains excluded from such benefits, and even with these agreements, a substantial number of workers still do not receive a living wage (Miller & Williams, 2009). Similarly, the increased involvement of the state in regulating labour conditions has set standards concerning working hours, health, safety, non-discrimination and child protections. However, these regulations often fall short of being fully enacted, as evidenced by the fact that work-related fatalities still outnumber casualties in wars (Piore & Schrank, 2018). Finally, although the end of colonisation and the rise of democratic institutions offer workers greater capacity to influence political systems in support of labour justice, many do not live in functioning democratic states, or are not franchised in the country where they work. Over the last thirty years, another wave of significant changes has affected labour justice, as described in the following sections.

Globalisation and the Rise of Global Value Chains

The 1990s ushered in a wave of globalisation marked by free trade, liberalised capital and neoliberal regulation. Goods, services, raw materials and manufactured component parts began crossing several borders before reaching their end consumer. Nearly all economic sectors experienced growth in the number of production stages (ILO, 2015). These 'global value chains' (GVCs) continued to increase in length until 2011 and have since persisted at a relatively stable rate (OECD, 2020; Zing, Gentile & Dollar, 2021). By 2015, one in five jobs was connected to a GVC (ILO, 2015).

Globalisation and GVCs shifted power dynamics in the global economy. In part, this is because the countries that had the most power to organise the new globalisation era (e.g., the United States and the G-20) also had the most to gain from allowing lead firms (which are largely located within their borders) to chase cheap labour (which is often found in poorer countries) (Held & McGrew, 2002). Today, around 70 per cent of international trade involves GVCs (OECD, 2023). Yet, GVC activity is concentrated among 15 per cent of large firms that account for 80 per cent of total trade flows (World Bank, 2020). This means that there are only a few large buyers or 'lead firms' while there are many 'suppliers' such as factories, fisheries, plantations and small farms (Anner, 2020). This situation creates asymmetric bargaining power: a lead firm can choose from many suppliers, while suppliers have few opportunities to find better buyers. Lead firms use this power to lock suppliers into low-paying contracts with poor terms and to alter contracts with little notice (e.g., decrease production time, increase volumes, cancel orders or revise specifications) (Locke, 2013). Suppliers are thus fiercely competing against one another by offering lower prices to win difficult contracts. One way they reduce production costs is to reduce the cost of labour. They pay less than minimum wages, offer poor working conditions, outsource, hire vulnerable groups, impede labour organising and facilitate bonded labour (Anner, 2020). Suppliers' demand for cheap labour has increased the portion of migrant, informal, and contract work, exacerbating vulnerability and disenfranchisement, as described in the section on the ILO's promotion of labour standards (Barrientos, 2008; Mayer & Phillips, 2017; Mayer et al., 2017).

Globalisation and Shifts in Global Economic Governance

The past three decades have also shifted *who* governs the global economy and *how*. Most notably, large multinational firms and investors gained social, economic and political power (ILO, 2013; Monaco & Pastorelli, 2013; Witherell, 2013; Mayer & Phillips, 2017; Bartley, 2022) while national governments face increased pressure to attract corporations and investors by promising cheap labour (Mosley, 2017; Anner, 2020). At the same time, labour organising is challenged by a decline in political resources (Sung et al., 2021) and an increase in contract, temporary and migrant work (Gold et al., 2020). In most regions of the world, union density (the portion of workers who are unionised) and union membership have declined (Schnabel, 2020).

The role of civil society has also changed. In the 1990s, global social movements emerged to bring people from all over the world together to take on collective action problems and solve complex governance issues at the international level (Bennett, 2012). Global social movements raised awareness about workers' rights (e.g., through anti-sweatshop campaigns) and helped link labour issues to environmental problems, indigenous rights and other movements (Brookes & Kinzel, 2019; Delautre et al., 2021; Séhier, 2023). At the same time, some argue that single-issue global social movements detracted attention from labour unions rather than bring them into the spotlight in part by focusing on civil society mobilisation rather than labour organising (Brookes & Kinzel, 2019).

The Rise of Private Economic Governance

By the end of the 1990s, many labour-oriented civil society organisations became frustrated with national governments and international organisations (e.g., the WTO) as venues for change. Unable to improve *legal* regulations, they began to shame companies into *voluntarily* adopting more responsible business practices (Bartley, 2007). Such attempts to (re)structure international business through non-governmental practices, agreements, and organisational forms is called 'private governance' (Ponte & Sturgeon, 2014). Private governance initiatives are now ubiquitous and significant in global economic governance. One of the first and most well-known examples of a private labour justice initiative is fair trade (Bennett, 2020). Fair trade aims to create 'a world in which justice and sustainable development are at the heart of trade structures and practices so that everyone, through their work, can maintain a decent and dignified livelihood and develop their full human potential' by promoting market access for marginalised groups, equitable trading relationships, capacity building for suppliers, and consumer awareness (WFTO & FTI, 2009; Raynolds & Bennett, 2015). In recent years, many other frameworks, perhaps most notably the SDGs, have emerged to support similar or overlapping goals (Tallontire and Anderson, 2020). Other private governance initiatives that commonly claim to improve labour justice include voluntary sustainability standards, social entrepreneurship, codes of conduct, and ESG (environmental-social-governance) reporting. Because lead firms, as described in the section on globalization and the rise of global value chains, occupy such a powerful role in the global economy, whether and how they engage in private governance is an important question (for more detail, see the section on private regulation and CSR).

The nature, power dynamics, efficacy, consequences, and future trajectory of private governance is intensely studied and contested (Cashore et al., 2021). More optimistic accounts suggest it may substitute for inadequate public regulation (Jackson & Apostolakou, 2010; Schrage & Gilbert, 2021), complement public policy (Moon, Crane & Matten, 2005; Knudsen & Moon,

2017) and/or support hybrid solutions and new policy innovations (Amengual, 2010; Locke, 2013; Eberlein et al., 2014; Sun, 2022). Where legal regimes are particularly unresponsive to or unsupportive of labour, this potential is particularly significant (Scherer & Palazzo, 2011; Brookes & Kinzel, 2019). In this perspective, global economic governance is now more collaborative and comprehensive, providing more opportunities for labour justice. More critical analyses point to ways in which private governance dilutes public regulation (Bair, 2017), compromises the state (LeBaron & Rühmkorf, 2019) and/or allows states to outsource regulatory responsibilities (Bartley, 2007; Mayer & Phillips, 2017). They also point out the hidden costs of transferring regulatory burden from states (which have regulatory capacity) to global social movements (which often lack resources and legitimate use of force) (LeBaron & Lister, 2021). In this perspective, firms now have more opportunities to regulate themselves and advance their interests, relative to voters, states, international organisations, and labour unions (Clapp & Fuchs, 2009).

Drawing on empirical analysis, many scholars warn against overestimating the efficacy of the private sector to voluntarily regulate itself (Selwyn, 2017; Amengual & Kuruvilla, 2020; Taggart, 2022). They show how private governance may *impede* sustainable development – for example, by narrowing the concept of sustainability to non-labour issues (Clapp & Fuchs, 2009) – more than support it (Ponte, 2020; Dauvergne, 2022).

LABOUR JUSTICE IN THE GLOBAL ECONOMY AND GLOBAL ECONOMIC GOVERNANCE

Labour Participation in Global Economic Governance

Overall, workers have *less* capacity to shape the global economy than thirty years ago. Although some public institutions remain accountable to labour, they are now competing with other actors for regulatory primacy (Moseley, 2017). And although many global social movements support unions, their effectiveness can be hampered by corporate intervention (Jaffee & Howard, 2010; Johns et al., 2019; LeBaron & Rühmkorf, 2019) or – in some contexts – state repression (Brookes & Kinzel, 2019; Fransen et al., 2021). And although new public–private collaborations may technically include worker organisations, they also limit labour influence, crowd out social dialogue with unions, and blur lines between interest groups (Bair, 2017; Mayer & Phillips, 2017; Delautre et al., 2021).

Socioeconomic Outcomes and Intergenerational Impacts on Labour

Globalisation and its governance have generated devastating consequences for labour (Bengtsson & Ryner, 2015; Mayer & Phillips, 2017; Sung et al., 2021). Working conditions are poor, labour rights are compromised (Appelbaum &

Lichtenstein, 2016; Anner, 2020; Delautre et al., 2021), and modern slavery is thriving (Crane et al., 2017; LeBaron & Phillips, 2019). Today more than 20 million people – many in the GVC-concentrated sectors of agriculture, manufacturing and mining – are forced to work, generating profits for their employers of over US $150 billion annually (Kara, 2017; LeBaron & Rühmkorf, 2019).

Gains from global economic growth are distributed very unevenly (Sung et al., 2021). Increasingly, more is going to capital investors than to labour (Piketty, 2014; Autor et al., 2017). Of the share going to labour, an increasing amount is paid to CEOs rather than typical workers. CEO compensation increased 940 per cent from 1978 to 2018, compared to a 12 per cent increase for workers (Mishel & Wolfe, 2019). This has contributed to rapidly increasing income and wealth inequality (see Malerba & Barrientos, Chapter 22 in this volume). In today's economy, being employed does not insure against being poor. About 6.4 per cent of people who are employed also live in extreme poverty (less than $2.15/day at 2017 purchasing power parity, according to the World Bank), and during the pandemic this increased to 7.2 per cent (ILO, 2022; UN, 2023).

Lead firms could distribute a greater share of profits to labour without significantly impacting bottom lines or consumer prices (Miller & Williams, 2009; Hall & Suh, 2020). One study suggests that if apparel brands paid ten cents more per t-shirt during the pandemic, the people making their garments would not have starved (Kyritsis & LeBaron, 2021). Yet, evidence clearly suggests that firms do not prioritise socioeconomic outcomes for labour. In the pandemic, many lead firms cancelled orders and withheld payments, passing the financial burden onto suppliers (Anner, 2021). Suppliers responded by withholding payments to workers, many of whom had few alternatives to unemployment, poverty, debt, and increased vulnerability to severe forms of labour exploitation (Kyritsis & LeBaron, 2021).

Socioeconomic outcomes for labour are terrible and getting worse. This reality raises questions about how the most powerful venues of economic governance are approaching labour justice. The following two sections examine this question in the context of the ILO (an international organisation initiated by states) and CSR (a strategy initiated by corporations). Together, they illustrate how public (governmental) and private (non-governmental) economic governance both play a role in excluding labour from economic governance and facilitating poor socioeconomic outcomes for labour.

PUBLIC REGULATION SPOTLIGHT: INTERNATIONAL LABOUR ORGANIZATION

ILO: Labour in the Democratic Process

The ILO is a UN body created in 1919 to develop labour standards and provide technical assistance to national governments. It is the only intergovernmental organisation in which states do not hold all decision-making power (Swepston, 2019). It has a tripartite governance structure that includes governments, employers, and workers (Posthuma & Rossi, 2017). The 'workers' group' is organised by the International Trade Union Confederation which represents 200 million unionised workers in 168 countries and over 300 national affiliate unions (ITUC, 2023). Although it aims to promote *all* workers' interests, it is formally accountable only to unions (Jakovleski et al., 2019; van der Linden, 2019) and opposes expanding the workers' group to include a broader population (Standing, 2008). Thus, ILO leadership excludes workers in the informal sector and unwaged labour, which is a significant portion of the workforce in many parts of the world – for example, more than 80 per cent in South Asia (Marshall, 2019). Although the ILO includes these groups in some programmatic work – such as the Decent Work programme (Vosko, 2002) – this is a significant deficit in democratic labour justice. An additional challenge for labour is that some member states are increasingly aligned with business interests and thus strengthen the employers' group by joining them in opposing fundamental rights such as freedom of association and the right to strike (Thomas & Turnbull, 2021).

The worker and employer groups have conflicting views on the ILO's response to globalisation. Labour asserts that GVCs and Export Processing Zones (EPZs)[3] pose unprecedented challenges to decent work. They advocate for a targeted ILO response and focus on human rights. Employers have been slower to recognise the distinct challenges posed by globalisation, less supportive of a human rights agenda, and more optimistic about the efficacy of voluntary private governance and 2010 UN Guiding Principles on Business and Human Rights (Posthuma & Rossi, 2017; Silva, 2022). In 2016, however, the groups agreed the ILO should increase attention to GVC-related labour issues and play a more active role in coordinating multi-stakeholder governance activities (Posthuma & Rossi, 2017).

ILO: Promotion of Labour Standards

One of the core functions of the ILO is to promote labour standards. It provides templates that other actors can draw on to design their own labour policies and legitimates the policies those actors create (van der Linden, 2019). ILO standards are integrated into public policy, collective bargaining agreements, labour advocacy positions, free trade agreements, and Global Framework Agreements between transnational corporations and global

[3] EPZs are industrial zones with special incentives set up to attract foreign investors, in which imported materials undergo some degree of processing before being exported again (ILO 2003). They are particularly challenging contexts in which to improve and enforce labour rights, especially freedom of association and collective bargaining (ILO 2003).

union federations (Fichter & Stevis, 2013; Posthuma & Rossi, 2017; Cho & Marzán, 2020). While the ILO's standards regime has expanded over the past three decades, coverage gaps remain. Perhaps most notably, the ILO has yet to develop standards holding lead firms liable for squeezing suppliers in ways that commonly lead to layoffs (Cho & Marzán, 2020).

By some measures, the ILO has been successful in promoting labour standards. Its 1998 Core Labour Standards include freedom of association and collective bargaining (Caraway, 2006). Today, they are incorporated (at least rhetorically) into most CSR initiatives (Posthuma & Rossi, 2017) and IMF and World Bank operations (Caraway, 2006). Similarly, the ILO's 1999 Decent Work programme – which focuses on marginalised worker groups and calls for quality jobs, dignity, equality, a fair income and safe working conditions – has been incorporated into the national economic, employment, and social policies and programmes of over 120 countries (Rantanen et al., 2020). Likewise, the ILO's 2014 Forced Labour Protocol, which obligates states to aid victims, support undocumented migrant workers and investigate forced labour practices, influenced the development of many national policies (Posthuma & Rossi, 2017). Today, labour rights are often recognised as human rights (Aeberhard-Hodges, 2019; Swepston, 2019).

At the same time, the ILO had limited success in compelling states to implement and enforce labour standards after adopting them (van der Linden, 2019). The issue of living wages is illustrative. Although the ILO is constitutionally mandated to support states in establishing a minimum wage sufficient to cover the costs of living, most countries' legal wage is below a 'living wage' (Anker & Anker, 2017; Guzi, 2021) and in many places it is poorly enforced (Anker, 2011; Marshall, 2019). One of the ILO's limitations is that it has no enforcement mechanism – it relies on the public to pressure governments, NGOs to provide oversight, and powerful states to use sanctions to hold other actors accountable (Mosley, 2010; van der Linden, 2019). Another challenge is inadequate resources, which increases risk of donor co-option (Standing, 2008).

ILO: Facilitation of Co-governance Experiments

In recent years, the ILO has played a facilitative role for multi-stakeholder groups attempting to improve labour conditions (Posthuma & Rossi, 2017). The Better Work Programme and the Accord on Fire and Building Safety in Bangladesh (the 'Accord') are examples of this experiment in bridging levels (national and international) and types (public and private) of governance to address GVC challenges (Bair et al., 2020).

The ILO and the International Finance Corporation launched Better Work in 2007 to support suppliers and supplier host countries in meeting standards and marketing their compliance to lead firms. Labour is represented on the governing Global Advisory Committee and each country's domestic advisory committee (Bair, 2017; Posthuma & Rossi, 2017). On one hand, Better Work is commonly identified as one of the more effective responses to GVCs because it incentivises brands to honour collective bargaining and privilege compliant suppliers (Mosley, 2017; Amengual & Kuruvilla, 2020). On the other hand, in some regions, the process of multiple actors interpreting labour standards and negotiating which infractions will 'count' as non-compliances has actually weakened domestic regulation and ratcheted down labour codes (Amengual & Chirot, 2016; Bair, 2017).

The ILO facilitated the Accord in the wake of the 2013 Rana Plaza disaster, in which an apparel manufacturing building collapsed, killing and injuring more than 1,000 and 2,000 workers, respectively (Saxena, 2020). The Accord is an agreement to improve worker safety signed by over 200 apparel brands, two global union federations (IndustriALL and UNI), eight Bangladesh trade unions, and four monitoring NGOs (Posthuma & Rossi, 2017; Bair et al., 2020). It includes worker organisations in its governance and legally requires brands to support remediation of unsafe factories and to source from them during the process (Amengual & Kuruvilla, 2020). On one hand, the Accord successfully engaged 2,000 factories and millions of workers in inspections, remediation and safety training, addressing over 100,000 building safety issues (Anner, 2018; Anner, 2020) – which surpasses the state response (Bair et al., 2020). On the other hand, outcomes for labour were compromised by state and industry actors reluctant to embrace labour organising (Bair et al., 2020). After five years the Accord's activities dissipated (Amengual & Kuruvilla, 2020). Fundamentally, it failed to address the broader structural issues that bring workers and factory managers to take deadly risks to comply with lead firm demands (Saxena, 2020).

Although Better Work and the Accord seek to improve labour justice in countries and sectors where there is unique potential for success, neither can compel lead firms or suppliers to participate. Some argue this non-global approach may erode the ILO's efficacy to improve labour standards *universally* (Jakovleski et al., 2019; Thomas & Turnbull, 2021) or is a symptom of the ILO's waning efficacy in global economic governance (van der Linden, 2019).

The last thirty years raised new questions about how the ILO can facilitate labour justice and whether private initiatives may have more success. The following section examines CSR from the labour justice perspective.

PRIVATE REGULATION SPOTLIGHT: CORPORATE SOCIAL RESPONSIBILITY

CSR: Objectives, Potential, Challenges

Corporate social responsibility (CSR) typically refers to private sector practices oriented around the concept of improving the workplace and society in ways that go above and beyond firms' legal obligations (Malik, 2015). Over the past thirty years, CSR has become a veritable industry and recognised professional domain. Virtually every major corporation allocates staff and resources to CSR (Bair & Palpacuer, 2015).[4] As described in the section on voluntary and mandatory CSR, some countries are now incorporating CSR into legislation, blurring lines between voluntary altruism and regulatory compliance (Gond et al., 2011; Knudsen et al., 2015; Knudsen & Moon, 2017).

Although CSR aims to simultaneously bolster profits and improve socioeconomic outcomes, these objectives often conflict with one another (Mayer & Gereffi, 2010; Crane et al., 2014; Gold et al., 2020). At best, this tension precludes CSR from achieving radical change and distributional justice (Steensen & Villadsen, 2020). At worst, it obscures the root causes of labour injustice (LeBaron & Lister, 2021), sidelines the issue of competitive, one-sided contracts (Barrientos, 2013), and resembles poverty profiteering (Barnett, 2019). In many cases, the gap between CSR rhetoric and action is substantial (Bromley & Powell, 2012; van der Ven, 2019), though some research points to ways in which overstated or aspirational claims may be motivating (Glozer & Morsing, 2020; Schoeneborn et al., 2020).

CSR: Unions and Democratic Justice

CSR is not typically driven by or accountable to labour (Chun & Shin, 2018; Martin et al., 2021; Séhier, 2023). In turn, unions are often sceptical of CSR activities, associating them with philanthropy, perceiving them as greenwashing and assessing them as less effective than supporting unions or defending workers' rights (Martin et al., 2021). At the same time, some unions leverage CSR to meet their own goals. They may use CSR training to disseminate information about labour rights, use CSR reporting to share union activities with external stakeholders, invoke CSR to embarrass companies into compliance or work with CSR-oriented NGOs to advance labour rights (Gold et al., 2020). Under some conditions, CSR may benefit unions by improving wage bargaining outcomes (Goerke, 2020) or attracting investors who are typically averse to unionised firms (Chantziaras et al., 2020).

CSR could do more to support democratic justice. Firms could collaborate with workers and unions when setting priorities, selecting strategies, developing codes of conduct, choosing certifications and designing complaint response mechanisms and monitoring and remediation plans (Amengual & Chirot, 2016; Graz et al., 2020; Martin et al., 2021). Additionally, multinational firms could negotiate collective agreements with global union federations or international trade unions that require firms to contract with unionised

[4] By some estimates, Fortune 500 Companies alone have spent more than US 20 billion dollars on CSR in one year (Dattani et al., 2015). Given the tremendous power of lead firms, widespread concern about inequality and climate change, and broad interest in promoting the Sustainable Development Goals, CSR has captured a great deal of attention and interest.

suppliers and offer reasonable purchasing prices and policies. These are called 'global framework agreements' or 'international framework agreements' (Stevis, 2010; Fichter & Stevis, 2013; Posthuma & Rossi, 2017). With clear, definitive language, they can improve outcomes for labour (Fichter & Stevis, 2013). Companies could also engage in 'worker-driven social responsibility' by legally committing to source from suppliers that follow codes of conduct developed by workers, such as the 'Food First' and 'Milk with Dignity' programmes in the United States (Mares & O'Neill, 2019; Ford & Nolan, 2020).

It should be noted that even if companies reorient CSR to support democratic justice *within* the firm, they may continue to challenge democratic justice externally (Stevis, 2017). Firms may lobby for public policies that limit workers' rights or labour organising (Lyon & Montgomery, 2015; Favotto & Kollman, 2021). They may also advocate for regulatory solutions that privilege private actors, sideline democratic participation (Goodman & Mäkinen, 2023) or weaken domestic or international institutions' regulatory power (Schrempf-Stirling, 2018).

CSR: Voluntary Sustainability Standards and Labour Justice Outcomes

CSR is sometimes compared to a 'fox guarding the henhouse' (Sasser et al., 2006, p. 10). Many doubt companies can develop rigorous codes of conduct, reliably audit their supply chains and sanction themselves for non-compliance. One solution is to bring companies, NGOs, industry associations and workers' groups together to develop industry-wide standards and have suppliers pay third-party auditors to verify compliance (e.g., examine a fishery's labour and environmental practices). The resulting 'certified' products are labelled to help consumers and businesses buy-cott responsible business practices. Examples of these 'voluntary sustainability standards' (VSS) systems include the Forest Stewardship Council (FSC), the Roundtable on Sustainable Palm Oil (RSPO) and Fairtrade International (Bennett, 2022). About 2 per cent of agricultural land is already certified, and this is rapidly increasing (UNFSS, 2020).

VSS generate mixed results for labour justice (Marx et al., 2024). Despite being dubbed 'multi-stakeholder initiatives', few VSS provide meaningful opportunities for labour unions, workers' associations, or labour NGOs to affect high-level decision-making (Bennett, 2017). The Small Producer Symbol (SPP) – which is led by smallholder farmers – and Fairtrade International are exceptional in this regard (Bennett, 2015; 2016; 2017). Although standard-setting processes typically include opportunities for stakeholder input, industry efforts to weaken standards tend to dominate (van der Van, 2022). Although VSS deliver some benefits for workers, under some conditions, in limited specific contexts, they largely fall short of improving socioeconomic incomes (MSI, 2020; Saxena, 2020; Bennett, 2022). Although some studies find that fair trade certifications address labour justice more than sustainability certifications

(Bennett, 2017; 2018; Raynolds, 2018), certifications of all kinds typically fail to distribute a great enough share of profits to suppliers to adequately remunerate their workforce (Grabs, 2020; Dietz & Grabs 2021). Effectiveness appears to be contingent on several highly dynamic variables including governance, standards content, audit practices, supplier capacity, supplier country conditions, consumer demand and – most critically – buyers' willingness to pay the cost of compliance (Grabs, 2020; Bennett, 2022).

The case of living wages is illustrative. Although some (mostly garment) companies have committed to paying living wages in supply chains, they typically do not even create the preconditions for implementation, such as extending order lead times, increasing prices and developing effective complaint mechanisms (Edwards et al., 2019; Khan & Richards, 2021; LeBaron et al., 2021). For many companies, supply chains include so many production sites and subcontractors that simply tracking how much workers are *actually* being paid is beyond their capacity (Edwards et al., 2019; Schrage & Gilbert, 2021). Although about twenty major global brands have signed on to ACT (the 'Action, Collaboration and Transformation' initiative) which rhetorically commits them to working with suppliers whose employees have collective bargaining agreements, ACT relies on self-regulation and has not made meaningful progress (Amengual & Kuruvilla, 2020; Ashwin et al., 2020a; 2020b; Coneybeer & Maguire, 2022). Although VSS are uniquely positioned to promote living wages in GVCs because they already audit labour conditions, only a third of high-profile VSS include living wages in their standards and none fully implements this in practice (Bennett, 2018; Edwards et al., 2019).

VSS could be reformed to improve labour justice. They could include workers in governance, raise standards, shift audit strategies, mandate living wages, hold buyers accountable for purchasing practices and reward countries that protect labour organising and enforce labour regulations (Bennett, 2022). They could also increase support for suppliers that are organised cooperatively, offer employees stock options or engage in profit-sharing schemes (Reed & McMurtry, 2009; Blasi et al., 2014; Bennett, 2024; Bennett & Grabs, 2024). Such reforms, however, may increase the costs of production beyond what companies are willing to bear.

CSR: From Voluntary to Mandatory?

Given the important role that corporations play in the global economy, the inadequacy of labour laws to protect workers and promote labour justice and apparent excitement about voluntary social responsibility initiatives, it is perhaps unsurprising that many countries and international organisations aim to make some CSR activities mandatory. Over the past two decades, several countries have passed new corporate accountability laws that encourage or require firms to engage in, report, raise spending on and/or improve CSR

(Gond et al., 2011; Phillips et al., 2018; Knudsen & Moon, 2017; Haslam, 2018; Bright et al., 2020).

This wave of legislation is in part motivated by new international norms regarding business responsibility. In 2011 the UN Guiding Principles on Business and Human Rights (UNGPs) established that UN member countries must hold corporations accountable for their impact on human rights abroad (Bueno 2019). The United States, for example, must hold Nike, an American footwear company, accountable for labour exploitation abroad. Although the UNGPs are soft law and thus not legally binding, they have initiated a wave of hard laws regarding 'human rights due diligence' (or HRDD) (Bright et al., 2020).

Corporate responsibility legislation varies widely in scope (e.g., single issue vs. human rights vs. all issues), requirements (e.g., prevention vs. reaction), monitoring (e.g., self-reporting vs. external audit) and consequence (e.g., none vs. legal sanction vs. civil liability). The 2017 French Duty of Vigilance Law, for example, requires companies to create, implement and publicly report their activities to identify, prevent and address human rights and environmental harms resulting from activities in their supply chain and it establishes a civil liability mechanism to facilitate accountability for non-compliance. The 2019 Dutch Child Labour Due Diligence Act, on the other hand, has narrower scope, focuses on response (not prevention) and has a weaker enforcement mechanism. It requires companies selling goods and services to Dutch end-users to take action to investigate suspicions, respond with action and issue a statement, and provides that non-compliant companies may be sanctioned (Bright et al., 2020).

Although no lead firm has, to date, been held liable for the business practices of suppliers in its value chain, recent case law has established that lead companies bear some responsibility for their subsidiaries, and this may pave the way for GVC accountability (Bright et al., 2020). On one hand, mandatory CSR may illustrate that corporations and states can collaborate on labour rights (Gond et al., 2011) and mark a shift away from decades of neoliberal regulation (Bright et al., 2020). On the other, poor enforcement mechanisms and few (if any) penalties for non-compliance make significant change unlikely (Mayer & Phillips, 2017; Bueno, 2019). Perversely, the resources companies allocate for compliance may actually detract from substantive changes, such as living wages (LeBaron & Rühmkorf, 2019). Full assessment is contingent on how implementation plays out (Weihraugh et al., 2022).

CONCLUSION

The globalisation era increased trade, expanded GVCs, consolidated power among a few lead firms and pressured suppliers to cut labour costs. The consequences for labour justice have been devastating. Unions are compromised, work is dangerous, modern slavery is thriving and many workers remain very poor, despite a growing global economy and billionaires' rapid accumulation of wealth.

This chapter described how labour has been excluded from economic governance and how democratic injustice has played a role in hindering progress toward better socioeconomic and intergenerational outcomes. Although the ILO has been successful in promoting labour standards and including (unionised) workers in governance, it faces challenges around including informal workers and enforcement mechanisms. And while CSR may put the issue of labour justice on the private sector agenda, it neither makes lead firms, suppliers or investors accountable to labour nor addresses the systemic pressures that facilitate exploitation.

Overall, this chapter concludes that the current situation of labour justice in the global economy is untenable and prospects for reform are grim. Many 'labour initiatives' seem to do more to ease the minds of the privileged than to fill the pocketbooks of the poor.

At the same time, it highlights that labour justice is not impossible. There are business models and supply chain management strategies that give workers a voice. Worker ownership, employee stock option plans, profit-sharing contracts, farmer cooperatives, collective bargaining, beneficiary-driven certification, worker-driven social responsibility and living wage policies can all be leveraged to improve labour justice. These and other labour-oriented strategies can be supported by national governments, international organisations, multinational lead firms, suppliers and civil society. Although these more effective initiatives are often overshadowed by more performative, aspirational and unenforceable approaches, that need not be the case. By asking 'who decides', 'who benefits, at what cost' and 'where will this leave us in five, ten or twenty years', labour advocates can assess which pathways are most likely to support labour justice.

REFERENCES

Aeberhard-Hodges, J. (2019). Workplace Gender Equality as a Human Right: The ILO Approach. In *Research Handbook on Labour, Business and Human Rights Law,* edited by Janice R. Bellace and Beryl ter Haar, 274–93. Edward Elgar.

Amengual, M. (2010). Complementary Labor Regulation: The Uncoordinated Combination of State and Private Regulators in the Dominican Republic. *World Development, 38*(3), 405–14.

Amengual, M., & Chirot, L. (2016). Reinforcing the State: Transnational and State Labor Regulation in Indonesia. *ILR Review: The Journal of Work and Policy, 69*(5): 1056–1080.

Amengual, M., & Kuruvilla, S. (2020). Editorial Essay: Introduction to a Special Issue on Improving Private Regulation of Labor in Global Supply Chains: Theory and Evidence. *ILR Review, 73*(4), 809–16.

Anker, R. (2011) *Estimating a Living Wage: A Methodological Review, ILO: Conditions of Work an Employment Series No. 29*. 29. Geneva. Available from: https://www.ilo.org/publications/estimating-living-wage-methodological-review (Accessed 15 September, 2024).

Anker, M., & Anker, R. (2017). Living Wages around the World: Overview of the Anker Living Wage Methodology. In *Living Wages around the World: Manual for Measurement*, 17–30. Edward Elgar.

Anner, M. (2018). *Binding Power: The Sourcing Squeeze, Workers' Rights, and Building Safety in Bangladesh since Rana Plaza*. Center for Global Workers' Rights.

Anner, M. (2020). Squeezing Workers' Rights in Global Supply Chains: Purchasing Practices in the Bangladesh Garment Export Sector in Comparative Perspective. *Review of International Political Economy, 27*(2), 320–47.

Anner, M. (2021). Three Labour Governance Mechanisms for Addressing Decent Work Deficits in Global Value Chains. *International Labour Review, 160*(4):,613–29.

Appelbaum, R. P., & Lichtenstein, N. (2016). *Achieving Workers' Rights in the Global Economy*. Cornell University Press.

Ashwin, S., Kabeer, N., & Schüßler, E. (2020a). Contested Understandings in the Global Garment Industry after Rana Plaza. *Development and Change, 51*(5), 1296–305.

Ashwin, S., Oka, C., Schüßler, E., Alexander, R., & Lohmeyer, N. (2020b). Spillover Effects across Transnational Industrial Relations Agreements: The Potential and Limits of Collective Action in Global Supply Chains. *ILR Review, 73*(4), 995–1020.

Autor, D., Dorn, D., Katz, L. F., Patterson, C., & Van Reenen, J. (2017). The Fall of Labor Share and the Rise of Superstar Firms. National Bureau of Economic Research.

Bair, J. (2017). Contextualising Compliance: Hybrid Governance in Global Value Chains. *New Political Economy, 22*(2), 169–85.

Bair, J., Anner, M., & Blasi, J. (2020). The Political Economy of Private and Public Regulation in Post-Rana Plaza Bangladesh. *ILR Review* 73 (4): 969–94.

Bair, J., & Palpacuer, F. (2015). CSR beyond the Corporation: Contested Governance in Global Value Chains. *Global Networks, 15*(s1), 1–19.

Barnett, M. L. (2019). The Business Case for Corporate Social Responsibility: A Critique and an Indirect Path Forward. *Business and Society, 58*(1), 167–90.

Barrientos, S. (2008). Contract Labour: The 'Achilles Heel' of Corporate Codes in Commercial Value Chains. *Development and Change, 39*(6), 977–90.

Barrientos, S. (2013). Corporate Purchasing Practices in Global Production Networks: A Socially Contested Terrain. *Geoforum, 44*, 44–51.

Bartley, T. (2007). Institutional Emergence in an Era of Globalization: The Rise of Transnational Private Regulation of Labor and Environmental Conditions. *American Journal of Sociology, 113*(2), 297–351.

Bartley, T. (2022). Power and the Practice of Transnational Private Regulation. *New Political Economy, 27*(2), 188–202.

Bengtsson, E., & Ryner, M. (2015). The (International) Political Economy of Falling Wage Shares: Situating Working-Class Agency. *New Political Economy, 20*(3), 406–30.

Bennett, E. A. (2012). Global Social Movements in Global Governance. *Globalizations, 9*(6), 799–813.

Bennett, E. A. (2015). Fairtrade International Governance. In Raynolds L. T., & Bennett, E. A., (eds.), *The Handbook of Research on Fair Trade*, 80–101. Edward Elgar.

Bennett, E. A. (2016). Governance, Legitimacy, and Stakeholder Balance: Lessons from Fairtrade International. *Social Enterprise Journal, 12*(3), 322–46.

Bennett, E. A. (2017). Who Governs Socially-Oriented Voluntary Sustainability Standards? Not the Producers of Certified Products. *World Development*, 91, 53–69.

Bennett, E. A. (2018). Voluntary Sustainability Standards: A Squandered Opportunity to Improve Workers' Wages. *Sustainable Development, 26*(1), 65–82.

Bennett, E. A. (2020). The Global Fair Trade Movement: For Whom, By Whom, How, and What Next. In Bell M., Carolan, M., Keller, J., & Legun, K., (eds.), *The Cambridge Handbook of Environmental Sociology*, 459–77. Cambridge University Press.

Bennett, E. A. (2022). The Efficacy of Voluntary Standards, Sustainability Certifications, and Ethical Labels. In Marx A., Van Calster, G., & Wouters, J., (eds.), *The Research Handbook on Global Governance, Business and Human Rights*, 176–203. Edward Elgar.

Bennett, Elizabeth A. 2024. Voluntary Sustainability Standards, Employee Ownership, and the Sustainable Development Goals: Can VSS Leverage EO to Accelerate Progress toward the SDGs? *International Review of Applied Economics*.

Bennett, Elizabeth A., and Janina Grabs. 2024. How Can Sustainable Business Models Distribute Value More Equitably in Global Value Chains? Introducing 'Value Chain Profit Sharing' as an Emerging Alternative to Fair Trade, Direct Trade, or Solidarity Trade, *Business Ethics, the Environment & Responsibility*.

Birchall, D. (2020). The Role of Civil Society and Human Rights Defenders in Corporate Accountability. In Deva, S., & Birchall, D., (eds.), *Research Handbook on Human Rights and Business, 182*, 422–45. Edward Elgar.

Blasi, J., Freeman, R., & Kruse, D. (2014). *The Citizen's Share: Reducing Inequality in the 21st Century*. Yale University Press.

Bright, C., Marx, A., Pineau, N., & Wouters, J. (2020). Toward a Corporate Duty for Lead Companies to Respect Human Rights in Their Global Value Chains? *Business and Politics, 22*(4), 667–97.

Bromley, P., & Powell, W. W. (2012). From Smoke and Mirrors to Walking the Talk: Decoupling in the Contemporary World. *Academy of Management Annals*, 1–48.

Brookes, M., & Kinzel, I. (2019). Global Labor Collective Action: An Evidence Review for Learning, Evaluation and Research Activity II. USAID.

Bueno, N. (2019). Multinational Enterprises and Labour Rights: Concepts and Implementation. In Bellace, J. R. & ter Haar, B., (eds.), *Labour, Business and Human Rights Law*, 421–38. Edward Elgar.

Caraway, T. L. (2006). Freedom of Association: Battering Ram or Trojan Horse? *Review of International Political Economy, 13*(2), 210–32.

Cashore, B., Knudsen, J. S., Moon, J., & van der Ven, H. (2021). Private Authority and Public Policy Interactions in Global Context : Governance Spheres for Problem Solving. *Regulation & Governance, 15*, 1166–82.

Chantziaras, A. E. D., Grougiou, V., & Leventis, S. (2020). The Impact of Labor Unionization on CSR Reporting. *Sustainability Accounting, Management and Policy Journal, 12*(2), 437–66.

Cho, S., & Marzán, C. F. R. (2020). Labor, Trade, and Populism: How ILO–WTO Collaboration Can Save the Global Economic Order. *American University Law Review, 69*(6), 1771–825.

Chun, H-M., & Shin, S.Y. (2018). The Impact of Labor Union Influence on Corporate Social Responsibility. *Sustainability, 10*(6), 1–17.

Clapp, J., & Fuchs, D., (eds.) (2009). *Corporate Power in Global Agrifood Governance*. MIT Press.

Coneybeer, J., & Maguire, R. (2022). Evading Responsibility: A Structural Critique of Living Wage Initiatives and Methodologies. *International Journal for Crime, Justice and Social Democracy, 11*(2), 15–29.

Crane, A., Lebaron, G., Allain, J., & Behbahani., L. (2017). Governance Gaps in Eradicating Forced Labor: From Global to Domestic Supply Chains. *Regulation and Governance*.

Crane, A., Palazzo, G., Spence, L. J., & Matten, D. (2014). Contesting the Value of 'Creating Shared Value'. *California Management Review, 56*(2), 130–53.

Dattani, P., Still, A., & Pota, V. (2015). *Business Backs Education.* Global Education and Skills Forum, Varkey Foundation, UNESCO, Dubai Cares.

Dauvergne, P. (2022). Is Artificial Intelligence Greening Global Supply Chains? Exposing the Political Economy of Environmental Costs. *Review of International Political Economy, 29*(3), 696–718.

Delautre, G., Manrique, E. E., & Fenwick, C. (2021). *Decent Work in a Globalized Economy: Lessons from Public and Private Initiatives.* International Labour Organization.

Dietz, T., & Grabs, J. (2021). Additionality and Implementation Gaps in Voluntary Sustainability Standards. *New Political Economy*, 1–22.

Eberlein, B., Abbott, K. W., Black, J., Meidinger, E., & Wood, S. (2014). Transnational Business Governance Interactions: Conceptualization and Framework for Analysis. *Regulation & Governance, 8*(1), 1–21.

Edwards, R., Hunt, T., & Lebaron, G. (2019). *Corporate Commitments to Living Wages in the Garment Industry.* University of Sheffield.

Favotto, A., & Kollman, K. (2021). Mixing Business with Politics: Does Corporate Social Responsibility End Where Lobbying Transparency Begins? *Regulation and Governance, 15*(2), 262–79.

Fichter, M., & Stevis, D. (2013). *Global Framework Agreements in a Union-Hostile Environment: The Case of the USA.* Friedrich Ebert Stiftung.

Ford, J., & Nolan, J. (2020). Regulating Transparency on Human Rights and Modern Slavery in Corporate Supply Chains: The Discrepancy between Human Rights Due Diligence and the Social Audit. *Australian Journal of Human Rights, 26*(1), 27–45.

Fransen, L., Dupuy, K., Hinfelaar, M., & Mazumder, S. M. Z. (2021). Tempering Transnational Advocacy? The Effect of Repression and Regulatory Restriction on Transnational NGO Collaborations. *Global Policy, 12*(S5), 11–22.

Glozer, S., & Morsing, M. (2020). Helpful Hypocrisy? Investigating 'Double-Talk' and Irony in CSR Marketing Communications. *Journal of Business Research, 114* (December 2019), 363–75.

Goerke, L., (2020). Trade Unions and Corporate Social Responsibility. Discussion Paper Series in Economics, 6.

Gold, M., Preuss, L., & Rees, C. (2020). Moving out of the Comfort Zone? Trade Union Revitalisation and Corporate Social Responsibility. *Journal of Industrial Relations, 62*(1), 132–55.

Gond, J. P., Kang, N., & Moon, J. (2011). The Government of Self-Regulation: On the Comparative Dynamics of Corporate Social Responsibility. *Economy and Society, 40*(4), 640–71.

Goodman, J., & Mäkinen, J. (2023). Democracy in Political Corporate Social Responsibility: A Dynamic, Multilevel Account. *Business and Society, 62*(2), 250–84.

Grabs, J. (2020). *Selling Sustainability Short? The Private Governance of Labor and the Environment in the Coffee Sector.* Cambridge University Press.

Graz, J. C., Nicole Helmerich, and Cécile Prébandier. (2020). Hybrid Production Regimes and Labor Agency in Transnational Private Governance. *Journal of Business Ethics, 162*, 307–21.

Guzi, M. (2021). Cost of Living, Living Wages, and Minimum Wages in EU-27 Countries. CELSI.

Hall, M. R., & Suh, S. (2020). How Large Is the Global Living Wage Gap and the Price Increase Needed to Close It? *Socio-Economic Review, 18*(2), 555–74.

Haslam, P. A. (2018). Beyond Voluntary: State-Firm Bargaining over Corporate Social Responsibilities in Mining. *Review of International Political Economy, 25*(3), 418–40.

Held, D., & McGrew, A. (2002). Introduction. In Held, D. & McGrew, A. (eds.), *Governing Globalization: Power, Authority and Global Governance.* Polity Press.

Hofmeester, K., & van der Linden, M., (eds.) (2018). *Handbook of Global History of Work*. Walter de Gruyter GmbH.
ILO. (2003). *Employment and Social Policy in Respect of Export Processing Zones*.
ILO. (2013). Trade Unions and Worker Cooperatives: Where Are We At? *International Journal of Labour Research*, *5*(2), 173–7.
ILO. (2019). *The Working Poor or How a Job is No Guarantee of Decent Living Conditions*. International Labor Organization.
ILO. (2022). *World Employment and Social Outlook: Trends 2022*.
ILO. (2023). *World Employment and Social Outlook: Trends 2023*.
ITUC (International Trade Union Confederation). (2023).
Jackson, G., & Apostolakou, A. (2010). Corporate Social Responsibility in Western Europe: An Institutional Mirror or Substitute? *Journal of Business Ethics*, *94*(3), 371–94.
Jaffee, D., & Howard, P. H. (2010). Corporate Cooptation of Organic and Fair Trade Standards. *Agriculture and Human Values*, *27*(4), 387–99.
Jakovleski, V., Jerbi, S., & Biersteker, T. (2019). The ILO's Role in Global Governance: Limits and Potential. *International Development Policy*, 1–17.
Johns, L., Pelc, K. J., & Wellhausen, R. L. (2019). How a Retreat from Global Economic Governance May Empower Business Interests. *Journal of Politics*, *81*(2), 731–8.
Kara, S. (2017). *Modern Slavery: A Global Perspective*. Columbia University Press.
Khan, R., & Richards, H. (2021). Fashion in 'Crisis' Consumer Activism and Brand (Ir) Responsibility in Lockdown. *Cultural Studies*, *35*(2–3), 432–43.
Knudsen, J. S., & Moon, J. (2017). *Visible Hands: Taking Responsibility for Social Development*. University of Cambridge Press.
Knudsen, J. S., Moon, J. & Rieneke, S. (2015) Government Policies for Corporate Social Responsibility in Europe: A Comparative Analysis of Institutionalisation', *Policy & Politics*, *43*(1), 81–9.
Kyritsis, P., & LeBaron, G. (2021). Hunger at the End of the Supply Chain. *Dissent*, *68*(2), 51–5.
LeBaron, G. (2021). Wages: An Overlooked Dimension of Business and Human Rights in Global Supply Chains. *Business and Human Rights Journal*, *6*, 1–20.
LeBaron, Genevieve., Remi Edwards, Tom Hunt, Charline Sempéré & Penelope Kyritsis. (2021). The Ineffectiveness of CSR: Understanding Garment Company Commitments to Living Wages in Global Supply Chains, *New Political Economy*, *27*(1), 1–17. Available at: https://doi.org/10.1080/13563467.2021.1926954.
LeBaron, G., & Lister, J. (2021). The Hidden Costs of Global Supply Chain Solutions. *Review of International Political Economy*, *29*(3), 669–95.
LeBaron, G., & Phillips, N. (2019). States and the Political Economy of Unfree Labour. *New Political Economy*, *24*(1), 1–21.
Lebaron, G., & Rühmkorf, A. (2019). The Domestic Politics of Corporate Accountability Legislation: Struggles over the 2015 UK Modern Slavery Act. *Socio-Economic Review*, *17*(3), 709–43.
Locke, R. (2013). *The Promise and Limits of Private Power: Promoting Labor Standards in a Global Economy*. Cambridge University Press.
Lyon, T. P., & Montgomery, A. W. (2015). The Means and End of Greenwash. *Organization and Environment*, *28*(2), 223–49.
Malik, M. (2015). Value-Enhancing Capabilities of CSR: A Brief Review of Contemporary Literature. *Journal of Business Ethics*, *127*, 419–38.
Mares, T., & O'Neill, B. (2019). Cultivating Comida: A New Day for Dairy? *Journal of Agriculture, Food Systems, and Community Development*, (April), 1–4.

Marshall, S. (2019). *Living Wage: Regulatory Solutions to Informal and Precarious Work in Global*. Oxford University Press.

Martin, I., Dufour-Poirier, M., & Villanueva, F. (2021). Against, before, or with Corporate Social Responsibility? Unions' Perception and Mobilization of CSR Regulation in Transnational Mining Enterprises. *Canadian Labour and Employment Law Journal, 23*(1), 37–70.

Marx, A. et al. (2024). Global Governance through Voluntary Sustainability Standards: Developments, Trends and Challenges, *Global Policy, 15*(4).

Mayer, F. W., & Gereffi, G. (2010). Regulation and Economic Globalization: Prospects and Limits of Private Governance. *Business and Politics*, 12(3), 1–25.

Mayer, F. W., & Phillips, N. (2017). Outsourcing Governance: States and the Politics of a 'Global Value Chain World'. *New Political Economy, 22*(2), 134–52.

Mayer, F. W., Phillips, N., & Posthuma, A. C. 2017. The Political Economy of Governance in a 'Global Value Chain World'. *New Political Economy, 22*(2), 129–33.

Miller, D., & Williams, P. (2009). What Price a Living Wage? Implementation Issues in the Quest for Decent Wages in the Global Apparel Sector. *Global Social Policy, 9*(1), 99–125.

Mishel, L., & Wolfe, J. (2019). CEO Compensation Has Grown 940% since 1978: Typical Worker Compensation Has Risen Only 12% during That Time. *Economic Policy Institute, 16*.

Monaco, M., & Pastorelli, L. (2013). Trade Unions and Worker Cooperatives in Europe: A Win–Win Relationship. Maximizing Social and Economic Potential in Worker Cooperatives. *International Journal of Labour Research, 5*(2), 227–50.

Moon, J., Crane, A., & Matten, D. (2005). Can Corporations Be Citizens? Corporate Citizen as a Metaphor for Business Participation in Society. *Business Ethics Quarterly*, 15(3), 429–53.

Mosley, L. (2010). *Labor Rights and Multinational Production*. Cambridge University Press.

Mosley, L. (2017). Workers' Rights in Global Value Chains: Possibilities for Protection and for Peril. *New Political Economy, 22*(2), 153–68.

MSI Integrity. (2020). *Not Fit-for-Purpose: The Grand Experiment of Multi-Stakeholder Initiatives in Corporate Accountability, Human Rights and Global Governance*.

OECD. (2020). Trade Policy Implications of Global Value Chains.

OECD. (2023). Global Value Chains and Trade.

Phillips, N., Lebaron, G., & Wallin, S. (2018). Mapping and Measuring the Effectiveness of Labour-Related Disclosure Requirements for Global Supply Chains. *ILO Research Department Working Paper No. 32*. International Labor Organization.

Piketty, T. 2014. *Capital in the Twenty-First Century*. Harvard University Press.

Piore, M. J., & Schrank, A. (2018). *Root-Cause Regulation: Protecting Work and Workers in the Twenty-First Century*. Harvard University Press.

Ponte, S. (2020). Green Capital Accumulation: Business and Sustainability Management in a World of Global Value Chains. *New Political Economy, 25*(1), 72–84.

Ponte, S., & Sturgeon, T. (2014). Explaining Governance in Global Value Chains: A Modular Theory-Building Effort. *Review of International Political Economy, 21*, 1–29.

Posthuma, A., & Rossi, A. (2017). Coordinated Governance in Global Value Chains: Supranational Dynamics and the Role of the International Labour Organization. *New Political Economy*, 22(2), 186–202.

Rantanen, J., Muchiri, F., & Lehtinen, S. (2020). Decent Work, ILO's Response to the Globalization of Working Life: Basic Concepts and Global Implementation with Special Reference to Occupational Health. *International Journal of Environmental Research and Public Health, 17*(10), 1–27.

Raynolds, L. T. (2018). Fairtrade Certification, Labor Standards, and Labor Rights. *Sociology of Development, 4*(2), 191–216.

Raynolds, L. T., & Bennett, Elizabeth A. (2015). *The Handbook of Research on Fair Trade. Handbook of Research on Fair Trade*. Edward Elgar.

Reed, D., & McMurtry, J. J. (2009). *Co-Operatives in a Global Economy: The Challenges of Co-Operation across Borders*. Cambridge Scholars Publishing.

Sasser, E. N., Prakash, A., Cashore B., & Auld, G. (2006). Direct Targeting as an NGO Political Strategy: Examining Private Authority Regimes in the Forestry Sector. *Business and Politics, 8*(3).

Saxena, S., (eds.) (2020). *Labor, Global Supply Chains, and the Garment Industry in South Asia: Bangladesh after Rana Plaza*. Routledge.

Scherer, A. G., & Palazzo, G. (2011). The New Political Role of Business in a Globalized World: A Review of a New Perspective on CSR and Its Implications for the Firm, Governance, and Democracy. *Journal of Management Studies, 48*(4), 899–931.

Schnabel, C. (2020). Union Membership and Collective Bargaining: Trends and Determinants. *IZA Discussion Paper Series, 13465*.

Schoeneborn, D., Morsing, M., & Crane, A. (2020). Formative Perspectives on the Relation between CSR Communication and CSR Practices: Pathways for Walking, Talking, and T(w)Alking. *Business and Society, 59*(1), 5–33.

Schrage, St., & Gilbert, D. U. (2021). Addressing Governance Gaps in Global Value Chains: Introducing a Systematic Typology. *Journal of Business Ethics, 170*, 657–72.

Schrempf-Stirling, J. (2018). State Power: Rethinking the Role of the State in Political Corporate Social Responsibility. *Journal of Business Ethics, 150*(1), 1–14.

Séhier, C. (2023). Promoting the Associational Power of Workers in Globalized Production Networks: A Missed Opportunity. *International Labour Review*, 162(1), 99–121.

Selwyn, B. (2017). *The Struggle for Development*. Polity Press.

Silva, V. (2022). The ILO and the Future of Work: The Politics of Global Labour Policy. *Global Social Policy, 22*(2), 341–58.

Standing, G. (2008). The ILO: An Agency for Globalization? *Development and Change, 39*(3), 355–84.

Steensen, K. Q., & Villadsen, K. (2020). From Social Gospel to CSR: Was Corporate Social Responsibility Ever Radical? *Organization*, 27(6): 924–42.

Stevis, D. (2010). *International Framework Agreements and Global Social Dialogue: Parameters and Prospects*. International Labor Organization.

Stevis, D. (2017). Investigating Those You Love: Labor and Global Governance. In Montgomerie, J., (ed.), *Critical Methods in Political and Cultural Economy*, 58–63. Routledge.

Sun, Y. (2022). *Certifying China: The Rise and Limits of Transnational Sustainability Governance in Emerging Economies*. MIT Press.

Sung, R., Owen, E., & Li, Q. (2021). How Do Capital and Labor Split Economic Gains in an Age of Globalization? *Review of International Political Economy, 28*(1), 232–57.

Swepston, L. (2019). How the ILO Embraced Human Rights. In Bellace, J. R., & ter Haar, B., (eds.), *Research Handbook on Labour, Business and Human Rights Law*, 295–313. Edward Elgar.

Taggart, J. R. (2022). Global Development Governance in the 'Interregnum'. *Review of International Political Economy, 29*(3), 904–27.

Tallontire, A., & Anderson, M. (2020). Guest Editorial: Special Issue on Fair Trade and the Sustainable Development Goals. *Food Chain, 9*(1), 1–7.

Thomas, H. & Turnbull, P. (2021) From a 'Moral Commentator' to a 'Determined Actor'? How the International Labour Organization (ILO) Orchestrates the Field of International Industrial Relations. *British Journal of Industrial Relations, 59*(3), 874–98. Available at: https://doi.org/10.1111/bjir.12578.

UNFSS (United Nations Forum on Sustainability Standards). 2020. *Scaling up Voluntary Sustainability Standards through Sustainable Public Procurement and Trade Policy.*

United Nations. (2023). *Inequality: Bridging the Divide.*

van der Linden, M. (2019). The International Labour Organization, 1919–2019: An Appraisal. *Labor: Studies in Working-Class History, 16*(2), 11–41.

van der Ven, H. (2019). *Beyond Greenwash: Explaining Credibility in Transnational Eco-Labeling*. Oxford University Press.

van der Ven, H. (2022). Effects of Stakeholder Input on Voluntary Sustainability Standards. *Global Environmental Change, 75.*

van Niekerk, A. J. (2020). Inclusive Economic Sustainability: SDGs and Global Inequality. *Sustainability, 12*(13), 1–19.

Vosko, L. (2002). 'Decent Work': The Shifting Role of the ILO and the Struggle for Global Social Justice. *Global Social Policy, 2*(1), 19–46.

Weihrauch, D., Carodenuto, S., & Leipold, S. (2022). From Voluntary to Mandatory Corporate Accountability: The Politics of the German Supply Chain Due Diligence Act. *Regulation and Governance.*

WFTO (World Fair Trade Organization) & FTI (Fairtrade International). (2009). *A Charter of Fair Trade Principles.*

Witherell, R. (2013). An Emerging Solidarity: Worker Cooperatives, Unions, and the New Union Cooperative Model in the United States. *International Journal of Labour Research, 5*(2), 251–68.

World Bank. (2020). *World Development Report 2020: Trading for Development in the Age of Global Value Chains*. World Bank.

Zing, Y., Gentile, E., & Dollar, D., (eds.) (2021). *Global Value Chain Development Report 2021: Beyond Production.*

Chapter 7

GLOBAL LABOUR (IN)JUSTICE

Sara Amighetti and Eszter Kollar

INTRODUCTION

Global labour (in)justice is a multifaceted issue that lies at the intersection of various dimensions of justice. As the world becomes increasingly interconnected through economic globalisation, the conditions that shape global labour markets as well as their regulation demand urgent attention. This chapter provides an overview of key questions and concerns about global labour injustice according to three main critical perspectives.[1]

The *socioeconomic perspective* considers the vast disparities in working conditions, wages and access to economic opportunities that exist between workers in different parts of the world. Philosophers taking this perspective examine the structures and policies that lead to these inequalities and propose solutions aimed at achieving a fairer distribution of economic gains, opportunities and power. The emphasis is on ensuring that all workers, regardless of their geographical location, can enjoy a fair share of the global economic pie.

The *political perspective* delves into the power dynamics and institutional frameworks that underpin global capitalism, specifically labour markets. It addresses the political disempowerment of workers, particularly in the face of powerful multinational corporations and neoliberal economic policies that favour capital over labour. Philosophers adopting this perspective are concerned with the erosion of workers' rights, the weakening of trade unions and the increasing difficulty of states to protect the workforce due to pressures from global capital. They advocate for measures empowering workers through robust political institutions, strong labour laws and the promotion of democratic participation in economic decision-making processes.

[1] While we have integrated feminist authors, we have not elaborated on the feminist perspective because we believe that providing a comprehensive treatment of it would necessitate a dedicated chapter.

The *historical perspective* focuses on the legacy and persistence of colonial structures in the international order. It examines how the historical exploitation and oppression of enslaved and colonised peoples continue to influence contemporary labour markets. The enduring economic disparities and power imbalances rooted in these historical injustices manifest in the ongoing marginalisation and exploitation of workers in former colonies and among racialised communities. Philosophers call for a reckoning with these historical wrongs through reparative measures, policies that address systemic inequalities and a commitment to dismantling the enduring structures of racial and economic oppression.

By examining global labour injustice through these three philosophical lenses, this chapter aims to provide a comprehensive understanding of the issue and highlight the interconnectedness of economic, political and historical factors. Each perspective offers unique insights and solutions, emphasising the need for a multifaceted approach to addressing the profound injustices faced by workers worldwide. Through this integrated analysis, we can better grasp the complexities of global labour injustice and work towards creating a more just global economy.

THE SOCIOECONOMIC PERSPECTIVE

Global labour justice has been widely discussed in normative political philosophy in the context of debates about global distributive justice, resulting in a variety of objections that often reflect the different theoretical orientations of global justice theorists. Below we overview a selection of the main arguments in the global justice debate, as they apply to labour (in)justice.

Labour standards have often been discussed as manifestations of severe poverty and inequality in the global order. Early contributions highlighted how workers in many parts of the world are employed under conditions that fail to meet the minimum standards of a decent life. This is a clear injustice since no one should live and work under conditions so dire that are incompatible with human dignity. Improving the conditions of the working poor is grounded in a concern for the well-being of others as a matter of common humanity and part of a duty to eradicate global poverty and to secure the basic conditions of freedom and human development (Sen, 1999).

A different set of critical arguments identifies labour injustice with the large disparities in work opportunities and wages between workers in impoverished and affluent states. For some, the problem with such disparities has to do with the moral arbitrariness of one's geographical location (e.g. Caney, 2005). For others, these large disparities are unjust because they are the manifestation of very unequal distributive patterns generated by the rise of global value chains (Bennett, Chapter 6 in this volume) and increasing economic integration at the global level (Beitz, 1999; Julius, 2006; Pogge, 2008).

A. J. Julius (2006) argues that through our economic activities, our actions directly or indirectly implicate distant others thus generating a demand of *equal concern* with their lives. The denser our interconnectedness, the more we owe others a justification for its distributive outcomes. For example, buying and consuming coffee every morning should lead us to afford equal concern to the interest of all the workers in the global value chain, that is, the coffee bean farmers, factory workers, transport and logistics staff etc., which requires distributing the benefits generated by the global value chain to the advantage of the least advantaged. In a similar vein, Thomas Pogge (2008) criticises the global economic system for creating rules that benefit the wealthy while leaving many workers in poverty. He argues that this system, which keeps producers in developing countries poor while making the Global North wealthier, is a form of systemic human rights violation. Based on these critical arguments, global egalitarians like Pogge and Julius propose solutions that rely on the responsibility of affluent guilty actors to redistribute global economic resources to poorer ones.

One limit of this approach is that it adopts what Iris Marion Young (2006) has called a liability model of responsibility which focuses too narrowly on identifying specific victims and perpetrators of global economic harms. She believes this oversimplifies the complex causal chains that lead to these harms, which involve direct and indirect forms of agency and differentiated social connections to the resulting injustice. For example, sweatshop labour is often a result of *structural injustice*, caused by millions of consumers following the global economy's rules and norms. Young suggests that instead of looking for individuals to blame, we should consider the different responsibilities of factory owners, retail companies, Western government elites and consumers. Her model of political responsibility takes into account the power and privileges of different agents, which shape their ability to influence global production and trade. Young's understanding of responsibility for sweatshop labour focuses on the power dynamics at play, highlighting the widespread objection that global labour dynamics are *exploitative*.

Exploitation, simply put, is *taking advantage of another.* However, what exactly makes exploitation a moral wrong and what should count as its proper remedy are questions subject to heated theoretical debates that resurface in the domain of global labour justice. For example, in the case of sweatshop labour, the wrong of exploitation cannot be easily captured through loss of income, because sweatshop workers are often thought to be (distributively) better off than they would have been, lest they entered the labour relation. Explaining the wrong of exploitation therefore requires the normative ideal of a fair distribution of burdens and benefits, which determines what should count as a fair wage (Vrousalis, 2018). In this view, exploitation occurs when workers are denied what they are morally entitled to through transactions in which one party unduly benefits by offering the other party an excessively low wage (Vrousalis, 2018; Wertheimer, 1999).

However, because this account of exploitation focuses on the normative features of the transaction and the resulting pay-offs, it is insufficient to capture what is unjust about sweatshop labour and it runs into several difficulties. First, the fact that the background circumstances between countries are unjust complicates what counts as a fair wage and a fair distribution of the added value. Global value chains operate under conditions of radical inequality; low-income countries mainly engage in processes of low-value-added production, such as resource extraction and manufacturing, from which they receive an unfair share of the surplus (van Apeldoorn, 2019). Second, beyond taking advantage of the weak bargaining power of workers, employers also take advantage of the worker's vulnerability due to structural injustice. By preying on another person's unjust disadvantage and turning it into profit, the employer becomes complicit in structural injustice (Malmquist, 2013). Moreover, employers are typically not morally neutral bystanders to this background injustice; they are either (indirectly) causally connected to it or they benefit from it, both of which aggravate the wrong of exploitation.

The focus on exploitative practices, such as sweatshop labour, tends to locate the injustice of the current global economy in the outsourcing of production to developing countries. But another trend that has attracted the scrutiny of philosophers in recent years is the organisation of labour through intensified labour mobility across countries. Low-skilled labour is in abundant supply and even more so when employers have access to a global pool of workers. When a low-skilled sector is opened up to labour immigration, increased supply negatively affects the price of labour. Lea Ypi (2016) argues that due to large inter-country differences between wages and what counts as a 'decent' wage, poorer migrant workers are willing to accept offers at wage levels the locals are no longer willing to work. According to Ypi, this is a form of class-based *structural exploitation* that maximises the profit of employers and at the same time limits the collective freedom of the local working class to negotiate better pay and working conditions.

There is now an influential debate focusing on the rights of migrant workers, especially in the context of temporary labour migration programmes and 'global care chains' that often restrict the rights of migrant workers. The debate is framed by the economic thesis known as the *numbers vs. rights trade-off*; the fewer rights are offered to migrant workers the more migrants are admitted by host countries (Ruhs & Martin, 2008). Some proponents think that if migrant workers consent to the terms of their employment and they are not forced or deceived, they could be seen as voluntarily forfeiting their rights (Pevnick, 2011). Others argue that accepting work visas with restricted rights is the second-best solution, which still improves the migrant worker's conditions compared to the alternative of not having access to the host state's labour market (Milanovic, 2016). Instead, opponents of rights restrictions argue that differentiating between the rights of one group of workers vs. another group of workers violates the democratic value of equal rights (Miller 2016), and puts migrant workers at greater risk of exploitation and domination (Lenard & Straehle, 2012). Still, others think that what migrant workers need is not equal rights but *special rights*, such as portable pensions and child-care contributions, to safeguard their mobility-related special interests (Ottonelli & Torresi, 2022).

Requirements of Global Labour Justice according to the Socioeconomic Perspective

What should be done to address some of these injustices related to global labour? Philosophers focusing on the socioeconomic perspective have traditionally advanced ambitious proposals for reform of the global economic system and its institutions aimed at a fairer distribution of opportunities and economic outputs. These go from the introduction of a global fund or tax (Pogge, 2008; Brock, 2009) to a universal basic income owed to every citizen of the world as a social dividend of the contribution of past generations, which would empower workers to decline exploitative offers (Van Parijs, 2018).

Other proposed measures focus instead on democratic states' complicity in the global and local exploitation of workers and aim at it. Typically, these measures justify the adoption of economic and political sanctions, such as trade embargoes and international boycotts, and they encourage forms of democratic disengagement practices with dictatorships, all of which are thought to put pressure on trade partners to comply with international labour standards (Pogge, 2008; Nili 2011; Wenar, 2016). Interestingly, the targets of these boycotts and divestment strategies are not limited to authoritarian states but include transnational corporations operating under the jurisdiction of liberal democratic states. Here there is a convergence with movements that call for greater corporate social responsibility (Marx et al., 2024).

A set of proposals specifically tackles the injustices of migrant workers through the introduction of greater safeguards such as (i) *portable* work visas: one's right to work in a foreign country should not be tied to one employer (as it is now), but should instead be *portable* within the same employment sector (Ruhs, 2013); (ii) special bundles of rights and benefits for migrant workers that can effectively safeguard their interest and vulnerabilities arising from their mobility (Ottonelli & Torresi, 2022); (iii) fast-tracking migrant workers statuses to permanent residency schemes (Lenard & Straehle, 2012).

THE POLITICAL PERSPECTIVE

As discussions framing global labour injustice mostly as a problem of socio-economic justice have deepened, their limits have also become more evident. Two critical insights have emerged: first, the traditional focus on the North/South divide has been criticised because it tends to represent the world in a binary way, dividing it into a wealthy, exploitative North and a poor, exploited South. Second, the dominant distributive paradigm focuses primarily on economic inequality and poverty, often neglecting the complex interplay between global economic structures, power dynamics and labour conditions. Consequently, some political theorists have begun paying greater attention to the political aspects of economic globalisation, such as the increasing inequality in power relations between labour and capital (in favour of the latter), and the erosion of the state's regulatory powers.

Economic Globalisation and Its Political Ramifications

The advent of unrestricted capital mobility and its implications on power relations between labour and capital. There has been a significant shift in global capital mobility from the Bretton Woods era's controlled capital flows to the late twentieth century's push for full capital account convertibility (FCAC) (Cordelli & Levy, 2022). Cordelli and Levy point out that unrestricted capital mobility, especially speculative movements, can cause significant harm, such as financial destabilisation, forgone economic development and increased inequality. The argument, briefly put, is that dependency on foreign private investments ultimately constrains the ability of states to implement policies that protect workers and promote equitable development. According to that view, restricting capital mobility is essential not only for economic stability but also for preserving the political autonomy and integrity of states.

In a similar vein, Miriam Ronzoni (2016) discusses the implications of unrestricted capital mobility by zooming in on the power distortions it creates (or in any case reinforces) in the relationship between capital and labour. She highlights how the increased international mobility of corporations allows capital to often bypass national regulations and erode labour standards. First, this mobility gives corporations significant bargaining power over workers and governments, as they can threaten to relocate production to countries with more favourable conditions. Second, countries, both developed and developing, engage in regulatory competition meaning that they compete to offer attractive conditions precisely to retain or attract corporate investment. Third, capital's ability to relocate and its associated ability to threaten domestic labour markets diminishes the effectiveness of unions and labour strikes, even in developed countries. In the context of regulatory competition between states, this provides states with additional incentives to adopt anti-union practices, which further contributes to the weakening of labour's political agency.

But global capitalism's quest to maximise competitiveness threatens workers also by pitting them against each other (Hussain, 2020). Indeed, the interplay between economic reforms promoting flexible jobs and welfare reforms promoting means-tested benefits has led to the rise of a new working class, the so-called precariat, whose members are in a condition of chronic insecurity, lacking social protection and political representation. The rise of the precariat further contributes to weakening labour, since it encourages the fragmentation of the workforce between workers with secure employment and rights and those without (Standing, 2011).

Unrestricted capital mobility and the erosion of domestic political agency. Some of the distortions in the power relations between capital and labour we have sketched above can also be captured in more general terms as threats to the political agency of state institutions and even to fundamental principles of contemporary political organisation, such as political equality and democracy. For example, one can argue that political influence is disproportionately held and exercised by private power (e.g., business corporations and the wealthy), thus undermining the core democratic value of political equality among citizens. The decline of trade unions can be seen as a key factor in this 'oligarchic shift', as unions historically provided a counterbalance to corporate power and represented the interests of the working and middle classes (O'Neill &White, 2018). Unions contribute to realising political equality by (O'Neill &White, 2018): (i) boosting voter turnout, especially among marginalised groups, with studies showing a link between union membership and voting rates (e.g., Radcliff & Davis, 2000); (ii) disseminating political information and enhancing informed participation; (iii) fostering collective identity and efficacy for democratic engagement beyond the workplace; (iv) cementing partisan alliances and building social trust. Since unions have historically supported political parties (especially those representative of working-class interests), they have worked to strengthen democratic representation; (v) diversify political leadership by recruiting from various backgrounds; (vi) advocating for interests and influencing public policy against corporate lobbying; (vii) facilitating international cooperation, unions help coordinate transnational political action to address global labour issues and promote solidarity across borders; (viii) promoting a more democratic control over capital, through the management of pension funds and financial activism. In sum, the overall impact of unions is to democratise power relations in society.

Concerns with how unregulated (or minimally regulated) economic structures at the global level negatively impact domestic political institutions and citizens' ability to exercise powers of democratic control have been expressed by political theorists interested in understanding contemporary forms of domination across borders. The neo-republican scholarship is perhaps the most prominent in this respect not only because it has drawn attention to how unchecked globalisation leads to new forms of domination where powerful states exert undue influence over weaker states, undermining their sovereignty and democratic processes, but also because it has emphasised the domination of non-state actors at the international level. For example, neo-republicans have focused on transnational corporations arguing that they exploit global market dynamics to influence domestic policies in their favour, often at the expense of domestic labour markets, public welfare and democratic accountability (e.g. Laborde & Ronzoni, 2016; Ronzoni, 2016). But they have also scrutinised international philanthropy (Blunt, 2022) and considered how international institutions like the IMF and WTO, can both mitigate or exacerbate economic domination, advocating greater democratisation of these institutions to minimise their domination potential over weaker states (Laborde & Ronzoni, 2016).

Requirements of Global Labour Justice according to the Political Perspective

Two implications follow from adopting the political perspective to diagnose global labour injustice. First, greater emphasis is placed on considering not just the economic outcomes of globalisation, but on the interplay between economic structures and political institutions. Key to this interplay is the problematisation of the increasing imbalance of political power between the public (the state, unions, citizens) and the private (capital investment banks and corporations). Second, addressing global labour injustices from the perspective of political justice requires taking action on multiple fronts. This entails a multifaceted approach that integrates global and domestic efforts to address the political and economic dimensions of labour injustices in a globalised economy. Below, we outline an ambitious agenda for reform towards robust global rules of transnational solidarity and stronger domestic institutions to counteract the negative effects of capital mobility on labour standards and workers' and citizens' political agency.

Introducing restrictions on capital mobility, while strengthening international regulation and institutions. One entry point is the introduction of permanent Capital Flow Management (CFM) measures targeting speculative capital movements and the creation of a new global Synthetic Hegemonic Currency (SHC) to replace the role of the US dollar (Cordelli & Levy, 2022). This currency would enhance the effectiveness of CFMs and support beneficial capital movements. Such practical measures could be part of a new international framework, akin to the Bretton Woods system, but with stronger enforcement mechanisms (Ronzoni, 2016). This framework would balance the need for openness in trade and markets with the need to protect domestic justice, fair distribution and states' autonomy, hence ensuring that states retain the ability to regulate labour markets effectively while also addressing the transnational nature of labour injustices.

Prioritising human mobility. Cordelli (2023) further develops the argument for restricting capital mobility by showing how the reasons which speak to constraining capital movement are stronger than those for restricting the free movement of people (and workers). Human mobility across borders should be largely liberalised due to its significant benefits for socioeconomic justice such as poverty reduction through remittances, and also because the cultural change brought about by immigration is often less disruptive and faceless than that caused by capital inflows.

Strengthening domestic institutions. Ronzoni's (2016) emphasis on restoring the regulatory capacity of states is crucial. This involves empowering domestic political institutions to enforce labour standards and protect workers' rights. Trade unions play a fundamental role in this, given how they contribute to democratising power relations in society. To address the oligarchic shift and enhance democratic resilience, O'Neill and White (2018) argue that states should not just remove obstacles to unionisation but actively support union formation and collective bargaining (e.g. easier union recognition) processes or duties on employers to engage in good faith bargaining.

Promoting transnational solidarity. The coordinated political action of workers and global campaigns are seen as of crucial importance to counteract the threats posed by capital and corporate mobility and global competition. An obvious way to initiate transnational political action is by leveraging existing collective organisations, such as workers' unions. To effectively counterbalance the power of capital, trade unions need to develop new transnational and multinational organising strategies, starting from more effective recruitment and fair representation of marginalised workers, such as migrant, temporary, typical and informal workers (Ottonelli & Torresi, 2022).

THE HISTORICAL PERSPECTIVE

A comprehensive critique of labour (in)justice must account for the historical and ongoing impacts of slavery and colonialism on economic inequalities, power imbalances and labour dynamics within the current global order. While it is beyond the scope of this chapter to fully address the extensive literature that critiques the global economic order from a historical standpoint, we will focus on a significant and growing body of work (Robinson, 2005; Virdee, 2019; Valdez, 2021) that examines the intertwined histories of slavery, colonialism and capitalism, and their persistent influence on global labour organisation, despite the formal abolition of these practices by international law.

According to these scholars, the slave trade and colonialism not only created vast material inequalities through the extraction of labour and resources but also entrenched race as a global sorting mechanism that organised labour systems and stratified human worth. This led to what Du Bois referred to as the 'global colour line,' highlighting the racial basis for denying over half the world the right to fully participate in modern civilisation (Du Bois, 1900). Indeed, one of colonialism's central mechanisms was dividing workers along racial lines and organising them into a hierarchical status system. Although racism predated this era, it gained 'material force' through the racialisation of labour, serving capitalist needs for cheap labour (Virdee, 2019, p. 13). Black workers were deemed to have inferior skills and capacities, legitimising discriminatory policies and the violent imposition of forced labour.

Contemporary capitalism's demand for cheap labour continues to rely on the racialised division of workers. Today, labour outsourcing to poorer countries (often former colonies) and immigration regimes reproduce a stratified workforce, differentiating between citizen workers with a full set of rights, migrant workers with fewer rights, high-skilled migrant workers with generous rights, and low-skilled migrant workers with increasingly restricted rights. At the bottom, temporary labour migration programmes typically recruit racialised workers from the Global South, who face both economic exploitation and a subordinate legal and social status as foreign temporary workers. The entanglement of labour supply and immigration policies, where work contracts are tied to the threat of deportation, exerts a disciplining effect, subjecting migrant workers to lower wages and poor working conditions (Valdez, 2021; Walia, 2021). This emerging scholarship reveals that global labour injustice is not merely a matter of contemporary economic inequality but is deeply rooted in the colonial legacy of racialised labour stratification and asymmetric mobility. These factors, intersecting with class, race, gender and migrant status, continue to shape the global economy and labour organisation, making workers *structurally vulnerable to exploitation* by their intersecting positions (Müller, 2024).

Addressing and disrupting these colonial patterns of distribution and domination require more than just apologies and the redistribution of resources and opportunities through reparations programmes. While reforming the international economic structure was once the focus, the current discourse has shifted towards the complex process of full-blown decolonisation, which involves epistemic changes and a thorough restructuring of global labour practices.

CONCLUSION

In this chapter, we have argued that understanding global labour injustice requires a comprehensive examination encompassing various normative concerns arising from the socioeconomic, political and historical perspectives, often intertwined and contradictory. Addressing these injustices entails monumental efforts. One thing that is already clear is that piecemeal isolated reforms tinkering at the edges of global economic forces will not suffice.

Global labour justice requires taming economic globalisation through the structural economic transformation of systems of production, exchange and distribution, common good-oriented joint political action through fair procedures at national and international levels, as well as socio-cultural effort to disrupt the intersectional social hierarchies of class, race and gender inherited from the past but still deeply entrenched in our present.

REFERENCES

Beitz, C. R. (1999). *Political Theory and International Relations*. Rev. ed. Princeton University Press.

Bennett, E. A. (2025). Labour Justice in the Global Economy and Global Economic Governance: A Broad Overview with Focus on the ILO and CSR. In A. Berger, C. Brandi, & E. Kollar (eds.), *Justice in Global Economic Governance: Normative and Empirical Perspectives on Promoting Fairer Globalization*. Edinburgh University Press.

Blunt, G. D. (2022). The Gates Foundation, Global Health and Domination: A Republican Critique of Transnational Philanthropy. *International Affairs, 98*(6), 2039–56.

Brock, G. (2009). *Global Justice: A Cosmopolitan Account*. Oxford University Press.

Caney, S. (2005). *Justice beyond Borders: A Global Political Theory*. Oxford University Press.

Cordelli, C. (2023). Freeing People; Restricting Capital. *British Journal of Political Science, 53*(4), 1093–107.

Cordelli, C., & Levy, J. (2022). The Ethics of Global Capital Mobility. *American Political Science Review, 116*(2), 439–52.

Du Bois, W. E. B. (1900, 2022). 'To the Nations of the World (1900)'. In Getachew, A., & Pitts, J., (eds.), *W. E. B. Du Bois: International Thought*, 18–21. Cambridge Texts in the History of Political Thought. Cambridge University Press.

Hussain, W. (2020). Pitting People against Each Other. *Philosophy and Public Affairs, 48*(1), 79–113

Julius, A. J. (2006). Nagel's Atlas. *Philosophy & Public Affairs, 34*(2), 176–92.

Laborde, C., & Ronzoni, M. (2016). What Is a Free State? Republican Internationalism and Economic Globalisation. *Political Studies, 64*(2), 279–96.

Lenard, P. T., & Straehle, C. (2012). Temporary Labour Migration, Global Redistribution, and Democratic Justice. *Politics, Philosophy & Economics, 11*(2), 206–30.

Malmqvist, E. (2013). Taking Advantage of Injustice. *Social Theory and Practice, 39*(4), 557–80.

Marx, A., Depoorter, C., Fernandez de Cordoba, S., Verma, R., Araoz, M., Auld, G., Bemelmans, J., Bennett, E. A., Boonaert, E., Brandi, C., & Dietz, T., (2024). Global Governance through Voluntary Sustainability Standards: Developments, Trends and Challenges. *Global Policy*.

Milanovic, B. (2016). *Global Inequality: A New Approach for the Age of Globalisation*. The Belknap Press of Harvard University Press.

Miller, D. (2016). *Strangers in Our Midst: The Political Philosophy of Immigration*. Harvard University Press.

Müller, M. (2024). *Global Sweatshops: A Feminist Theory of Exploitation and Resistance*. Oxford University Press.

Nili, S. (2011). Democratic Disengagement: Toward Rousseauian Global Reform. *International Theory, 3*(3), 355–89.

O'Neill, M., & White, S. (2018). Trade Unions and Political Equality. In *The Philosophical Foundations of Labour Law*. Oxford University Press.

Ottonelli, V., & Torresi, T. (2022). *The Right Not to Stay: Justice in Migration, the Liberal Democratic State, and the Case of Temporary Migration Projects*. Oxford University Press.

Pevnick, R. (2011). *Immigration and the Constraints of Justice: Between Open Borders and Absolute Sovereignty*. 1st ed. Cambridge University Press.

Pogge, T. (2008). *World Poverty and Human Rights: Cosmopolitan Responsibilities and Reforms*. 2nd ed. Polity.

Radcliff, B., & Davis, P. (2000). Labour Organisation and Electoral Participation in Industrial Democracies. *American Journal of Political Science, 44*(1), 132–41.

Robinson, C. J. (2005). *Black Marxism: The Making of the Black Radical Tradition*. University of North Carolina Press.

Ronzoni, M. (2016). Global Labour Injustice: A Critical Overview. In Y. Dahan, H. Lerner, & F. Milman-Sivan (eds.), *Global Justice and International Labour Rights*, 27–52. Cambridge University Press.

Ruhs, M. (2013). *The Price of Rights: Regulating International Labour Migration*. Princeton University Press.

Ruhs, M., & Martin, P. (2008). Numbers vs. Rights: Trade-Offs and Guest Worker Programs. *The International Migration Review, 42*(1), 249–65.

Sen, A. (1999). *Development as Freedom*. Oxford University Press.

Standing, G. (2011). *The Precariat: The New Dangerous Class*. Bloomsbury Academic.

Valdez, I. (2021). Socialism and Empire: Labour Mobility, Racial Capitalism, and the Political Theory of Migration. *Political Theory, 49*(6), 902–33.

van Apeldoorn, L. (2019). Exploitation, International Taxation, and Global Justice. *Review of Social Economy, 77*(2), 163–83.

Van Parijs, P. (2018). *Basic Income and the Left: A European Debate*. Social Europe Edition. Social Europe Ltd.

Virdee, S. (2019). Racialised Capitalism: An Account of Its Contested Origins and Consolidation. *The Sociological Review, 67*(1), 3–27.

Vrousalis, N. (2018). Exploitation: A Primer. *Philosophy Compass, 13*(2), e12486.

Walia, H. (2021). *Border and Rule: Global Migration, Capitalism, and the Rise of Racist Nationalism*. Haymarket Books.

Wenar, L. (2016). *Blood Oil: Tyrants, Violence, and the Rules That Run the World*. Oxford University Press.

Wertheimer, A. (1999). *Exploitation*. Princeton University Press.

Young, I. M. (2006). Responsibility and Global Justice: A Social Connection Model. *Social Philosophy and Policy, 23*(1), 102–30.

Ypi, L. (2016). Taking Workers as a Class: The Moral Dilemmas of Guestworker Programs. In S. Fine & L. Ypi (eds.), *Migration in Political Theory: The Ethics of Movement and Membership*, 151–74. Oxford University Press.

Chapter 8

JUSTICE IN FINANCE: FINANCIAL STABILITY VS FAIRNESS

Paola Subacchi

WHO PAYS FOR BANKS' FAILURE?

Should failing banks be bailed out? When the Silicon Valley Bank (SVB) collapsed in March 2023 after holding approximately $150 billion in uninsured deposits, the US Treasury promptly organised the backstop through the Federal Deposit Insurance Corporation's (FDIC) 'Deposit Insurance Fund', stating that this was not a bailout and taxpayers' money was not used.

The US Treasury Secretary Janeth Yellen committed to extend guarantees to all deposits, even those above the threshold of $250,000 – these were 93 per cent of the total domestic deposits at the SVB. By the end of March 2023, following the closure of SVB and the creation of the Silicon Valley Bridge Bank, the FDIC agreed on behalf of all depositors of the latter to move their deposits to the First-Citizens Bank & Trust Company. Moreover, the Fed, the US Central Bank, created the 'Bank Term Funding Program', which offers up to one-year loans to banks, savings associations, credit unions, and other eligible depository institutions to prevent more bank runs (Board of Governors of the Federal Reserve System, (n.d.), Bank Term Funding Program).

This episode starkly highlights the complex decisions that policy-makers need to grapple with when financial stability is at stake. In the specific case of the SVB the high level of debt in the non-banking financial sector was a concern as the US monetary policy needed to remain constrained to keep inflation under control. The US Treasury and the Fed acted on the assumption that there was no choice, but to curb from the beginning a banking crisis. In doing so, however, they set aside other considerations such as whether rescuing a bank that was not deemed to have a systemic impact – that is, if it failed it would not bring down the entire banking and financial system – was fair and just. Of course, the distributive impact of the decision to extend the Fed's safety net to the SVB was negligible because no public funds were used; this was because by stepping in as guarantor of all deposits the Fed would fend off any bank run. In doing so, however, the US Treasury and the Fed shifted the risk threshold for banks and their clients and implicitly endorsed bad practices in risk management and poor governance. Above all, they set the clock back to the period that preceded the global financial crisis and the unmanageable level of risk that was propped up by the idea that banks were too big to fail.

This chapter discusses how the policy goal of financial stability often tramples on broader public policy considerations, with outcomes that are often inequitable and unjust. Because banking crises have always caused deep recessions due to their impact on the real economy (Reinhart & Rogoff, 2011), it is critical to deal with them promptly and decisively. This is the lesson from the global financial crisis of 2007/8. When the system is on the verge of collapse any consideration of moral hazard is out of place; the central banks need to act as lenders of last resort with no ifs nor buts. The need to rescue banks, however, is often followed by a period of fiscal austerity that disproportionally hits the poorest in our societies. This, again, is what happened after the global financial crisis. This chapter discusses this challenge and how it can be addressed.

As the international financial system has become more integrated, one important result is that bank failures can have a cross-border systemic impact. Crisis prevention should therefore be better embedded in global financial governance. We also need an international financial safety net that is broader and more comprehensive than what the multilateral financial institutions, that is, the International Monetary Fund (IMF), can currently provide. Moreover, the G20 also plays an essential role. Since its inception as a leaders' forum in November 2008, the G20 focused on preventing crises through a more robust regulatory framework under the supervision of the Financial Stability Board. The safety net was improved through the extension of flexible, non-conditional credit lines in April 2009 and a general allocation of Special Drawing Rights (SDRs), that is, supplementary international exchange reserve assets maintained by the IMF, equivalent to about 650 billion dollars in 2021. In addition, the G20 at the Rome Summit approved 100 billion dollars of voluntary contributions to poor countries. However, progress on injecting more resources into the IMF as the provider of the multilateral financial safety net has been stuck.

I will first explore the dilemma around whether to rescue or not the investment bank Lehman Brothers during the global financial crisis that started in 2007 and argue that public policy considerations cannot be left to when a crisis is underway. I will carry on discussing lessons learned from the global financial crisis and the impact on economies and societies as a whole of measures necessary to avoid financial instability. This leads me to consider crisis prevention vs crisis resolution as a more effective way to maintain financial stability without the need to redistribute of public resources and negative impact on welfare. I will conclude by looking at the potential tension between global markets and nation-states.

TOO BIG TO FAIL

Surely the ghost of 2008 was behind the decision to support SVB. In September 2008, the US financial authorities decided not to rescue the investment bank Lehman Brothers to avoid the moral hazard implicit in the expectation that it was 'too big to fail'. But the collapse of Lehman shook almost fatally the US banking sector and this triggered a broad and deep financial crisis with worldwide ramifications and impact. It is worth rewinding those events.

During the summer of 2008, Lehman Brothers – a medium-size investment bank first established as a dry goods store in 1844 – was in serious trouble. The bank's position in the subprime and other lower-rated mortgage-backed securities market had left it largely exposed to the 2007 crisis. A loss of $2.8 billion had emerged, to mitigate which Lehman had to sell off $6 billion in assets. As a result, the value of its stocks had dropped by 73 per cent. Senior executives, however, remained confident that they would be able to find a new partner willing to put some fresh capital into the ailing bank. At the end of August 2008, it looked like a deal with the Korea Development Bank was imminent, but then the negotiations collapsed, and the stock price took another deep plunge – this time by 45 per cent. The risk was material, but many capital markets practitioners and commentators remained persuaded that there was nothing to be worried about. Eventually, it was thought, the Fed would bail out Lehman Brothers to avert a deeper crisis. In other words, the troubled bank was too big to fail.

But the Fed was aware of the dilemma that Lehman's fate was tied to. Was it fair and just to bail out a financial organisation that was deemed to profit from risk-taking? Would such a bailout end up underwriting and even encouraging moral hazard? To prevent moral hazard – and discourage the belief that all insolvent institutions would eventually be saved – the Fed decided not to intervene and let Lehman cave in. The Fed was surely right about avoiding underwriting Lehman's losses and de facto 'institutionalising' moral hazard, but its call almost brought down the entire US banking and financial system with rippled effects to the rest of the world. Concerns about a specific banking institution morphed into fear that no banks were safe. The liquidity crisis, caused by the subprime mortgage crisis the previous year, had turned into a global credit crunch and stock market crash.

In the end, the Fed had to give up. The day after the collapse of Lehman Brothers, it bailed out and nationalised the insurance giant AIG, out of concerns that, had it allowed AIG to fail, the consequences for insurance contracts on securities would be systemic. By then, however, financial contagion was difficult to rein in. By early October, the crisis had spread to Europe. The global interbank market had ceased functioning. In the UK, the authorities responded by pumping capital into domestic banks, guaranteeing all interbank deposits and providing massive amounts of liquidity. The other EU countries responded in a similar fashion and the US Treasury followed suit. They injected 250 billion dollars into the US banks, providing insurance to senior interbank debt and unlimited deposit insurance for non-interest-bearing deposits.

This episode brings up two critical features of the banking and financial system. The first is its deep interdependencies as capital is constantly intermediated – and huge profits come from this intermediation – and 'recycled' in different types of instruments. This explains how widespread delinquencies in the subprime section of the US mortgage market transmitted through the US banking system – and that of other countries as well – and brought it to the edge of collapse.

The second feature is the snowball effect, taking into account the speed at which insolvencies in one part of the system can transmit to others. Everybody knows that a credit-based system runs into trouble if everybody makes claims at the same time, and so incentives are skewed towards getting out as soon as strains materialise. Solvent institutions can become victims of bank runs. For example, the guarantee on bank deposits of £32,000 proved not to be enough, and the threshold was raised to £85,000 through the British Financial Services Compensation Scheme (FSCS). In addition, banks in the UK can now be bailed in, so that investors bear losses rather than the taxpayers (Bank of England, n.d.). Other countries also introduced more regulation. At the same time, these new regulations in the UK and beyond, have not reduced financial imbalances or the potential for instability, as recent episodes have shown us.

THE ASYMMETRY OF BANKS' LOSSES AND PROFITS

The lesson from Lehman Brothers was clear, when the banking system is on the verge of collapse prompt intervention, 'whatever it takes', is needed to avoid the worst. But this means avoiding any consideration around distributive impact and fairness that are typical of any public policy intervention. The story of the Royal Bank of Scotland (RBS) illustrates the fundamental unfairness that is implicit in the dilemma between financial stability and moral hazard, or 'too big to fail'. At the same time, the decision to bail out the bank shows the policy and political consequences of socialising banks' losses while profits remain private.

Until the early 2000s, RBS remained a solid bank with limited international outreach. Following some successful mergers and acquisitions, by 2008 RBS had become the largest bank in the world, with a balance sheet that matched the size of the German economy (Morris & Megaw, 2018). This achievement, however, was only to be short-lived. Towards the end of 2007, RBS agreed to take over the Dutch bank ABN Amro for £49 billion – a record high. The takeover stretched RBS's financial resources to breaking point. In April 2008, RBS was forced to undergo a £12 billion debt and equity restructuring, or recapitalisation, but to no avail. The bank had become too reliant on short-term wholesale funding, that is, funding from other banks and the capital markets, which – together with its considerable use of low-quality capital and losses in trading activities – had left it extremely vulnerable. When Lehman Brothers collapsed in September, the following loss of confidence that affected all banks proved to be fatal for RBS. Considered too big to fail, the UK government decided to intervene to prevent the collapse of RBS which could have brought down the domestic banking and financial system. By October, RBS needed to be bailed out to the tune of £15 billion as an emergency measure. During 2009, the UK Treasury injected a further £30 billion into RBS, resulting in it holding an 86 per cent stake in the bank by the end of the year. Halifax Bank of Scotland and Lloyds Bank also needed to be bailed out and the UK government ended up allocating £500 billion to an overall bank rescue package. The bank bailout package drained Britain's public resources and had long-term implications for the country's public finances. But what was the alternative?

The bailout prevented a banking collapse and helped the economy to restore confidence. Britain was one of the best-performing countries in Europe, while the periphery of the euro area was in the grip of the debt sovereign crisis. The downside was that the British government's net borrowing massively expanded to 10 per cent of GDP in 2009 (on debt, see also Berensmann, Chapter 14 in this volume). The fact that taxpayers' money was used for the bailout did not seem to bother the banking sector; in February 2009 RBS – now a majority state-owned bank – announced that it had every intention of distributing £1 billion in bonuses in extra compensation for its senior executives as per usual.

RULES FOR THE PEOPLE OR FOR MARKETS?

Extraordinary measures that are necessary at times of crisis increase public deficits and bloat central banks' balance sheets. In 2010, for instance, the G20 agreed on a programme of spending cuts and fiscal austerity to rein in the public debt that had grown significantly. In the UK, the newly elected Conservative and Liberal Democrat coalition government implemented a tough programme of spending cuts.

This austerity programme, however, begs the question of how much debt is too much. It is widely conceded that debt levels were too high in the run-up to the financial crisis and that this is one of the factors that started the downward spiral. Yet, debt is not necessarily bad if it is intended to drive long-term economic development and create prosperity for all, rather than generating short-term returns for some.

As a result of extremely accommodative monetary policy and constrained fiscal policy capital flew into Britain from all over the world, supporting a run-up in prices of all assets. House prices skyrocketed, especially in the most dynamic areas of the country, making it difficult for many young people and low-middle income families to secure decent and fairly priced accommodation. The austerity programme, which was felt necessary after the banks' bailout, undermined the post-crisis recovery and disproportionally affected low-income families and local communities

DEEP FINANCIAL INTEGRATION

The collapse of Lehman Brothers triggered a domestic crisis in the USA that soon spiralled down and became a major global crisis that required a huge effort of cooperation among the world's largest economies – hence the elevation of the G20 to head of state/government level. This crisis revealed how deeply interconnected banks and non-bank financial institutions are through cross-border capital flows. This is historically unprecedented. Cross-border financial positions more than tripled as a share of world GDP between the mid-1990s and the global financial crisis in 2008. The pace of financial integration remains strong in historical terms even if it was slower in the decade after 2010 (Milesi-Ferretti, 2022).

Cross-border interconnectedness in banks and non-bank financial institutions means that stress in some markets could spill over to different markets and jurisdictions. The system is intrinsically vulnerable because of the pace of structural changes that are underway. Fintech, digital currencies and crypto assets have emerged in the years after the global financial crisis and remain unregulated. In addition, shocks such as the war in Ukraine have exposed new vulnerabilities for financial stability. In its annual report, the Financial Stability Board (FSB), an international body that was established by the G20 in 2009 and that monitors the global financial system, identifies vulnerabilities in the non-bank financial intermediation sector, in risk management of financial institutions, in unregulated crypto assets and climate-related financial risks (FSB, 2022). To tackle these vulnerabilities the report stresses the importance of deeper international cooperation, coordination and information-sharing.

As van 't Klooster and Mayer (Chapter 9 in this volume) stress, the goal of financial stability can be justified by appealing to the no-harm principle as banking and financial crises dampen activity, reduce jobs and increase poverty. As shown by the examples discussed above, there are costs in resolving crises. Crisis prevention is a much better and fairer option than crisis resolution as it allows measures that can be assessed against their overall impact on public welfare. Regulations are the largest bulk of preventive measures. Rather than drawing on public resources, they focus on reducing the scope for arbitrage and risky behaviour, often curbing excessive risk-taking and so profits. Since the global financial crisis, there has been significant progress in strengthening financial regulations, even if more can be done.

Financial safety nets are also critical to help countries that face an economic or financial crisis and reduce the global systemic risk by preventing crises from spreading and avoiding the related adverse consequences for the real economy. It is often the case that countries with strong fundamentals experience a liquidity shortage on the back of episodes of strong capital outflows. This is the direct consequence of cross-border capital flows that I have discussed above. The complexity of financial instability since 2008 – their size and potential for contagion through the highly integrated international system – has highlighted the importance of ensuring plenty of liquidity at times of dwindling market confidence. In 2013, for instance, when the Fed indicated a change in its monetary policy stance, capital flowed out of the large developing countries. An effective financial safety net would have been needed to provide liquidity rapidly.

Historically, the international financial safety net has been organised mainly around the IMF, where resources have predominantly been mobilised (IMF, 2016). At the London Summit in April 2009, the G20 expanded the global safety net with a non-conditional Precautionary and Liquidity Line for countries with sound economic fundamentals and a Flexible Credit Line for countries with structurally sound economies. Countries with a temporary shortage of liquidity can now access these lines and restore market confidence without going through the procedure of a fully-fledged IMF rescue. Non-conditionality has not, however, removed the stigma attached to requesting support from the IMF. Only a handful of countries to date have used these credit lines.[1]

IMF assistance is conditional on the country's government making the necessary adjustments to ensure that the underlying causes of financial imbalances are addressed so that the financial help can eventually be repaid. This approach responds to the need to manage moral hazard risks that are inevitably associated with the provision of financial resources to countries that struggle to get access to credit. For instance, private sector lenders are required to share some of the losses, thereby removing possible incentives to take up excessive and unsustainable lending knowing that official financing

[1] In addition, regional components such as the European Stability Mechanism and the Chiang Mai Initiative (CMI) in Asia – later to become Chiang Mai Initiative Multilateralization (CMIM) (IMF, 2016) – have emerged. The regional and bilateral components of the international financial safety net are appropriate instruments for addressing the recent crises, and they reduce, in principle at least, the scope for IMF interventions.

will eventually bail out the private sector, as happened with banks in Europe. The need to mitigate moral hazard for lenders makes IMF interventions and the process from insolvency to financial sustainability painful and politically difficult. People resent external interventions and see them as a diminution of national sovereignty, especially when such interventions require fiscal sacrifices such as considerable cuts in public expenditure or tax increases.

Some costs and risks are linked to providing a global financial safety net (Subacchi, 2020). A commitment to lend represents a contingent liability, and in the case of IMF quotas, paid-in capital is required. Paid-in capital and assets lent to the IMF earn interest – less than those from commercial assets. Similarly, accumulating foreign exchange reserves – a favourite of many developing countries – carries both direct financial and opportunity costs. Participation in bilateral currency swaps carries credit, foreign exchange and sovereign risks that are difficult to mitigate. Furthermore, taxpayer money committed to the safety net carries an opportunity cost as this money cannot be used for other purposes.

Although the IMF acts as a lender of last resort, it is not a central bank and it cannot print money. It has about 1 trillion dollars for the coming years in quota subscriptions, new arrangements to borrow, and fixed-term borrowing agreements. This capacity to lend needs to be strengthened. But financial capacity is linked to governance so IMF members need to be persuaded to pay in more resources – and the way to do this is to reform the structure of voting rights.

The IMF as well as the World Bank remains dominated by the United States which holds veto rights. The influence of the BRICS and other developing countries is constrained in both organisations. However, to provide an effective safety net and coordinate international policy action, the IMF needs to be representative and accountable, offering democratic space at the regional and global levels (Rodrik, 2018). If not, the gap between international policy action and domestic policy preferences will continue to widen, impairing international policy cooperation at the time when it is most urgent.

FINANCE AND DEMOCRACY

The need to maintain financial stability 'whatever it takes' highlights the intrinsic contradiction and potential tension between global markets and nation-states. Where are the trade-offs in channelling national financial resources – or, taxpayers' money – in supporting global banks to restore financial stability?

The global financial crisis thus marked a turning point. Unlike previous episodes of financial instability, the 2008 crisis originated in Wall Street and put under the spotlight global markets and global capitalism while questioning the 'free market' doctrine and the governance – including the burden sharing – that ensures the functioning of global capitalism (Subacchi, 2020). It also raised the issue of setting up a new system – indeed a new Bretton Woods as some suggested (Brown & Sarkozy, 2008) – to underpin the functioning of global markets and governance, with rules to avoid excessive risk-taking and moral hazard, and the infrastructure to provide financial safety nets and so restore financial stability.

The moral of the tale is that financial stability and capital markets' preferences – to ensure smooth capital flows – are often at odds with collective welfare and even with democracy and thus with political justice. Governments are often painfully aware of the restraints and the inability, in democracy, to square long-term market commitments with short-term advantages that derive from having plenty of capital and debt funding to grow their economies. The distributive impact of policy measures that are required to 'stay in the market' is broadly skewed against the poorest members of society. These individuals and families tend to disproportionately rely on public welfare and benefits, and so they experience significant losses when public spending on welfare is axed. In addition, there are people with limited or no financial assets, so unable to gain from the rapid increase in asset prices that materialised on the back of the monetary policy stance in the years after the global financial crisis and during the pandemic. The widespread inability to take care of the poorest in our societies – for example, by increasing taxation – speaks volumes about unfairness, inequality, and lack of socioeconomic justice that is embedded in short-term speculative finance.

REFERENCES

Bank of England. (n.d.). *The Financial Crisis – 10 Years On: What Happened, and What Has Been Done Since?*

Board of Governors of the Federal Reserve System. (n.d.). Bank Term Funding Program. https://www.federalreserve.gov/financial-stability/bank-term-funding-program.htm#:~:text=The%20Bank%20Term%20Funding%20Program,needs%20of%20all%20their%20depositors.

Brown, G., & Sarkozy, N. (2008). *New Bretton Woods*. Financial Times.

Financial Stability Board. (2022). *2022 Annual Report*.

International Monetary Fund. (2016). *Adequacy of the Global Financial Safety Net*.

Milesi-Ferretti, G. M. (2022). *2021 Was a Year of Strong Global Capital Flows: Updating External Wealth of Nations Database with Year-End 2021 Data*. Brookings Institution, Commentary.

Morris, S., & Megaw, N. (2018). *RBS Drops off List of World's Most Important Banks. Financial Times*.

Reinhart, C. M., & Rogoff, K. S. (2011). *This Time Is Different: Eight Centuries of Financial Folly*. Princeton University Press.

Rodrik, D. (2018). *Straight Talk on Trade: Ideas for a Sane World Economy*. Princeton University Press.

Subacchi, P. (2020). *The Cost of Free Money*. Yale University Press.

Chapter 9

JUSTICE IN GLOBAL FINANCIAL GOVERNANCE

Jens van 't Klooster and Marco Meyer

INTRODUCTION

In 2015, the Nigerian government awarded grants of around $50,000 to over seven hundred randomly selected small firms (McKenzie, 2017). In the years that followed, these firms did dramatically better than those who did not receive the grants. The firms hired more workers, made new investments, and increased profits on average by 25 per cent. One winner pivoted from selling paint from the trunk of her car to setting up a small factory producing paint. Access to money expanded the possibilities for these entrepreneurs. The grants made Nigeria a richer country, yielding ample returns on the initial investment.

Low-income countries, the experiment illustrates, are rife with opportunities for economic growth, which go unrealised in the absence of finance. Most low-income governments cannot finance large budget deficits. The benefits of a grant could also be achieved through private credit, but assessing creditworthiness is difficult and costly. Global financial regulation often prioritises financial stability over financial inclusion. Therefore, the global financial system today lets many investment opportunities go to waste.

Over the last decades, governments have agreed to international rules and created institutions to regulate the global financial system. Looking at these regulatory efforts through the lens of global justice yields a mixed picture. The structures of global banking governance seek to facilitate access to finance. To this end, regulators have set up a global financial architecture that allows for cross-border financial flows. However, regulators have also come to acknowledge the risks of financial crises.

In the first section, we discuss the goals of global financial regulation. Currently, global financial regulation is focused on enabling cross-border financial flows and safeguarding financial stability. Yet we argue in favour of looking beyond financial stability to global priorities that finance can help advance. The following three sections focus on three such priorities: socio-economic justice, political justice and intergenerational justice, respectively. The final section outlines a reform proposal to shift the priorities of global financial regulation from an exclusive focus on financial stability to a broader focus on financial priorities.

GLOBAL BANKING AND FINANCIAL STABILITY

As the Bretton Woods system of strict capital controls slowly unravelled during the 1970s, a tight-knit network of central bankers and globally active banks built a predominantly dollar-denominated global financial order (Helleiner, 1996).

Although the objectives of policy-makers have evolved, their efforts can be described as focused on balancing two types of regulatory objectives. The first is that policy-makers seek to facilitate the creation of a global banking system. In the 1970s, international banks came to increasingly offer services of financial intermediation to the global economy. They started lending to governments and large firms in the developing world with little in the way of regulatory oversight – often to low-income countries that imported oil. These same banks would also offer dollar-denominated deposits – to large multinational companies and oil-exporting countries. The financial system that facilitates such flows is situated primarily offshore in those banks outside the jurisdiction of the USA issuing new dollar deposits in the act of granting loans. More minor offshore banking activities also exist for other currencies.

Enabling offshore and otherwise international banking activities requires extensive collaboration between regulators and banking supervisors. To this end, the Basel Committee and a host of other transnational standard-setting bodies came into being to coordinate rules. Equally important is the support from jurisdictions that issue core currencies such as the US dollar. Already in the 1970s, offshore banks received emergency credit in foreign currencies through global collaboration between central banks. Today, the world's largest central banks lend to each other via so-called swap lines. The International Monetary Fund (IMF) and the World Bank provide credit directly to governments but have also taken up various roles to intermediate between low-income countries and the global financial system.

Global finance, properly regulated, has a clear potential to improve prosperity by advancing economic development. A sound and effective financial system can play an important role in helping to reduce poverty and advance economic development (Beck, 2011). As Elizabeth Anderson has remarked, trade credit has been necessary for nearly every occupation in the transatlantic economy since the nineteenth century (Anderson, 2004, p. 349). Cross-border finance plays an important role in enabling international trade. Alexander Hamilton, one of the founding fathers of the United States, argued that 'banks were the happiest engines that ever were invented for advancing trade' (Cowen & Sylla, 2018, p. 33).

This harmonious conception of the financial system, however, is only part of the story. A global financial system, where money flows across jurisdictions, is not easy to regulate. Hence, where regulators have gone beyond merely facilitating free capital flows, their efforts have been focused on what is today described as financial stability; the absence of financial *in*stability – at a minimum, the absence of financial crises (Allen & Wood, 2006). In fact, global financial regulation largely developed through regulatory cooperation in response to crises and banking failures. In 1974, the messy liquidation of a German bank briefly brought down the global payment system. This resulted in the creation of the Basel Committee for Banking Supervision in the same year. During the 1980s, Latin American countries defaulted on the loans they received to import oil resulting in the infamous'lost decade'. It led the IMF to develop its structural adjustment programmes and the Basel Committee to issue the Basel rules. The Basel rules set global minimum standards for bank capital requirements, that is, the amount of capital banks must hold to protect against becoming insolvent. Basel II, created in 2004, updated the Basel I rules with a more sophisticated risk modelling approach. The new risk modelling approach could not prevent, and may even have contributed to, the financial crisis of 2008/9 (Green et al., 2011). Basel III, adopted in 2010 and regularly updated since then, attempts to correct the deficiencies of Basel II, with a focus on ensuring financial stability by introducing higher capital requirements – if not nearly as high as demanded by some important voices in the debate (Admati & Hellwig, 2013). The jury is still out as to whether Basel III and other regulations introduced by central banks and governments are sufficient to ensure financial stability.

The goal of financial stability can be justified by appealing to the no-harm principle. Financial crises cause enormous wreckage to economies, leading to job losses, poverty and the destruction of wealth at an enormous scale (Kindleberger, 2011). Along these lines, Aaron James uses a powerful analogy to drive home the importance of financial stability (James, 2012, p. 253). James invites us to imagine a powerful bio-agent that is the source of cheap power and therefore economic savings. But the technology is also dangerous. At regular intervals, the use of the bio-agent breaks out into highly contagious diseases with serious social and economic costs, leading to unemployment, the shrinking of economies, and the explosion of public debt – in a way that hits the least well-off hardest. The contagion does not stop at country borders, and as a result, even countries that do not use the dangerous technology suffer its downsides. Over time, we got better at managing the dangers of the technology. By introducing stringent regulation, we had kept outbreaks at bay for nearly three decades. Yet recently, after undoing much of the regulation that had kept outbreaks at bay, we were subject to one of the worst outbreaks we have ever witnessed. James invites us to conclude that using this bio-agent is far from morally innocent. In the very least, we would be foolish to not re-establish the regulation that worked well in the past. This hypothetical bio-agent is a lot like global finance. Between 1945 and 1970, there were only three banking crises (India 1947, Brazil 1963, and Uruguay 1971). Between 1970 and 2017, there were 151. There were also 236 currency crises and seventy-nine sovereign debt crises (Laeven & Valencia, 2020). To date, bank capital requirements have not stopped repeated crises, nor have the IMF and the World Bank been particularly effective in resolving them.

James' analogy suggests that financial stability is a really important goal from the perspective of global justice – insofar as the point and purpose of global justice is on global well-being. He takes a contractualist approach to global justice, asking whether citizens can reasonably reject the imposition of risks of unemployment and other financial disadvantages on citizens. He argues that lax regulation does not afford most global citizens advantages that make the harms of financial crises justifiable. Yet we should not conclude that financial stability should be the exclusive focus of global financial regulation. It is clear why advanced economies would take financial stability to be the main concern for global banking activities: they do not want their banks to make losses that necessitate bailouts. But, as we now show, this narrow focus on financial stability sidelines a range of other considerations of justice. We will use the three components of global justice introduced in this volume to assess to what extent global financial regulation is heading in the right direction: socioeconomic justice; political justice; and intergenerational justice.

GLOBAL FINANCIAL REGULATION AND SOCIOECONOMIC JUSTICE

Global socioeconomic justice concerns the reduction of poverty and exploitation, as well as reducing global economic inequality. The hierarchical structure of the existing financial system hinders such efforts and confronts states with the risk of financial stability as the price of accessing credit. Financial globalisation does not impact all countries equally. For one, the impact of global finance on inequality is mediated by state-level institutions. A financial system where firms and states can access credit under favourable conditions is likely to decrease inequality *between* countries. It enables less-developed economies to grow faster than advanced economies, which means that inequality between countries trends downwards (Beck et al., 2007). Yet how global finance impacts inequality *within* countries is contingent on domestic institutions such as the tax regime (Claessens & Perotti, 2007).

How global finance impacts domestic justice is also intimately tied up with the broader distributive effects of globalisation. Because the primary benefits of globalisation are concentrated in some parts of the population and not others, inequality within countries can increase. In advanced economies, there is increasing evidence that the negative impact of globalisation falls disproportionately on the 'middle class' as certain types of jobs shift to less-developed economies (Rodrik, 2017; Klein and Pettis, 2022).

Turning to the financial system itself, how financial flows affect the lives of people depends crucially on the position of states within the global financial system. Today's monetary system is one of market-driven monetary competition, where states compete to ensure widespread usage of their national unit of account (Herzog, 2019; Svartzman & Althouse, 2020; Murau & van 't Klooster, 2022). Some currencies are widely used as a means of payment and store of value. The United States, in particular, has a pivotal role as the US dollar serves as the world's reserve currency (Bernes et al., 2014). Roughly half of all cross-border loans and international debt securities are denominated in dollars (Davies & Kent, 2020). Other key currencies are the euro, the UK pound and the Japanese yen. Issuers of core currencies can more easily deal with shocks and offset fluctuations in their trade balance as they can borrow at low rates from international lenders. A major reason for their ability to borrow at low rates is that lenders are confident in the creditworthiness of governments that issue core currencies. Their central banks can issue more currency to repay loans and there will always be demand for these currencies.

Towards the periphery of the global financial system, we find currencies that investors are much more reluctant to hold; usually, they do so with an eye to yields when converted back into a core currency. For states issuing debt in these currencies, or borrowing in core currencies themselves, being embedded in the global financial system increases the risk of financial and economic crises (Korinek, 2011). Because trade and key financial flows are denominated in dollars, their domestic economic and monetary policy is generally tightly constrained by the need to stabilise their currency against the dollar.

The global banking system reflects the hierarchy of currencies (Jones, 2020). Its main financial institutions are almost exclusively located in core currency areas. These institutions play an important role in determining which states are creditworthy, and which are forced to default. When returns in core currencies are low and appear to be higher elsewhere, money flows into the rest of the world looking for higher yields; so-called 'hot money' flows. As financial conditions in the core improve, these flows often reverse, leaving recipient countries vulnerable to crises (Naqvi, 2019).

The risks that come with global funding raise clear questions of justice. The dangers of global credit flows can be mitigated, but often only by reducing the availability of funds for investment. One way to ensure financial stability would be to prohibit them entirely. Such an extreme measure would be difficult to implement in a world of global trade flows, and would itself require regulatory cooperation. If successful, the measure would exclude large parts of the world from access to finance and thereby reduce their development prospects.

Another way to stop hot money flows, which is what many countries do today, is to hold large foreign exchange reserves. Consider Bangladesh, not long ago one of the poorest countries in the world, which holds foreign currency reserves valued at over $43 billion (Bangladesh Bank, 2021). To build such reserves, it must run large trade surpluses, that is, export more than it imports in goods and services. Holding reserves means that the country lends to the USA and other core jurisdictions. Because of the pressure to ensure financial stability, Bangladesh is hindered from investing in the productive capacity of its economy. The Nigerian grants programme mentioned in the introduction could be funded hundreds of times from its current reserves.

The issue of hot money flows illustrates that the structure of the global financial system today is skewed against large parts of the world. The underlying problem is that focusing on financial stability alone is myopic. A financial system is desirable to the extent that it is stable *and* furthers rather than hinders global justice. Any solution to hot money flows and other forms of financial instability cannot just be to reduce access to finance for the Global South.

GLOBAL BANKING REGULATION AND POLITICAL JUSTICE

States at the periphery face financing conditions subject to foreign rules and decisions made by actors outside their jurisdiction. What should we make of this situation from the perspective of political justice?

The first observation to make is that existing structures of global banking governance are anything but democratic (Jones, 2020). Consider the Basel rules as crafted by the Basel Committee. When the Basel process started in the 1970s, the committee was constituted exclusively by representatives of countries with advanced economies. By now, the Basel Committee consists of forty-five members from twenty-eight jurisdictions, with South Africa the only member from Africa. Proponents may argue that the rules crafted by the committee are only binding on its members, who are all represented in the committee. The Basel standard's demanding reporting requirements ensure that banks meet minimal capital standards, which is not a concern in most developing countries. Sophisticated enforcement of capital requirements is much less of a concern towards the periphery of the financial system. Moreover, the Basel Committee has crafted a governance mechanism to engage with non-members through the Basel Consultative Group, ensuring the voice of non-members in the standard-setting process. Hence proponents may argue that the governance of the Basel Committee ensures the creation of financial stability as a global public good, in a way that imposes the regulatory burden exclusively on affluent member countries.

But even if no obligation exists to implement the rules, this assessment leaves out two key concerns. First, many non-members decide to implement

Basel standards anyway, due to concerns about reputation and regulatory competition. Put simply, non-members face a choice: either, to implement rules that are ill-suited to their regulatory environment. Or, to signal to global investors that they are less than full members of the global financial system (Jones, 2020). Second, even if states do not implement the rules for their own banks, it will still affect them. Periphery states and their domestic firms are often dependent on lenders outside their jurisdiction. Hence, they access funds under market conditions that they cannot shape. In a globalised world, non-members cannot simply watch from the sidelines.

Other institutions at the heart of global financial regulation are subject to the same shortcomings. The IMF and the World Bank are dominated by the issuers of core currencies. The monetary policy of the US Federal Reserve and other core central banks set the pace for the world economy, but do so serving the narrow priority of domestic price stability (Mishra & Rajan, 2016).

Despite ample room for improvement, the root causes of these democratic deficits are not easy to fix. They reflect a fundamental mismatch between a financial system that is global and democratic institutions tied to local jurisdictions. Cross-border financial flows by their nature involve economic activities regulated in multiple jurisdictions. The struggles to create a European public sphere illustrate the limits of supranational democratic participation (van Parijs, 2019). Hence, there may be no simple way to make global banking governance democratic.

Political justice, however, does not only require democratic global regulation. It also mandates supporting democratic decision-making domestically. The global legal order is based on formal sovereignty, that is legislative self-determination without outside interference (Murau & van 't Klooster, 2022). Most states retain 'monetary sovereignty' understood as the ability to issue and regulate a national currency. However, for societies to make meaningful democratic choices they also need effective sovereignty understood as 'the substantive problem-solving capacity of states and . . . their ability to make meaningful and genuinely discretionary choices on a range of political, legal and socioeconomic issues' (Ronzoni, 2012). The hierarchical structure of global finance limits states' democratic self-determination by making their economic policy dependent on global capital markets.

Global banking regulation can further democratic self-determination by supporting the effective sovereignty of democratic governments. One way in which global banking regulation can do this is to develop regulatory regimes that apply better across a range of stages of economic development. The current system of financial governance is not set up with an eye to less-developed countries. Rules are crafted with advanced economies' interests in mind; they are designed for complex, large banks at the core of the financial system. Widely accepted Basel standards that fit a broader range of stages of development would help less-developed countries attract more long-term investment. It would allow banking regulation to be geared toward domestic priority, hence improving the scope for self-determination. However, doing so will require broadening the objectives of global banking governance, which to date remain limited to facilitating cross-border financial flows and ensuring financial stability.

GLOBAL BANKING REGULATION AND INTERGENERATIONAL JUSTICE

Global financial regulation is a key determinant of the economic and natural resources we transmit to future generations. John Rawls proposed the'just savings principle' to determine how much economic and natural resources current generations minimally ought to transmit to future generations (Rawls, 2001, 159ff.). The principle requires that current generations should leave future generations enough to meet the material preconditions of living as free and equal citizens under just institutions.

The just savings principle has implications for global justice. By failing to support sustainable development in the Global South, advanced states endanger the living conditions of future generations. The economic effects of climate change are likely to be disproportionately larger in developing countries, both because they are likely to experience the strongest increase in temperature, and because they are more vulnerable to extreme weather events and sea-level rise. Higher vulnerability to climate risks is expected to have a significant impact not only on political development but also on political stability in developing countries, which threatens the capacity of developing countries to set up or maintain just institutions (Volz et al., 2020).

For global banking regulation to contribute to socioeconomic, political, and intergenerational justice, it must also promote decarbonisation. The Basel rules require banks to accurately monitor risk and hold sufficient capital to offset potential losses. Potentially, merely asking banks to effectively screen transition risk could already make a major contribution to offsetting climate change (Carney, 2015; Mercure et al., 2018). Still, overall bank lending is to date far from sustainable as billions still flow to coal plants and other investments incompatible with the objectives of the Paris Agreement (Mercure et al., 2018). Since the Paris Agreement was signed, the largest sixty globally active banks have still provided $3.8 trillion in loans to new fossil fuel infrastructure (RAN, 2021).

These enormous financial flows are only possible because the risk management techniques at the heart of Basel II and III fail to take climate impact sufficiently into account (Smoleńska & van 't Klooster, 2020; Chenet et al., 2021). Being narrowly focused on financial stability, environmental and climate-related considerations have no role in setting bank capital requirements. However, Basel rules do badly even when judged on the criterion of financial stability. The Basel standards rely on historical default rates to estimate future potential losses. Because they are in this sense backward-looking, they ignore the risk that has not historically occurred. Fossil fuels remain at the heart of advanced economies, resulting in high and reliable profits to date. Extreme weather events are defined as those at the extremes of historical observations. In the absence of techniques to assign a probability distribution to future outcomes, the Basel rules mostly lead supervisors to ignore the climate impact of bank lending.

Meanwhile, the hierarchical structure of global finance exacerbates ecological imbalances (Svartzman & Althouse, 2020). Today, fast-growing economies are often focusing on ecologically unsustainable industries, as in China. Or, returning to the example of Nigeria, focusing on fossil fuel extraction. These industries, we hope, will soon be either transformed or replaced by less carbon-intensive modes of production. That, in turn, will require major global investments, which even advanced economies are currently struggling to pull off. The fight against climate change will require more global capital flows, rather than less.

In sum: a more just financial system today is a key precondition for the well-being of future generations. To that end, global banking regulation must move beyond its narrow focus on enabling cross-border capital flows and financial stability.

REFERENCES

Admati, A., & Hellwig, M. (2013). *The Bankers' New Clothes: What's Wrong with Banking and What to Do about It*. Princeton University Press.

Allen, W. A., & Wood, G. (2006). Defining and Achieving Financial Stability. *Journal of Financial Stability*, 2(2), 152–72.

Anderson, Elizabeth. 2004. Ethical Assumptions in Economic Theory: Some Lessons from the History of Credit and Bankruptcy. *Ethical Theory and Moral Practice*, 7(4), 347–60. https://doi.org/10.1007/s10677-004-2202-7.

Bangladesh Bank. (2021). *Foreign Exchange Reserve (Monthly)*.

Beck, T. (2011). *The Role of Finance in Economic Development: Benefits, Risks, and Politics*. Social Science Research Network, 2011, 161–203.

Beck, T., Demirgüç-Kunt, A., & Levine, R. (2007). Finance, Inequality, and the Poor. *Journal of Economic Growth*, 12(1), 27–49.

Bernes, T. A., Jenkins, P., Mehrling, P., & Neilson, D. H. (2014). *China's Engagement with an Evolving International Monetary System: A Payments Perspective: Special Report*. Centre for International Governance Innovation (CIGI) and Institute for New Economic Thinking (INET).

Carney, M. (2015). *Breaking the Tragedy of the Horizon: Climate Change and Financial Stability*. Speech given at Lloyd's of London, 220–30.

Chenet, H., Ryan-Collins, J., & Van Lerven, F. (2021). Finance, Climate Change, and Radical Uncertainty: Towards a Precautionary Approach to Financial Policy. *Ecological Economics*, 183, 106957.

Claessens, S., & Perotti, E. (2007). Finance and Inequality: Channels and Evidence. *Journal of Comparative Economics*, 35(4), 748–73.

Cowen, D., & Sylla, R. (2018). *Alexander Hamilton on Finance, Credit, and Debt*. Columbia University Press.

Davies, S., & Kent, C. (2020). *US Dollar Funding: An International Perspective*. Bank for International Settlements. CGFS Papers, 65.

Green, C. J., Pentecost, E. J., & Weyman-Jones, T. G., (eds.) (2011). *The Financial Crisis and the Regulation of Finance*. Edward Elgar Publishing.

Helleiner, E. (1996). *States and the Reemergence of Global Finance: From Bretton Woods to the 1990s*. Cornell University Press.

Herzog, L. (2019). Global Reserve Currencies from the Perspective of Structural Global Justice: Distribution and Domination. *Critical Review of International Social and Political Philosophy*, 1–23.

James, A. (2012). *Fairness in Practice: A Social Contract for a Global economy*. Oxford University Press.

Jones, E. (2020). *The Political Economy of Bank Regulation in Developing Countries: Risk and Reputation*. Oxford University Press.

Kindleberger, C. P. (2011). *Manias, Panics, and Crashes: A History of Financial Crises*. John Wiley & Sons.

Korinek, A. (2011). *Hot Money and Serial Financial Crises*. IMF Economic Review, 59(2), 306–39.

Laeven, L., & Valencia, F. (2020). Systemic Banking Crises Database II. *IMF Economic Review, 68*(2), 307–61.

McKenzie, D. (2017). Identifying and Spurring High-Growth Entrepreneurship: Experimental Evidence from a Business Plan Competition. *American Economic Review, 107*(8), 2278–307.

Mercure, J. F., Pollitt, H., Viñuales, J. E., Edwards, N. R., Holden, P. B., Chewpreecha, U., & Knobloch, F. (2018). Macroeconomic Impact of Stranded Fossil Fuel Assets. *Nature Climate Change, 8*(7), 588–93.

Mishra, P., & Rajan, R. (2016). Rules of the Monetary Game. *Reserve Bank of India Working Paper Series, 4*.

Murau, S., & van't Klooster, J. (2022). Rethinking Monetary Sovereignty: The Global Credit Money System and the State. *Perspectives on Politics, 21*(4), 1–18. https://doi.org/10.1017/S153759272200127X.

Naqvi, N. (2019). Manias, Panics, and Crashes in Emerging Markets: An Empirical Investigation of the Post-2008 Crisis Period. *New Political Economy, 24*(6), 759–79.

RAN (Rainforest Action Network). (2021). *Banking on Climate Chaos: Fossil Fuel Finance Report 2021*. RAN.

Rawls, J. (2001). *Justice as Fairness: A Restatement*. Harvard University Press.

Rodrik, D. (2017). *Straight Talk on Trade: Ideas for a Sane World Economy*. Princeton University Press.

Ronzoni, M. (2012). Two Conceptions of State Sovereignty and Their Implications for Global Institutional Design. *Critical Review of International Social and Political Philosophy, 15*(5), 573–91.

Smoleńska, A., & van 't Klooster, J. (2022). A Risky Bet: Climate Change and the EU's Microprudential Framework for Banks. *Journal of Financial Regulation* 8 (1), 51–74.

Svartzman, R., & Althouse, J. (2020). Greening the International Monetary System? Not without Addressing the Political Ecology of Global Imbalances. *Review of International Political Economy*, 1–26.

Van Parijs, P. (2019). Just Europe. *Philosophy & Public Affairs, 47*(1), 5–36.

Volz, U., Beirne, J., Ambrosio Preudhomme, N., Fenton, A., Mazzacurati, E., Renzhi, N., & Stampe, J. (2020). *Climate Change and Sovereign Risk*. SOAS University of London, Asian Development Bank Institute.

Chapter 10

TOWARDS A GLOBAL ARCHITECTURE FOR SUSTAINABLE FINANCE?

Kathrin Berensmann and Ulrich Volz

INTRODUCTION

Climate change is deeply unjust. Not only are the physical impacts of climate change felt the most by poorer countries and those at the base of the economic pyramid within countries, but poorer countries and poorer segments within societies have also contributed the least to global warming and are least capable of investing in resilience and adaptation. Moreover, climate change is diminishing the development prospects of future generations, which have not contributed to the problem at all.

The financial sector sits at the heart of the problem. It has financed economic activities that have contributed to climate change, and it continues to do so. For the time being, the financial sector is also channelling too few resources into investment in climate resilience and adaptation. Article 2.1c of the Paris Agreement calls for 'making finance flows consistent with a pathway towards low greenhouse gas emissions and climate-resilient development'. (UN, 2015). As highlighted by Mark Carney, the UN Special Envoy on Climate Action and Finance, estimates suggest that presently 'the financial system as a whole is funding temperature increases of over three degrees centigrade' (Carney, 2020). To make finance consistent with the Paris climate goals and other sustainability goals will require bold policy actions both at the national and international levels. This chapter discusses the challenges of aligning the global financial system with sustainability goals and introduces governance structures and policies that contribute to this end. It will also discuss the contributions that finance can make towards facilitating a just transition towards low-carbon economies and lifestyles.

A just global sustainable financial system assumes two roles. First, the financial system should adhere to environmental, social and governance (ESG) standards and should not finance activities that run contrary to the Sustainable Development Goals (SDGs) and the Paris Agreement such as fossil fuel extraction, activities related to deforestation or other forms of environmental degradation, or exploitation of labour. Second, the financial system should actively contribute to attaining the SDGs and facilitating a just transition by financing sustainable economic activities. Essentially, the financial system should take on an enabler role. Importantly, a just global sustainable financial system entails that international financial flows should contribute to sustainable development in recipient countries. To align finance with the SDGs, ESG criteria need to be integrated into all lending, investment and underwriting decisions. For this to happen, we need appropriate governance structures at the national and international levels.

The next section discusses the shortcomings of the current global financial system and outline attempts at introducing sustainability elements into global financial governance. The following section assesses sustainable finance from the perspective of political, socioeconomic and intergenerational justice. The final section offers policy recommendations for developing a global governance framework for sustainable finance.

THE CURRENT SYSTEM IS FLAWED AND EXACERBATES INEQUALITY

Currently, large parts of the financial system are not aligned with sustainability goals and prevent the transition towards a sustainable and more resilient global economy. ESG risks are not adequately priced, and adverse impacts of non-sustainable investments are often not accounted for. Rather, we see a misalignment between the interests of a financial system that is mostly driven by a short-term interest in maximising profits and the long-term investment and development needs of communities and countries, such as those associated with environmental change.

Emerging markets and developing economies (EMDEs) are disproportionately impacted by global environmental change. The physical impacts of climate change are not only greater in developing countries (Buhr et al., 2018; Volz & Ahmed., 2020), but businesses in climate-vulnerable developing countries also face higher costs of capital, hindering private sector development (Kling et al., 2021). In essence, climate-vulnerable developing countries suffer twice from a problem they did not cause: through higher loss and damage from environmental change, and a 'climate risk premium' they have to pay in financial markets because of elevated vulnerability.

Despite being the worst affected, most EMDEs have little to no influence over decisions that are shaping financial market structures and outcomes. Decision-making on the evolving global architecture for sustainable financial governance has been concentrated in the hands of a small number of key players in developed countries and large emerging markets.

GLOBAL SUSTAINABLE FINANCIAL GOVERNANCE FROM THE PERSPECTIVE OF JUSTICE

(a) Political Justice

Participation in decision-making processes shaping the emerging sustainable financial governance system varies substantially depending on institutions, instruments, countries and regions. However, more often than not decision-making has been concentrated among developed countries and large emerging markets and on a small number of key players, as is also the case for other fields of the global financial system such as the global debt governance system (Berensmann, 2024).

Indeed, many EMDEs are not adequately represented in central decision-making bodies shaping the global sustainable financial governance architecture, including the MDBs, the International Monetary Fund (IMF) and the Financial Stability Board (Berensmann, 2024). This lack of representation means that these countries have little or no say in the decisions that affect them. Private actors from industrialised countries and large emerging markets, such as the International Capital Market Association or the Institute of International Finance, have often disproportionate influence over the norms and rules that shape the global sustainable financial governance system.

One reason for the limited involvement of EMDEs in the decision-making processes of the global sustainable financial architecture is that these decisions are made in existing institutions, such as the Financial Stability Board or the G20, where EMDEs are underrepresented. One example is the Task Force on Climate-related Financial Disclosures (TCFD), which was established in 2015 by the Financial Stability Board (FSB) to improve and increase reporting of climate-related financial information by companies, banks and investors (TCFD 2017). The TCFD has become the most important standard-setter for climate-related financial disclosures but the thirty-two members of the TCFD included only representatives from large private financial institutions across the G20 countries.

(b) Socioeconomic Justice

Global rules and standards should contribute to mobilising financial resources that enhance sustainable development and resilience. Moreover, they should contribute to lowering the damages caused by global environmental change, mitigating the risks associated with climate change and nature loss, and reducing the disproportionate effects that climate change has on climate-vulnerable developing countries.

Finance will have to play an important role in achieving the transition to net zero greenhouse gas emissions, by rapidly phasing out the financing of activities that are not aligned with the Paris climate goals, while scaling up investment in renewable energy, energy efficiency, the retrofitting of existing building stock, and low-carbon transport systems. The financial sector will also have to ramp up adaptation finance. It is needed to facilitate investments in resilience and new opportunities for the people and communities adversely affected by the low-carbon transition or the physical effects of environmental change (Volz & Ahmed, 2020). Those at the bottom of the economic pyramid tend to be disproportionately impacted by environmental change, and they require particular support. Financial services directed to the specific needs of those exposed to the physical or transition impacts of environmental change can support adaptation, foster mitigation and help to realise new opportunities and sustain livelihoods. Inclusive green finance can help to empower also the base of the economic pyramid to be a driver of transition, thus making it 'just'. For instance, pay-as-you-go financing schemes can help micro, small and medium enterprises switch to more environment-friendly technologies, helping them to save costs and improve their competitiveness while reducing their environmental footprint. Global financial governance should contribute to providing the framework conditions to align both national and global financial flows with climate and other sustainability goals and facilitate a just transition to more resilient and inclusive economies.

One important example is the case of the cost of capital. Global environmental change has a disproportionate effect on developing countries. Not only are the physical impacts of climate change stronger in developing countries. Empirical evidence also shows that developing countries must pay higher interest rates on their sovereign borrowing because of their climate vulnerability, limiting fiscal space and the governments' ability to invest in crucial areas of development (Buhr et al., 2018). Likewise, corporations in climate-vulnerable developing countries face a higher cost of capital, holding back private sector development (Kling et al., 2021). Developing countries, whose historic contributions to global warming are negligible, are thus being punished twice: by the physical impacts of climate change and by financial markets.

A just global sustainable financial system should enable investment in climate resilience and adaptation to address this injustice. Indeed, the United Nations Framework Convention on Climate Change, the Kyoto Protocol and the Paris Agreement calls for financial assistance from countries with greater financial resources – which are also the ones who have historically contributed the most to climate change – to those who are less endowed and more vulnerable. Under the Paris Agreement, the industrialised countries made an international commitment to provide USD 100 billion per annum from 2020 onwards to support climate protection and adaptation measures in the poorest countries. Although several bodies – most importantly the Global Environment Facility, the Green Climate Fund, the Special Climate Change Fund, the Least Developed Countries Fund and the Adaptation Fund – were set up alongside the multilateral development banks to provide international climate finance, the amounts provided by advanced countries have fallen short of commitments. Moreover, efforts to mobilise private capital for investment in EMDEs through blended finance have disappointed (Attridge & Engen, 2019). Greater efforts are needed to scale up finance for adaptation and resilience and also develop insurance and risk transfer solutions.

(c) Intergenerational Justice

Environmental destruction and social inequity undermine the prospects of future generations. Catastrophic global warming will have severe consequences for the livelihood of the following generations. At present, financial markets tend to operate within a short-term horizon, focusing on short-term returns and largely ignoring medium- and long-term risks, although these risks, such as those stemming from climate change, are well understood and recognised. Mark Carney, the former governor of the Bank of England, has famously termed this problem the tragedy of horizons (Carney, 2015). A global governance framework for sustainable finance should facilitate the adoption of long-term risk analysis approaches. At the essence, a global governance framework for sustainable finance should prevent the financing of actions that will undermine future generations' well-being.

One case in point is the challenge of accounting for long-term risks and impacts. To integrate long-term risks into financial decision-making, central banks and supervisors have started to develop long-term scenario analysis and a growing number of central banks are now demanding that financial institutions do the same. Conventional risk management approaches based on historical data are unsuitable for assessing climate-related financial risks given the non-linear nature of climate change and the resulting radical uncertainty associated with these risks. Scenario analysis is a tool to evaluate forward-looking risks for a range of hypothetical outcomes by considering alternative plausible future states under a set of assumptions. The Network of Central Banks and Financial Supervisors for Greening the Financial System (NGFS) has developed several scenarios that an increasing number of NGFS members are starting to use for their risk analysis but also as a basis for climate stress tests that financial firms are asked to conduct. The integration of long-term risk into financial analysis through mandatory risk disclosures and stress testing is an important way of overcoming the tragedy of horizons and trying to make sure that both transition risks and the impacts of today's investment and lending decisions on future generations are at least partially accounted for. Besides mandatory stress tests, supervisory authorities could adjust prudential frameworks and require all regulated financial institutions to submit net zero transition plans laying out how they will achieve decarbonisation of their portfolios (Robins et al., 2021).

TOWARDS A GLOBAL SUSTAINABLE FINANCIAL GOVERNANCE SYSTEM

Several steps are needed to create a global governance framework for sustainable finance that can make the global financial system more just in terms of political, socioeconomic and intergenerational outcomes. To improve political justice in global sustainable financial governance, the fairness of decision-making processes should be enhanced. Global policy-making institutions and forums shaping the design of the emerging global sustainable financial governance system do not sufficiently represent the perspectives and interests of EMDEs. To enhance the fairness of the set of rules and standards governing sustainable finance and investment, the representation and voice of developing countries in the institutions setting these rules and standards needs to be strengthened.

To enhance socioeconomic justice, significantly more financial resources must be made available for investment in climate protection and adaptation measures in the poorest countries, honouring the commitments made under the United Nations Framework Convention on Climate Change, the Kyoto Protocol and the Paris Agreement. Without international support, many climate-vulnerable countries, which are already facing a higher cost of capital in international capital markets because of their climate vulnerability, are at a risk of facing a vicious circle of greater climate vulnerability, a growing climate risk premium in financial markets and less fiscal space for investment in resilience. Greater international efforts are therefore needed to scale up finance for adaptation and resilience and also develop insurance and risk transfer solutions.

To enhance intergenerational justice, national and international financial authorities need to inhibit lending and investment in areas that put the livelihood of future generations at risk and integrate long-term risk analysis into the rules and conventions that govern finance. Prudential frameworks need to be adjusted to account for sustainability risks (Dikau et al., 2020). As guardians of macroeconomic and financial stability, central banks and supervisors need to take a long-term perspective going beyond the usual financial cycle and introduce explicit strategies to support the transition to net zero (Robins et al., 2021). The NGFS as the preeminent forum of central banks and supervisors can forge a new consensus and establish best practices in this respect. Likewise, the central international standard-setting and oversight bodies, including the Bank for International Settlements, the Financial Stability Board, the International Association of Insurance Supervisors, the International Organisation of Securities Commissions and the Organisation for Economic Co-operation and Development should mainstream sustainability risks in their supervisory frameworks, recommendations and guidance. As the preeminent institution overseeing the stability of the international financial system, the IMF ought to integrate sustainability risks in all of its operational work, comprising surveillance, technical assistance and training, and emergency lending and crisis support (Volz & Ahmed, 2020; Volz, 2021; Volz, 2022).

The sustainable finance standards and rules that are being developed by the institutions dominating global financial governance will shape public policies and have a profound impact on markets around the world. It is hence of critical importance that these rules are just, and that they will help to create the framework conditions that will align finance with sustainability goals and mobilise sufficient capital for attaining the SDGs. Global standards and rules will have to be complemented by international development and climate finance and national and international policies that enhance financial inclusion and help communities and countries to become more resilient.

REFERENCES

Attridge, S., & Engen, L. (2019). *Blended Finance in the Poorest Countries: The Need for a Better Approach.* ODI Report.

Berensmann, K. (2024). How Should Sustainable Finance Standards Be Designed for Developing Countries? In Boubaker, S., & Le, T. H., (eds.), *Green Finance and Sustainable Development Goals*, 145–66. World Scientific Publishing Company.

Buhr, B., Volz, U., Donovan, C., Kling, G., Lo, Y. C., Murinde, V., & Pullin, N. (2018). *Climate Change and the Cost of Capital in Developing Countries.* UN Environment, Imperial College London, and SOAS University of London.

Carney, M. (2015). Breaking the Tragedy of the Horizon–Climate Change and Financial Stability. *Speech given at Lloyd's of London, 29.*

Carney M. (2020). From Climate Crisis to Real Prosperity. The Reith Lectures, BBC.

Dikau, S., Robins, N., & Volz, U. (2020). A Toolbox of Sustainable Crisis Response Measures for Central Banks and Ssupervisors. 2nd ed.: Lessons from Practice. *INSPIRE Briefing Paper*

Kling, G., Volz, U., Murinde, V., & Ayas, S. (2021). The Impact of Climate Vulnerability on Firms' Cost of Capital and Access to Finance. *World Development, 137*(1), 105131.

Robins, N., Dikau, S., & Volz, U. (2021). Net-Zero Central Banking: A New Phase in Greening the Financial System. SOAS, University of London.

TCFD (Task for Climate-related Financial Disclosure). (2017). Recommendations of the Task Force on Climate-related Financial Disclosures.

UN (United Nations). (2015). The Paris Agreement. *United Nations.*

Volz, U. (2021). The IMF and the Macro-criticality of Climate Change. In Gallagher, K. P., & Gao, H., (eds.), *Building Back a Better Global Financial Safety Net,* 108–18. Global Development Policy Center.

Volz, U. (2022). Climate-Proofing the Global Financial Safety Net. *Journal of Globalization and Development. 13*(1). https://doi.org/10.1515/jgd-2020-0085.

Volz, U., & Ahmed, S. J. (2020). Macrofinancial Risks in Climate-Vulnerable Developing Countries and the Role of the IMF: Towards a Joint V20-IMF Action Agenda. *SOAS Centre for Sustainable Finance, Global Center on Adaptation, and Munich Climate Insurance Initiative.*

Chapter 11

CLIMATE FINANCE, THE RIGHT TO PROMOTE SUSTAINABLE DEVELOPMENT AND RESPONSIBILITY

Darrel Moellendorf

INTRODUCTION

Achieving net zero carbon emissions by 2050 is a massive undertaking. The speed and the scale of the transition are breathtaking. In under three decades, every form of production, mode of transportation, and all heating and cooling systems in the world that can be powered by electricity must be, and all of the electricity used must be generated by renewable energy. Meanwhile, energy consumption across the globe must increase significantly to overcome energy poverty. Some 785 million people lack access to electricity, and 2.6 billion do not use clean cooking fuels (IEA [International Energy Agency], 2021, p. 17)[1]. According to the International Energy Agency (IEA), building the capacity for the amount of energy needed is 'equivalent to installing the world's current largest solar park roughly every day' (IEA, 2021, p. 14). The IEA projects that $5 trillion annually will soon be required to achieve this world-historical transition (IEA, 2021, p. 22). Financing this is crucial, not only for purely economic reasons but also for moral ones.

Climate finance to low and medium-income countries can play three crucial roles. One is to aid in mitigating climate change by subsidising a rapid transition to a zero-carbon economy to avoid a slowing in human development. Another is to fund development projects that build social resilience to a rapidly changing climate thereby helping communities to adapt. And finally, financing is required to fund climate-related loss and damage schemes. All three of these roles are important for respecting the Right to Promote Sustainable Development recognised in the United Nations Framework Convention on Climate Change (UNFCCC) (hereafter the Convention).

The right to promote sustainable development is a fundamental norm of international justice that constrains and directs climate policy. It serves the forward-looking aim of human development progress. I offer moral reasons to believe that this is an important aim of international justice below. It is noteworthy, however, that the right to promote sustainable development is a central feature of the framework treaty governing climate change negotiations. To appeal to the right does not involve invoking a norm that is foreign to the activities of climate politics. The right is not a proclamation of a philosopher king or an external critic. It is also not the product of a cosmopolitan theory of ideal global justice. Rather, it is an international norm accepted by the parties that have ratified the Convention (Moellendorf, 2016).

THE RIGHT TO PROMOTE SUSTAINABLE DEVELOPMENT

Article 3 paragraph 4 of the Convention affirms that:

> The Parties have a right to, and should, promote sustainable development. Policies and measures to protect the climate system against human-induced change should be appropriate for the specific conditions of each Party and should be integrated with national development programmes, taking into account that economic development is essential for adopting measures to address climate change. (UNFCCC [United Nations Framework Convention on Climate Change], 1992, p. 10)[1]

The right is a liberty right that low and medium-income countries can claim against high-income ones in the context of the cooperative effort to prevent dangerous climate change (Moellendorf, 2022, p. 82). Insofar as the Right to Promote Sustainable Development is a claim of some states against others, it is a principle of international justice and has significant implications for responsibility for climate finance.

Development has many understandings and measures. Measures of development solely in terms of economic activity have no direct moral significance. It would be implausible then to think that international justice protects the promotion of development in that sense. A much more plausible conception of development is that of human development, which the United Nations Human Development Programme (UNHDP) employs. The UNHDP's Human Development Index (HDI) ranks states using a mean of the three different measures. One is health, measured by the life expectancy at birth; another is education, measured by a combination of the mean years of schooling for adults and the expected years of schooling for children just starting school; and the final one is income per capita. The central idea behind the HDI is to broaden or humanise the idea of development.

There are several reasons to value human development. Being well-educated is valuable in part in the pursuit of other things of value. It allows us to pursue meaningful work, to advance other personal aims, and to respond intelligently to our social and political environments. When we consider the relationship between education and, say, meaningful work, education seems valuable as a means. In that sense, education has instrumental value. But there's more. To become educated is to come to possess knowledge. And having knowledge is plausibly valuable for its own sake regardless of whether it helps us to do valuable things or whether it augments our freedom. Knowledge is intrinsically valuable. Similar claims regarding the instrumental and intrinsic value of health are equally plausible. Unlike education and health, income seems valuable only instrumentally, only for the pursuit of other goods that it enables. Amartya Sen's discussion of the value of human development highlights the instrumental value of the constituents. Sen interprets human development 'as a process of expanding the real freedoms that people enjoy' (Sen, 2000, p. 36). Development, accoridng to Sen, consists of the expansion of real or substantive freedoms, including the powers to act in morally valuable ways, for example, to assess and pursue a rewarding way of life.

If we understand development, then, as human development, the value of developmental progress for a country is that in aggregate the citizens of such a country are healthier, better educated and better able to pursue valuable aims. As an aggregate measure, high human development does not ensure that the goods of education, health and income are equally or even adequately secured for all citizens. But a very high level of human development is indicative of the preconditions of the adequate enjoyment of these goods for all.

CLIMATE POLICY AND THE RIGHT TO PROMOTE HUMAN DEVELOPMENT

The liberty to pursue human development can be infringed by mitigation policies that raise the costs of providing energy. Human development is immensely energy intensive. This can be easily appreciated by comparing the HDI to the Energy Development Index (EDI) devised by the IEA. The EDI comprises four measures, per capita commercial energy consumption, per capita residential electricity consumption, the percent age of modern fuels in total residential energy use, and the percent age of the population with access to electricity (IEA, 2011, p. 6). In effect, the EDI is a measure of access to and consumption of modern forms of energy, electricity and cooking fuels. A comparison of eighty developing and underdeveloped countries reveals a strong correlation between HDI and EDI ranks (IEA, 2012, p. 547).

The direction of causation is not established by noting a correlation between the HDI and the EDI. Modern energy consumption could result in human development progress, or human development could drive people to consume more energy (Stern, 2011, pp. 18–19). The causal influence may run in both directions. In any case, however, on balance, the evidence suggests that progress in human development goes along with expanding modern energy access and use.

Attention to particular cases dramatises the relation between human development and energy consumption. In 1990 China had a low level of Human Development with an HDI of 0.499. By 2015 China's HDI had improved to a high level of 0.738 (UNDP [United Nations Development Programme], 1990–2015). The transformation that occurred involved an eightfold increase in per capita electricity consumption from 0.51 MWh/person to 4.05 MWh/person (IEA, 2015a). The case of Thailand is similar. In 1991 Thailand's HDI was 0.574; by 2015 it had risen to 0.740, a less dramatic rise than China's, but still impressive (UNDP, 1990–2015). Fuelling the HDI improvement was an over threefold increase in electricity consumption from 0.71 MWh/person to 2.62 MWh/person (IEA, 2015b). The evidence is compelling then that human development progress is energy intensive.

This correlation between development progress and energy consumption, along with the comparatively low costs of fossil fuels explains the insistence by developing and underdeveloped countries that their right to promote sustainable development be safeguarded by the UNFCCC. Once again, the Chinese and Thai cases are instructive. During the period in which China made the human development progress noted above, its per capita CO_2 emissions rose from 1.83 tons in 1990 to 6.59 tons in 2015 (IEA, 2015a). In Thailand, emissions rose from 1.43 tons per person to 3.64. For countries seeking to make poverty-eradicating developmental gains, the use of fossil fuels has been especially attractive.

As cited above Article 3 Paragraph 4 of the Convention holds that 'Policies and measures to protect the climate system against human-induced change should be appropriate for the specific conditions of each Party . . . taking into account that economic development is essential for adopting measures to address climate change' (UNFCCC, 1992, p. 10). The requirement that measures be appropriate to the conditions of the country and consistent with national development programmes supports the view that the right to promote sustainable development is in the first instance a liberty of states to pursue national development programmes. Insofar as an energy transition requires not fully utilising existing fossil fuel capacity and making new investments in infrastructure, and to the extent that the comparative cost of renewable energy is higher than that of fossil fuels (which is often no longer the case), reconciling the liberty to pursue sustainable development with climate change mitigation requires subsidising the transition to a zero-carbon economy. This echoes a familiar point in global justice discussions that even so-called negative rights can have positive obligations (Shue, 2020, pp. 35–40).

The right to promote sustainable development is morally relevant, as we have seen, to the cooperative effort to mitigate climate change. It is also relevant to climate change adaptation and the financing of loss and damages. Human development is threatened not only by policies that raise the costs of energy but also by the ravages of an unstable climate. Climate change adaptation policies aim to protect people against climate instability, and loss and damage funds can finance the repair of what is destroyed. As the planet warms, more investment will be required for adaptation and loss and damage. The countries that are the most exposed to the ravages of an unstable climate also tend to be those that have the least financial capacity to protect against the problem (Moellendorf, 2022). Climate change threatens to immiserate hundreds of millions of people in these countries. Hence, financing both protective adaptation projects and funds to repair loss and damages is a matter of respecting the right to promote sustainable development.

Since adaptation schemes will be limited, even if well-funded, a way of prioritising expenditures is needed. What I call 'the pro-poor formula' offers guidance in that regard. It ranks projects according to three factors: 1) the likelihood of project success in protecting the poor, 2) the number of people the policy would serve, and 3) the depth of poverty of those served. The formula is the following:

$R = (E \times n \times P)$, *or*
Rank = Effectiveness × *Number of people affected* × *Poverty gap*

The poverty gap is the ratio of an agreed-upon international poverty line (in terms of income) to the amount by which the average income of the population group falls below that line (Moellendorf, 2022, pp. 104–6). The further their incomes are below the poverty line, the larger the poverty gap.

Even if the pro-poor formula were accepted, familiar moral questions would remain. For some people, a higher aggregate number of poor people helped is more valuable than prioritising the poorest of the poor, whereas for others the opposite is the case. In terms of the pro-poor formula, this is a question of whether n or P should be preceded by a multiplier, in other words, whether the formula should include '$2n$' or '$2P$' rather than merely 'n' or 'P'. The formula is useful for incorporating relevant considerations in prioritising adaptation projects to protect the poor, but it does not settle the need to come to terms with fundamental normative ethical controversies about aggregation and prioritarianism.

THREE REASONS IN FAVOUR OF THE RIGHT TO PROMOTE SUSTAINABLE DEVELOPMENT

The moral importance of the right to promote sustainable development can be supported by three arguments. First, the right protects development efforts seeking to eradicate poverty. The history of poverty-eradicating national development strategies in the twentieth century, as exemplified in the cases of China and Thailand, gives reason to believe that poverty eradication is tremendously energy intensive. In order not to prevent or slow poverty eradication efforts, the liberty of states to increase their energy usage must be respected. In short, the paramount importance of eradicating poverty requires that states have the liberty to pursue human development.

Second, fairness in the cooperative international project of mitigating climate change requires recognising the right. Ensuring a stable climate system using climate change mitigation would be a benefit to all states, but especially to developing and underdeveloped states because climate change threatens to exacerbate poverty. But yielding the benefit will require that all, or most, states assume some costs. It would be unfair to require any state to unnecessarily assume costs that would threaten to outweigh the benefit gained by the cooperative enterprise itself. Preventing a state from the pursuit of poverty-eradicating human development would threaten to do that. No state should be made to unnecessarily sacrifice poverty-eradicating human development for climate change mitigation. The parties to the international project cannot simply avoid their obligations of fairness by demanding less of themselves and all other parties, thereby increasing the need for adaptation. To the extent that climate change adaptation is required due to a failure to mitigate climate change sufficiently, fairness also requires adaptation expenses to be subsidised to compensate for the destruction of the natural basis of human development due to climate change.

Third, respect for the right to promote sustainable development in climate policy is a promissory obligation deriving from the ratification of the Convention, which entered into force in 1994. Because the right is recognised in the treaty document, any state ratifying the treaty, without specifically exempting itself from the obligation, is obliged to respect the right. A state proposing international climate measures within the UNFCCC context that failed to respect the liberty of states to pursue poverty-eradicating human development would be showing contempt for the prior agreement and the parties who had ratified it in good faith (Moellendorf, 2016).

FROM JUSTICE TO RESPONSIBILITY

Justice and responsibility are interconnected. Conceptions of justice concern who is owed what and in virtue of what. They are accounts of the moral creditors. Conceptions of responsibility are accounts of the moral debtors, of who must pay or perform and why. The claim of international justice that states are at liberty to pursue human development within a cooperative practice aimed at avoiding dangerous climate change has important implications for how we think about responsibility for financing climate policies.

If the point of the right to sustainable development is to secure liberty for states to pursue poverty-eradicating human development, then responsibility for financing climate policies should fall primarily on those states that have already achieved a very high level of development. States should be assigned responsibility based on their capacity to contribute to a financing mechanism without requiring reductions in the human development level of those states. Responsibility in the climate change mitigation regime must fall firstly and mainly on states with a greater capacity to carry the burden without incurring human development losses. This is an ability-to-pay conception of responsibility, in which ability, or capacity, is a function of human development level. This is consistent with the language of the Convention in Article 3 paragraph 1, which affirms that states should be assigned burdens 'on the basis of equity and in accordance with their common but differentiated responsibilities and respective capabilities' (UNFCCC, 1992, p. 9).

This ability-to-pay conception of responsibility is fully consistent with the right to promote sustainable development. Justice protects the pursuit of human development for countries that are not yet at the highest level, and responsibility assigns financing costs to countries in proportion to their level of human development, leaving only the very highest carrying significant burdens. Responsibility according to such an account is not based on fault. The history of, or how, the very high level of human development was acquired is not scrutinised. Such a scheme resembles progressive taxation schemes within states. Such schemes do not suppose that those with high incomes are at fault for their earnings. Their proportional higher tax liability is a function of nothing other than their higher income. Reducing income inequality produces greater justice. Similarly, the justification of the assignment of responsibility to states with the highest levels of human development is solely to serve the aim of justice in securing the liberty of states to pursue human development progress.

Other conceptions of responsibility are less reliable in serving the right to promote sustainable development. Consider assigning responsibility to states based on their historical emissions. The year 1990 is sometimes used as the date from which to assign fault for historical emissions because the first Assessment Report of the Intergovernmental Panel on Climate Change was published that year. If responsibility should track fault, and if fault requires knowledge, then there is reason to think that the 1990 benchmark is reasonable. Most of the growth in global emissions since 1990, however, has been in countries that the World Bank refers to as *Upper Middle-Income Countries*. (World Bank, 2018). Indeed, by 2007 so-called non-Annex 1 countries (mostly low and medium-income countries) were emitting more CO_2 than Annex 1 countries (high-income countries) (Friedrich & Damassa, 2014). Hence assigning responsibility to states on their emissions since 1990 would lay a heavy burden on developing countries, which burned fossil fuels to make significant human development gains, but remain well below the most highly human-developed countries. It is not surprising that the no-fault ability-to-pay principle and the fault-based historical emissions principle would result in different sets of responsible states. It would be much more surprising if that were not the case.

A principle of historical responsibility that places the benchmark for counting emissions back to the beginning of the Industrial Revolution would align better with ability to pay. The most highly human-developed states include those that industrialised earliest. A historical principle employing a benchmark that far back, however, would lack the *prima facie* attraction of assigning responsibility based on fault since knowledge of the problem of climate change cannot be attributed to states at the beginning of the Industrial Revolution (e.g. Moellendorf, 2014). Whether responsibility for historical emissions aligns with the right to promote sustainable development is contingent on the cut-off date for counting emissions. In contrast, the attraction of the ability-to-pay conception of responsibility, where ability is measured by human development level, is that it non-contingently serves the right to promote human development.

CONCLUSION

As a matter of international justice, financing climate change mitigation and adaptation programmes and funds to repair loss and damages should respect the right to promote sustainable development. State responsibility for climate finance should be assigned according to an ability-to-pay conception of responsibility that requires that the most highly human-developed countries be primarily responsible for funding climate finance. But securing the amount of money needed, on the order of $5 trillion annually, will require not only drawing on public coffers but also directing private investment and lending. Although respecting the right to sustainable development in climate finance is crucially about the financial responsibilities of very highly human-developed states, it is also about the policies that incentivise private investments and the lending practices of international financial institutions. Discussions of these very important matters are to be found in other chapters of this volume.

REFERENCES

Friedrich, J., & Damassa, T. (2014). The History of Carbon Dioxide Emissions. *World Resources Institute.*

IEA (International Energy Agency). (2011). *World Energy Outlook 2011*. IEA.

IEA (2012). *World Energy Outlook 2012*. OECD Publishing.

IEA (2015a). *China Indicators 2015*. IEA

IEA (2015b). *Thailand Indicators 2015*. IEA.

IEA (2021). *Net Zero by 2050: A Roadmap for the Global Energy Sector.*

Moellendorf, D. (2014). The Moral Challenge of Dangerous Climate Change: Values, Poverty, and Policy. *Cambridge University Press*, 164–73.

Moellendorf, D. (2016). Taking UNFCCC Norms Seriously. In Roser, D. & Heyward, C., (eds.), *Climate Change and Non-Ideal Theory*, 104–24. Oxford University Press.

Moellendorf, D. (2022). *Mobilizing Hope: Climate Change and Global Poverty*. Oxford University Press.
Sen, A. (2000). *Development as Freedom*. Alfred A. Knope.
Shue, H. (2020). *Basic Rights: Subsistence, Affluence, and US Foreign Policy*. Princeton University Press, 35–40.
Stern, D. I. (2011). The Role of Energy in Economic Growth. In Guruswamy, L., (ed.), *International Energy and Poverty*, 18–19. Routledge.
UNDP (United Nations Development Programme). (1990–2015). *Human Development Data 1990–2015. UNDP.*
United Nations Framework Convention on Climate Change. Secretariat. (1992). *United Nations Framework Convention on Climate Change*. UNFCCC.
World Bank. (2018). *Atlas of Sustainable Development Goals 2018: From World Development Indicators*.

Chapter 12

JUSTICE IN GLOBAL TAX GOVERNANCE: ASSESSING THE ROLE OF TAX EXPENDITURES

Christian von Haldenwang and Sabine Laudage Teles

INTRODUCTION

The international tax system forms a regime in global economic governance that governs the allocation of taxing rights for cross-border transactions between countries. The regime is based on domestic tax laws, bilateral or regional tax treaties, non-binding guidelines, and multilateral agreements. There is no global institution such as an international tax organisation, although discussions on a new UN tax convention are currently underway (Laudage Teles & von Haldenwang, 2023). The key challenges for global justice are harmful tax competition between countries, as well as tax avoidance and tax evasion by multinational corporations and wealthy individuals. Such practices are facilitated by the widespread use of tax expenditures, referring to preferential tax treatments that favour specific sectors, activities or groups of taxpayers. At an international scale, the use of tax expenditures strips countries of desperately needed public revenues and deepens inequalities between tax havens and countries with high-income tax rates.[1]

Following the world economic crisis of 2009, global tax governance and tax competition have received a growing share of academic attention (Dietsch & Rixen 2014; 2016; Dietsch 2015; Genschel & Seelkopf 2016). The key concern is that tax competition has intensified over time and generates overall welfare losses. In addition, seminal studies on the impact of tax avoidance and evasion on global inequalities find that tax competition, avoidance and evasion are increasing global inequalities within and between countries and create large losses in governments' revenues (Piketty, 2014; Zucman, 2014). In the normative literature on tax competition, with few exceptions, there is a broad consensus on global tax

[1] It might also affect inequality within countries and undermine domestic social justice (see Ronzoni, Chapter 13 in this volume).

competition being unjust (Dietsch, 2015; Dietsch & Rixen, 2014; see also Ronzoni, Chapter 13 in this volume).

Governments engage in international tax competition via three main channels. First, they compete for investments using decreasing statutory corporate tax rates (Laudage, 2020). Second, sometimes they provide spaces of secrecy, facilitating tax avoidance along with tax evasion, money laundering and other criminal activities. Third, they offer generous tax incentives to corporations to attract investment and capital. These tax expenditures can be based on laws and double-tax agreements (DTAs), but also on contracts with individual companies. Digitalisation and the growing relevance of intangibles in value creation further intensify the call for adequate taxation of multinational enterprises (MNEs) and a fair allocation of taxing rights between countries. This has led to the historic agreement in 2021 on the implementation of a global minimum corporate income tax within the OECD/G20 Inclusive Framework on Base Erosion and Profit Shifting (BEPS) (OECD, 2021).

This chapter assesses the impact of one of the three channels mentioned above, namely tax expenditures, across different dimensions of global justice. Tax expenditures are departures from the benchmark tax structure, designed to favour a particular industry, activity or group of persons. They are a widely used, though often overseen, instrument of international tax competition. Empirical cross-country studies on tax expenditures for foreign direct investment (FDI), which include only a few developing countries so far, remain inconclusive on the effect of tax expenditures on FDI (e.g. Klemm & Van Parys, 2012; Abbas & Klemm, 2013). Another strand of literature assesses research and development (R&D) tax expenditures (Appelt et al., 2020) and finds that these incentives help increase R&D activity in firms, but may also be used for profit shifting (Haufler & Schindler, 2020).

Since tax expenditures are still largely neglected in the global tax justice debate, this chapter aims at linking these two debates. While other aspects of the international tax system are currently being reformed (for example the G20/OECD BEPS project), no global reform agenda for tax expenditures has yet been presented. However, international initiatives and organisations such as the UN Tax Committee or the Addis Tax Initiative have identified tax expenditures as a key feature of inequality, opacity and unfairness in international tax matters. The Global Tax Expenditures Database (GTED) is the first to shed light on the scale of tax expenditures and tax expenditure reporting worldwide (von Haldenwang et al., 2021). We use the GTED data in this chapter to present a descriptive analysis of tax expenditures worldwide.

THE INTERNATIONAL TAX EXPENDITURE REGIME

Until recently, the use of tax expenditures was hardly institutionalised at the international scale. Tax expenditures were provided under the sovereignty of domestic tax laws or specified in bilateral agreements between jurisdictions and large firms or industries. Governments were requested to notify the World Trade Organisation (WTO) on the use of subsidies (including tax expenditures) under the WTO Agreement on Subsidies and Countervailing Measures (WTO, 1994), but reporting has been fairly inconsistent and typically did not include any figures on revenue forgone (Gulotty, 2022). Previous attempts to curb harmful tax competition (e.g. European Commission, 2016; OECD, 1998) have only insufficiently accounted for tax expenditures.

The picture has gradually changed over the last few years. In 2021, 136 out of the 140 member countries of the Inclusive Framework on Base Erosion and Profit Shifting (BEPS) under the roof of the OECD[2] agreed on an international tax reform that includes the introduction of a global minimum tax rate of 15 per cent for large MNEs (OECD, 2021). The new agreement marks a shift in international tax cooperation, acknowledging the realities of a truly globalised and digitalised world economy. The global minimum tax will have a significant impact on the way governments use tax incentives for investment, in particular those mechanisms that lower the tax burden on profits (González Cabral et al., 2023). In a similar vein, the EU's new Foreign Subsidies Regulation (2022), will subject tax incentives granted to companies to increased scrutiny (Luja, 2023). At a regional scale, the West African Economic and Monetary Union (WAEMU) is implementing a set of common standards on benchmark systems and tax expenditures in its member countries (ATI, 2022).

Still, governments make widespread – and often uncontrolled – use of tax expenditures to pursue a wide range of public policy goals. The difference between the regular tax and the tax benefit provided can be calculated as a revenue loss. In theory, revenue losses should be compensated by revenue gains resulting from growing welfare and increased economic activity. However, few governments assess the true costs and benefits of the tax expenditures they grant.

While all tax expenditures are provided at the domestic country level, their beneficiaries can be domestic (for example households or firms) or foreign stakeholders (for example multinational firms). Though most tax expenditures have third-country effects, we focus on those mechanisms that affect in particular cross-border business and investment and have a direct impact on the conditions of tax competition between countries (e.g. tax expenditures for FDI and R&D).

Practically all countries use tax expenditures to stimulate investments and attract foreign capital, among other objectives. Income tax expenditures

[2] The OECD is the global standard-setter for international tax rules since the 1960s, providing guidance for its member countries and beyond.

typically reduce taxable income or lower the tax burden of foreign investors for a predefined amount or a specific period of time. Mechanisms include tax holidays, tax credits, preferential tax rates or special economic zones (Klemm, 2010). Consumption tax expenditures, such as exemptions on import VAT or customs duties, may be granted for specific goods and services. Experts argue that harmful tax expenditures (e.g. for fossil fuels) reduce public revenues without producing any relevant benefits, particularly in developing countries (Redonda et al., 2018). Therefore, the impact of tax expenditures on tax revenue and investment needs to be studied further.

A major initiative on this matter is the Global Tax Expenditures Database (GTED), a joint project of the Council on Economic Policies (CEP) and the German Institute of Development and Sustainability (IDOS), which aims to promote transparency on tax expenditures worldwide (Redonda et al., 2021). Based on official data published by governments, the database includes information on tax expenditures of 105 countries and identifies an additional 113 non-reporting countries. Tax expenditures are categorised according to *type* (e.g. deduction, deferral, exemption, reduced rate, credit), *tax type* (e.g. taxes on income, goods and services, property), *beneficiaries* (e.g. businesses, households, NGOs, public sector), and *policy objectives* (e.g. promote investment, facilitate access to basic goods and services, provide disaster relief, promote sustainability). Data collected by the GTED shows that revenue forgone due to tax expenditures amounts to 3.8 per cent of GDP or 23.0 per cent of total tax revenue over the period 1990 to 2021 (unweighted world average of reporting countries). In total, 25,774 individual tax expenditure provisions are currently gathered in the GTED. The following section links empirical insights gained from this database to discussions on global justice of tax expenditures.

TAX EXPENDITURES FROM THE PERSPECTIVE OF JUSTICE

Tax expenditures tend to belong to the hidden part of the tax competition iceberg: even countries that do not qualify as tax secrecy jurisdictions use them to attract investments, often without providing information on the size, cost and range of the benefits they grant. In those cases where information is available, the public often perceives tax expenditures as unfair, because large (multinational) companies frequently use their market power to obtain particularly generous benefits. Existing scientific evidence tends to support a critical view. For instance, James (2013) finds that in some African countries the redundancy rate, referring to the share of investment projects that would have been realised even without any tax incentives, is higher than 90 per cent (von Haldenwang et al., 2021). Other studies have shown that even social welfare-driven tax expenditures may have a regressive distributional impact (Redonda et al., 2023).

Hence, it is important to differentiate between harmful and beneficial tax expenditures. In this section, we assess tax expenditures in light of different dimensions of justice (see Hilbrich & Kollar, Chapter 1 in this volume):

(i) Political justice (process-related): What is the level of transparency of a country's tax expenditure regime? Are tax expenditures based on law and subject to periodical legislative oversight and public debate? Do tax expenditures have sunset clauses (defined termination dates)?
(ii) Socioeconomic justice (outcome-related): Does the government conduct cost-benefit analyses on their tax expenditures? Does it assess the expected positive and negative spillovers (both domestic and cross-border)? Do tax expenditures effectively increase economic outcome variables, such as FDI or R&D?
(iii) Intergenerational justice (goal-oriented): Do governments introduce tax expenditures to promote sustainable development, or are they used in a beggar-thy-neighbour approach to competing over scarce investment?

Political Justice

The international tax system is based on unilateral decision-making and bilateral negotiation shaped by power relations. Due to the lack of a global institution for tax governance, tax competition between countries has taken a largely uncoordinated path. No global reform agenda on tax expenditures has been set at this stage.

The Inclusive Framework on BEPS, the Global Forum on Transparency and Exchange of Information for Tax Purposes, both based at the OECD and the UN Tax Committee, are attempts to be more inclusive in discussing international tax issues and push forward reforms on the exchange of information between tax administrations (Global Forum) and on combating tax avoidance (Inclusive Framework on BEPS). The OECD also works on tax expenditures (e.g. for fossil fuels and R&D). The OECD-centred initiatives are mainly driven by a few powerful states and their networks. Smaller and poorer countries still have less voice in international tax cooperation due to the weakly institutionalised character of the international tax regime (Christensen et al., 2020). The UN has taken on this call for more inclusive international tax cooperation and is currently discussing how to draft a future UN tax convention (Laudage Teles & von Haldenwang, 2023). Should decision-making power on tax move to the UN in the future, tax expenditures need to be an element of the global tax reform agenda.

At the domestic level, tax expenditures are often granted in an undemocratic way. Frequently, their design is influenced by powerful corporations or business associations that enjoy privileged access to political decision-making. Furthermore, governments report quite differently on tax expenditures. For

Figure 12.1 The Global Tax Expenditures Transparency Index.
Source: https://gteti.taxexpenditures.org/

instance, among the 105 countries that provide any information on their tax expenditures, only forty-two publish regular reports with disaggregated data at the provision level while 113 countries do not report at all on their tax expenditures (see Redonda et al., 2023).

A more fine-grained assessment of tax expenditure reporting is provided by the *Global Tax Expenditures Transparency Index* (GTETI) (Millan et al., 2023). Figure 12.1 shows how countries score on the GTETI for the most recent year of reporting, where higher scores indicate higher levels of transparency in tax expenditure reporting. The GTETI dimensions that deal with the public availability of reports, the institutional framework and tax expenditure assessments cover several relevant aspects of political justice. Tax expenditure assessment, for instance, refers to information on revenue forgone as well as evaluations of tax expenditures. This is the dimension with the lowest average score, a sign of generally low levels of transparency on the costs and benefits of tax expenditures.

Heterogeneity in reporting standards can be a reflection of country-specific approaches to tax expenditures, but in combination with a general lack of encompassing information in so many countries, it can also be seen as an indicator of the fact that tax expenditures are deliberately used as a hidden element of tax competition. While small countries with weak domestic markets, for example, Caribbean island states, may lower overall statutory tax rates as their main approach to compete for foreign investments, countries with significant income tax revenue from domestic activities often prefer to use tax expenditures instead (Genschel & Seelkopf, 2016). Since most tax expenditures create third-country effects, the current global regime of tax expenditures is under-regulated and uncoordinated. A mid-term solution could be the elaboration of non-binding guidelines for fair negotiations and transparency standards on tax expenditures involving governments and corporations, as well as jointly agreed standards on the definition of benchmark systems.

Socioeconomic Justice

The current international tax system generates global welfare losses in the form of revenue forgone as well as growing inequalities between and within countries (Piketty, 2014; Zucman, 2014). The revenue lost due to BEPS is estimated at about 4–10 per cent of global corporate income tax revenue (Bradbury et al., 2018). Developing countries are affected to a greater extent by tax avoidance because of their higher reliance on corporate tax in their revenue mix (Johannesen et al., 2020). While tax expenditures create additional revenue forgone as an immediate effect, this does not necessarily imply a net loss of public revenue as some measures may have a positive effect on FDI, employment and economic growth, though the available evidence suggests that these effects are rather tenuous (Kronfol & Steenbergen, 2020).

In the context of tax competition, tax expenditures can have detrimental distributive effects. Similar to BEPS, they create winner and loser countries concerning economic outcomes. While countries engaging in harmful tax competition can sometimes be identified by their high level of financial secrecy and notoriously low corporate income tax rates, unjust tax expenditures are much harder to identify. There are no established mechanisms to assess the spillover effects of tax expenditures on third countries, and no blacklist of countries with harmful tax expenditures has ever been produced. The GTED is a first step in the direction of quantifying tax expenditures worldwide and assessing their effects on socioeconomic outcome variables such as investment and income inequality. The revenue forgone reported by countries in the GTED varies from below 1 per cent to more than 10 per cent of GDP.

Regarding social and economic effects, tax expenditures can be beneficial or harmful. For example, beneficial tax expenditures can reduce global income inequalities and enhance economic growth without harming third countries. These often include mechanisms that mainly target the domestic economy, for example, income tax credits for the unemployed or tax deductions for businesses in crisis. In contrast, harmful tax expenditures increase global economic inequalities by attracting investment that would have otherwise flown into another country with a better investment environment. Thus, harmful tax expenditures fuel aggressive tax competition and negatively affect third countries.

The spillover effects of tax expenditures are hard to quantify. Due to lacking data on effective tax rates, research on tax-related spillovers in low- and middle-income countries takes statutory tax rates as a proxy. Further, only a few empirical studies assess the effects of tax expenditures on FDI (e.g. Klemm & Van Parys, 2012) and R&D (e.g. Appelt et al., 2020).

Intergenerational Justice

Tax expenditures affect the welfare of current as well as future generations. This intergenerational dimension can be linked to questions regarding the underlying goals of tax expenditures, such as promoting sustainability, innovation and R&D. At the same time, this perspective needs to take into account that tax expenditures may also incentivise harmful behaviour such as increased carbon emissions or rent-seeking.

At the country level, purely domestic tax expenditures can promote intergenerational justice, for instance by making education expenses tax-deductible. At the global level, some tax expenditures can increase intergenerational justice by promoting the production or provision of global public goods such as environmental sustainability, biodiversity or energy transformation (e.g. subsidies for environmentally sustainable innovations). In contrast, other tax expenditures can jeopardise intergenerational justice by violating such sustainability principles (e.g. subsidies for fossil fuels).

The GTED database shows that governments across the world grant tax expenditures with a broad range of different policy objectives. However, only twelve countries have published information on the policy objectives of 75 per cent or more of their tax expenditures since 1990. Less than a third of all provisions gathered in the GTED state both the policy objective they are supposed to serve as well as the revenue forgone they imply. Countries reporting on investment and growth-related tax expenditures spend an average of 0.45 per cent of GDP and 2.8 per cent of tax revenue on this policy objective. These descriptive statistics reveal that more transparency is needed regarding the mid-and long-term policy goals of tax expenditures.

Tax expenditures can affect intergenerational justice in many ways. For example, tax expenditures without sunset clauses decrease the fiscal space of future generations. The decisions of governments taken today on tax expenditures affect the social welfare of future generations through their distributional impact, the spillover effects they create as well as their impact on present and future public budgets.

REFORM PROPOSALS FOR TAX EXPENDITURES

Our analysis has shown that the current tax expenditures regime can undermine political, socioeconomic and intergenerational global justice. A reform of the global tax expenditures regime is needed. We propose reforms in line with the three assessment criteria mentioned above: process, outcome and goal.

First, regarding the process dimension, the GTETI discussed above is based on a set of standards that go beyond reporting and cover elements of sound tax expenditure management. In this sense, regular, public and comprehensive reporting is a necessary, but certainly not sufficient requirement. Other elements include clear procedural rules and responsibilities for the design and set-up of tax expenditures, their embeddedness in medium-term budget planning and revenue strategies as well as regular monitoring of the cost and take-up of individual measures.

Second, governments should create joint frameworks for ex ante cost-benefit and spillover assessments (that is, before deciding on tax expenditures) as well as ex post evaluations of the mechanisms in place. Primarily, investment incentives should be non-tax incentives (e.g. good infrastructure, stable political regime, tax certainty, etc.). Furthermore, more international coordination on tax expenditures is needed to reduce harmful tax competition between countries, which generates large revenues forgone.

Third, governments should state the short-, medium-, and long-term goals of the tax expenditure provisions they offer. International guidelines are needed to reduce harmful tax competition via tax expenditures (IMF, 2019). While the new global minimum tax will likely limit the use of certain tax incentives for investment, as discussed above, it can be expected that at least some governments and MNEs might actively look for options to sidestep those rulings and engage in harmful tax competition by implementing alternative tax-related mechanisms instead. Peer reviews in line with the current procedure of fighting harmful tax practices (BEPS Action 5) under the roof of the OECD (OECD, 2020) could perhaps help to identify those mechanisms that negatively target third countries.

REFERENCES

Abbas, S. A., & Klemm, A. (2013). A Partial Race to the Bottom: Corporate Tax Developments in Emerging and Developing Economies. *International Tax and Public Finance, 20*, 596–617.

Appelt, S., Bajgar, M., Criscuolo, C., & Galindo-Rueda, F. (2020). The Effects of R&D Tax Incentives and Their Role in the Innovation Policy Mix: Findings from the OECD microBeRD Project, 2016–19. *OECD Science, Technology and Industry Policy Papers No. 92*. OECD.

ATI (Addis Tax Initiative). (2022). *Report on the First Regional Workshop on Tax Expenditures.*

Bradbury, D., Hanappi, T., & Moore, A. (2018). Estimating the Fiscal Effects of Base Erosion and Profit Shifting: Data Availability and Analytical Issues. *Transnational Corporations, 25*(2), 91–106.

Christensen, R. C., Hearson, M., & Randriamanalina, T. (2020). At the Table, off the Menu? Assessing the Participation of Lower-Income Countries in Global Tax Negotiations. *ICTD Working Paper 115.*

Dietsch, P. (2015). *Catching Capital: The Ethics of Tax Competition.* Oxford University Press.

Dietsch, P., & Rixen, T. (2014). Tax Competition and Global Background Justice. *Journal of Political Philosophy, 22*(2), 150–77.

Dietsch, P., & Rixen, T. (eds.). (2016). Global Tax Governance: What Is Wrong with It and How to Fix It. *ECPR Press.*

European Commission. (2016). Communication from the Commission to the European Parliament and the Council on an External Strategy for Effective Taxation. *European Union.*

Genschel, P., & Seelkopf, L. (2016). Winners and Losers of Tax Competition. In P. Dietsch & T. Rixen (eds.), *Global Tax Governance: What Is Wrong with It and How to Fix It*, 55–75. ECPR Press.

González Cabral, A. C., O'Reilly, P., van Dender, K., & Zawisza, T. (2023). Tax Incentives and the Global Minimum Tax. In C. von Haldenwang, A. Redonda, & F. Aliu (eds.), *Tax Expenditures in an Era of Transformative Change.* GTED Flagship Report 2023.

Gulotty, R. (2022). WTO Subsidy Disciplines. *World Trade Review, 21*(3), 330–41.

Haufler, A., & Schindler, D. (2020). Attracting Profit Shifting or Fostering Innovation? On Patent Boxes and R&D Subsidies. *CESifo Working Paper 8640.*

IMF (2019). Tax Expenditure Reporting and Its Use in Fiscal Management: A Guide for Developing Economies. *How to Notes 19/01.*

James, S. (2013). Tax and Non-tax Incentives and Investments: Evidence and Policy Implications. *The World Bank Group.*

Johannesen, N., Tørsløv, T., & Wier, L. (2020). Are Less Developed Countries More Exposed to Multinational Tax Avoidance? Method and Evidence from Micro-data. *The World Bank Economic Review, 34*(3), 790–809.

Klemm, A. (2010). Causes, Benefits, and Risks of Business Tax Incentives. *International Tax and Public Finance, 17*(3), 315–36.

Klemm, A., & Van Parys, S. (2012). Empirical Evidence on the Effects of Tax Incentives. *International Tax and Public Finance, 19*(3), 393–423.

Kronfol, H., & Steenbergen, V. (2020). *Evaluating the Costs and Benefits of Corporate Tax Incentives: Methodological Approaches and Policy Considerations.* World Bank.

Laudage, S. (2020). Corporate Tax Revenue and Foreign Direct Investment: Potential Trade-offs and How to Address Them. *IDOS Discussion Paper 17/2020.*

Laudage Teles, S., & von Haldenwang, C. (2023). Advancing International Tax Cooperation: Towards a UN Tax Convention? *IDOS Current Column.*

Luja, R. (2023). The Foreign Subsidies Regulation: The Challenge of Notifying Non-selective Tax Expenditure. *Competition Law & Policy Debate, 8*(1), 13–21.

Millan, L., Redonda, A., von Haldenwang, C., & Aliu, F. (2023). The global tax expenditures transparency index: Taking Tax Expenditure Scrutiny to the Next Level. In C. von Haldenwang, A. Redonda, & F. Aliu, Eds., *Tax Expenditures in an Era of Transformative Change*, 26–45. GTED Flagship Report 2023.

OECD (Organisation for Economic Co-operation and Development). (1998). *Harmful Tax Competition.* OECD Publishing.

OECD. (2020). *Harmful Tax Practices – Peer Review Results: Inclusive Framework on BEPS: Action 5.* OECD/G20 Base Erosion and Profit Shifting Project, OECD Publishing.

OECD. (2021). *Statement on a Two-Pillar Solution to Address the Tax Challenges Arising from the Digitalisation of the Economy.* OECD Publishing

Piketty, T. (2014). *Capital in the 21st Century*. Harvard University Press.

Redonda, A., & Axelson, C. (2021). Assessing Pension-Related Tax Expenditures in South Africa. *WIDER Working Paper 2021/54.*

Redonda, A., Diaz de Sarralde, S., Hallerberg, M., Johnson, L., Melamud, A., Rozemberg, R., Schwab, J., & von Haldenwang, C. (2018). Tax Expenditure and the Treatment of Tax Incentives for Investment. *G20 Argentina Policy Brief.*

Redonda, A., von Haldenwang, C., & Aliu, F. (2023). Global Tax Expenditures Database (GTED). *Zenodo.*

von Haldenwang, C., Redonda, A., & Aliu, F. (2021). Shedding Light on Worldwide Tax Expenditures. *GTED Flagship Report 2021.*

von Haldenwang, C., Redonda, A., & Aliu, F. (eds.). (2023). Tax Expenditures in an Era of Transformative Change. *GTED Flagship Report 2023.*

WTO (World Trade Organization). (1994). Agreement on Subsidies and Countervailing Measures. *WTO.*

Zucman, G. (2014). Taxing across Borders: Tracking Personal Wealth and Corporate Profits. *Journal of Economic Perspectives, 28*(4), 121–48.

Chapter 13

IS THE RIGHT OF THE STATE TO TAX AN ILLUSION?

Miriam Ronzoni

INTRODUCTION

The case for regulating, and indeed taming global tax competition is overwhelming. The capacity of powerful actors to avoid or evade taxation enables mind-blogging levels of global wealth to be hidden away; it undermines the capacity of states to fund public services and exacerbates both domestic and global inequalities. Indeed, the case seems to be overdetermined: current forms of global tax competition appear unjust from a broad range of different understandings of justice. The asymmetrical and unilateral capacity of certain actors (mainly extremely wealthy individuals and transnational corporations) to avoid taxation seems to constitute a clear violation of the duty to contribute to forms of social cooperation one benefits from (Dietsch, 2016). The difficulty it poses for the capacity of states to provide public services (healthcare, social welfare, infrastructure, you name it) is at odds with the widespread belief that an adequate provision of those very services is something to which people living in political communities have a justice-based claim. Its unequalising effects are deeply problematic from an array of conceptions of distributive justice, well beyond the most demanding forms of egalitarianism. Finally, by externally imposing these pressures on jurisdictions in a way that severely constrains the range of feasible policy options, unregulated tax competition appears to be a very severe obstacle to genuinely democratic decision-making.

In the normative literature on tax competition, an additional reason for the case being overdetermined has come to light: its potential to be fairly ecumenically embraced by many statist and cosmopolitan conceptions of justice alike (Dietsch, 2011, 2015; Dietsch & Rixen, 2014; Laborde & Ronzoni, 2016; Rixen, 2011; Ronzoni, 2014, but see also 2009, 2012). Unregulated tax competition surely exacerbates global inequality but puts pressure on domestic distributive patterns as well, and generally threatens the problem-solving capacity, internal democracy and self-determination of states. Indeed, this might be one of the very few areas where many (if not all) statists and cosmopolitans might largely converge on the same verdict, and agree on a significant range of solutions, if not on the full picture.

Some recent work, however, has questioned this hardly won consensus (Risse & Meyer, 2019; Kern, 2020). Risse and Meyer (2019) argue that a blanket condemnation of tax competition commits the 'Independence Fallacy' (p. 481) of postulating that each jurisdiction has a fiscal right over what its own gross national income would be *absent* such competition. This is unwarranted because, given global interdependence, states and their members 'must be prepared to devote some of their resources to matters of more than purely domestic concern' (Risse & Meyer, 2019, p. 481). Whether tax competition is unjust, they conclude, depends on whether it leads to overall more unjust or just outcomes, according to an overall theory of justice which takes the fact of interdependence into account. From this perspective, the likely verdict will be that some forms of tax competition are more justified than others. Kern (2020) similarly argues that the Capture Principle (p. 155), according to which 'states which host an economic activity should have rights to tax it' (Kern, 2020, p. 154), is unjustified. This is not necessarily because the fundamental ideal of reciprocity, upon which it rests, is misguided, but because such an ideal does not necessarily imply that the state in which a given economic activity takes place is the site where reciprocity is due. Again, appeal is being made to global interdependence: even if it is true that 'when some people sacrifice to make another's prosperity possible, they are entitled to share in her good fortune' (Kern, 2020, p. 155), it is not obvious who those people are, nor what exactly they are owed. Once again, global interdependence is invoked. Kern's view, however, is less aimed at showing that some forms of tax competition might be justified after all, and more at making the point that, even if they are not, the way to combat them is not by insisting on the Capture Principle. We should instead be open to more inventive, ramified and possibly even extra-jurisdictional, forms of taxation.

This chapter aims to provide a restatement of the view according to which we should restore the capacity of the state to tax – one which takes, among other things, such challenges into account. The chapter starts off by providing a brief summary of the case against unregulated tax competition in the name of state fiscal self-determination, as well as of the critical views just sketched. It then argues that two challenges, even if correct, miss the point. The case for restoring the fiscal self-determination of states is not so much grounded in a state's fundamental right to tax whatever economic surplus is produced within one's borders, but rather in what restoring such fiscal capacity *achieves*. Broadly speaking, fiscal capacity enables states to realise certain aims that many conceptions of justice consider essential – in particular, it allows them to provide certain public services and realise certain distributive patterns and social relations among those of its members. Additionally, and for some even more crucially, it enables them to do so in a way that is responsive to the view of its members, rather than to external pressures. In other words, what we want is to restore, and protect, the capacity of state institutions to be agents of both justice and democracy. Of course, if it is true that reciprocity pulls, despite appearances, in a different and more ramified direction, then the aim of restoring the fiscal capacity of states might need to be tamed and qualified in important ways. And there may well be other moral reasons to qualify such capacity in important – yet limited – ways. However, it is important to understand what the strongest justification for it is to begin with. This, in turn, enables us to see, *pace* (Risse & Meyer, 2019) that the stronger arguments in favour of restoring the fiscal self-determination of states do not commit the Independency Fallacy after all. Their point is not to postulate a claim to some fixed disposable national income in a way that disregards global interdependence, but to make sure that states remain capable of realising justice (including political justice, i.e., democracy) within such a context – an aim that Risse and Meyer (2019) also explicitly champion. The last section concludes by a) addressing some rejoinders and making some qualifications; as well as b) arguing that, if the reason to regulate tax competition is primarily to restore the capacity of states as agents of justice and democracy in a globalised economy, some surprising policy implications follow.

FOR AND AGAINST THE REVIVAL OF THE STATE IN DEBATES ON TAX COMPETITION

Tax competition occurs when, in a context of high capital and business mobility – allowed by current levels of financial and economic globalisation – different jurisdictions design tax systems to attract investment and tax bases from different jurisdictions. This can take many forms: changes in the tax rate and tax base: offers of tax breaks, exceptions and expenditures to particularly desirable actors; a loosening of enforcement in tax law; and the implementation of high levels of banking secrecy.

The 'rational' expectation (according to orthodox rational choice and game theory) within such a context is that 'countries will attempt to undercut one another in tax burdens' (Rixen, 2011, p. 449). This, in reality, does not lead to a simple 'race to the bottom' (Dietsch & Rixen, 2014; Genschell & Seelkopf, 2016; Ronzoni, 2014); what actually happens is, however, no less worrying. To start with, tax competition affects different countries differently. Established economies (mainly, OECD countries) are usually capable of preserving their tax rate, or at least to prevent it from reaching intolerably low levels. To do so, however, they usually need to shift the tax base – for example from capital to labour, and from income and wealth to consumption (for example, VAT). This allows such jurisdictions to preserve a decent level of public service provision, if not to maintain the desired level entirely; but at the cost of accepting a much higher degree of domestic inequality. Using Dietsch and

Rixen's helpful terminology, developed countries are capable of preserving the 'size of the budget' (2014, pp. 6–7), but not of maintaining the distributive patterns among their residents which they desire, and which their citizens might express a democratic preference for. What we end up with are, in a nutshell, much more unequal societies which, however, still manage (some better than others) to provide the level of public services that one would expect an advanced economy to offer to its residents. What is more, advanced economies, especially when they are liberal democracies and when they are already enmeshed in forms of multilateral and supranational governance (such as EU member states), far from behaving like 'rational actors' in a game theory scenario, instead establish various forms of cooperation to resist tax competition – above all by harmonising their tax regimes (Genschell, 2002). However, decisions on tax harmonisation often happen in forms of supranational governance which are not only less than perfectly democratic in and of themselves, but also deprive domestic democratic publics of the power to decide on their tax rate and their fiscal outlook more broadly. In other words, harmonisation prevents races to the bottom but still takes fiscal self-determination away from the people.

Developing countries, instead, have a hard time even preserving the size of the budget, simply because they often lack the institutional, administrative and infrastructural capacity to change their tax base in effective and reliable ways (Keen & Simone, 2004). Many of them have also, so far, been less successful in engaging in effective forms of harmonisation. What we face in many of these cases is, therefore, a proper challenge to state capacity itself. Thus, the evidence suggests that tax competition affects *both* domestic and global inequalities: it (by and large) makes societies more unequal internally *and* it affects poorer countries more severely. This is one of the main reasons why it would seem that those who think that social justice is primarily a state-level affair and those who endorse a more cosmopolitan picture could actually profitably link arms here: fighting global tax competition could make individual societies more just, and the world less unequal.

If what I have said above is true, there is an ecumenical range of reasons to try and regulate, and indeed reduce tax competition. Of course, one way of doing so could be to move the power to tax one level up, by levying taxes at a supranational level and then distributing them according to some relevant normative criterion. This, however, is a non-starter if we want to capitalise on the potential coalition between statists and cosmopolitans. Luckily, however – while disagreements may remain about whether some forms of regional or global taxation might persist – we need not go there. First of all, most cosmopolitans about the scope of justice would agree that moving the power to tax income and wealth too high up has very problematic implications in terms of loss of democratic control, accountability and technocratic capture. Second of all, if – as we have seen – reducing tax competition has beneficial effects in terms of both domestic and global inequality (with the potential exception of small poor countries, to which I shall turn below), then maybe we just do not need to engage in such grand projects of revolutionary global institutional design. Dietsch and Rixen (2014), for instance, argue that honouring what they call the Membership Principle and the Principle of Fiscal Policy Constraint would do the trick. The principles are defined as follows:

> Membership Principle (MP): Natural and legal persons (that is, individuals and corporations) are liable to pay tax to the state(s) of which they are a member; they are not liable to pay tax to any other entities.
>
> Fiscal Policy Constraint (FPC): Any fiscal policy of a state is unjust and should be prohibited if it is both strategically motivated and harms the aggregate fiscal self-determination of other states. (Dietsch, 2015, p. 80)

The two principles, when combined, would prevent all forms of 'poaching', but only intentional and harmful forms of 'luring'. Poaching occurs when tax regimes are designed to entice individuals or companies to take their wealth or profits somewhere else, even though they have not registered their residency or undertaken economic activity there – this is what happens when individuals and corporations park their wealth and profits in tax havens. In the current global tax regime, some poaching is perfectly legal (this is why actors who respond positively to poaching are said to engage in tax 'avoidance', rather than tax 'evasion'); some is illegal but poorly enforced. The Membership Principle rules out any form of poaching. 'Luring' occurs when states engage in competitive behaviour to encourage attractive actors to *change membership* by relocating to a different jurisdiction – company relocations are the prime example here. The Fiscal Policy Constraint determines that luring is unjustified when intentionally aimed at undermining the fiscal self-determination of other political communities and succeeds in doing so.

While sympathetic to Dietsch and Rixen's (2015) motivation and to several aspects of their proposal, which is very congenial and partly inspired by a general perspective on global justice I developed elsewhere (Ronzoni, 2009; 2012), I disagree with some self-contained but important aspects (Ronzoni, 2014). I shall turn to them further below. What is crucial at this juncture is that the framing of these two principles has led critics to believe that what is being posited is some form of natural ownership right over the wealth created within its territory. I believe this is a misunderstanding.

As already sketched, Risse and Meyer (2019) make this point very straightforwardly, by arguing that views such as Dietsch and Rixen's (2014) commit the Independence Fallacy: they are wrongly committed to the view that a state's disposable (that is, taxable) national income corresponds to its gross national income or, better still, to what its gross national income would be in the absence of tax competition. This is implausible because, in a context of global interdependence, each country's national income is the product of a complex nexus of transactions and interactions. It is also normatively unwarranted because we should not ground verdicts on the justifiability of different global tax regimes on isolated claims of purported natural ownership: what justifies a tax regime is whether it tends to lead to overall more just outcomes than its alternatives (Risse & Meyer, 2019, p. 492). And once we shift to this approach, we realise (at least) two things. First, many forms of tax competition are unjust, but simply because they enable certain actors to pay much less tax than is needed to realise justice, period – regardless of *where* exactly those revenues are due. Second, some forms of tax competition are justified – especially when poor countries, or very small countries who otherwise would not stand a good chance to prosper, use it to their own advantage (Risse & Meyer, 2019, pp. 490, 496–8). In the battle between David and Goliath, certain unconventional fighting strategies become fair.

Here, Risse and Meyer (2019) make several different moves that are not explicitly distinguished – it is therefore worth disentangling them for a moment. First, they imply that a broadly Lockean, or libertarian, story, according to which states have an acquired ownership right over their national income, is *factually* incorrect, due to global interdependence. Second, they claim that we should assess tax regimes from a justice perspective anyway – here, however, they are making two claims at once. They are implicitly ruling out the possibility of a libertarian conception of justice based on historical entitlements and they are suggesting that we should look instead at what kinds of patterns different tax regimes produce. In other words, they are not suggesting to replace a false Lockean story (national income belongs to states) with a factually correct one (global surplus is produced in a more complex way), but to endorse a more pattern-based conception, within the broad liberal egalitarian family. They then argue that the correct pattern is inspired by a pluralist account along the lines of Risse's Grounds of Justice theory (Risse, 2012) – which we shall not explore further here for space reasons. Finally, they conclude that, from this point of view, some forms of tax competition should be condemned, but for different reasons compared to those put forward by views that commit the Independence Fallacy, while others are all things considered acceptable. The likes of Singapore and Panama, for instance, might well be largely off the hook.

Kern's argument relies on a similar starting point as Risse and Meyer's: the Capture Principle, as he defines it, is broadly in line with the Independence Fallacy:

> Capture Principle: Each state ought to have a package of rights, *Ri*, to tax income generated from economic activities within its borders.

> The value of *Ri* ought to be proportionate to the amount of income generated from the economic activities hosted by *i*. (Kern, 2020, p. 155)

There are, however, two important differences. First, the Capture Principle makes no reference to what the economic activities hosted by *it would* be *in the absence of tax competition* – whereas Risse and Meyer (2019) want to explore that scenario, as well. As such, then, the principle only concerns cases of poaching, not of luring. Second, Kern (2020) does not claim that the principle relies on a fallacy, but rather goes through a list of possible justifications for it, and argues that they all fail. The argument, roughly, runs as follows. Kern (2020) starts off by suggesting that the intuitive pull of the Capture Principle relies on some formulation of the ideal of reciprocity. He argues that reciprocity is unpacked in roughly three ways in the academic literature and in policy-making discourse – in terms of fair play, compensation and contribution. He then proceeds to show that all three accounts fail to show that the right way to make sure that reciprocity is honoured is by implementing the Capture Principle.

The principle of fair play cannot do the trick because it simply claims that one must not free-ride; it is, however, neutral as to whom in particular one takes advantage of by free-riding, and what not free-riding would exactly mean. People who hide away their taxes in tax havens are surely free-riding, but honouring fair play would be compatible with 1) their money being taxed by an international agent; and 2) in principle, different tax rates. Fair play as such is silent on those issues – a substantive theory on the content and scope of justice must be plugged in. Compensation, in turn, requires that agents compensate for the burdens they impose on other members of social cooperation. Again, however, these are not necessarily fellow citizens and residents only; what is more,'there is nothing close to a 1:1 relation between the income earned from business activities within a state and the marginal burdens that those activities place on that state's public sector' (Kern, 2020). Some investors can make a lot of money without seemingly burdening anyone and the other way around. Finally, the principle of contribution might plausibly suggest that 'each state's share of global economic resources ought to be proportionate to its members' contributions to the global surplus' (Kern, 2020, p. 167). Kern's argument here comes closest to Risse and Meyer's: in a globally interconnected economy, the contribution of people to the global surplus does not neatly match their country's national income in any reliable way. When, say, I move to a country different from the one where I was born and raised, the surplus I thereby create is always a joint product of the infrastructure offered by the hosting country, the education and know-how that my country of origin has provided, the technology produced in a third country still, the opportunities made possible by international trade and so on – the list is endless. Thus, it is not clear whether obligations of reciprocity are owed to fellow citizens and residents, to residents of the country where a given economic activity (rather than the people profiting from it) is located, the country where a certain person has been trained, the one where a technology necessary for a certain type of business has been developed or a mix of all of the above.

The policy conclusions that Kern (2020) draws from this diagnosis are, however, very different from those suggested by Risse and Meyer (2019). First, Kern's aim is not to defend (some forms of) tax competition but rather to replace the Capture Principle as the right way to combat it with more plausible alternatives. Second, and following directly from the first point, such plausible alternatives will have a much stronger cosmopolitan and transnational flavour. Kern (2020) entertains, for instance, the possibility of a 'Progressive Formulary Apportionment' (p. 178), according to which member states of a free trade area (such as the EU) are assigned more generous taxing rights when it comes to taxing companies operating within the trade area if they are relatively worse off. A less revolutionary, but still fairly radical, alternative is the Bhagwati Tax (Bhagwati, 1979), a proposed measure to contain brain drain according to which skilled migrants who move from developing to developed countries should be required to pay some or all of their taxes to their country of origin.

TALKING ACROSS PURPOSES

The present section is crucial, yet it is also surprisingly short. The reason is quite simple: I shall not engage in a detailed rebuttal of Risse and Meyer's and Kern's argument, but I shall claim, instead, that their challenges are mistargeted. The strongest arguments in favour of protecting states from tax competition are not grounded in a putative 'right' of states to their own national income or their national income in the absence of tax competition; but rather in the conviction that preserving the fiscal self-determination of states is essential for justice, however we conceive it – or at least, across a range of broadly egalitarian views. The justification, therefore, is instrumental: we want to tame and slow down tax competition not because it deprives states of what is rightfully theirs, but because it makes it prohibitively difficult for them to be agents of justice and democracy. The aim is the forward-looking one of securing a capacity, rather than the backward-looking one of securing a right – tax competition should be countered because, and *to the extent that*, it secures this capacity.

If this is the aim, we can see how both challenges unpacked in the previous section misfire. Let me quickly address both in turn. *Pace* (Risse & Meyer, 2019), a strategy aimed at restoring state capacity does not commit the Independence Fallacy. First of all, it is very much grounded in the aim of acknowledging interdependence, and recognising that *new duties* arise from it (Dietsch, 2011): in an interdependent world, states have an obligation not to undermine each other's fiscal self-determination, which in turn requires both refraining from undertaking certain actions and setting up common rules (Dietsch, 2011). Secondly, to the extent that the goal is to restore fiscal capacity, and through it the capacity of states to deliver justice and be democratically responsive to their own citizens (rather than to global pressures), this approach is very much in line with the ostensibly justice-based one championed by Risse and Meyer (although it does not necessarily endorse the very same substantive conception of justice). To appreciate that, note how Risse and Meyer propose the following principle as the guiding ideal for designing a global taxation regime:

> Global Justice Principle (GJP): Any state should design its fiscal policy to advance justice, both domestic and global. This means funds are generated to that effect and no policies are adopted that frustrate the realisation of justice, unless necessary as part of an overall policy package that advances justice. (Risse & Meyer, 2019, p. 492)

In their view, this constitutes a stark contrast with views such as Dietsch's, Rixen's, and my own. Note, however, that this is simply inaccurate. The approaches being challenged are committed to the very same principle according to which the aim is to approximate justice – they simply rely on an empirical diagnosis (Dietsch & Rixen, 2014; Ronzoni, 2014) according to which an overall significant reduction of tax competition throughout will do just that, in that it will reduce domestic and global inequalities, secure the capacity of *all* states to deliver important public services and secure better democratic control. This may well be a source of disagreement, but it has nothing to do with the Independence Fallacy.

The same is true, *mutatis mutandis,* about Kern's challenge. The claim that the capacity of states to deliver justice and democracy needs a significant curtailing of tax competition need not rely on any intrinsic commitment to the Capture Principle. Dietsch and Rixen's Membership Principle in particular seems to imply that this principle (and the Fiscal Policy Constraint) are explicitly endorsed as *policy guidelines* which, in their view, will lead overall to more just outcomes (2014, p. 150) and not as trumping moral imperatives which must be respected no matter what the consequences are. They are better rules of the game, part of a project of institutional design which, in their view, will prevent injustice from occurring more effectively. Note how Kern sketches what he thinks is a more promising way of thinking about the issue (2020, pp. 179–84) – on which, in a nutshell, assesses different global tax regimes according to how they will affect state capacity, and the value of state capacity according to what it entails for the realisation of justice (independently defined). This is *exactly* what Dietsch, Rixen and I do, as well – we just reach the substantive conclusion that an overall regime where the fiscal capacity of all states is better protected from aggressive tax competition is better (if not perfect) from a wide range of perspectives of justice.

And while it is true that some formulations (Dietsch, 2016, p. 236) lend themselves to Kern's interpretation, a more charitable reading clearly exposes how the project is one of institutional design grounded in the idea that a world with less tax competition is a world where rights to public services, just distributions and democratic control can better be maintained. My own previous work on the matter is fairly adamant on this point – we want a world that is not dominated by tax competition because it is a world where the preconditions to joint and effective sovereignty of all political communities are less severely undermined, both in distributive and in democratic terms (Ronzoni, 2009; 2012; 2014).

This can of course be something one might want to take issue with, as we shall see in the last and final section – but it is a very different kind of debate compared to the one that both critiques point at.

WHERE THE REAL ISSUE IS

I have argued that a focus on an alleged ownership right that states have over their national income misses the point: critics of tax competition in the justice literature are rather preoccupied with what the loss of state capacity means for justice and democracy overall. This, however, exposes a new problem: while Risse, Meyer and Kern might have mistargeted their critiques, many of their points seem to reveal an important, if different, disagreement – a disagreement about whether it is really true that restoration of state capacity due to a reduction of tax competition will lead to more just outcomes. Since I have started off by suggesting that the appeal of the case for regulating tax competition is its ecumenical nature, this is seemingly quite a blow – if a different one from what was originally intended. While such a topic would lead us too far, I will offer some very brief thoughts in response to this alternative challenge. I then conclude by offering a sketch of some surprising implications that the case for taming tax competition in the name of restoring state capacity would entail, in a way that reveals some 'family disagreements' with Dietsch and Rixen's (2014) solution.

I have argued that authors such as Dietsch, Rixen, and myself, who think we should try to restore the fiscal self-determination of states, are primarily motivated by the thought that this would be better for justice from a wide range of different perspectives – not by a commitment to some ownership right which states have over their national income. Thus, while Risse, Meyer and Kern largely mistarget their challenges, their arguments reveal that they disagree on this very issue. Let me provide a quick response to each.

Risse and Meyer's (2019) main area of disagreement seems to be about whether it is true that all forms of tax competition are at least pro tanto bad for justice. They claim, for instance, that once we move away from an 'ownership over national income' perspective to one of justice, we must admit that tax competition engaged in by poor countries, by small countries and especially by countries that are both poor and small, might lead to more rather than less just outcomes. If it is true, for instance, that the citizens of poor countries currently have fewer of the world's resources than their fair share would envisage, then tax competition targeted at wealthier countries might be one way of claiming some of them. Small countries, in turn, might just be one of the very few cards they have in a world where they must often just comply with rules made by others and which largely disadvantage them. For countries that are both poor and small, the case is overdetermined.

As we have seen, the argument that poor countries in general can benefit by engaging in tax competition seems to be empirically shaky (Keen & Simone, 2004). Despite some apparent short-term gains, tax competition makes these economies more fragile in a variety of ways. It not only makes them more unequal but also threatens their very capacity to control the 'size of the budget', and thus their capacity to deliver public services. As I acknowledged above, however, things are trickier for small countries, especially those who are also poor – those who can obtain a net benefit in revenue levels from engaging in tax competition. Here the case is more complex, but still by far not as straightforwardly in favour of tax competition as Risse and Meyer (2019) appear to suggest. First of all, relying on one's own tax haven status – especially when those hiding their money away are breaking the law in their country of residence by doing so, or when other countries are actively trying to devise systems to end a regime when doing so is legal – is extremely unstable and unreliable. It does not constitute, to put it mildly, a long-term growth or development strategy within such a volatile global environment. What is more, even if that were not the case, these small countries would be increasing their state capacity at the expense of many others – including many other poor states, with large populations. This need not mean that tax competition is always wrong and that small countries might not still use it in their favour. Risse and Meyer (2019) argue that critics of tax competition are too black and white and that we should recognise how some tax competition can be justified. I would like to turn the table on them: dividing tax competition into good and bad is also too simplistic; we should assess both its quality and its amount. The case for regulating tax competition is about having *less* of it, and a slower, less volatile overall dynamic which does not render states powerless and pre-empt internal democratic decision-making. It is not about eliminating it altogether.

Kern's argument is different and, in a way, more non-committal. He does not subscribe to a specific perspective of justice but offers a research agenda instead (2020, pp. 179–84). However, what is clear in his view is that a) restoring state capacity need not always be the only solution; and b) when it is, it is not clear that the way to do it is by allowing states to tax *their own* national income. With respect to (a), he appears open to multilevel tax regimes; with respect to (b), he seems to regard forms of extra-jurisdictional taxation as promising. Again, an in-depth treatment of both topics would lead us too far. What must be noted, however, is that the less radical proposals in the literature which Kern criticises are put forward from a perspective that takes feasibility and real-world considerations into account. The point is not to assess how a policy model would work in a vacuum. Thus, while the case needs wider treatment, it is quite clear that both the 'Progressive Formulary Apportionment' proposal and the Bhagwati Tax would encounter large resistance, and would be difficult to control democratically in a way that escapes technocratic capture. With the Bhagwati Tax in particular, one further consideration is in order: if justice also requires establishing certain social relationships between members, the co-existence of people who live in the same jurisdiction but are liable to different packages of obligations, needs to be assessed much more thoroughly.

The argument of this chapter is thereby concluded. Risse, Meyer and Kern's objections to the case for restoring the fiscal capacity of states are largely addressed by a claim that such a case never makes. And while their points indirectly reveal that the case for restoring state capacity might not be as unquestionably ecumenical as initially suggested, such a case still has more ammunitions than its critics suggest. By means of conclusion, let me now move on to a brief sketch of what the case for regulating tax competition in the name of state capacity does and does not entail. As we shall see, some of the implications are not obvious. In particular, the intention of certain policies aimed at encouraging tax completion does not matter that much; and there may indeed be some significant if limited space for some global tax governance, in terms of both taxation and tax harmonisation.

First of all, the point is not to eliminate tax competition altogether, but to regulate it and to slow it down. What matters is not so much to justify which competition is fair and which is unfair, but the effects it has on state capacity. This might reveal some differences between the position I would favour and the one put forward by Dietsch and Rixen (2014), for instance. Rather than a blanket prohibition of both poaching and certain kinds of luring, for instance, we might want to opt for measures that lead to the reduction of both – looking at the effects rather than at reasons based on a logic of fairness or entitlement. This might lead to a scenario where, *pace* (Dietsch & Rixen, 2014) some poaching (much less than the current one, of course) is allowed, and when some forms of luring are disallowed or disincentivised regardless of their intentions. Secondly, we might favour certain forms of harmonisation if they are overall beneficial to state capacity: for instance, a global minimal tax rate might both slow down tax competition and enable states to decide more freely what to do above that rate – including making different choices depending on domestic circumstances and democratic preferences (Ronzoni, 2014). Finally, certain forms of supranational taxation might be justified overall, either as a means to solve global problems (say, in the case of climate change or health), or as a way to slow down tax competition itself (as, for instance, a tax on transnational financial transactions might do). In other words, if the point of taming tax competition is to strengthen state capacity, rather than to respect some alleged right that states have to their own national income, the toolkit of policy options is a little more diversified than critics might think – if still structured along a leading guiding principle.

REFERENCES

Bhagwati, J. N. (1979). International Migration of the Highly Skilled: Economics, Ethics and Taxes. *Third World Quarterly, 1*(3), 17–30.

Dietsch, P. (2011). Rethinking Sovereignty in International Fiscal Policy. *Review of International Studies, 37*(5), 2107–20.

Dietsch, P. (2015). *Catching Capital: The Ethics of Tax Competition*. Oxford University Press.

Dietsch, P. (2016). Whose Tax Base? The Ethics of Global Tax Governance. In Dietsch, P. & Rixen, T., (eds.), *Global Tax Governance: What Is Wrong with It and How to Fix It*, 231–51. ECPR Press.

Dietsch, P., & Rixen, T. (2014). Tax Competition and Global Background Justice. *Journal of Political Philosophy, 22*(2), 150–77.

Genschel, P. (2002). Globalization, Tax Competition, and the Welfare State. *Politics & Society, 30*(2), 245–75.

Genschel, P., & Seelkopf, L. (2016). Winners and Losers of Tax Competition. In Dietsch, P. & Rixen, T., (eds.), *Global Tax Governance: What Is Wrong with It and How to Fix It*, 55–76. ECPR Press.

Keen, M., & Simone, A. (2004). Is Tax Competition Harming Developing Countries More Than Developed? *Tax Notes International, 34*(13), 1317–25.

Kern, A. (2020). Illusions of Justice in International Taxation. *Philosophy & Public Affairs, 48*(2), 151–84.

Laborde, C. and Ronzoni, M. (2016). What Is a Free State? Republican Internationalism and Globalisation. *Political Studies, 64*(2), 279–96.

Risse, M. (2012). *On Global Justice*. Princeton University Press.

Risse, M., & Meyer, M. (2019). Tax Competition and Global Interdependence. *Journal of Political Philosophy, 27*(4), 480–98.

Rixen, T. (2011). Tax Competition and Inequality: The Case for Global Tax Governance. *Global Governance, 17*(4), 447–67.

Ronzoni, M. (2009). The Global Order: A Case of Background Injustice? A Practice-Dependent Account. *Philosophy & Public Affairs, 37*(3), 229–56.

Ronzoni, M. (2012). Two Conceptions of State Sovereignty and Their Implications for Global Institutional Design. *Critical Review of International Social and Political Philosophy, 15* (5), 573–91.

Ronzoni, M. (2014). Global Tax Governance: The Bullets Internationalists Must Bite – and Those They Must Not. *Moral Philosophy and Politics, 1*(1), 37–59.

Ronzoni, M. (2016). Tax Competition: A Problem of Global or Domestic Justice. In Dietsch, P. & Rixen, T., (eds.), *Global Tax Governance: What Is Wrong with It and How to Fix It*, 201–14. ECPR Press.

Chapter 14

JUSTICE IN GLOBAL DEBT GOVERNANCE IN DEVELOPING COUNTRIES

Kathrin Berensmann

INTRODUCTION

The debt situation in developing countries (low- and middle-income countries) has come under immense stress. The International Monetary Fund (IMF) and World Bank have estimated that the proportion of low-income countries (LICs) that are at high risk of debt distress or are already in debt distress has increased from 30 per cent in 2015 to more than 50 per cent in 2024 (IMF, 2024). About 25 per cent of middle-income countries (MICs) are also at risk. There are many reasons for this, including the Covid-19 pandemic and the climate crisis. However, some countries have taken on excessive debt in the good times, in some cases on unfavourable terms. The rise in interest rates over the last two years has further increased the debt burden and made refinancing more difficult. Despite this mounting debt crisis, recent debt restructurings have been slow to materialise and has so far been limited to very few countries.

This chapter assesses key elements of global debt governance and argues that its instruments for resolving over-indebtedness are inadequate. The current system has often led to delayed, disorderly inefficient debt restructuring processes that could contribute to different dimensions of injustice, namely socioeconomic, political and intergenerational injustice. The chapter starts by providing a brief overview of key instruments of global debt governance to resolve debt crises. It outlines the challenges of the current system and then discusses today's global debt governance in light of questions of socioeconomic, political and intergenerational justice by assessing the debt treatment mechanism of the G20. The final section discusses reform proposals for the G20's approach to resolving debt crises.

KEY ELEMENTS OF THE CURRENT SYSTEM OF GLOBAL DEBT GOVERNANCE

Global debt governance can be defined as the development of a system of institutions and rules and new mechanisms of international economic cooperation and transactions with regard to international relations between creditors and debtors, be they private or public (Berensmann, 2018). The current system of global debt governance consists of instruments for preventing and for resolving sovereign debt crises. Policy instruments for resolving sovereign debt crises become relevant when a country has unsustainable external debt.

There are two entry points for improving the financing situation of highly indebted countries. Firstly, the international financial system can provide more funds for developing countries. This is one of the key elements of the ongoing reform of World Bank and Multilateral Development Banks (MDBs), which involves better utilisation of existing capital and the provision of additional financial resources by shareholders (primarily in the form of guarantees). Secondly, the international community can adopt instruments resolving debt crises, which are in the spotlight of this chapter and become relevant when a country has unsustainable external debt including collective action clauses, debt moratoria (e.g. the G20 Debt Service Suspension Initiative, DSSI), debt restructuring/relief initiatives such as the G20 Common Framework for Debt Treatment beyond DSSI (Common Framework), codes of conduct and debt swaps. For example, the HIPC and related multilateral initiatives have relieved thirty-seven participating countries of more than $100 billion in debt. But since such systematic debt relief initiatives for a large number of countries would typically place a heavy burden on the national budgets of creditor countries and is therefore only likely to be taken up by political decision-makers if they fear a worldwide debt crisis. Mainly because of collective action problems, it is unlikely that the international community will agree on a new systemic debt relief initiative in the medium term. For these reasons, a reform of the so-called G20 Common Framework, currently the key instrument for resolving debt crises in developing countries and the focus of this chapter, is particularly necessary.

In 2020, the G20 established the Common Framework, which sets forth the rules for future debt restructuring, that is, changing the terms on loans to make them easier to pay back, and for debt relief (G20, 2020b) to deal systematically with highly indebted LICs. Under the Common Framework, the G20 and Paris Club (a group of major creditor countries aiming to tackle debt problems in debtor countries, which dates back to 1956) agreed to coordinate and cooperate on debt treatment for LICs. A key objective was to ensure not only the participation of Paris Club members, that is, bilateral official creditors of Western industrialised countries, but also of G20 bilateral official creditors that are not members of the Paris Club, including India, China, Turkey or Saudi Arabia (Berensmann et al., 2022; Siaba Serrate et al., 2024).

DIFFERENT DIMENSION OF INJUSTICE IN THE GLOBAL DEBT GOVERNANCE SYSTEM

The existing global debt governance framework is inadequate in its ability to prevent and address over-indebtedness in developing countries. Major challenges include collective action problems, unequal participation in decision-making processes, information asymmetry among creditors as well as between creditors and debtors, and a missing link to sustainable development.

In particular, collective action problems have resulted in the uncoordinated and delayed restructuring of debt, which can lead to an unfair distribution of burdens. Over the past two decades, collective action problems have become increasingly frequent, in large part due to the increased heterogeneity of the creditor base for sovereign debt. This is primarily due to the growing influence of non-Paris Club public creditors and private creditors, which has led to an increase in coordination difficulties in the context of sovereign debt restructuring (Berensmann, 2018; 2022). For example, a collective action problem may manifest in the form of a 'holdout problem', whereby a majority of creditors are held up by a minority of creditors. This occurs when the latter group declines to be involved in a restructuring process that would result in losses for them. The minority of creditors may choose to withhold their participation in the restructuring process until its conclusion, at which point they may seek to enforce their claims to the full extent of the law. In this instance, the minority would receive their full claims, while the majority would waive part of theirs. This represents an unequal and unfair treatment of the various creditors.

A second challenge is the unequal participation of different stakeholders in decision-making processes on debt restructurings in the context of decision-making procedures between (i) creditors and debtors, (ii) inter-creditor fairness and (iii) fairness between different actors in the debtor country. The extent of participation in relevant decision-making processes varies significantly depending on the different institutions and actors involved as well as the instruments chosen. Typically, decision-making power is concentrated in the hands of a small number of key players such as high-income countries and large emerging markets (including their forums such as the G20) and powerful international institutions and private associations including the Institute of International Finance. Unequal participation in the decision-making process of debtors undergoing debt restructuring can also result in unfair burden sharing between debtors and creditors, which could potentially lead to socioeconomic injustice. Likewise, different stakeholders in debtor countries could unequally be involved in decision-making processes, which could have unfavourable distributional effects and harm poor people.

A third major challenge of the global debt management system is the unequal distribution of the burden between the different generations in the debtor countries. The concept of intergenerational injustice in the context of debt arises from the fundamental nature of debt. The issue of intergenerational equity in the area of debt concerns the extent to which the current generation is allowed to take on debt that future generations will have to repay. Since a high debt burden forces future generations to service that debt, these payments divert budgetary resources from investments needed to finance critical sectors that support future and long-term development, including social and health sectors, infrastructure and human capital. In this respect, the instruments of the global debt governance system should help to ensure that a country's debt service is not too high so that servicing the debt does not crowd out government spending on social policies or other important investments for sustainable development (Loko et al., 2003).

A fourth challenge in the context of intergenerational justice is that climate and other sustainability risks are often insufficiently taken into account in debt sustainability analyses albeit the prospects of future generations are undermined by these risks. This is highly problematic as the risks of climate change can endanger a country's financial stability and thus also generate sovereign risks (Volz et al., 2020; Volz, 2022). The global debt governance systems need to address these different types of injustice.

CURRENT DEBT RESTRUCTURING MECHANISM FROM THE PERSPECTIVE OF JUSTICE: THE G20 COMMON FRAMEWORK

The challenges and the resulting different dimensions of injustice are illustrated by a typical example of a debt rescheduling mechanism, the G20 Common Framework that the G20 endorsed mainly in cooperation with the Paris Club members and the IMF, in response to the COVID-19 pandemic in 2020/2021. It lays down the rules for future debt restructuring and/or relief and offers LICs with unsustainable debt the opportunity to restructure their debt including debt relief on a case-by-case basis with a broad participation of bilateral official creditors including the call for private creditors' participation.

One main advantage of the new Framework is that it also included non-Paris Club members in debt treatments because for many developing countries non-Paris Club countries have become the main creditors, in particular China in the past fifteen years. The landscape of creditors has changed over the previous decade. While in the early 2000s, the Paris Club members and the IFIs were the main creditors for developing countries, this has changed in the previous decade. New official and private creditors have increased their lending to developing countries. In addition, many of the Paris Club creditors have shifted from providing loans to offering a large part of their financial support as grants. For these reasons, it was important to not only limit debt treatment to Paris Club members, but also include G20 countries that are not Paris Club members.

As there have been collective action problems in the coordination with non-Paris Club members during debt restructurings, the G20, the Paris Club and the IMF established the Common Framework. Accordingly, the primary goal was to guarantee the involvement of both the Paris Club, which represents the bilateral official creditors of Western industrialised countries, and other G20 bilateral official creditors, including non-Paris Club members such as India, China, Turkey or Saudi Arabia.

However, only four debtor countries – Chad, Ethiopia, Ghana and Zambia – have adopted the Common Framework three and a half years after its implementation. The principal reasons for this low level of participation have been the typical challenges associated with debt rescheduling mechanisms, namely collective action problems, unequal participation of different creditor groups and debtors in debt restructuring decision-making processes, the missing link to climate risks and information asymmetries among stakeholders, which have generated socioeconomic, political and intergenerational injustice. In this respect, this example is representative of other debt rescheduling mechanisms that exist in the global system of debt governance.

According to the IMF, implementation has been delayed because of collective action problems, foremost the difficulty of coordinating Paris Club creditors and other creditors, as well as the many government institutions and agencies in creditor countries. In addition, some private creditors are not participating or have delayed participation. For example, in Chad, the restructuring of a large private loan is delayed (Georgieva & Pazarbasioglu, 2021). In the absence of private creditors participating in the debt restructuring process, an unequal burden sharing among creditors occurs.

In addition, there has been an unequal participation of different creditor groups and debtors in debt restructuring decision-making processes because the main decisions were made by a small number of official bilateral creditors belonging to the G20 and the IMF and debtors were hardly involved in the decision-making process. Private creditors also had little or no involvement (Berensmann et al., 2022). Firstly, the decision on the participation of the debtor country and the debt restructuring envelope that is required is subject to the IMF–World Bank Debt Sustainability Analysis (DSA) and collective assessment of the official creditors' taking part in the restructuring. Debtors are not involved in the DSAs that could generate an unfair burden sharing between the debtor and creditor. Secondly, private creditors have been largely excluded from the design of the Common Framework and the decisions on the Debt Sustainability Analysis, albeit in 2021, private creditors received 49% of the debt service paid by countries eligible for the Common Framework (World

Bank, 2023). This is because their loans are more expensive and have shorter terms. This limited participation of private creditors has been a contributing factor to the reluctance of private creditors to engage in debt restructurings under this framework, which could result in an inequitable distribution of the burden of debt repayment among creditors.

Moreover, there have been information asymmetries among stakeholders, which have generated socioeconomic, political and intergenerational injustice. One further impediment to the implementation of the Common Framework is the lack of transparency in loan agreements, which is essential for the equal treatment of creditors in the context of debt restructuring. Enhanced transparency is intertwined with creditor coordination, which, in turn, would facilitate more effective creditor coordination. According to the World Bank, almost 40 per cent of low income developing countries have either never published debt data on their websites or have not updated their data in 2019 and 2020. (Rivetti, 2021; Berensmann et al., 2022). The availability of debt data is often constrained to the liabilities of the central government, excluding lower levels of government, public companies including the central bank and publicly guaranteed debt taken on by wholly or partially owned state enterprises, as well as privately owned companies. Upon comparison of public debt data across available sources, discrepancies in the order of up to 30 per cent of GDP can be identified (Rivetti, 2021; Berensmann et al., 2022).

One further challenge of the Common Framework is that debt restructurings and/or relief are not aligned with sustainability goals. Given the risks to debt sustainability posed by climate change, debt sustainability analysis for LICs for debt treatment under the Common Framework conducted by IMF / World Bank must include sustainability criteria. Although the IMF has begun incorporating climate stress testing into its DSAs for LICs, these stress tests primarily focus on physical risks such as climate-induced natural disasters. They do not take into account investment requirements for climate adaptation and resilience or transition risks. Similarly, these debt sustainability analyses also do not consider the increasing cost of capital because of climate dangers and the risk of stranded assets (Volz et al., 2020; Maldonado & Gallagher, 2022; Volz, 2022).

REFORM OPTIONS FOR GLOBAL DEBT GOVERNANCE

As it will not be politically feasible to introduce alternative instruments in the short or medium term, most stakeholders believe that reforming the G20 Common Framework is the only feasible solution (albeit not the first-best solution). While the Common Framework has the great advantage of including non-Paris Club members such as China, India and Saudi Arabia, it is cumbersome and has not yet brought the expected successes.

First, all creditors and debtors should be involved such that not only G20 creditors but also non-G20 countries and private creditors as well as the debtors are part of the decision-making process to increase political fairness. To improve incentives for private creditors to participate in the restructuring process, the G20 should agree to provide legal safeguards for debt restructurings and limit opportunities for holdouts. In addition, the G20 could invite the World Bank and the Multilateral Investment Guarantee Agency (MIGA) to establish a facility to provide partial guarantees to private creditors on restructured debt (Volz et al., 2022). Moreover, all private and public creditors should publicly commit to complying with the principle of comparable treatment. This commitment should exclude recognised preferential creditors, such as MDBs, who should contribute towards debt treatment deals through newly identified sources of financing (Siaba Serrate et al., 2024). To guarantee the continued cooperation of sovereign debtors, the creditor majority and the IMF should require these debtors to commit, as part of programme conditionality, to refrain from servicing holdouts until they agree to provide comparable treatment (Henning, 2023). Moreover, to improve participation in restructuring processes, there should be parallel and coordinated negotiations by public and private creditor committees, which could promote coordination among creditors and speed up the restructuring process. (Siaba Serrate et al., 2024). In addition, the recently established Global Sovereign Debt Roundtable, co-chaired by the IMF, the World Bank and the G20 Presidency, which includes official bilateral creditors, private creditors and borrowing countries, is a good measure to broaden participation in debt restructuring but it also promotes information exchange and transparency on debt contracts (Siaba Serrate et al., 2024). To further address collective action problems and information asymmetries, a complementary universal code of conduct should be developed under the Financial Stability Board to reinforce governance by establishing common, overarching principles throughout the entire debt engagement process (Siaba Serrate et al., 2024). The code of conduct should include transparency and timely information flows, coherent financial support, including capacity building, and regular dialogue between sovereign debtors and creditors (Berensmann, 2022).

To improve intergenerational justice, the G20 Common Framework's debt treatment should be linked to investments in the SDGs and climate. In addition, IMF / WB monitoring and assessment tools, such as debt sustainability analyses, should take into account sustainability risks such as climate change, and should also consider the level of investment in climate adaptation, as these investments decrease the risks associated with climate change (Berensmann et al., 2022; Volz et al., 2022).

REFERENCES

Berensmann, K. (2018). The Global Debt Governance System for Developing Countries: Deficiencies and Reform Proposals. *Third World Thematics: A TWQ Journal*, *2*(6), 863–81.

Berensmann, K. (2022). How Could a New Universal Code of Conduct Prevent and Resolve Sovereign Debt Crises? Proposals for Design and Implementation. *Journal of Economic Surveys*, *37*(3), 747–88.

Berensmann, K., Heitzig, C., Ekeruche, M., Ordu, A., & Senbet, L. 2022. Resolving Debt Crises in Developing Countries: How Can the G20 Contribute to Operationalising the Common Framework? *T20 Policy Brief.*

G20 / Paris Club (2020). Common Framework for Debt Treatments beyond DSSI, Paris, https://clubdeparis.org/sites/default/files/annex_common_framework_for_debt_treatments_beyond_the_dssi.pdf.

Georgieva, K. & Pazarbasioglu, C. 2021. The G20 Common Framework for Debt Treatments Must Be Stepped Up. IMF Blog, 2. December 2021, https://www.imf.org/en/Blogs/Articles/2021/12/02/blog120221the-g20-common-framework-for-debt-treatments-must-be-stepped-up.

Henning, C. R. (2023). How to Make Sovereign Debt Restructuring Work Now. *CIGI Policy Brief No. 179*. Centre for International Governance Innovation.

IMF. (2024). *List of LIC DSAs for PRGT-eligible Countries*. International Monetary Fund.

Loko, B., Montfort, M., Raj, N., & Kadima, K. (2003). The Impact of External Indebtedness on Poverty in Low-Income Countries. *IMF Working Paper, lokoWP/03/61*. International Monetary Fund.

Maldonado, F. & Gallagher, K. P. (2022). *Climate Change and IMF Debt Sustainability Analysis*. The Task Force on Climate, Development and the IMF.

Rivetti, D. (2021). *Debt Transparency in Developing Economies*. World Bank.

Siaba Serrate, J., Berensmann, K., Carey, R., Weber, R., Alexandroff, A., Bradford, C., Estevão, M., Henning, R., Thornton, S., Wihardja, M. & Yu Ye (2024): How Can the G20 Contribute to Debt Sustainability in Low- and Middle-Income Countries? *T20 Policy Brief.*

Volz, U., Akhtar, S., Gallagher, K. P., Griffith-Jones, S. & Jörg Haas, with a contribution by Moritz Kraemer (2020). *Debt Relief for a Green and Inclusive Recovery: A Proposal*. Heinrich Böll Foundation; Center for Sustainable Finance, SOAS, University of London; Global Development Policy Center, Boston University.

Volz, U. (2022). Climate-Proofing the Global Financial Safety Net. *Journal of Globalization and Development*. *13*(1), 1–30.

World Bank. (2023). *International Debt Statistics*. Washington.

Chapter 15

FAIRNESS IN THE GLOBAL SOVEREIGN BORROWING REGIME

Juri Viehoff

INTRODUCTION

One of the most persistent calls for reform of the global financial system relates to the issue of poorest-country debt: for many years, a broad coalition of ideologically diverse actors, ranging from globalisation critical civil society players like ATTAC (Association for the Taxation of Financial Transactions and Citizens' Action) over (some) UN agencies to the Catholic Church, have demanded an across-the-board cancellation of such sovereign debt and a comprehensive reform of the existing legal system that enables the enforcement of such putative obligations. Yet, as this chapter will show, the problem of poorest-country-debt is but one of the normative issues that arise in the context of reflecting on the fairness and justice of the global borrowing regime (GBR). Indeed, I will suggest that although debt relief is arguably the most pressing issue, it is, morally speaking, one of the less complex ones given that insistence on repayment of such debt is morally wrong for a host of reasons, and, conversely, the moral case for cancellation is multiply overdetermined.[1] Nonetheless, analysing paradigmatic cases of this overdetermined kind can be helpful to lay bare the anatomy of those values that should inform a just and fair GBR generally.

The next section organises the questions that form part of a normative assessment of any borrowing regime. I then turn to the domain of global economic governance and describe the existing ground rules of sovereign borrowing. In the subsequent section, I look at some recent criticisms of the GBR, both concerning poor-country debt and sovereign debt more generally, and list suggestions for improvement based on normative arguments. I do note, however, two worries about existing normative arguments about sovereign debt regimes in the section after that. Building on these worries,

[1] None of this is to suggest that there are not complex empirical questions here about how to best execute such relief (see Berensmann, Chapter 14 in this volume).

I propose some directions for future research at the nexus of global justice and sovereign debt.

DEBT AND BORROWING: BACKGROUND AND METHODOLOGICAL ISSUES

Debt and Borrowing Regimes

Debt-making and debt-related financial phenomena are ubiquitous. Still, some clarifying of the relevant terrain and defining of terms is essential: first, 'debt' (or 'debt obligation', 'debt contract') refers to a bi-directional legal and economic relationship in which some agent (called 'debtor' or 'borrower') has received some financial or non-financial asset and, as a result, has incurred a legal obligation to pay some financial or other contribution to another agent (called 'creditor' or 'lender') in the future. Typically, but not necessarily, borrowers incur an obligation to repay more than the amount received (the 'principal'). Interests are assets owed over and above the principal. Transactions through which debt is created can take on many different forms, ranging from simple promissory notes to highly complex financial instruments, for example, contingent convertible bonds, collateralised debt obligations, etc. More narrowly, debt is typically distinguished in commercial contexts from other securities in terms of its payment structure: as a fixed-income instrument, debt requires repayment of predetermined amounts on a set schedule. As opposed to loans, *bonds* – either commercial or public-issued – are standardised debt securities that are transferable/tradeable.

The logical correlative of debt is credit: whenever a debt is created in the economy, some agent assumes the structural position of the debtor and another that of the creditor. By a *borrowing regime,* I mean the totality of laws, rules, conventions and systemic constraints that determine how agents distinguished by their structural position as debtor or creditor interact in the process of creating and repaying credit/debt obligations. So, for example, the backbone of the debt-making regime of domestic capitalist states are the legal rules governing private contracts (which determine, inter alia, who can enter a debt contract and grants contracting parties extensive freedom to set their own terms in making loans), but also more specific regulations governing debt (for example maximum permissible interest rates for consumers, rules for asset-backed lending, etc.). These legal rules operate against the structural features of the broader capitalist economic and financial system. Under contemporary capitalism, the allocation of capital to productive assets is set by financial markets, and banks (but not individuals) act as financial intermediaries and create deposit money by extending credit to agents in the real economy.

Key Normative Issues

The concept of 'debt' is, for better or worse, pervasive in everyday talk and is deeply coloured by moral assessments: we speak of 'moral debt' towards others, whereby we mean, roughly, that the other whom we owe is due moral gratitude, or that we would wrong them if we did not 'repay' them what they are owed. The problem to which this dual use gives rise is a frequent equivocation between 'financial debt' and 'moral debt'. Whereas facts about what we morally owe to others are set by the moral reason we have, facts about financial debt are set by prevailing conventions. When we ask about the *fairness* or *justice* of some borrowing regime, we ask, in effect, in what relationship prevailing (legal, customary, economic) conventions about the repayment of financial liabilities stand to convention-independent standards of morality. Amongst these standards of moral assessment, we can distinguish between the following dimensions.

When we assess the *justice* or *fairness* of a regime, we pass judgement on the substantive results in terms of the interpersonal distribution of burdens and benefits that the regime foreseeably creates/permits. If, on the other hand, we assess the *legitimacy* (or procedural/political justice) of a regime, we judge whether the procedures by which the conventions that generate fair/unfair consequences are created are morally adequate. Finally, both fairness/justice and legitimacy play their part in assessing what we might call the *overall justifiability* of a regime. In other words, we weigh all the moral reasons (procedural and substantive) that speak for or against these or alternative conventions, and we deem a regime justifiable in case it is the most justifiable arrangement or at least a sufficiently close approximation.

In this piece, I look at the *macro-level* issues of debt-making and public borrowing practices in the international public domain. Within it, we should distinguish procedural and substantive issues: amongst the *procedural* issues, I count the question of who ought to make the rules governing the substantive questions, and who gets to adjudicate on whether legal norms have been respected.[2] Procedural matters capture the normative dimension of whether those subject to these rules have pro tanto reasons to accept them, quite independently of their substantive outcomes. Amongst *substantive* ones, I count (i) how sovereign debt is created and by whom, (ii) who bears duties to repay such debt, (iii) under what conditions such duties cease to exist, and (iv) who is entitled to demand and enforce payment of debt obligations. These

[2] I do not discuss normative micro- and intermediate-level questions, for example whether or not, at a micro-level, international human rights legislation should include a 'human right to credit' and what the implication of such a right would be (Padgett Walsh & Lewiston, 2020). Nor can I engage here with some intermediate-level questions of sovereign-debt making, for example which *types* of conditionalities lending agents may impose on borrower states (Barry, 2011; Fabre, 2018).

are 'substantive' issues because, even though they relate to specific rules that govern the permissibility of individual agential behaviour, particular ways of filling out their content foreseeably lead to particular distributions of benefits and burdens amongst different categories of agents (for example borrowers vs. creditors) and, ultimately, between real human beings.

THE GLOBAL BORROWING REGIME WE HAVE

Procedural Features

To morally evaluate the current GBR, we first need an account of what its most important features are, both procedurally and substantively. Let us begin with its procedures, most importantly:

> *Fragmentation*: There is no single coherent set of rules and decision-making/decision-enforcing institutions that applies to all participating states and non-state actors equally.

This first assumption may sound surprising, given that all states are subject to international law, and international law contains norms about debt repayment. Nonetheless, fragmentation turns out to be the best characterisation when we compare basic procedural components to that which prevails for state-level borrowing regimes of a (capitalist) state mentioned above: the GBR is at best a primitive legal system. As a result, it has no centralised authority that can enact, enforce, and adjudicate substantive principles. It is thus piecemeal, consisting of some basic principles and norms of international law that apply to all sovereigns, the de facto reigning practices that have developed between sovereign borrowers and lenders, as well as a complicated net of litigating bodies and national courts that rely on other state and non-state agents to abide by and enforce their decisions. Beyond this, there is one set of borrowing practices for states without access to sovereign debt markets that are governed by rules of global economic governance institutions (World Bank, International Monetary Fund, regional development banks) and quite another one for fiscally more sovereign states (within the latter, it is also important to distinguish between those that can issue debt in their currency and those that cannot). Each of these distinct spheres has its own rules – and none of them exhibit the systematic and transparent structure of accountability and functional differentiation between norm-making, norm-interpretation, and norm-enforcement comparable to state-level borrowing regimes. Moreover, *Fragmentation* goes hand in hand with:

> *Power Asymmetry:* The vast majority of rules (both formal and informal), that govern the GBR are set by creditors and capital-exporting states.

Whether we look at the internal decision-making rules of IMF and World Bank (voting share based on paid-in capital), the location and state-affiliation of international arbitration bodies and national courts that decide on important matters regarding sovereign debt, or the agents capable of collectively enforcing such rulings (commercial banks, lender governments, etc.), there is overwhelming evidence that decision-making power is highly concentrated amongst one side in the structural debtor/creditor divide.

Substantive Features of the GBR

Core substantive elements of the existing GBR (insofar as they apply to all agents, see above), concern the issue of (i) who can incur sovereign debt, (ii) who is subsequently obligated to repay it, (iii) what substantive duties creditors and debtors incur through sovereign debt contracts, and (iv) who is legally empowered and de facto capable of enforcing such debt obligations. In relation to (i) and (ii), one fundamental cornerstone is:

> *Permissive attribution*: When a duly authorised state official concludes a sovereign debt obligation with lenders, that obligation is incurred by the state as a collective (as principal) through the official's actions (as agent).

The idea is straightforward: states are collective agents, and they can incur legal obligations when those vested with decision-making authority act on their behalf. Decision-making authority here is understood as a valid form of legal representation analogous to fiduciary relations in domestic law. But the principle is labelled one of 'permissive' attribution because, in contrast to fiduciary transactions in nearly all domestic legal systems, those *receiving* state consent need not, legally speaking, engage in any significant due diligence regarding the propriety of the claimed authorisation relation between the nominal borrower (the government official) and the agent incurring a duty to repay ('the state' and, ultimately, the citizens that will repay the debt), nor must the creditor act on evidence that the official is violating a fiduciary duty to act in the principal's interests (Dimitriu, 2017, p. 80).

Perhaps the most widely discussed principle governing sovereign debt contracts is a rigid norm of contractual obligations, namely:

> *Pacta sunt servanda*: Debt obligations are binding, even against significant changes in circumstances. There is a strong presumption against alteration or avoidance.

In the words of Odette Lienau, when it comes to the GBR, 'basic expectations resolve into one background rule: sovereign borrowers must repay, regardless of the circumstances of the initial debt contract, the actual use of loan proceeds, or the exigencies of any potential default' (2014, p. 1). This key principle is enshrined in international treaties that are considered customary international law (that is, binding on states, not parts of these treaties), it is de facto entrenched in virtue of the global financial marketplace that 'punishes' those in breech; and it is part and parcel of the (tacitly assumed) normative outlook of policy-makers, international governance institutions, as witnessed, for example, in the framing of the vocabulary on debt-contract alterations in terms of 'relief', 'forgiveness', 'assistance' and so forth (Barry & Tomitova, 2007, p. 54).

Most sovereign debt obligations typically have various protection, acceleration and blanket default clauses. These allow lenders not only to 'call' the bond, that is, insist on immediate repayment when a payment on *that specific instrument* is missed, but to do so and claim various forms of creditor protection in case a state discontinues payment on *any single outstanding instrument* of its total debt obligations (Wollner, 2018, p. 346). As a combined consequence of pacta sunt servanda and creditor-favouring norms, states that do encounter payment difficulties typically either default and largely lose access to credit and become subject to various decentralised enforcement measures (for example the case of Argentina at various historical points), or they have to subject themselves to significant foreign control and embark on austerity (e.g. in the case of Greece after 2009) (Viehoff, 2018, 388).

MAJOR MORAL SHORTCOMINGS OF THE EXISTING GBR

Of those philosophers writing about the GBR, none have maintained that it is anywhere close to a (sufficiently) justified institutional regime. Starting with the procedural features of the system, each of the elements described above has received sustained criticism. Below I briefly refer to these various criticisms before noting some open questions and tentatively proposing a more unified framework for ordering our normative judgements about what a justified (or, at any rate, significantly *more* justified) GBR would look like.

Problems of Procedural Justice in the GBR

Both *fragmentation* and *power asymmetry* strongly indicate a lack of procedural legitimacy of the existing GBR: first, because of how its fundamental ground rules are *nominally* made. Second, because of who is de facto subject to what set of formal and informal norms. Third, because of who is de facto capable of enforcing rules governing the GBR. On the first: there is no fair and representative legislative process by which the applicable norms of public international law are made. Rather, core provisions (for example *pacta sunt servanda*) stem from a time that precedes the legal existence of many debtor states as sovereigns, and, these norms being deemed to form part of customary international law, they legally bind all states irrespective of their democratically declared will. Second, as per *fragmentation*, there are several borrowing regimes in place, and those rules that govern poor-country debt in particular are not made or enforced in a procedurally just way. For example: states unable to access global capital markets to issue debt crucially depend on the global financial governance institutions (World Bank and IMF) but voting power within these institutions is dramatically skewed towards creditor states. It is thus unsurprising that several scholars have criticised the legitimacy of decision-making procedures in these institutions (e.g. Woods & Narlikar, 2001). Third, as per *power asymmetry*, even if it were the case that these global financial governance institutions had more equitable legislative procedures in place, it is far from clear that creditor states and creditors more generally (lending banks, investments funds, etc.) could be compelled to comply with their rules. Thus, the GBR is procedurally unjust.

Importantly, this verdict holds irrespective of whether one adopts a more cosmopolitan-individualist or a statist-internationalist perspective on matters of global justice: whether we look at state-level interactions or the effect that these rules have on individuals in borrowing states, the proper diagnosis is one of structural *domination* of *subordination*: it is an instance of individual and collective *domination* because one type of agent can arbitrarily and (typically) unilaterally exercise unchecked power over other collective agents and their members. This seems true on most Republican variants of how to spell out the arbitrariness condition, for example in terms of 'not being forced to track the subjects' interests, in terms of 'not being bound by rules', or in terms of 'not being subject to a democratic will' (e.g. Pettit, 2012). It is an instance of *subordination* because the entrenched de facto power asymmetry inherent in the GBR, lacking any adequate justification, expresses or can be reasonably taken to express a hierarchy of worth between those persons who wield power (creditors) and those subject to it (borrowers) (Kolodny, 2014).

Problems of Substantive Fairness

First, consider the underlying logic and expectable consequences of the norm of permissive attribution: not only does it allow corrupt public officials to legally incur debt on behalf of (frequently poor) populations that have neither authorised nor will benefit from such obligations, but it also perpetuates, through the benefits that can be derived from this 'borrowing privilege', their corrupt and authoritarian rule, and it burdens transitional democratic regimes with paying for the ill-gotten gains of their tyrannic predecessors. Moreover, the existing GBR incentivises parties engaged in civil conflict to ruthlessly pursue full control over the government machinery the sovereign borrowing privilege being one major element in the spoils of war.

Thomas Pogge suggests that this predictable process of resource misattribution and prolongation of conflicts foreseeably and avoidably causes poor people in countries to be worse off than they could otherwise be, and he, therefore, maintains that the existing GBR's features of *pacta sunt servanda* and *permissive attribution* are unjust and should be revised (Pogge, 2005a, 2005b). On this first reading then, the GBR is substantively unfair because it avoidably imposes serious burdens on those already worse off from a global distributive perspective.

Whilst Pogge's position seems plausible, it comes with the argumentative burden that, for the GBR to be unjust, it must be shown that (a) its present features contribute to unjust (because subsistence-rights-violating) outcomes and (b) that there is a feasible alternative that would avoid these outcomes. Especially (b) may be considered tricky to establish, as any borrowing regime exists of voluntary transactions between debtors and creditors so that any shift in rules about who may borrow, or on what terms repayment needs to proceed could significantly alter the de facto practices of sovereign debt. For example, increasing borrower protection may cause sovereign-debt-making opportunities for poor states to diminish or dry up as creditors opt for less risky, more profitable alternative investments.

Others have suggested that rather than faulting the existing GBR for its contribution to perpetuating poverty and global inequality, we should deem it inappropriate for the moral failures inherent in the way in which it attributes liability, *whether or not* these ways lead to inequality and poverty. Dimitriu for example, draws an analogy to domestic agency law and argues that any set of rules where a (purported) agent can incur unjustified and uncontrolled obligations for a principal in a principal–agent relationship is unfair towards the principal. Likewise, a system is unfair and flawed when those benefiting from transacting with the (putative) agent have no duty of care to verify whether the agent is representing the principal or acting in their best interest (Dimitriu, 2015; 2019). By violating basic moral principles underpinning domestic agency/fiduciary laws and wider principles of acting for others, the GBR is unfair and unjust.[3] Whilst Dimitru offers important insights into how sovereign-debt-making practices can be unfair without causing poverty and harm, it faces two difficulties: first, it cannot plausibly account for why illegitimately incurred debt for poor countries strikes us as *especially* morally troubling. The most plausible answer seems to be that such obligations are problematic because of the cost they impose on those already badly off. A second challenge arises when we ask why we should accept a system of acting for others in the first place: isn't the point of agency laws that they make the lives of those on whose behalf the government acts *better*, that is, aren't

[3] On the moral foundations of acting for others, see Viehoff (2022).

the right rules of who should be liable for what actions incurred by others about which set of rules produces the best consequences after all?[4]

Other authors have combined assessments of unjust rules and harmful outcomes: both Barry and Tomitova (2007) and Wiedenbrüg (2018a; 2018b) argue that odious debt violates basic constraints of fairness *because* those who now have to repay it (current populations in poor countries) have *neither* benefited nor voluntarily accepted these liabilities (Barry & Tomitova, 2007; Wiedenbrüg, 2018a; 2018b). Beyond the issue of odious debt, the GBR also suffers, because of the incredible strictness of the 'pacta sunt servanda' provision, from basic fairness in terms of the respective duties that creditors and debtors incur. Perhaps most notably, the existing regime unfairly fails to hold wealthy states and agents accountable for what we may call 'creditor hazard': irresponsible lending is not institutionally punished, but burdens are systematically shifted towards borrowers (Wiedenbrüg, 2018b; Wollner, 2018).

FUTURE DIRECTIONS FOR JUSTICE AND THE GBR

Difficulties with Interpersonal / Domestic Analogies

Most existing approaches, perhaps with the exception of Pogge's, rely on the idea that we can build our moral assessments of the GBR from the application of either (i) interpersonal moral principles or (ii) the one-for-one transfer of specific legal institutions of domestic legal systems (most notably contract law, but also agency law, bankruptcy law, tort, and so on) to the global domain. I want to suggest that both (i) and (ii) are problematic and that future research should seek to develop an 'integrationist' framework that pays better attention to the GBR's embeddedness in other features of the world economy.

First, it is problematic to derive moral conclusions for a macro-domain like the GBR from imperfect analogies to the morality of interpersonal behaviour, most notably the morality of promising. This is in effect what those who have tried to vindicate *pacta sunt servanda* have typically done: like individuals, states should keep their promises, including their promises to repay debt. But as Shiffrin has pointed out, even the institution of domestic contract law is only indirectly connected to the morality of promising (Shiffrin, 2012). Any legal regime, domestic or global, must pay attention to a plurality of values and pragmatic considerations. Whether or not a person (or collective) is morally bound to keep their promise is a different issue from whether or not a public system of rules should be organised in such a way that promises are enforced against the promisor. Any moral assessment of the GBR ought to be evaluating

[4] The strict demands on agents/fiduciaries to avoid conflicts, for example, may be more of a response to what keeps an effective system of acting for others in place rather than a perfectly fair balancing of the principal and the agent's interests.

it holistically, that is as a social arrangement that must pay attention to a number of values including, but certainly not limited to the morality of promising, the respect for rights, the total amount of well-being that different rules are likely to produce and how this well-being is distributed, and so forth.

Second, it is likewise problematic to assess the GBR by evaluating whether or not it observes seemingly moral principles inherent in specific legal constructs of domestic law, for example agency law or tort law. What this neglects is the fact that, in domestic legal systems, those legal institutions to which authors appeal for reform of the GBR (say the rules governing fiduciary obligations) exist alongside each other and are, at least in well-functioning legal systems, complementary and co-dependent. For example: fiduciary/agency law is what it is because we need, in commercial contexts, to strike a balance between, on the one hand, allowing private persons to gain the benefits from being represented and, on the other hand, limiting cases in which attribution fails and counterparties are left without a remedy. But how these factors are normatively evaluated depends on what other legal and social institutions there are (for example welfare state provisions, opportunities to appeal decisions, etc.). Likewise, there is no guarantee that the relevant values and interests in the global case correspond closely to those we find domestically. So merely appealing to the benefits and justifiability of existing domestic institutions is insufficient as a normative argument about how to reform the GBR.

An Integrationist Approach to the GBR?

The last point above helps to relate the issue of the GBR to a wider theoretical issue in current debates about global justice, namely the question of *internalist* vs. *integrationist* approaches to specific domains. Perhaps the right way of thinking about the GBR is not in terms of unique features that make the practices of sovereign-debt-making fair or just, but in terms of the contribution that it can make to the overall realisation of certain more abstract distributive goals. 'Integrationist' approaches have, for example, recently been proposed for the domains of climate change governance, but also for international tax governance and transnational trade (Caney, 2012; 2016; Kern, 2020; Walton, 2020). In relation to the sovereign debt regime, integrationist approaches potentially also hold the promise of resolving a methodological difficulty that reflection on any borrowing regime brings into focus, namely whether and how it possibly describes the GBR's core features in isolation, independent of other pertinent features of the global economy system, most notably the fact that it is one of *financial* capitalism that exhibits a dramatic core-periphery dynamic.

Let me give one crucial example: standardly, creditors have claims to future income streams from the debtors that are monetary. So, debt obligations are ultimately claims on another financial asset class, currency. One resulting complication is that sovereign debt-related normative questions thereby necessarily become interwoven with monetary questions, both in their substantive and their procedural dimension: since, substantively, we are concerned with the distributive effects that debt obligations have on some more fundamental measure (say well-being, or resources, or human capabilities), changes in the relationship between the fiat currency in which the debt is denominated and the correct standard of distributive justice matter for how we should assess their fairness. And since *control* over the fiat money in which debt must be repaid amounts to control over the distributive effect of debt obligations, questions of procedural justice by which rules governing borrowing regimes should be made are shaped by who controls *currency*.

This matters for any real-world assessment of the GBR because there are two options about who controls the currency in which sovereign debt is denominated: if a government issues local currency debt, then it is, at least to some extent, within the control of the debtor how costly repayment of the bond is going to be. At least theoretically, a government can reduce the 'real' costs of repayment by inflating the debt-denominating currency. Alternatively, sovereign debt can be (and frequently is) issued in some global reserve currency, as a result of which neither borrower nor lender have any significant control over debt inflation. But this alternative too shapes justice-relevant issues. For example, reserve-currency-denominated debt increases the risk of the state defaulting on its obligations, which carries very serious consequences for the borrowing state's ability to access credit markets in the future. And at a systemic level, the existence of global reserve and debt-issuing currencies that are controlled by (and benefit) some states over others raises thorny issues of monetary fairness. The upshot of all this is that under financial capitalism, it seems quite ad hoc to propose rules governing GBR independent of a fuller consideration of the embedding system of capital and credit creation.

What would an integrationist approach to justice of the GBR look like? We would start with the core interests that individuals and states have in being able to access credit: what makes access to credit valuable is, ultimately, the ability to intertemporally distribute spending, which matters for leading an autonomous life. How well this particular interest is satisfied constitutes one element in the overall advantage that individuals (and, when organised as a collective, their state) enjoy in the international realm. Understanding what a fair or just GBR looks like will then require us to assess what absolute level of capabilities and what level of advantage people ought to have, and to design institutions that integrate the demands for fairness across different domains.

CONCLUSION

I have focused on the core objections that philosophers have advanced against the existing GBR, documenting the multiple reasons for which demands that poor countries repay their debt are morally problematic. Having pointed to some difficulties that different arguments face, I have suggested that, perhaps, a more integrationist approach to sovereign debt that pays closer attention to the overall distribution of benefits and burdens in the global economy (not just about sovereign debt-making) promises to resolve some of these difficulties. My discussion only amounts to a few pointers of where future researchers may fruitfully connect the issue of the GBR to wider debates in global justice. Re-orienting the debate in this way would, I hope, pave the way to more systematic and morally sound proposals for governance reform of the GBR.

REFERENCES

Barry, C. (2011). Sovereign Debt, Human Rights, and Policy Conditionality. *Journal of Political Philosophy, 19*(3), 282–305.

Barry, C., & Tomitova, L. (2007). Fairness in Sovereign Debt. In Barry, C., Herman, B. & Tomitova, L., (eds.), *Dealing Fairly with Developing Country Debt*, 41–79. Blackwell Publishing.

Caney, S. (2012). Just Emissions. *Philosophy and Public Affairs, 40*(4), 255–300.

Caney, S. (2016). The Struggle for Climate Justice in a Non-ideal World. *Midwest Studies in Philosophy, 40*(1), 9–26.

Dimitriu, C. (2015). Odious Debts: A Moral Account. *Jurisprudence, 6*(3), 470–91.

Dimitriu, C. (2017). Agency Law and Odious Debts. *Ethics & Global Politics, 10*(1), 77–97.

Dimitriu, C. (2019). The Irrelevance of Poverty for the Morality of the Lending System. *Critical Review of International Social and Political Philosophy*, 1–15.

Fabre, C. (2018). Economic Statecraft: Human Rights, Sanctions, and Conditionality. *Harvard University Press.*

Kern, A. (2020). Illusions of Justice in International Taxation. *Philosophy & Public Affairs, 48*(2), 151–84.

Kolodny, N. (2014). Rule over None II: Social Equality and the Justification of Democracy. *Philosophy & Public Affairs, 42(4)*, 287–336.

Lienau, O. (2014). Rethinking Sovereign Debt. *Harvard University Press.*

Padgett Walsh, K., & Lewiston, J. (2020). Human Capabilities and the Ethics of Debt. *The Journal of Value Inquiry.*

Pettit, P. (2012). *On the People's Terms: A Republican Theory and Model of Democracy*. Cambridge University Press.

Pogge, T. (2005a). Real-World Justice. *The Journal of Ethics, 9*(1–2), 29–53.

Pogge, T. (2005b). Recognized and Violated by International Law: The Human Rights of the Global Poor. *Leiden Journal of International Law, 18*, 717.

Shiffrin, S. (2012). Are Contracts Promises. In Marmor, A., (ed.), *Routledge Companion to Philosophy of Law*. Routledge.

Viehoff, D. (2022). Legitimate Injustice and Acting for Others. *Philosophy & Public Affairs, 32*(1).

Viehoff, J. (2018). Eurozone Justice. *Journal of Political Philosophy, 26*(3), 388–414.

Walton, A. (2020). Trade Justice: An Argument for Integrationist, Not Internal, Principles. *Journal of Political Philosophy, 28*(1), 51–72.

Wiedenbrüg, A. (2018a). What Citizens Owe: Two Grounds for Challenging Debt Repayment. *Journal of Political Philosophy, 26*(3), 368–87.

Wiedenbrüg, A. (2018b). What Creditors Owe. *Constellations*, *25*(1), 101–16.
Wollner, G. (2018). Morally Bankrupt: International Financial Governance and the Ethics of Sovereign Default. *Journal of Political Philosophy*, *26*(3), 344–67.
Woods, N., & Narlikar, A. (2001). Governance and the Limits of Accountability: The WTO, the IMF, and the World Bank. *International Social Science Journal*, *53*(170), 569–83.

Chapter 16

DISTRIBUTIONAL EFFECTS OF A GLOBALISED DIGITAL ECONOMY

Florian Hett and Jakob Schwab[1]

INTRODUCTION

Digital technologies are used in arguably all sectors of the economy and the private sphere. They connect people all over the world, alter production structures and facilitate new business models. As the digitalisation of the economy has the potential to profoundly change global economic interactions, it is likely to also change distributional outcomes.

This chapter analyses possible distributional consequences of the globalised digital economy along different dimensions, including intra- and intergenerational socioeconomic distributions and the distribution of political control. We discuss the resulting national and international policy options to address potentially undesired distributional consequences. Specifically, we offer empirical predictions that can be evaluated against normative theories of justice, thereby contributing to the analysis of justice in global economic governance. Our conjectures build on the application of basic economic theory to what we consider characteristic, specific features of the digital economy.

Analysing the distributional effects of the digital economy first requires identifying its inherently novel features. To do so, we consider a simple but powerful definition of digitalisation: 'Digital technology is the representation of information in bits' (Goldfarb & Tucker, 2019). Technologically, this implies that information (narrowly captured in the form of 'data') is available in larger amounts and at higher speed, which – in essential economic terms – implies data to be cheaper. Accordingly, business models that rely on data ('data-driven') are a substantial and characteristic element of the digital economy. While we agree with Johannes Himmelreich (in this volume) that many companies of the digital economy supply some form of infrastructure, we argue that business models based on the collection of data entail some specific features that justifies putting the focus on them. We argue that the

[1] We thank Erik Faller for excellent research assistance.

fact that the transfer of information is central to the interaction between firms and customers leads to distributional outcomes that are specific to the digital economy of data-driven business models.

While data-driven markets comprise a rather broad range of products and services, they also share some common features. First, many markets are characterised by strong concentration with only one, or a few, large supplying firm(s) serving most of the global demand. The headquarters of these firms are typically also geographically concentrated, most of them in the US, many in California but more recently also increasingly in China. Of the largest digital platforms (valued above 1 billion US dollars in 2015), only two come from Latin America or Africa, representing less than 1 per cent of all platforms by number and market valuation (UNCTAD, 2019).

Second, the explicit pecuniary prices of digital products are typically comparatively low or even zero, and many firms often still incur operating losses. Nevertheless, the corresponding stock market valuations of these companies are very high and mostly increasing: the Price-to-Earnings ratio, which indicates how much a company is valued by the market compared to the profits it currently incurs, is on average roughly 33 per cent higher for companies of the MSCI World and S&P 500 Information Technologies indices than for their traditional core counterparts (numbers for 2021). Companies like X (formerly Twitter) and Spotify are still in red numbers, despite their strong market power and broad customer base.[2]

Third, the markets for digital products cannot easily be – and are consequently largely not – regulated. There is no international organisation that is responsible for governing the global digital market. The only international organisation which has enacted an explicit policy is the WTO, which has manifested the non-regulation of the international transfer of digital products across borders in its Moratorium on Digitally Transferred Goods (ICC/ITC, 2023).

We argue that taken together, these characteristics – market concentration, low prices, operating losses, and lack of regulation – imply distinct distributional consequences. As digital markets in principle comprise the entire world, these consequences affect the distribution of economic profits and participation between high-income and low-income countries, where the different outcomes of firms and consumers are most prominently also manifested in a between-country division. In reference to the opening chapter, we analyse these distributional consequences along three dimensions:

- the contemporary, intragenerational, socioeconomic dimension (distributional effects between countries, as well as between firms and consumers),

[2] Source: Own computations using data from www.ishares.com.

- an intergenerational socioeconomic perspective (discussing to what extent the transactions of the digital economy have external effects on future generations),
- a political perspective (discussing the fact that many transactions in the digital economy are non-monetary and thus not observable, rendering them hard to control democratically).

In the next section, we outline the characteristics of the digital economy as a basis for the analysis that follows. The subsequent sections describe the distributional outcomes that our stylised digital economy implies, which we structure along the three dimensions of justice. Finally, we discuss the insights and policy options that arise from our analysis.

ECONOMIC CHARACTERISATION OF THE DIGITAL ECONOMY

Analysing distributional effects of the digital economy first requires conceptualising its characteristic features. As digitalisation has reached almost all parts of the economy, a clear delineation is not easy to make. In line with the definition by Goldfarb & Tucker (2019) from above, we therefore consider a company to be part of the digital economy if its business model critically depends on the utilisation of large amounts of data.

The corresponding markets are characterised by significant scale economies. First, products and services based on data typically exhibit large fixed costs and very small or even zero marginal costs, constituting *supply-side economies of scale*. For instance, consider a company which supplies a digital service. While the digital service may be bundled with other physical products or components, its central feature is typically an algorithm, whose development costs are high, but the marginal costs of supplying an additional consumer with the same service are very low. Second, digital services often entail network effects, also described as *demand side economies of scale*. For instance, many companies in the digital economy can be interpreted as platforms, where the users of the platform value the platform higher, the more other users are active on different sides of the same platform. Taken together, supply and demand side economies of scale imply strong tendencies for natural monopolies, as competitiveness increases with increasing production and sales. This explains the popular notion of 'winner-takes-all' markets inherent in many parts of the digital economy, as one or a few large firms can undercut competitors simply by being large (Shapiro & Varian, 1998).

The combination of demand- and supply-side economies of scale and the accompanied monopolistic tendencies are not a delimiting feature of data-driven business models as they are also present in other sectors and industries. However, we argue that they exhibit an additional and unique 'scale economy' mechanism: when a firm following a data-driven business model sells a product or a service, it reaps an additional benefit on top of the pecuniary price: it acquires additional consumer data while providing the service and executing the transaction. This data is of specific value to the firm as it reveals something about the tastes and demand structure of the respective customer. Together with the according data from other transactions from other customers, this allows the firm to improve its ability to price discriminate, that is, to adjust product and service features and in particular the prices in future transactions with this or other customers (Bergemann & Bonatti, 2019, Fudenberg & Villas-Boas, 2012). Ultimately, this allows the firm to acquire a larger share of the surplus of the transaction and increase profits at the cost of the net benefit of consumers (Belleflamme & Peitz, 2015). If the ability to price discriminate and hence the value of transaction data increases in the amount of customer data (Grunes & Stucke, 2016), this represents a further scale effect for firms with data-driven business models: the more transactions they carry out, the better they are in acquiring larger shares of the transaction surplus in the future.

Importantly, this additional benefit for the firm represents an externality from the perspective of the corresponding customer: the information generated through the transaction does not affect the conditions of the transaction itself, but could only be used in future transactions, which may or may not be with the same individual. Hence, even a rational consumer will typically not take this effect into (full) account. What is more, recent literature shows that in fact consumers are often not necessarily deciding rationally with respect to their personal data and privacy – a phenomenon referred to as the 'digital privacy paradox'. This makes it unlikely that consumers demand an appropriate compensation for implicitly revealing their data while acquiring a digital service (see Acquisti et al., 2016, for an overview).

DISTRIBUTIONAL OUTCOMES OF THE DIGITAL ECONOMY

We now analyse theoretically how the digital economy as characterised above induces which types of distributional effects. We consider a 'North-South' setting, as the most relevant dimension of global distribution is arguably that of benefits between high-income (the Global North) and low-income countries (the Global South).

There are several reasons to assume that new digital products and services are first developed and marketed in countries of the Global North: due to comparatively high development costs for new digital products and services, access to capital markets is imperative for financing upfront costs. Typically, firms in developed countries obtain this access much more easily, for instance due to more developed domestic financial markets or higher levels of collateral and larger expected domestic profits (Holmstrom & Tirole, 1997). Finally, differences in the level of human capital between developed and developing countries make it more likely that new business ideas are first developed and then domestically brought to the market in the North.

Once a new market emerges, the monopolistic tendencies described above provide the incumbent firm(s) with a competitive advantage, such that other firms are effectively inhibited to enter if no regulation is in place. Because transport costs for digital products and services are low or even zero, 'natural' barriers to trade across borders – a crucial feature of classic industries – are almost non-existent. Companies from the Global North can easily expand internationally to countries of the Global South. Companies in the South face the same barriers to market entry in their own domestic markets as do potential competitors in the home country of the incumbent monopolist.

To facilitate market entry by firms from the Global South in their home markets, one would need to prohibit foreign firms from entering markets in the respective developing country. In what follows, we consider such a situation of de facto *internationally closed digital markets* as the relevant theoretical counterfactual for identifying distributional effects of the globalised digital economy. This approach saves on taxonomical exposition and provides the basis for a more nuanced discussion of the policy options after the analysis of the distributional outcomes along the three dimensions.

INTRAGENERATIONAL DISTRIBUTION

The most obvious distributional effects concern the division of income between active, contemporaneous economic agents: who benefits from open digital markets as compared to de facto internationally closed digital markets?

Standard microeconomic theory of monopolistic behaviour states that a monopolist with stronger scale economies and lower marginal costs produces larger quantities and/or qualities and sells at lower prices. Hence, an already existing monopolist from the North will offer the respective digital product or service at lower prices (or higher quality, or both) than a potential domestic counterpart. The increasing value of consumer data implies that firms with a larger existing user base (and hence a larger existing stock of consumer data) also have a higher value of taking on additional customers. Hence, they are willing to sell their services at even lower prices to acquire the accompanied data.

As a result, we see that an incumbent monopolist from the North will always be able to sell more units at lower prices to domestic consumers than a smaller local firm, even if the latter had the same technology available. As many digital services are free of direct monetary costs, it seems noteworthy that this does not prevent the described effect from playing out. If a firm already operates at the zero-lower bound of prices ('selling' its services for free), it has an incentive to invest more in improving the quality of the service to be competitive to obtain beneficial consumer data. These unambiguous effects on quantities, prices and quality of the digital products and services offered by the monopolist from the North represent a clear benefit for contemporaneous consumers in the South as compared to a situation where (only) a domestic firm serves the market: they get better products at better prices.

Moving to the perspective of (the owners of) firms, the increase in contemporaneous consumer welfare does not come at the cost of firm profits. In fact, realising the efficiency gains from scale effects allows the larger firm from the North to generate even higher additional profits than a domestic supplier would do, such that overall firm profits increase. However, it is likely that these increased profits ultimately do not represent income of domestic economic agents, as Northern firm ownership typically does not lie in the South. This represents a negative distributional effect from a Southern perspective: while firm profits generally increase due to the opening of digital markets, these profits are leaving the country. In comparison, profits of a domestic firm would, albeit being smaller, be more likely to remain domestically owned.

Comparing the two effects, it is not obvious whether the gains for domestic consumers outweigh the losses for owners of domestic firms and thus, whether the developing country overall suffers or profits from opening. Nevertheless, it is possible to identify factors making one or the other more or less likely. First, we consider the domestic market size: the larger the domestic market becomes, the more likely are the losses to domestic firms to outweigh the benefits for consumers when a foreign monopolist enters: for a domestic firm, the size of its local market determines the strength of scale economies it can realise – if the domestic market is small it will be served at higher prices. Therefore, the entering of a foreign firm reduces product prices, the stronger the smaller the domestic market, letting consumers in small domestic markets benefit more from opening. Moreover, the smaller the domestic market, the smaller are the (total and per-unit) profits for firms it could capture by serving the market by itself. Hence, in smaller domestic markets there are also lower domestic profits lost if a foreign firm enters. In sum, the larger the Southern country, the more likely it is to lose overall by opening its digital markets and vice versa.

Second, we consider the economic value of data. As argued above, consumers are not appropriately compensated for the value of the data that accrues during the economic transaction with the firm. Hence, a larger economic value of data reflects higher economic profits for supplying firms. Accordingly, the higher the value of data, the stronger bears the outflow of firm profits if the market is supplied by a foreign firm. Overall, this creates the paradoxical situation that while low prices and high qualities offered by a firm from the North seem to indicate particularly high benefits of its entrance, the country as a whole is actually worse off as the lost monopoly profits a domestic supplier could have earned (and kept domestically) are particularly large. Thus, as tempting as the technological leap may look that developing countries can achieve by attracting global monopolists into their markets, it might shift the distribution of benefits from international trade even more towards developed countries.

INTERGENERATIONAL DISTRIBUTION

Next, we turn to intergenerational distributional effects and ask how future consumers are affected by the opening of digital markets today. As argued above, detailed information about consumer characteristics and the corresponding demand behaviour improve a firm's ability to predict demand behaviour of subsequent consumers. These improved predictions allow adjusting product features and prices to absorb a higher share of the realised surplus from the economic transaction. Initially, this improved ability to price discriminate can even benefit consumers as it facilitates economic transactions that would not take place if firms were only able to offer uniform products and prices. However, with more data the precision by which the monopolist can tailor its offers to the preferences of individual consumers improves and its profits are increasingly fuelled by the forgone benefits of consumers (see Belleflamme & Peitz, 2015). As a result, with increasing amounts of data, the value this data represents for the possessing firm reflects a direct welfare loss of future consumers.

This implies a direct intergenerational redistribution inherent in economic transactions of digital products and services. While initial consumers benefit from low prices and high qualities as they give away their data, future consumers suffer from the intensified price discrimination enabled by the data originating in previous transactions. Importantly, both these effects – reduced prices and improved qualities for consumers today and lower consumer welfare in the future – are reflected in a higher value of consumer data. This means that the more a specific sector adheres to our characterisation of the digital economy by relying on utilising data as its business model, the more severe these intergenerational redistribution effects are.

These theoretical considerations are consistent with the commonly observed combination of very high stock market valuations of companies with data-driven business models despite relatively low operating profits or even losses. While the low to negative operating profits reflect the aggressive pricing necessary to acquire customer data, the corresponding high market valuations indicate the expectation that this data represents substantial opportunities for creating profits in the future.

DISTRIBUTION OF POLITICAL CONTROL

Next, we consider distributional implications along the political dimension. Democratic control is a resource which can be defined as the ability to politically influence procedures that affect oneself. In the digital economy many transactions affect people not directly taking part in them (external effects), both over time and across regions, thereby depriving these people of democratic control. What is already inherent to 'traditional' economic globalisation, namely that mobility of some (non-labour) factors of production implies less scope for democratic control, is even more pronounced in the digital economy: with the free transferability of data, its impact can be effective over greater distance and regulatory reach.

The collection of personal data does not only affect those from whom the data originated. Once companies obtain information about a critical mass of people, statistical methods allow extrapolating to others and predict their behaviour and characteristics (Acemoglu et al., 2022, Bergemann et al., 2022, Garratt & Van Oordt, 2021, Choi et al., 2019). This implies that even if the *collection* of data is regulated to protect those directly providing it, other individuals who are external to the specific transaction and therefore not able to influence this regulation are nonetheless affected. To provide these people with the corresponding democratic control would hence require regulating the *usage* of data. However, this seems much harder to implement.

The non-monetary character of transactions in the digital economy also implies a loss of control opportunities. When consumers use platforms without paying for them, there is no monetary value explicitly attached to the data transferred within this transaction that could be observed from outside the firm. Consequently, this type of interaction cannot be easily regulated by most traditional instruments, be taxed, or controlled via customs. In international taxation, the nexus principle dominates the division of profits by multinational firms. It states that their corporate taxes should accrue where the respective value added is created. Because this value added is measured in monetary terms, a consumer base that contributes to value added by supplying its personal data does not count for added value in the sense of the nexus principle. Similarly, the WTO agreement not to apply customs to digitally transferrable goods and services restricts developing countries to regulate cross-border activities of digital companies through established instruments of economic policy.

The institutional background of the international tax system is provided by the OECD (OECD 2018), and that on trade policy by the WTO. Both institutions are often criticised for not being democratically legitimised and not representing the interests of developing countries adequately, which remain underrepresented in decision processes (see Fung, 2017, for the OECD, and Narlikar, 2005, and Risse, 2012, Ch. 18, amongst others, for the WTO). The institutions creating rules of international conduct that restrict domestic democratic control of regulations of the digital economy and the data economy are thus themselves constituted without democratic control of those affected by their governance. Thus, the little democratic control that the digital economy still allows for is also skewed towards developed countries.

CONCLUSION AND POLICY IMPLICATIONS

The arguments made in this chapter suggest that an unregulated global digital economy has distributional effects that are overall to the disadvantage of developing countries. First, concurrently, because global digital monopolists serve markets all over the world and accrue resulting monopolistic rents that are particularly large when obtaining data is key to the business model. This income is consequently not accruing to producers in developing countries and likely outweighing the gains for consumers from the entry of a foreign monopolist. Secondly, the intergenerational distributional effects are also skewed to the disadvantage of developing countries: the firms who profit at cost of future consumers are concentrated in the Global North, while consumers are both in developed and developing countries. Thirdly, regulation of the digital economy is globally neglected or even inhibited, and those that are affected by it have no say in the rule-making procedures. This applies particularly for agents in developing countries and their representatives.

These predictions on adverse distributional effects critically hinge on the interpretation of the digital economy as one of data-driven business models. As far as the distributional outcomes derive from market failures, they are also globally inefficient. This applies to the external effects that occur towards non-participants in digital transactions today and tomorrow. One solution that is proposed is to give people the right to their data (see Jones & Tonetti, 2020). This would also tackle distributional issues between developed and developing countries because value creation by data provision could then be priced (and taxed) accordingly. However, because price discrimination is also possible from information about others than the affected, regulating how obtained data can be *used* may be imperative to improve economic outcomes, both in terms of efficiency and in terms of distribution.

The adverse outcomes can hardly be tackled by individual countries' regulation alone. The dominance of monopolists from a few countries in global markets of digital services amplifies an economic imbalance between North and South. Closing their markets to protect their own digital infant industries may not be a valid (or even beneficial) option for many, particularly smaller, developing countries. The case of China, who did exactly that by many measures of strict regulation combined with massive subsidisation of domestic digital giants, shows, that it can be an option for larger developing countries to participate in the gains from data accumulation. A measure implemented by many countries are data localisation requirements, which demand that foreign companies physically store data about their customers in the country of operation. This only ensures political control, however, but leaves the economic property rights untouched. Many developed countries also have or are planning to implement digital services taxes, among them the EU. Besides the agreed-upon minimum taxation of globally operating (digital) firms, a proposal on taxation of digital service provision by customer base is currently under discussion under the Inclusive Framework of the OECD in which more than 140 countries participate. While such a measure would help internalising some external effects, it requires much information by the governments on business models and consumer preferences and the discussions are prone to be tangled up in conflicts of interest.

The data economy is – in contrast to current practice – not only in need of economic regulation as any other market which involves market failures or stark distributional effects, but some of its characteristics make its regulation even more necessary. Its global reach calls for an international body to address the distributional consequences laid out in this chapter. A political regulation is particularly important because of the intergenerational consequences that this entails. It is then important to also include developing countries in this rule-making process over the regulation of global digital markets. This would enable them to politically influence a sphere they are greatly affected by and thus more democratically distribute political control of an area that will become even more central to the lives of all citizens of the world.

REFERENCES

Acemoglu, D., Makhdoumi, A., Malekian, A., & Ozdaglar, A. (2022). Too Much Data: Prices and Inefficiencies in Data Markets. *American Economic Journal: Microeconomics, 14*(4), 218–56.

Acquisti, A., Taylor, C., & Wagman, L. (2016). The Economics of Privacy. *Journal of Economic Literature, 54*(2), 442–92.

Belleflamme, P., & Peitz, M. (2015). *Industrial Organization: Markets and Strategies*. Cambridge University Press.

Bergemann, D., & Bonatti, A. (2019). Markets for Information: An Introduction. *Annual Review of Economics, 11*, 85–107.

Bergemann, D., Bonatti, A., & Gan, T. (2022). The Economics of Social Data. *The RAND Journal of Economics, 53*(2), 263–96.

Choi, J. P., Jeon, D. S., & Kim, B. C. (2019). Privacy and Personal Data Collection with Information Externalities. *Journal of Public Economics, 173*, 113–24.

Fudenberg, D., & Villas-Boas, J. M. (2012). In the Digital Economy. In Peitz, M. & J. Waldfogel (eds.), *The Oxford Handbook of the Digital Economy*, 254, Oxford University Press.

Fung, S. (2017). The Questionable Legitimacy of the OECD/G20 BEPS Project. *Erasmus Law Review*, 2.

Garratt, R., & Van Oordt, M. R. (2021). Privacy as a Public Good: A Case for Electronic Cash. *Journal of Political Economy, 129*(7), 2157–80.

Goldfarb, A., & Tucker, C. (2019). Digital Economics. *Journal of Economic Literature, 57*(1), 3-43.

Grunes, A., & Stucke, M. (2016). *Big Data and Competition Policy*. Oxford University Press.

Holmstrom, B., & Tirole, J. (1997). Financial Intermediation, Loanable Funds, and the Real Sector. *The Quarterly Journal of Economics, 112*(3), 663–91.

ICC/ITC (2023). The WTO Moratorium on Customs Duties on Electronic Transmissions: What Is Really at Stake? *Joint Policy Brief.*

Jones, C. I., & Tonetti, C. (2020). Nonrivalry and the Economics of Data. *American Economic Review, 110*(9), 2819–58.
Narlikar, A. (2005). *The World Trade Organization: A Very Short Introduction* (Vol. 135). Oxford University Press.
OECD (2018). *Tax Challenges Arising from Digitalisation – Interim Report 2018.*
Risse, M. (2012). *On Global Justice.* Princeton University Press.
Shapiro, C., Carl, S., & Varian, H. R. (1998). *Information Rules: A Strategic Guide to the Network Economy.* Harvard Business Press.
UNCTAD (2019). *Digital Economy Report 2019.*

Chapter 17

JUSTICE IN THE GLOBAL DIGITAL ECONOMY

Johannes Himmelreich

DIGITAL ECONOMY AS DIGITAL INFRASTRUCTURE

A first step is to get clear on what we are talking about: what is meant by 'digital economy'? For the purposes of this chapter, the digital economy is understood as consisting of those companies that produce infrastructure goods, which are provided or accessed online.[1] In a slogan, the digital economy is the *digital infrastructure*.

Consider some examples. Amazon is not only a retail operation but an online marketplace and fulfilment company. Google and Facebook, through their advertising networks, allow companies to track and influence customers. Cloud computing companies offer backend services like database hosting, fraud detection, code analysis, or budget management. Microsoft and others sell their software 'as a service'. Whether it is office apps, YouTube, Netflix, Spotify or Apple Music – the digital economy provides diverse resources for businesses' backend operations and the private production of leisure.

In short, the digital economy should be thought of as *infrastructure that is provided or accessed online*. The digital economy fits the three conditions of what it means for a resource to be an 'infrastructure' (Frischmann, 2013, p. 61). First, the resources can be consumed non-rivalrously. Second, the 'demand for the resource is driven primarily by downstream productive activity that requires the resource as an input'. Third, the 'resource may be used as an input into a wide range of goods and services, which may include private goods, public goods and social goods'. Moreover, the digital economy exhibits key features of infrastructures as they are investigated by infrastructure

[1] This chapter benefited from detailed comments by and thoughtful discussions with Lisa Herzog, Seth Lazar and Marco Meyer. Amir Arturo Javier Castellanos and Tatevik Khachatryan provided valuable research assistance. Potential conflict of interest disclosure: from 2017–2019 the author held a postdoctoral fellowship at Stanford University which was sponsored by Apple Inc, during which the author participated in activities at Apple University.

studies. The digital economy is ubiquitous, users can rely on it, the resources provided become invisible and, in case of a breakdown, the effects are profound (Plantin et al., 2018, p. 294).

The 'digital economy' could also instead be understood as consisting of those companies whose business model 'critically depends on the utilisation of large amounts of data' (see Hett & Schwab, Chapter 16 in this volume). However, the assets of companies like Amazon, Google, Apple, or Facebook include crucial physical ones: data centres, networks of high-bandwidth cables, specialised chips, and power generation facilities (to meet their high demands for electricity). Moreover, insofar as data is crucially important for most economic activity, this definition risks including 'in modern economies, the entire economy' (IMF, 2018, p. 7).

Yet, regardless of whether 'digital economy' is defined as being about data or about infrastructure, the economic analysis is similar: search and transaction costs are very low and data travels for free (Goldfarb & Tucker, 2019). When the infrastructure is not only accessed electronically – as in online shopping – rather the infrastructure goods are delivered or consumed online – as with cloud computing services – then the infrastructure has global reach. To make matters worse, because of high fixed costs and economies of scale, the digital economy tends to give rise to natural monopolies (see Hett & Schwab, Chapter 16 in this volume).

Notwithstanding this overlap in economic analysis, emphasising the infrastructure aspects of the digital economy over its dependence on data has two advantages.

First, it narrows the aperture and thereby brings certain aspects into focus. This invites researchers to use approaches and tools that were developed for infrastructures and platforms specifically (e.g. Plantin et al., 2018). For normative analyses, the topic of privacy moves into the background: privacy, of course, matters because digital infrastructures harvest and exploit data. But harvesting and exploiting data is something that, these days, most enterprises do.

Second, seeing the digital economy as digital infrastructure makes clear why the digital economy matters for justice. The digital economy provides powerful resources. It enables the production of goods across all aspects of life. It lubricates economic activities, such as setting up new businesses; but it also provides resources for political goods – facilitating participation, spreading misinformation, or building solidarity – as well as social goods, such as maintaining friendships. In short, in virtue of being an infrastructure, the digital economy is an ingredient for economic, political and social goods. Giving individuals access to it is a matter of justice.

To keep things short, this survey about justice in the global digital economy is selective and schematic. It is geographically selective in that I concentrate mostly on America, Europe and Africa, and it is topically selective in that I leave aside issues of domestic socioeconomic justice as well as racial and gender justice. The survey is schematic in that, by dividing the world into the Global North and South, I omit important distinctions within and between these two groups.

JUSTICE IN THE GLOBAL DIGITAL ECONOMY

The global digital economy raises problems of justice on many fronts. I will focus on three: on the front of socioeconomic justice, the digital economy increases global inequality. On the front of intergenerational justice, one generation may give up their data at the expense of the next (see Hett & Schwab for both points, Chapter 16 in this volume). On the front of political justice, the global digital economy raises four potential problems: it (1) abridges state power, (2) degrades political relations, (3) supports authoritarian politics, and (4) exacerbates American global political power.

These problems are largely familiar. Some of them even come in familiar proportions: global inequality is a long-standing and persistent problem; so is shifting burdens onto later generations. One thing is different, however: issues in political justice that are familiar domestically – such as antitrust and corporate power – now scale up to global proportions. *The global digital economy thus opens a new chapter of colonialism*. Both Chinese and the US multinational companies today are seen as colonial powers in the Global South – because of their control of the digital infrastructure (Kwet, 2019; Gravett, 2020). Yet the bigger picture that emerges from the injustices described below, especially the political ones, may still be this: colonialism – at least recognised by its mark of denying members of a political association 'equal and reciprocal terms of cooperation' (Ypi, 2013) – is back.

Global Monopolies, Global Inequality

Socioeconomically, the digital economy leads to an unjust distribution. The monopolies of the digital economy will reside in the Global North, which, consequently, will *on average* likely see greater income and better access to resources and opportunities (see Chapter 16 in this volume). This is a matter of distributive justice. To start with, this is a matter of *equality* – or, rather, lack thereof. Even if philosophers disagree about the equality of what – income, welfare, resources, opportunities – equality, at least within some measure, is widely taken to be one component of justice. But moreover, this global disparity could also be a matter of *sufficiency*. The issue would then be not that some have too much, but that others do not have enough (Frankfurt, 1987). Insofar as the digital economy is a basic good, individuals have strong claims to get enough of it.

Of course, inequality is not always unjust – in fact, there can be justice-based reasons for inequality – and equality is not the only value that matters. But distributive justice is still of paramount importance in the digital economy.

The relevant things to look at, the *distribuenda*, may not be income or opportunities, but instead *standing* (whether individuals relate to each other as equals) or *power* (whether one can impose their will on another). Even if everyone had sufficient access to the digital economy, the *way* in which this access is provided might be unjust. Equality can be provided in a way that is demeaning (Anderson, 1999); and power asks not only what you have and how you got it, but whether somebody could take it away (cf. Pettit, 1997).

Power over infrastructures might be the harder problem than *access* to them. Because the digital economy is a business, and because the Global South is a market, there is a buck to be made. Thus, given the existing economic regimes, the Global South will get access to the digital infrastructure – and pay for it. And those who own the digital economy will have power over those who merely get to use it.

Price Discrimination against Future Generations

The companion piece identifies a potential problem of intergenerational justice: today, consumers pay for digital services with their data. Present consumers hence 'benefit from low prices' while 'future consumers suffer from the intensified price discrimination' (Hett & Schwab in draft of companion chapter) (cf. Steinberg, 2020).

Price discrimination is a less pressing problem than it may seem – yet it is interesting to consider why: to start with, even if present generations disadvantage future generations in this way, future generations may still benefit on balance, all other things being equal. Just as future generations inherit cultural and technological capital, they inherit whatever good comes from the digital economy. Price discrimination on future generations might be a way in which these generations compensate the present generations for the things the present generations leave behind.

Moreover, price discrimination is not wrong. Price discrimination is when a seller charges different people different prices for the same product. Price discrimination is very common: discounts for students and senior citizens; travel tickets that get more expensive over time; journals to which university libraries can subscribe only in bundles; university tuition support that varies with household income; and hardcover books are examples. Price discrimination can lead to greater welfare and efficiency (Steinberg, 2020, pp. 99–104; but see Huang, 2005), it makes industries with high fix costs profitable (Elegido, 2011, p. 637), and hence enables products that otherwise might not exist. It allows monopolists – instead of maximising profit by restricting supply – to offer as much of their product as they would on a competitive market (Steinberg, 2020, p. 103).

The problem is, or so some might think, that price discrimination offends against a norm of equality: equality demands that everyone pays the same.

Not quite. In fact, price discrimination may make things equal: it allows that each consumer gets the equal surplus value for some good (Marcoux, 2006). The fact that someone gets more welfare out of a product and can afford to pay more, is a reason that they should pay more. By the same principle, global pharmaceutical companies charge higher prices in rich countries, and thereby – in addition to making significant profit – fund the development of new medication.

Abridgement of State Power

At the beginning of the SARS-CoV2 pandemic, Apple and Google developed low-level software that could have been used for contact tracing. But the companies only allowed the software to be used for exposure notifications. The companies legally barred public health authorities from using the gathered information to identify individuals in a chain of transmissions. In this way, the companies took an important public health policy option off the table.

This illustrates a general problem: companies in the digital economy have power over states. The companies control how their infrastructure is used – in this case: phone operating systems. In addition to such direct control, when digital infrastructure is critical, companies wield significant indirect bargaining power. Companies can threaten to restrict infrastructure access and thereby influence policy options that are not under their direct control.

This is an example of how state power is suffocated by corporate power (cf. Claassen & Herzog, 2021). To put corporate power in perspective, one can think of it either as a matter of market concentration or of size. *Market concentration* is measured by the Herfindahl–Hirschman Index (HHI) and has been rising in the public cloud computing market. Concentration is nearing the US Department of Justice's highest category. Going by size – by market valuation – digital economy companies are the largest companies in the world. As of early 2021, Microsoft is valued at $1.76tn, followed by Amazon at $1.59tn, followed by Alphabet at $1.41tn. In terms of revenue, they dwarf states. Apple's annual revenue in 2020 approached $300bn, Amazon's was over $380bn. For comparison, the median annual total GDP is Afghanistan's at around $19bn.

Of course, size and power are not as such morally problematic. But when companies are powerful enough to escape or profoundly limit the jurisdiction and governance of states, the companies yield their power illegitimately and without proper authority (Lazar, 2022). Regardless of what they decide and why, companies are just not the right agents to make policy decisions – they lack authority – and they do not do so in the right way – they act illegitimately. And, because power consists in possibility, this problem of political justice persists, even if companies do not actually influence policy-making.

This abridgement of state power is particularly acute on the global scale. Power likely correlates with existing advantages. Those states that are already victims of injustice may come to live under the shadow of the digital economy.

Degradation of Economic Opportunities and Political Relations

Global corporate power has effects for economies domestically. For one, corporate power can degrade economic opportunities by stifling competition and innovation (Khan, 2018). Large companies in the digital economy have *gatekeeper power*. Large corporations can keep competitors out of markets, for example, by acquiring them – think of Facebook and Instagram. Second, large corporations have *leveraging power*, that is, they can establish an advantageous position in ancillary markets. For example, the Amazon retail platform may have given its own book publishing division an advantage in its competition with other publishers. Third, large corporations have *information exploitation* power to practice forms of price discrimination. Finally, the digital economy can degrade economic opportunities on labour markets – salaries diverge, workers are made contingent, and unions are busted.

Secondly, the power of the digital economy moreover negatively affects political relations. This starts at work: labour relations are political relations because they transfer authority over important aspects of an individual's life. Because the workplace is rife with oppression, these relations are already defective (Anderson, 2017). As the political power of employers increases – not only through institutions but also through technologies, such as, workplace surveillance – these relations are bound to degrade further. Corporate power moreover degrades political equality between citizens also outside of the workplace. Large corporations influence legislative, regulatory or judicative processes and outcomes. With the digital economy, this old story of regulatory capture is now told anew (Shughart & Thomas, 2019). Finally, large corporations can escape the 'ordinary mechanisms of political accountability' (Rahman, 2018, p.1629).

When the digital economy is placed before this backdrop of colonialism, two problems of political justice on a global scale stand out: how the digital economy supports authoritarian politics and how it subsequently exacerbates American global political power.

Support of Authoritarian Politics

The digital economy can be a force for democracy (Himmelreich, 2022). Social media lubricated civil society movements in the Philippines in 2001, in Ukraine in 2004 (the Orange Revolution), in Lebanon in 2005 (the Cedar Revolution), in Tunisia, Egypt and others during the Arab Spring, as well as during the Gezi

Park and Occupy protests around 2010–11 (Diamond, 2010, p. 78; Howard & Hussain, 2011; 2013; Tufekci, 2017).

However, the digital economy can also be a force in the opposite direction – and support authoritarianism. One example for this is Facebook's role in Myanmar's humanitarian crisis in 2018. For many of Myanmar's 18 million internet users, Facebook is indistinguishable from the internet (Mozur, 2018). Facebook, hence, was the ground on which the Myanmar military rolled out an Astroturf ultranationalist Buddhist movement that spread misinformation and vilified the Muslim Rohingya minority in Rakhine State (Fink, 2018). This led to a 'textbook example of ethnic cleansing' according to a UN report (quoted in Mozur, 2018). In the eyes of one member of a civil society group, Facebook had a responsibility 'to take proper actions to avoid becoming an instigator of genocide'; Facebook 'acknowledged it had been too slow to act' (Mozur, 2018).

Whereas Facebook's involvement here may have been unintentional, elsewhere the company seemed to cooperate deliberately. In Vietnam, Facebook 'agreed to restrict access to dissident political content deemed illegal [by the government] in exchange for the government ending its practice of disrupting Facebook's local servers, which had slowed the platform to a crawl' (Horwitz & Newley, 2020). Likewise, in India – where Facebook has more users (280m) than in any other country, including the USA (190m) – Facebook may have engaged in 'a broader pattern of favoritism . . . toward Mr. Modi's Bharatiya Janata Party and Hindu hard-liners.' (Horwitz & Newley, 2020).

These cases, since they are anecdotal evidence, do not show the problem's extent, but they suggest its magnitude. They illustrate how companies in the digital economy can prop up authoritarian politics. That social media are 'tilting dangerously towards illiberalism' because they offer regimes means of surveillance and control, has been observed systematically in other contexts (Shahbaz & Funk, 2019). And what goes for social media goes, likewise, for cloud services. China, for example, requires 'foreign firms . . . to submit source code, undergo security audits and localize data and equipment' (Parasol, 2018, p. 86).

The structural problem in these cases is that the business interests of companies in the digital economy align with the interests of authoritarian regimes: to stifle opposition and political competition and to consolidate their power. The companies and these authoritarian interests support each other. Authoritarian powers enable companies to stay in business, and these companies help the regimes to stay in power.

Exacerbation of American Global Power

Finally, the global digital economy affects political justice in that it indirectly increases the USA's international power. Because many large players in the digital economy are US companies, they are under direct jurisdiction of, or are at least politically beholden to, the US government. In fact, as of 2019, US companies control around 68 per cent of the worldwide public cloud market. To the extent that these companies provide critical infrastructure to other countries, this increases the effect of potential sanctions, and hence the bargaining power of the USA.

This is not a hypothetical concern. Even without sanctions, US domestic politics has restricted foreign access to digital infrastructure. On July 25, 2019 GitHub started blocking Iranian nationals from accessing their code repositories and, reportedly, their pages (Motamedi, 2019a). Just weeks later, Iranian users had been locked out of Amazon's cloud products, Amazon Web Services (AWS). Because AWS powers virtual private networks – which are crucial for circumventing governmental internet surveillance and restrictions – this move by Amazon may have adversely affected the Iranian civil society (Motamedi, 2019b). These restrictions were only the latest additions after other companies, such as Google, Apple and Slack, had reportedly already restricted their services in Iran (Motamedi, 2019b). Although the US Office of Foreign Assets Control (OFAC) had *allowed* companies to export services to Iran in 2014, according to reports from Al Jazeera, Iranian citizens are effectively still 'locked out' from many internet services. The US-based digital economy tends to 'overcomply' with US sanctions against the Iranian government – be it for political reasons or because of the administrative burden associated with exporting services (Motamedi, 2019b; 2019a).

The digital economy hence leverages the international political power of those states that are their primary political home – generally, this means often: the power of the USA. Without adjudicating this particular instance of US sanctions, this power leverage raises concerns for political justice. In the digital economy, export restrictions can affect the economic and social opportunities of citizens in distant countries directly. Such international power might be illegitimate or substantially unjust.

CONCLUSION

This chapter outlined a framework for thinking about justice in the global digital economy. The framework consists of three main points. First, the digital economy should be thought of as a digital infrastructure. Second, the digital economy compounds existing concerns of socioeconomic injustice – issues of global inequality and insufficiency. Third, the digital economy raises four problems of political justice. The power wielded by the digital economy restricts what states can do, it deepens defects in domestic economic participation, political representation, and labour relations, it finds itself contributing to anti-democratic currents and exacerbates the diplomatic power of already powerful states.

The point of identifying problems of justice is to do something about them. What can be done? To fix price discrimination, a first route goes via competition. In a perfectly competitive market, price discrimination would be impossible. If Amazon charges you more for premium cat litter because they know your willingness to pay, Amazon's competitors might try to make you a better offer – given that the competitor knows about Amazon's offer. So, price discrimination can be addressed by lowering search costs. Moreover, price discrimination could be addressed by distinguishing between permissible and impermissible price discrimination and enforcing a ban on the latter. However, given the difficulty of drawing this distinction, this latter avenue seems less promising.

The problems of socioeconomic injustice, as suggested in the companion piece to this chapter, could be addressed through a digital services tax. On such a tax, each country has the right to tax a digital services company's global income proportional to the revenue that the company generated in this country. Normative arguments for such a policy and proposals for a global tax regime are being developed (Dietsch, 2015; Kern, 2020). The process of setting up such a tax may entail – that is, it may either presuppose or lead to the situation – that the balance of power shifts from economic interests to states.

The problems of political justice play out both domestically and internationally. Domestically, states should renew their efforts to reign in economic power. The powers that the digital economy wields domestically are not novel and may be hemmed in with known tools of antitrust and competition regulation. Internationally, the picture is different. A relatively easy start would be for the USA to use its domestic power over the digital economy to shape how the companies behave abroad. This, of course, exploits the potential injustice of American global power instead of addressing it. But this may be a first step towards a recommendation that has to be – unfortunately – as vague as it is trite: effective global governance is needed.

Thus, even though key problems of the digital economy have been identified and potential reforms sketched, the hard work remains yet to be done – intellectually, to articulate the procedural and substantive norms that injustices violate; and practically, to develop specific reforms and organise for their implementation.

REFERENCES

Anderson, E. (1999). What Is the Point of Equality? *Ethics, 109*(2): 287–337.

Anderson, E. (2017). *Private Government: How Employers Rule Our Lives (and Why We Don't Talk about It).* Princeton University Press.

Claassen, R., & Herzog, L. (2021). Making Power Explicit: Why Liberal Egalitarians Should Take (Economic) Power Seriously. *Social Theory and Practice.*

Diamond, L. (2010). Liberation Technology. *Journal of Democracy, 21*(3), 69–83.

Dietsch, P. (2015). *Catching Capital: The Ethics of Tax Competition*. Oxford University Press.

Elegido, J. M. (2011). The Ethics of Price Discrimination. *Business Ethics Quarterly, 21*(4), 633–60.

Fink, C. (2018). Dangerous Speech, Anti-Muslim Violence, and Facebook in Myanmar. *Journal of International Affairs, 71*(1.5), 43–52.

Frankfurt, H. (1987). Equality as a Moral Ideal. *Ethics, 98*(1), 21–43.

Frischmann, B. M. (2013). *Infrastructure: The Social Value of Shared Resources*. Oxford University Press.

Goldfarb, A., & Tucker, C. (2019). Digital Economics. *Journal of Economic Literature, 57*(1), 3–43.

Gravett, W. (2020). Digital Neo-Colonialism: The Chinese Model of Internet Sovereignty in Africa. *African Human Rights Law Journal, 20*(1), 125–46.

Himmelreich, J. (2022). Should We Automate Democracy? In Véliz, C., (ed.), *The Oxford Handbook of Digital Ethics*, Oxford University Press.

Horwitz, J., & Newley, P. (2020). Facebook's Hate-Speech Rules Collide with Indian Politics. *Wall Street Journal*

Howard, P. N., & Hussain, M. M. (2011). The Upheavals in Egypt and Tunisia: The Role of Digital Media. *Journal of Democracy, 22*(3), 35–48.

Huang, M-H. (2005). Unequal Pricing in the Information Economy: Implications for Consumer Welfare. *Journal of Business Ethics, 56*(4), 305–15.

IMF. (2018). *Measuring the Digital Economy. Staff Report*. International Monetary Fund.

Kern, A. (2020). Illusions of Justice in International Taxation. *Philosophy & Public Affairs, 48*(2), 151–84.

Khan, L. M. (2018). Sources of Tech Platform Power. *Georgetown Law Technology Review*, 2(325), 10.

Kwet, M. (2019). Digital Colonialism: US Empire and the New Imperialism in the Global South. *Race & Class, 60*(4), 3–26.

Lazar, S. (2022). Power and AI: Nature and Justification. In Bullock, J. B., Chen, Y-C., Himmelreich, J., Hudson, V. M., Korinek, A., Young, M. M., & Zhang, B., (eds.), *The Oxford Handbook of AI Governance*, Oxford University Press.

Marcoux, A. M. (2006). Much Ado about Price Discrimination. *Journal of Markets and Morality, 9*(1).

Motamedi, M. (July 31, 2019a). Locked out: Did US Tech Company Overcomply with Iran Sanctions? *Aljazeera*.

Motamedi, M. (October 2, 2019b). Locked out: Why Is Amazon Blocking Iranians from Its Services? *Aljazeera*.

Mozur, P. (October 15, 2018). A Genocide Incited on Facebook, with Posts From Myanmar's Military. *The New York Times*.

Parasol, M. (2018). The Impact of China's 2016 Cyber Security Law on Foreign Technology Firms, and on China's Big Data and Smart City Dreams. *Computer Law & Security Review, 34*(1), 67–98.

Pettit, P. (1997). *Republicanism: A Theory of Freedom and Government*. Oxford University Press.

Plantin, J-C., Lagoze, C., Edwards, P. N., & Sandvig, C. (2018). Infrastructure Studies Meet Platform Studies in the Age of Google and Facebook. *New Media & Society, 20*(1), 293–310.

Rahman, K. S. (2018). The New Utilities: Private Power, Social Infrastructure, and the Revival of the Public Utility Concept. *Cardozo Law Review, 39*(5), 1621–89.

Shahbaz, A., & Funk, A. (2019). *Freedom on the Net 2019*. Freedom House.

Shughart, W. F., & Thomas, D. W. (2019). Interest Groups and Regulatory Capture. In Congleton, R. D., Grofman, B. & Voigt, S., (eds.), *The Oxford Handbook of Public Choice, Volume 1*, 584–603. Oxford University Press.

Steinberg, E. (2020). Big Data and Personalized Pricing. *Business Ethics Quarterly*, 30(1), 97–117.

Tufekci, Z. (2017). *Twitter and Tear Gas: The Power and Fragility of Networked Protest*. Yale University Press.

Ypi, L. (2013). What's Wrong with Colonialism. *Philosophy & Public Affairs*, *41*(2), 158–91.

Chapter 18

GLOBAL INTELLECTUAL PROPERTY GOVERNANCE: AN ASSESSMENT OF ITS TERMS

Madison Cartwright and Jean-Frédéric Morin

INTRODUCTION

Our understanding of intellectual property (IP) in global economic governance has undergone a major shift over the past few decades. For most of the twentieth century, international IP law was seen as an obscure and technical issue. However, since the end of the 1990s, the global distributive impact of IP has come into sharper focus. Today, IP is highly politicised and constitutes a key component of several global justice campaigns, including access to education, health, agriculture and environmental technologies.

Yet, the fundamental principles of IP laws remain largely unchanged. IP grants exclusive rights to individuals and entities for the commercialisation of intangible assets. It comes in various forms including (1) copyright, which protects creative and literary works; (2) patents, which protect inventions; (3) trademarks, which protect distinctive signs. Each of these rights allows IP holders to prevent third parties from selling products that are identical to their protected products. As a result, IP holders can increase their products' sale prices.

In this way, IP can be interpreted as a breach of the liberal precepts of a free market and open competition. Several liberal thinkers from the nineteenth century heavily criticised IP laws for being interventionist and protectionist (Machlup & Penrose, 1950).

IP was widely accepted and uncontroversial throughout most of the twentieth century, largely thanks to an 'instrumentalist' narrative that justifies IP as a means to incentivise knowledge production in the market (Drahos, 2016). According to this instrumentalist narrative, IP rights are public policy instruments, limited in scope and duration, designed to provide economic incentives for innovation and creativity. This justification has become so deeply ingrained in global economic governance that the inclusion of IP provisions in trade agreements does not appear incoherent to most trade analysts.

The chapter assesses how well the instrumentalist justifications underlying the global IP regime match its actual outcomes. It argues that the global

IP regime is failing on its terms. For several countries, 1) IP laws tend to serve the private interests of the most powerful players; 2) they provide little incentive for local innovation and creativity; and 3) their duration is extended beyond reasonable limits. As such, the global IP regime is failing in its principles of political justice, socioeconomic justice and intergenerational justice. The recent contestation over the global IP regime was sparked by these mismatches between the instrumentalist narrative, which attempts to justify and legitimise global IP governance, and the actual outcomes of the IP regime.

POLITICAL JUSTICE: A NATIONAL INSTRUMENT OR AN EXTERNALLY DICTATED POLICY?

Different countries have different interests in IP protection. The most advanced knowledge economies have an interest in providing and promoting strong IP standards to build on their competitive advantage. Developing countries, on the other hand, have an interest in providing lower levels of IP protection to acquire foreign technologies. If IP is a public policy instrument, as the instrumentalist narrative on IP suggests, we would expect to see different levels of IP protection across countries (Kim et al., 2012).

In principle, the global IP regime is consistent with this expectation. IP law is based on the principle of territoriality, that is the protection granted by a state exists within its territory alone. Inventors cannot obtain a global patent and creators cannot acquire a global copyright that would be universally enforceable as a single property right. Instead, they obtain a series of distinct property rights in each country. Multilateral IP treaties exist, but they aim to harmonise certain aspects of domestic IP systems, rather than create universal property rights.

However, the level of IP protection offered in several developing countries is not the result of domestic deliberations. Instead, IP reforms are often 'externally dictated' by powerful foreign actors (Miller, 2003, p. 847). This arrangement is counter to the principles of political justice and has a long history in IP. Patent and copyright laws were first introduced in several developing countries during colonialism to serve the interests of European powers. This was particularly the case at the end of the nineteenth century when France and Great Britain transplanted their IP systems in Africa and Asia. This colonial legacy is still visible in the contemporary IP laws in several developing countries (Okediji, 2003).

The first international IP treaties were also adopted during the nineteenth century, including the Paris Convention for the Protection of Industrial Property (1883). All these treaties prohibit states from offering greater IP protection to their nationals than to foreigners. Initially, they were negotiated by European powers and extended to their then colonies (Okediji, 2003). To this day, most developing countries cannot design an IP system that favours their inventors and creators over foreign IP holders.

The early IP treaties were initially administered by the United International Bureaux for the Protection of IP, which later became the World Intellectual Property Organization (WIPO). WIPO joined the United Nations system in 1974, nearly ninety years after the conclusion of the Paris Convention. Thus, WIPO came to the UN with a long history and a well-established view of its mission. Although WIPO's mandate was amended when it joined the UN to include the promotion of technology transfer and economic development, it took several decades to change its organisational culture (May 2007). For a long time, WIPO saw itself as an organisation that primarily aimed to defend and protect the interests of IP holders, sometimes to the detriment of IP users. As recently as 2003, the Director General of the WIPO wrote that IP laws are 'an essential component of economic strategy regardless of whether the country is developed or developing' (Idris, 2003, p. 133).

Unlike most UN organisations, WIPO's funding comes primarily from the private sector, specifically from IP holders. WIPO provides services to individuals and businesses that complete an IP application in exchange for a fee. In 2024, WIPO expects to receive 930 million Swiss francs in fees, representing 95 per cent of its overall budget (WIPO, 2024). In contrast, civil society organisations representing the interests of IP users (librarians, educators, consumers, etc.) do not have a privileged channel to influence the WIPO.

In 1994, the Agreement on Trade-Related Aspects of Intellectual Property (TRIPs) was adopted at the World Trade Organization (WTO). When compared with agreements administered at WIPO, the TRIPs agreement provided more detailed and restrictive rules on IP. These rules reflected the standard of protection in force in the USA and Europe at the time. Their implementation in developing countries required major reforms and IP protection was significantly strengthened as a result (Deere, 2008). Developing countries could take advantage of transitional periods, but ultimately, they were obliged to meet the same obligations as high-income countries.

Different accounts explain how and why developing countries accepted the TRIPs agreement (Sell, 2003). One narrative claim that the USA used coercion, threatening to impose unilateral trade sanctions on developing countries that favoured lower IP standards. Another narrative presents the TRIPs agreement as a concession agreed by developing countries in exchange for greater access to markets for textiles and agricultural products in high-income countries. Both narratives highlight the importance of IP's emergence as a trade issue. This has both made the level of IP protection subject to trade sanctions, including now through the WTO's Appellate Body, and opened IP up to economic horse-trading in the framework of trade negotiations, where economies with larger markets have the advantage. Several developing countries accepted the TRIPs agreement knowing that it did not reflect their best economic interests.

Moreover, in the last two decades, the USA and the European Union have included a wide variety of 'TRIPs-plus' provisions in their bilateral trade agreements with developing countries. In so doing, by using their asymmetrical market power to their advantage in bilateral settings, they pressurise their trading partners into adopting IP standards similar to their own (Cartwright, 2019; Sell, 2010). According to a recent account, there are currently more than 126 trade agreements with TRIPs-plus provisions (Morin & Surbeck, 2019). There is also a positive correlation between the degree of power asymmetry among negotiating parties (measured by the difference in their GDP) and the number of TRIPs-plus provisions included in a trade agreement (Morin & Surbeck, 2019). A further study reveals that the inclusion of TRIPs-plus provisions in trade agreements is one of the main explanations for domestic IP reforms in developing countries since 2000 (Morin & Gold, 2014; Deere, 2008).

In the 1990s and early 2000s, coalitions of developing countries and civil society groups mobilised against the global IP regime's built-in bias in favour of IP holders and advanced knowledge economies (Helfer, 2004; Morin, 2010; Dobusch & Quack, 2013). They organised campaigns on a variety of specific issues, including access to patented medicines, farmers' right to use protected seeds, and indigenous communities rights over their traditional knowledge. These campaigns improved the political representation of civil society interests in global IP forums. Their claimed successes also include the adoption of the 2001 Doha Declaration on Public Health at the WTO, the 2004 WIPO Development Agenda and the 2013 Marrakesh Treaty to Facilitate Access to Published Works for Persons Who Are Blind. That said, according to some accounts, the diversity of stakeholders involved in global IP politics peaked in 2007 and has decreased since then (Morin, 2020). Meanwhile, the main IP treaties have remained unchanged, and bilateral TRIPs-plus agreements, which extend IP protection in developing countries, are still being concluded every year.

The participation of diverse stakeholders representing both IP owners and users is required to achieve political justice. In addition, IP laws should be designed with the national interest in mind, rather than following the dictates of foreign countries. The instrumentalist narrative of IP suggests that, by the territorial principle, each country is free to design its IP system and its political procedures, which are in line with its interests. However, in practice, international IP institutions have promoted a uniform approach modelled on the US and EU systems, which is applicable in every country, irrespective of their level of development (Shi, 2010). Global IP governance is organised increasingly in the framework of trade forums, which is an advantage for high-income economies. As a result, some of the poorest countries that have no major industries and that could benefit from strong IP protection, have standards similar to those found in the USA or EU (Deere, 2008). For these countries, IP law is, at best, a trade concession, and at worst, evidence of neo-colonialism. It is not a policy instrument designed to serve the local population.

SOCIOECONOMIC JUSTICE: AN INCENTIVE FOR ALL OR A RENT FOR THE FEW?

The instrumentalist narrative assumes that IP generates net social benefits. More specifically, it argues that the prospect of obtaining an IP right incentivises innovation and creativity. Presumably, market actors would not invest in the production of knowledge if the result of their efforts could be cheaply replicated by competitors. By allowing market actors to reap the financial benefits of their investments, IP addresses this perceived market failure and directs private capital towards knowledge production. The goal of IP is not to make IP owners wealthy but to generate knowledge that contributes to better collective socioeconomic outcomes. In other words, despite using IP to privatise the gains of innovation and creativity, the instrumentalist narrative's primary focus is ostensibly the broader public interest. This does not mean that the instrumentalist narrative denies the fact that IP comes with social costs. IP implies restricted competition, which often translates into higher consumer prices. From the instrumentalist perspective, these social costs are an acceptable price to pay for the social benefits generated by greater innovation and creativity.

However, in practice, the relation between IP protection and knowledge creation is not linear. Too much IP protection can impede rather than incentivise knowledge creation because creativity and innovation are cumulative processes. Each new artistic creation or technological invention builds on pre-existing work. If the latter is protected by IP, it may dissuade creators and inventors from developing innovations. In some cases, when there is no IP protection, the knowledge that is freely accessible can even stimulate innovation, as illustrated by the constant refinement of open-source software (Boldrin & Levine, 2008). The extent to which IP incentivises knowledge creation without obstructing it remains unclear (Hudson & Minea, 2013).

Although the optimal level of IP protection is uncertain and contested, most experts agree that it varies across both sectors and countries. First, some innovations have more social value than others. For example, the development of antiretroviral medications to treat HIV/AIDS has a far greater social value than the development of the five-blade razor. However, the global IP system restricts the capacity of states to calibrate the level of IP protection about social value. The TRIPs agreement, for example, prohibits discrimination based on the field of technology (art. 27(1)). All inventions must receive the same level of patent protection and all artistic creations must receive the same level of copyright protection. Second, the optimal level of protection also varies across countries because their needs and their capacities differ. However, the global IP regime, particularly in the post-TRIPs era, sets extremely detailed IP standards that limit the capacity of each jurisdiction to design its IP laws according to its specific circumstances. A series of multilateral and

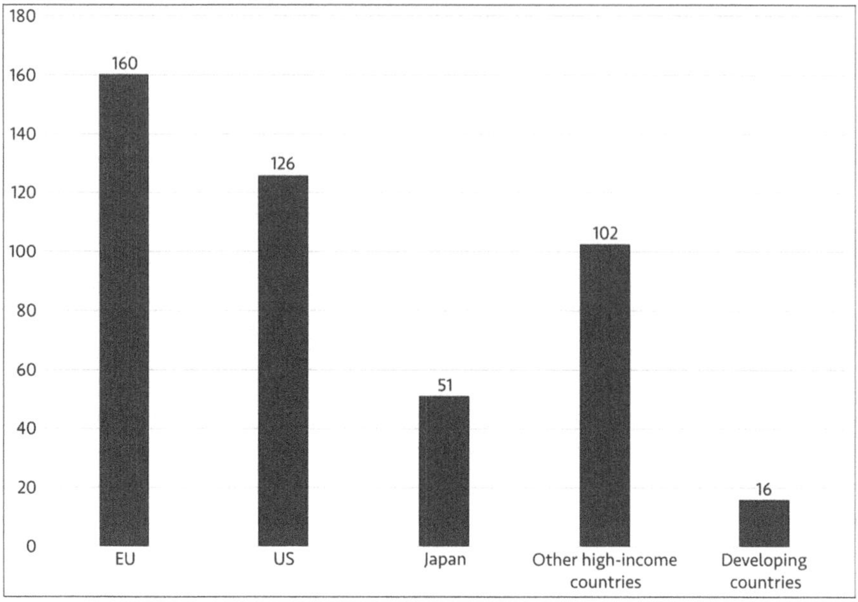

Figure 18.1 Global distribution of receipts for the use of IP (2023).
Source: World Bank indicator.

bilateral treaties require developing countries to align their domestic law with the standards of the most advanced economies.

The advanced economies have used international treaties to set the level of IP protection in developing countries because they have a commercial interest in doing so. In 2019, international flows for royalties and licensing fees reached US$ 397 billion, and 97 per cent of this amount was captured by high-income countries (Figure 18.1). The USA alone received more than US$ 129 billion in international royalties and licensing fees in 2019. It paid US$ 57 billion to other countries for a net gain of US$ 74 billion. In contrast, all developing countries combined paid US$ 77 billion and received US$ 10 billion, for a net loss of US$ 60 billion in international royalties and licensing fees. To put these numbers in perspective, developing countries paid almost twice as much in international royalties and licensing fees compared to what they received in development assistance from the USA (US$ 34 billion in 2019). In short, the global IP regime allows IP owners in high-income countries to extract rent from developing countries.

However, while today tens of billions of dollars in royalties and licensing fees flow from low-income to high-income countries every year, most of these same high-income countries developed their economies by offering little IP protection, especially for foreigners (Wade, 2003). In the nineteenth century, the US patent and copyright systems were highly discriminatory against foreigners and it did not accede to the Berne Convention until 1989. Even in the 1970s, Korea had an IP system designed to encourage the reproduction of foreign technologies. Today, the USA, Korea, and other high-income countries prevent developing countries from doing the same. This is partly because IP is an increasingly important feature of the world economy and the international revenue it generates is growing rapidly. Since the adoption of the TRIPs agreement in 1994, world GDP increased threefold, but international flows of royalties and licensing fees increased tenfold. As IP becomes more lucrative in the global economy, high-income countries are intensifying their pressure on developing countries to protect foreign-held IP.

Not only were high-income countries able to develop free from the strict IP restrictions now placed on developing countries, but they also continued to benefit from significant advantages in the global competition for knowledge production. An entire economic ecosystem is required to sustain a high level of knowledge production. One important component of this economic ecosystem is the support of public funding and proactive government intervention (Drahos, 2016). For example, the US public sector spent US$133 billion in research and development (R&D) in 2018, which represents 23 per cent of its total national R&D expenditure (UNESCO). Developing countries (with the notable exception of China) cannot compete with this level of public support for knowledge creation.

Moreover, the US government does not simply fund knowledge production. It also fosters its commercial application by brokering partnerships in the private sector, facilitating market creation, and transferring the IP ownership of government-funded innovations to private enterprises (MacNeil, 2013). Notoriously, the development of the various components of the iPhone was funded by the US military, including the internet, the GPS, the touchscreen and cellular technology (Mazzucato, 2013). This unequal footing raises profound implications for the socioeconomic justice of global IP harmonisation. The prevalence of public funding also undermines the founding principle of the instrumentalist narrative, which states that the gains from innovation and creativity must be privatised to incentivise investment in knowledge production.

INTERGENERATIONAL JUSTICE: LIMITING DURATION OR EVERGREENING?

The perennial dilemma for the instrumentalist narrative is how to achieve a balance in IP law that maintains the appropriate market incentives for knowledge production while also minimising the social costs created by private ownership of knowledge. One mechanism for achieving this balance is limitations and exceptions that restrict the scope of IP protection (Baldwin, 2014). The major limitation for any form of IP right is duration. Patent, copyright, trademark and other IP rights are not granted in perpetuity, but for only as long as is deemed sufficient to incentivise knowledge production. Therefore, there is a trade-off built into the IP system between short-term social costs – during which IP holders can exercise their exclusive rights for their private gain – and long-term social gain – that is the expansion of our knowledge base, which ultimately falls into the public domain. This could be interpreted as an intergenerational transaction, that is the current generation pays the price of limited competition, while future generations will have access to a greater pool of knowledge.

IP rights also come with obligations. In exchange for obtaining a patent, inventors must agree to disclose their invention. This legal obligation is conducted by governmental patent offices, which publish all the patent applications they receive. These applications include a detailed description of the invention, allowing competitors to gain knowledge even before the patent expires and they are authorised to replicate it. In the absence of a patent system or if the inventor does not fill out a patent application, inventors might try keeping their invention secret for as long as possible. In some fields of technology, it is not easy for competitors to reverse-engineer an invention, which means that the initial inventor has an indefinite period of exclusivity. However, there is always a risk that a competitor will be able to replicate an undisclosed invention. Thus, patents are a form of social contract: states give exclusive rights to patent holders for a limited period in exchange for the immediate disclosure of their invention. Here again, exclusive rights are supposed to represent a short-term social cost for a long-term social gain.

However, international treaties disrupt this delicate balance between short-term cost and long-term gain. In the 1980s, several developing countries offered a copyright duration of up to thirty years after the death of an author. This was to ensure that the author's children could benefit financially from the copyrighted work. When developing countries joined the Berne Convention and the TRIPs agreement, they had to extend copyright protection to fifty years after the death of an author, as this is the minimal length provided in these multilateral agreements. More recently, at least thirty-six TRIPs-plus agreements extended the term of protection to seventy years after the author's death (Morin & Surbeck, 2020). These extended durations are unlikely to provide additional incentives for creators.

Figure 18.2 illustrates the expansion in international commitments for longer copyright term lengths since the Berne Convention was negotiated in the late nineteenth century. As it shows, the Berne Convention's initial minimum copyright length was ten years, which was later expanded to the life of the author plus fifty years in 1908. Whilst some countries had twenty-five years as the longest internationally obligated copyright term under the Universal Copyright Convention of 1952, this began to decline from the mid-1990s as these states joined either the Berne Convention or the WTO (or both) and committed to longer terms. Meanwhile, the life of the author plus

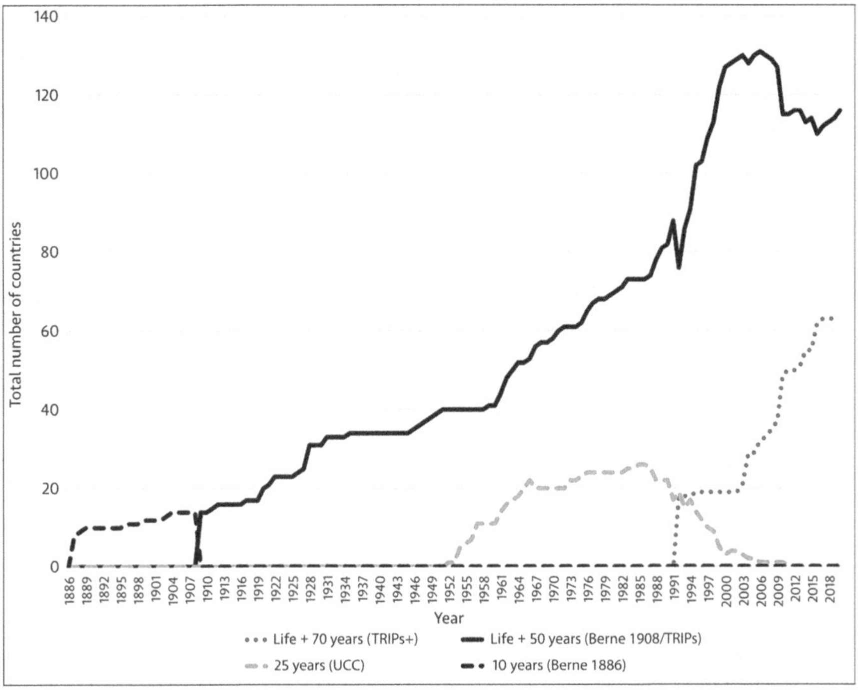

Figure 18.2 Longest copyright term length committed to under international treaties (number of countries).

Source: TRIPS-plus data from Morin & Surbeck (2023).

fifty years declined in 1992 and then from the 2000s as more countries committed to higher TRIPs-plus terms. By 2020, a combined 179 states had committed to a minimum copyright term of either life of the author plus 50 years and/or 70 years through international agreements.

Few novelists, filmmakers or musicians consider the economic well-being of their great-grandchildren when they make artistic decisions. However, these extensions are important for corporations that own copyrights on artistic creations made more than fifty years ago. Famously, Mickey Mouse was created in 1928 and would have come into the public domain in the 1980s if Disney and other corporations had not succeeded in extending the length of copyright protection.

Disney's persistent lobbying to extend its copyright terms exposes a contradiction in the instrumentalist narrative, which undermines intergenerational justice. IP rights do not incentivise knowledge production as much as they incentivise the monetisation of the rights themselves. The rules governing the allocation of resources generated by IP rights are mutable. Thus, the owners of IP rights have the incentive to change the rules to extract more rents (Drahos, 2016). This can consolidate ownership among large commercial owners, to the detriment of other IP-owning interests (Benkler, 2001). Meanwhile, the gradual expansion of IP rights reduces the available knowledge that future would-be creators and innovators can build on. For example, the practice of 'sampling' short segments of a song was made popular by rap and hip-hop artists. However, this has since become risky with the emergence of so-called 'copyright tolls', which aim to obtain financial windfalls through copyright litigation against artists 'sampling' other music or even non-musical sounds. This has had a chilling effect on emerging artists, robbing them of the creative expression enjoyed by artists in the past (Weldon, 2017).

A similar pattern occurred for patents. Before the conclusion of the TRIPs agreement, several developing countries limited the term of a patent to twelve or fifteen years. The TRIPS agreement forced them to be more generous towards IP holders because it states that 'the term of protection available shall not end before the expiration of a period of 20 years' (art. 33). More recently, no fewer than forty-two TRIPs-plus agreements required the extension of patent terms to compensate for the administrative delays during which patent holders cannot market their invention (Morin & Surbeck, 2020).

IP holders can also use various strategies to extend their period of protection. First is 'evergreening', which involves filling a second patent for an existing patented invention about the discovery of a new use for the same product or the design of a slightly improved formula. In the case of pharmaceutical products, several TRIPs-plus agreements require a five-year protection period for data that is submitted to governmental agencies to obtain market approval (Morin & Surbeck, 2020). In some cases, pharmaceutical companies can use this form of data protection to extend further the effective period of exclusivity, which protects them from the competition of generic producers. Second, owners can use one form of IP rights to extend the privileged market position associated with another form of IP rights. For example, when the patent on a pharmaceutical drug expires, its trademark remains. The medical community often continues to refer to the drug using the original trademark and prescribes the original drug more often, even when generic producers offer the same molecule at a lower price.

These are some of the strategies that contradict the principle that IP rights are short-term social sacrifices to expand the public domain for future generations. International IP agreements focus almost exclusively on extending the rights conferred to IP holders and rarely combine these extensions with greater limits and exceptions (Cartwright, 2019). Therefore, they breach the social contract underlying the instrumentalist narrative of IP.

REFORM IDEAS

The above analysis shows that the global IP regime is failing on its terms. Several reforms could be adopted to address this. First, international forums should facilitate greater participation of the various stakeholders involved in IP, particularly IP users, that are currently largely excluded from official forums. Improving the representation of civil society groups in international forums could greatly enhance their political legitimacy. However, this would not be sufficient to change state interests or the fact that the most powerful states generally want stronger IP protection. In addition, IP owners have outsized influence within powerful states. Therefore, it is also important to ensure that there is more diverse representation at the domestic level.

There will always be more powerful and less powerful states. However, some forums particularly enhance power asymmetries (MacNeil, 2013). Thus, a second reform to improve justice in international IP governance would be to favour procedures and forums that lessen the impact of power asymmetries. Forums with only a few members make power asymmetries starker and, therefore, they should be avoided. Meanwhile, multilateral forums allow smaller states to act collectively against more powerful states, thus, reducing the imbalance. IP governance should also be organised at the multilateral level through a wide variety of forums related to IP, such as the WHO (health), UNESCO (education and culture), and the UNFCCC (climate). Although this will not eliminate power asymmetries, it would help mitigate them.

Third, the relationship between IP, incentives, and economic growth is uncertain and complex. However, the instrumentalist narrative, which is the main institutionalised frame seeking to legitimise the current global IP regime, fails to acknowledge this. It assumes that innovation depends on IP protection. Therefore, IP governance should be more explicit about acknowledging the complexities of how IP affects socioeconomic outcomes. It should also be open to new evidence that questions the relationship between IP and global welfare. This will require fully acknowledging the fact that the effects of IP vary from one country to another, from one sector to another, and from one period to another. In other words, the one-size-fits-all model should be rejected to maintain flexibility in IP governance.

One approach to achieving greater recognition might be to institutionalise an international panel of IP experts to explore and expose the diverse and complex connections between IP and welfare. Such a panel would function similarly to the Intergovernmental Panel on Climate Change, incorporating both experts and policy-makers and reviewing current peer-reviewed research. It would also coordinate across the various forums that address IP, as discussed above. Currently, assessment of IP and welfare occurs on a more ad hoc basis to address specific issues. One example was the Commission on Intellectual Property Rights set up by the British government in May 2001 to 'look at how intellectual property rights might work better for poor people and developing countries' (IPR Commission). It provided significant credibility to the 'access to medicines' campaign led by civil society and developing countries in the late 1990s and early 2000s (Morin, 2014).

Fourth, IP treaties should be revised to strengthen international commitments to technological transfer. Several agreements only mention technology transfer as an aspiration. The TRIPs agreement simply states that 'Developed country Members shall provide incentives to enterprises and institutions in their territories to promote and encourage technology transfer to least-developed country Members to enable them to create a sound and viable technological base' (Art. 66(2)). If developing countries are required to model their domestic IP law along American and European standards, high-income countries should be required to make concrete commitments to technology transfers, including educational, health, agricultural and environmental technologies. These commitments should be supported by treaties that champion limitations and exceptions to IP, specifically by protecting the public domain from (re)privatisation and promoting open science.

Last, IP is one way to facilitate innovation and knowledge production but there are others. Indeed, governments have invested large amounts of public funds in research and development, whilst some industries have benefited greatly from the availability of public knowledge. Governments have access to many policy instruments. They should be encouraged, not hindered, by global IP governance. Alternatives include advance market commitments and prize contests, which can and should be implemented globally. Furthermore, these policy instruments should be recognised as alternatives to IP protection. For example, knowledge produced through public funds should not be privatised and should be made publicly available.

CONCLUSION

IP has become one of the most controversial and politicised areas of global governance. The criticisms of the current regime have been the subject of both public and academic debate, particularly in the aftermath of the TRIPS agreement. This chapter argues that the controversies surrounding global IP governance stem from its failure to legitimise how it has or has not balanced private incentives with the broader public good. By examining political, socioeconomic and intergenerational dimensions, the chapter illustrates that the instrumentalist narrative, which seeks to justify the current regime, has failed to match its 'actual' effects. The global IP regime has not only created unjust outcomes, but it has created outcomes that are unjust in its terms.

Reforming the system is difficult. The power of IP owners is tremendous and their interests have been largely institutionalised in a global governance framework. IP-owning industries are also increasingly profitable and economically powerful. Furthermore, the influence of IP owners is particularly pronounced in the most powerful states. The USA and EU have focused on IP in their trade initiatives since the TRIPS agreement. They have given priority to maximalist IP agendas. Nevertheless, the clear disconnect between the institutionalised narratives used to justify the current IP regime and the regime's 'actual' outcomes will continue to erode its legitimacy.

REFERENCES

Baldwin, P. (2014). The Copyright Wars: Three Centuries of Trans-Atlantic Battle. *Princeton University Press.*

Benkler, Y. (2001). A Political Economy of the Public Domain: Markets in Information Goods versus the Marketplace of Ideas. *Expanding the Boundaries of Intellectual Property: Innovation Policy for the Knowledge Society, 267,* 270.

Boldrin, M., & Levine, D. K. (2008). Against Intellectual Monopoly (Vol. 62). *Cambridge University Press.*

Cartwright, M. (2019). Preferential Trade Agreements and Power Asymmetries: The Case of Technological Protection Measures in Australia. *The Pacific Review, 32*(3), 313–35.

Cartwright, M. (2021). Business Conflict and International Law: The Political Economy of Copyright in the United States. *Regulation & Governance, 15*(1), 152–67.

Deere, C. (2008). *The Implementation Game: The TRIPS Agreement and the Global Politics of Intellectual Property Reform in Developing Countries.* Oxford University Press.

Dobusch, L., & Quack, S. (2013). Framing Standards, Mobilizing Users: Copyright versus Fair Use in Transnational Regulation. *Review of International Political Economy, 20*(1), 52–88.

Drahos, P. (2016). *A Philosophy of Intellectual Property.* Routledge.

Helfer, L. R. (2004). Regime Shifting: The TRIPs Agreement and New Dynamics of International Intellectual Property Lawmaking. *Yale Journal of International Law, 29,* 1.

Hudson, J. and Minea, A. (2013). Innovation, Intellectual Property Rights, and Economic Development: A Unified Empirical Investigation. *World Development, 46,* 66–78.

Idris, Kamil. 2003. *Intellectual Property: A Power Tool for Economic Growth,* 2nd edition. Geneva: World Intellectual Property Organization.

Kim, Y. K., Lee, K., Park, W. G., & Choo, K. (2012). Appropriate Intellectual Property Protection and Economic Growth in Countries at Different Levels of Development. *Research Policy, 41*(2), 358–75.

Machlup, F., & Penrose, E. (1950). The Patent Controversy in the Nineteenth Century. *The Journal of Economic History, 10*(1), 1–29.

MacNeil, R. (2013). Seeding an Energy Technology Revolution in the United States: Reconceptualising the Nature of Innovation in 'Liberal-Market Economies'. *New Political Economy,* 18(1), 64–88.

Miller, Jonathan M. A. (2003). Typology of Legal Transplants: Using Sociology, Legal History and Argentine Examples to Explain the Transplant Process. *The American Journal of Comparative Law, 51*(4), 839–86.

Morin, J.-F. (2010). The Two-Level Game of Transnational Networks: The Case of the Access to Medicines Campaign. *International Interactions, 36*(4), 309–34.

Morin, J.-F. (2014). A Paradigm Shift in the Global IP Regime: The Agency of Academics. *Review of International Political Economy, 21*(2), 275–309.

Morin, J.-F. (2020). Concentration despite Competition: The Organizational Ecology of Technical Assistance Providers. *The Review of International Organizations, 15*(1), 75–107.

Morin, J.-F. and Gold, E. R. (2014). An Integrated Model of Legal Transplantation: The Diffusion of Intellectual Property Law in Developing Countries. *International Studies Quarterly, 58*(4), 781–92.

Morin, J.-F. et Surbeck, J. (2020). Mapping the New Frontier of International IP Law: Introducing a TRIPS-Plus Dataset. *World Trade Review, 19*(1), 109–22.

Okediji, R. L. (2003). The International Relations of Intellectual Property: Narratives of Developing Country Participation in the Global Intellectual Property System. *Singapore Journal of International & Comparative Law*, *7*, 315.

Sell, S. K. (2003). *Private Power, Public Law: The Globalization of Intellectual Property Rights* (Vol. 88). Cambridge University Press.

Sell, S. K. (2010). The Rise and Rule of a Trade-Based Strategy: Historical Institutionalism and the International Regulation of Intellectual Property. *Review of International Political Economy*, *17*(4), 762–90.

Shi, W. (2010). Globalization and Indigenization: Legal Transplant of a Universal TRIPS Regime in a Multicultural World. *American Business Law Journal*, *47*, 455.

UNESCO UIS (n.d). https://uis.unesco.org/.

Wade, R. H. (2003). What Strategies Are Viable for Developing Countries Today? The World Trade Organization and the Shrinking of 'Development Space'. *Review of International Political Economy*, *10*(4), 621–44.

Weldon, C. (2017). The De Minimis Requirement as a Safety Valve: Copyright, Creativity, and the Sampling of Sound Recordings. *New York University Law Review*, *92*, 1261.

World Intellectual Property Organization, Program of Work and Budget for 2024/25, Geneva, WIPO https://www.wipo.int/about-wipo/en/budget/.

Chapter 19

JUSTICE IN GLOBAL INTELLECTUAL PROPERTY GOVERNANCE

Annabelle Lever and Cristian Timmermann

INTRODUCTION

The twentieth century has seen a striking expansion in the scope, application and geographic reach of intellectual property rights (IPR) – that is, of legal rights that enable the rights holder to use, withhold, license and transfer ideas for profit, in exchange for registering them publicly. There is widespread consensus that the Agreement of Trade-Related Aspects of Intellectual Property Rights (TRIPS, 1994) in the World Trade Organization marked a turning point in the globalisation of minimum standards of intellectual property protection applicable to all countries after a ten-year transition time (Drahos & Braithwaite, 2003). By linking intellectual property protection to trade agreements, exclusive rights holders from strong economies gained the ability to enforce the protection of their interests through trade sanctions, rather than, as previously, through lawsuits for infringement of property rights. Countries building up their industries are now prevented from designing intellectual property policies that are tailored to their stage of technological development although, historically, countries in the Global North had significantly different IP policies as they industrialised. (Boyle, 2008; Khan, 2005; May 2007 see Cartwright & Morin, Chapter 18 in this volume).

These developments highlight the fluidity but also the political and economic significance of IPRs and remind us that an ethical evaluation of their properties is important for global justice broadly conceived. In this chapter, we identify the different stakeholders in IPRs, examine their conflicting interests, and analyse shortcomings in deliberation processes over IPRs. We also sketch ways to address several problems with the current IP regime.

STAKEHOLDERS AND THEIR CONFLICTING INTERESTS

A widely held philosophical justification of intellectual property rights appeals to a hypothetical contract between society and innovators, where society grants innovators temporary exclusivity about the information on how to replicate their invention (Murray, 2006). In this view, innovators should be allowed to recoup their costs and make profits during the time they enjoy market exclusivity and, in return society benefits by having more information become part of the public domain. Yet, as philosophers reflecting on the nature and limits of mutually beneficial consensual exchanges argue, even mutually beneficial consensual exchanges can have adverse effects on others.

For IPRs to be consistent with demands of justice, whether domestically or globally, they ought to reflect the legitimate interests of the following groups, at least:

> *Innovators (producers of new ideas)* have an interest (i) in being recognised as authors, (ii) in the material benefits coming from the invention, (iii) in the diffusion of the invention, and (iv) in participating in scientific advancement (for example, follow-up innovation, access to science).
>
> *Consumers of those ideas* have an interest (i) in accessing the invention, (ii) in the availability of creative solutions for their problems, and (iii) in socially, environmentally and scientifically responsible innovation.
>
> *Investors* have an interest (i) in a return on their investments, (ii) in the fulfilment of their legitimate expectations, and (iii) in the freedom to engage in mutually beneficial joint ventures.
>
> *People outside the global market*: who (i) want to maintain their knowledge-exchange practices (for example indigenous seed exchange networks, open-source software), and (ii) do not want to be exposed to appropriation of their knowledge by outsiders. The fourth group is often overlooked but their legitimate interests deserve attention. Those people, usually the very poor but also some marginalised indigenous groups, neither use nor benefit from the global market and their various contributions to the creation of ideas/products remain largely unrecognised by the market.

As we discuss in what follows, the interests of the different groups affected by IPR regimes may diverge and sometimes conflict.

Investors: Current global property regimes are heavily slanted towards the interests of innovators and investors in high-income countries and against consumers both in developing countries and in high-income ones. Among the advantaged groups, current rules favour investors over innovators, insofar as the producers of patentable ideas are generally employees of corporations and usually have to cede IP rights to their employers as part of their contract (Lemley, 2012).

Innovators, that is producers of ideas, have an interest in being recognised as creators, an interest in preventing unconscionable uses of their ideas, as they see fit, and an interest in promoting uses of ideas that they favour (Timmermann, 2020). These non-material interests of innovators are poorly protected by existing intellectual property regimes, even when their material interests are safeguarded. Formally, creative workers have a right to attribution of authorship and to the integrity of expressive work. However, institutional support to enforce such rights is often unavailable, leaving early-career scientists in academia, smallholders and indigenous people vulnerable to the misattribution and misappropriation of their intellectual contributions by others. Legally, when it comes to the future use of exclusive rights, the moral interests of authors are understood in a highly restricted sense (Prifti, 2016). For example, permitting usurious licensing practices, and indifference to the needs of the worst-off by current patent holders, regardless of the desires and hopes that may have animated inventors.

Moreover, copyright laws make it all but impossible for *innovators* to experiment with Samuel Becket's plays, for example, however brilliant, respectful and appealing those experiments, because copyright protection extends to seventy years after the death of an author and means that the author's estate can withhold permission to directors and productions that do not meet with their approval (Wyver, 2020). Innovators can find themselves constrained by patent law because the institutions in which they work may seek to prevent the sharing of samples and ideas with peers, or the timely publication of research results, to protect the patentability of research.

Material and non-material interests in being recognised as authors, autonomy in deciding how the invention is used and diffused, and creative freedom to cooperate with others and reuse inventions have a role in explaining the moral case for IPR (Drassinower, 2008; Biron, 2012; Lametti, 2012). Existing rules for global IP fail adequately to protect these interests, in part because of the way that the creative industries are currently structured (Demuijnck, 2012), and because the costs of seeking and enforcing licences are prohibitive. As Hettinger says 'In our society . . . most patents and copyrights are owned by institutions . . . Independent authors or inventors who earn their living by selling their writings or inventions to others are increasingly rare' (Hettinger, 1989, p. 46).

Consumers of inventive ideas are often greatly disadvantaged by existing IP rules, even in rich countries (Boyle, 2008). Although medicines, like surgical techniques, used to be unpatentable (Noonan, 1995), their patentability has facilitated the creation of life-saving knowledge, at the cost of rendering their price prohibitively expensive for a large part of the global population. Lack of access to life-saving medicines for those most affected by ill health is a major ethical challenge. It highlights the problem that a large part of the world population does not suffer from unavoidable (natural) threats to their health but from the avoidable (human-made) consequences of an institutional order that gives insufficient weight to their interests and leaves their basic needs unfulfilled (Pogge, 2005; Jaggar, 2010). Patents interfere with the mechanism of market 'demand' as a vehicle for signalling needs that are particularly evident (Pogge et al., 2010). For example, patents may adversely affect the development of much-needed products, including medicines, because patent-holders may simply refuse to develop products themselves or to license them to others. (Heller & Eisenberg, 1998; Hall et al., 2012).

Moreover, pressures on farmers to use patented seeds, which need to be bought each year, can exacerbate problems of precarity, indebtedness and food security, especially in the Global South. Farmer suicides in India testify to the tragic results of seeds that cannot be reused from year to year with often unscrupulous sales practices, and unrealistic claims made about the benefits of such products (Thomas & De Tavernier, 2017). Although IP rights are thought to limit *use*, not *access* to ideas, controlling use necessarily limits access to ideas by those who cannot set aside resources to purchase the end products, go to patent offices, access their online sites or whose academic institutions cannot afford expensive copyrighted books and prohibitively priced journals.

Intellectual property governance can neither ignore existing inequalities in terms of financial, legal and scientific resources, nor the urgency with which some major global challenges need to be confronted by widely diffusing technological innovations. In a world of extreme inequality of purchasing power, innovators from the Global South have few chances of benefiting from the IP system to market their inventions. Moreover, reliance on intellectual property regimes, as opposed to other ways of protecting and promoting ideas, inherently constrains public choice and accountability concerning the legal definition of property, and over the direction and access to research and technology (Resnik, 1997; Nuffield Council on Bioethics, 2002; Lever, 2008; Dutfield, 2012).

WAY FORWARD

The first way forward builds on the idea that, conceptually and normatively, we can distinguish rights of recognition and control over one's ideas from rights to profit from using those ideas oneself or from licensing them to others (Biron, 2012). We must recognise and use the flexibility inherent in IPR rights which, like other property rights, can be thought of as a bundle of different rights rather than as an indissoluble whole (Munzer, 2001; Waldron, 2020). Thus, as John Christman suggested, we can distinguish two large groups of property rights for conceptual, moral and political purposes – *control* rights, which determine our ability to use, alienate, destroy and transform objects, and *income* rights, which are rights to profit from the use of our control rights (Christman, 1994). In the IP context, we might also want to distinguish rights to license or not to license one's invention – given that one does not presuppose the other conceptually or normatively, and their relationship is at stake in arguments over compulsory licensing.

We might also consider the scope for the compulsory licensing of inventions to international agencies on especially favourable terms, without supposing that inventors must otherwise lack strong rights in their ideas (Wilson, 2012; Christman, 2012). There is nothing in the concept of IP itself that precludes fairly stringent regulations of intellectual property rights to better reflect the legitimate claims of those who are ignored or poorly protected under existing legal and political arrangements (Beitz, 2005). Even those legal conventions that treat intellectual property rights as human rights, such as the protocol to the European Convention on Human Rights, acknowledge that these rights are not absolute and that they must be protected by other rights.

Indeed, the flexible character of IP rights, and scope for improved protection of legitimate global claims, can be seen in the international legal recognition granted to traditional knowledge (TK) (Christman, 2012; Munzer, 2012). Of course, granting IP rights over indigenous knowledge is not sufficient to ensure that the legitimate claims of indigenous communities to use, transmit and profit from their knowledge are adequately protected. However, IP rights in TK reflects abhorrence at the idea of Western countries patenting the fungicidal properties of the Neem tree and then legally excluding indigenous communities, who had identified the tree's potential for agricultural pest control, from using their knowledge as before (Hamilton, 2006). Indigenous communities should not be induced to sell their patents on severely disadvantageous terms and, by that means, be prevented from using their knowledge because the licence fees are beyond their means. It might be unreasonable to say that IP rights in traditional knowledge can never be sold, only licensed. However, it seems clear that the case of indigenous knowledge shows both the scope for improving IP law and the urgency of improving the protections for indigenous peoples.

The dramatic power differentials that characterise our world are a crucial barrier to designing legal permissions, duties and claims that would safeguard the legitimate interests of the worst-off. The dramatic neglect and exploitation of indigenous knowledge is the result of centuries of colonial rule. Colonisation not only imposed foreign rule on and extracted raw materials from the colonised. It also created a global hierarchy of human values with some cultures, knowledge and ways of life considered to have less value than others. Indigenous farming communities' centuries-old methods have been discounted or ignored as forms of knowledge (Altieri & Toledo, 2011). In addition to minimising political and economic power differentials, then, there is a need to rethink colonial biases in the global hierarchy of knowledge production and to properly recognise formerly marginalised methods and cultures.

The second way forward addresses the problem that the costs of protecting against patent infringement, or of arguing for rights of legal access to ideas, are prohibitive for many producers, consumers and investors in ideas, whether they are members of rich or poor countries, and whether the claims that they seek to vindicate are national or international. It is particularly unfair that groups who do not use or benefit directly from the IP system need to spend scarce resources to protect their knowledge and expressions from appropriation by setting up large databases to show prior art (Kidd, 2012). It is necessary, then, to rethink the ways that IP rights are enforced to prevent large companies from bullying smaller companies or weaker governments and to ensure adequate protection for individual consumers, producers and investors in ideas. Particularly when property boundaries between different patent owners are unclear, as is the case in patents involving genes (Safrin, 2004), large companies can use their superior economic and legal strength to threaten smaller companies over infringement and to create delays to court cases that drain their opponents' resources.

At national and international levels this might suggest a centralised agency, akin to a public prosecutor and defender, to ensure that moral and legal claims over intellectual property are fairly protected. The agency could be financed from a combination of national taxation and a graduated tax on IP receipts by rights holders. Such an agency could also be required to propose measures to prevent 'nuisance' lawsuits amongst companies that turn IPRs into a tool of business competition at the cost of their ability to recognise and support creative ideas. Markets in intellectual property rights themselves have become dissociated from the protection and use of the products – inventions, expressions and distinguishing marks – whose encouragement, access and use formed their *raison d'être*. Speculative markets in IPRs can threaten future funding for research, as companies are bought and sold for their patent portfolio rather than for their present and future capacities to innovate (Bessen et al., 2011) and access to knowledge becomes one more asset in existing forms of casino capitalism.

The third way forward addresses the problem of *political injustice* in designing the rules of IP governance. Our globally enforced IP regimes are not the result of careful deliberation about the interests of industrialised, emerging and subsistence economies. Instead, the powerful get to impose their interets against those of the less powerful, often in conflict with global priorities, such as the rapid diffusion of green technologies. Political power was used to shift debates on IP to more advantageous forums and superior legal expertise, and political connections facilitated the exclusion of dissenting voices in increasingly complex negotiations (Kuyper, 2015).

To address this political injustice, the rules covering IPR at the national and international levels need to be determined in circumstances that are more open, inclusive and accountable than they currently are (Lever, 2008). Doing so can help to prevent prolonged fights over the morality of particular patentable inventions (Liddell, 2012), over the consequences of patent rights granted for cultural norms in the Global South, and prevent biopiracy in cases that are not as self-evidently abusive as the recent effort by a US company to patent traditional basmati rice (Orozco & Poonamallee, 2014). Furthermore, mechanisms need to be established so that provisions to protect the interests of vulnerable populations, such as the right to issue compulsory licences, remain in place and are not rescinded when negotiating binational and regional trade agreements (Dutfield, 2008).

CONCLUSIONS

At present, there is relatively little scope for distinctly moral considerations in the adjudication of IP claims (Liddell, 2012), in part because of the legal assumption that there must be *no* morally acceptable use for an idea if it is to be denied IP protection. The justification for such a high standard is that governments are perfectly free to determine what patent and copyright holders are then entitled to do – or not do – with their IP-protected ideas. This distinction looked like a helpful way to recognise the creation of innovative ideas and expressions, while (at least in principle) creating considerable flexibility in regulating their use in light of concerns for their morality, safety or efficacy – though TRIPS has effectively prevented that. However, to focus only on that aspect of current rules misses the point that some objections to IP are motivated by the belief that some things should not be treated as *private* property, and therefore seen as subject to the exclusive use and control of anyone (Ossorio, 2002). In other cases, the concern is that IP rights treat and turn into property things that should not be thought of as property to begin with. (Lever, 2008). Both worries about the moral implications of IP can be found in opposition to patents on human genes and other life forms, on medicines as well as surgical techniques and in the treatment of TK, and point to the ways that implicit ideas of morality underpin the discovery/invention distinction which provides the central criterion of patentability (Liddell, 2012; Wilson, 2012).

There is wide support for the idea that some goods need to be considered *public goods* normatively (cf. O'Neill, 2018), such that nobody ought to be excluded from benefiting from them, and that at least some inventions fall under that rubric. This was also the understanding that was defended by Jonas Salk who developed the first polio vaccine (van den Belt & Korthals, 2013), and that explains the urgency felt by John Sulston and others who wanted the sequence of the human genome to be freely available to all (Sulston & Ferry, 2002; Ferry 2018). More recently, the idea that some inventions should be treated as public goods morally, given their importance to human rights, figured in arguments for lifting exclusive rights over the Covid-19 vaccines to allow wider access to them (Club de Madrid, 2021). In other cases, considerations of *intergenerational justice* combined with the urgency of addressing climate change, raise concerns about the way IP rights might prevent the rapid introduction and use of green innovations and technologies in poor, as well as rich, countries. (Biddle, 2016). We simply do not have the time to wait for patents to expire – let alone copyrights – before making energy-saving as well as green energy technologies more widely available.

In short, some innovations are not merely commodities for private consumption but concern the prerequisites and necessities of human life. IP, at least as currently constituted, makes it extremely difficult adequately to recognise and act on this morally fundamental distinction. It is therefore urgent to establish suitably inclusive, deliberative settings at national and international levels to address ethical problems in our current IP regime. This is necessary to prevent the unreflective global imposition of what are, at best, only some amongst a potentially infinite set of morally permissible norms of IP. And it is necessary to prevent the worst: where global rules of IP actively foster and enforce immoral and dangerously misguided ideas about the worth of human lives, capacities, activities and relationships with each other and with the non-human world.

REFERENCES

Altieri, M. A., & Toledo, V. M. (2011). The Agroecological Revolution in Latin America: Rescuing Nature, Ensuring Food Sovereignty and Empowering Peasants. *Journal of Peasant Studies, 38(3)*, 587–612.

Beitz, C. R. (2005). The Moral Rights of Creators of Artistic and Literary Works. *Journal of Political Philosophy, 13(3)*, 330–58.

Bessen, J., Ford, J., & Meurer, M. J. (2011). The Private and Social Costs of Patent Trolls. *Regulation, 34*, 26–35.

Biddle, J. B. (2016). Intellectual Property Rights and Global Climate Change: Toward Resolving an Apparent Dilemma. *Ethics, Policy & Environment, 19(3)*, 301–19.

Biron, L. (2012). Public Reason, Communication, and Intellectual Property. In Lever, A. (ed.), *New Frontiers in the Philosophy of Intellectual Property*, 225–60. Cambridge University Press.

Boyle, J. (2008). *The Public Domain: Enclosing the Commons of the Mind*. Yale University Press.

Christman, J. (1994). *The Myth of Property: Toward an Egalitarian Theory of Ownership*. Oxford University Press.

Christman, J. (2012). Autonomy, Social Selves, and Intellectual Property Claims. In Lever, A. (ed.), *New Frontiers in the Philosophy of Intellectual Property*, 33–57. Cambridge University Press.

Club de Madrid. (2021). *Former Heads of State and Nobel Laureates Call on President Biden to Waive Intellectual Property Rules for COVID Vaccines.*

Demuijnck, G. (2012). Illegal Downloading, Free Riding, and Justice. In Lever, A. (ed.), *New Frontiers in the Philosophy of Intellectual Property*, 261–83. Cambridge University Press.

Drahos, P., & Braithwaite, J. (2003). *Information Feudalism: Who Owns the Knowledge Economy?* New Press.
Drassinower, A. (2008). Authorship as Public Address: On the Specificity of Copyright vis-à-vis Patent and Trade-Mark. *Michigan State Law Review,* 199–232.
Dutfield, G. (2008). Delivering Drugs to the Poor: Will the TRIPS Amendment Help? *American Journal of Law & Medicine, 34(2–3),* 107–24.
Dutfield, G. (2012).'The Genetic Code Is 3.6 billion Years Old: It's Time for a Rewrite': Questioning the Metaphors and Analogies of Synthetic Biology and Life Science Patenting. In Lever, A. (ed.), *New Frontiers in the Philosophy of Intellectual Property,* 172–202. Cambridge University Press.
Ferry, G. (2018). John Sulston (1942–2018). *Nature, 555*(7696), 588–9.
Hall, B. H., Helmers, C., von Graevenitz, G., & Rosazza-Bondibene, C. (2012). A Study of Patent Thickets: Final Report Prepared for the UK Intellectual Property Office. *Report, National Institute of Social and Economic Research.*
Hamilton, C. (2006). Biodiversity, Biopiracy and Benefits: What Allegations of Biopiracy Tell Us about Intellectual Property. *Developing World Bioethics, 6(3),* 158–73.
Heller, M. A., & Eisenberg, R. S. (1998). Can Patents Deter Innovation? The Anticommons in Biomedical Research. *Science, 280(5364),* 698–701.
Hettinger, E. C. (1989). Justifying Intellectual Property. *Philosophy & Public Affairs, 18(1),* 31–52.
Jaggar, A. M. (2010). *Thomas Pogge and His Critics.* Polity Press.
Khan, B. Z. (2005). *The Democratization of Invention: Patents and Copyrights in American Economic Development,* 1790–920. Cambridge University Press.
Kidd, I. J. (2012). Biopiracy and the Ethics of Medical Heritage: The Case of India's Traditional Knowledge Digital Library. *Journal of Medical Humanities, 33(3),* 175–83.
Kuyper, J. (2015). Deliberative Capacity in the Intellectual Property Rights Regime Complex. *Critical Policy Studies, 9(3),* 317–38.
Lametti, D. (2012). The Virtuous P(eer): Reflections on the Ethics of File Sharing. In Lever, A. (ed.), *New Frontiers in the Philosophy of Intellectual Property,* 284–306. Cambridge University Press.
Lemley, M. A. (2012). The Myth of the Sole Inventor. *Michigan Law Review, 110,* 709–60.
Lever, A. (2008). Is It Ethical to Patent Human Genes? In Gosseries, A., Marciano, A., & Strowel, A. (eds.), *Intellectual Property and Theories of Justice,* 246–64. Palgrave Macmillan.
Liddell, K. (2012). Immorality and Patents: The Exclusion of Inventions Contrary to Ordre Public and Morality. In Lever, A. (ed.), *New Frontiers in the Philosophy of Intellectual Property,* 140–71. Cambridge University Press.
May, C. (2007). The Hypocrisy of Forgetfulness: The Contemporary Significance of Early Innovations in Intellectual Property. *Review of International Political Economy, 14(1),* 1–25.
Munzer, S. R. (ed.). (2001). *New Essays in the Legal and Political Theory of Property. Cambridge University Press.*
Munzer, S. R. (2012). Corrective Justice and Intellectual Property Rights in Traditional Knowledge. In Lever, A. (ed.), *New Frontiers in the Philosophy of Intellectual Property,* 58–87. Cambridge University Press
Murray, K. N. (2006). Rules for Radicals: A Politics of Patent Law. *Journal of Intellectual Property Law, 14,* 63–110.
Noonan, W. D. (1995). Patenting Medical and Surgical Procedures. *Journal of the Patent & Trademark Office Society, 77,* 651–64.
Nozick, R. (1974). *Anarchy, State, and Utopia. Basic Books.*

Nuffield Council on Bioethics. (2002). The Ethics of Patenting DNA: A Discussion Paper. *Nuffield Council on Bioethics.*

O'Neill, John. 2018.'Food, Needs and Commons'. In Vivero-Pol, J. L., Ferrando, T., De Schutter, O., & Mattei, U. (eds.), *Routledge Handbook of Food as a Commons*, 103–20. Routledge.

Orozco, D., & Poonamallee, L. (2014). The Role of Ethics in the Commercialization of Indigenous Knowledge. *Journal of Business Ethics, 119*, 275–86.

Ossorio, P. N. (2002). Property Rights and Human Bodies. In Magnus D., Caplan, A., & McGee, G. (eds.), *Who Owns Life?*, 223–42. Prometheus Books.

Pogge, T. (2005). Symposium on World Poverty and Human Rights. *Ethics and International Affairs, 19*(1). https://onlinelibrary.wiley.com/doi/abs/10.1111/j.1747-7093.2005.tb00484.x

Pogge, T., Rimmer, M., & Rubenstein, K. (eds.). (2010). Incentives for Global Public Health: Patent Law and Access to Essential Medicines. *Cambridge University Press.*

Prifti, V. (2016). Die Rolle des öffentlichen Interesses an Pflanzenpatenten: Eine europäische Perspektive. In *Biopatente*, 55-74. Nomos Verlagsgesellschaft mbH & Co. KG.

Resnik, D. B. (1997). The Morality of Human Gene Patents. *Kennedy Institute of Ethics Journal, 7*(1), 43–61.

Safirin, S. (2004). Hyperownership in a Time of Biotechnological Promise: The International Conflict to Control the Building Blocks of Life. *American Journal of International Law, 98(4)*, 641–85.

Sulston, J., & Ferry, G. (2002). *The Common Thread: A Story of Science, Politics, Ethics, and the Human Genome*. Bantam Press.

Thomas, G., & De Tavernier, J. (2017). Farmer-Suicide in India: Debating the Role of Biotechnology. *Life Sciences, Society, and Policy, 13*, 8.

Timmermann, C. (2020). *Social Justice and Agricultural Innovation*. Springer.

Van den Belt, H., & Korthals, M. (2013). The International Patent System and the Ethics of Global Justice. In Arapostathis, S., & Dutfield, G. (eds.), *Knowledge Management and Intellectual Property: Concepts, Actors, and Practices from the Past to the Present*, 235–51. Edward Elgar Publishing.

Waldron, J. (2020). Property and Ownership. In Zalta, E. N. (ed.), *The Stanford Encyclopedia of Philosophy*.

Wilson, J. G. S. (2012). On the Value of the Intellectual Commons. In Lever, A. (ed.), *New Frontiers in the Philosophy of Intellectual Property*, 122–39. Cambridge University Press.

Wolff, J. (1991). *Robert Nozick: Property, Justice and the Minimal State*. Polity Press.

Wyver, K. (2020). Not Waiting for Godot: New Show Tackles Beckett's Ban on Women. *The Guardian, 18*.

Chapter 20

GLOBAL ECONOMIC AND EARTH SYSTEM GOVERNANCE: A CALL FOR PLANETARY JUSTICE

Clara Brandi, Defne Gönenç, Prakash Kashwan, Frank Biermann, Aarti Gupta and Chukwumerije Okereke

INTRODUCTION

The disruptions to the earth's system have reached an unprecedented scale, posing enormous challenges around the globe. The world has entered the Anthropocene, a new geological age in which human activity is recognised as the dominant force driving the negative changes in climate and environment, and the very earth system upon which our existence depends. In such an era of planet-wide transformation, some scholars have argued for a new model for planet-wide environmental politics: earth system governance (Biermann, 2007). Earth system governance is broader than traditional environmental policy and emphasises the complexities of integrated socio-ecological systems (for a focus on natural resources, see Armstrong, Chapter 21 in this volume). Key concerns of earth system governance are broad and often include interdependent challenges such as land use change, food system disruptions, climate change, environment-induced migration, species extinction and air pollution.

Global economic governance cannot remain stagnant in the face of these existential challenges. It needs to focus much more on concerns of planetary stewardship and earth system governance than in the past. This, in turn, requires, however, more attention also to issues of *planetary justice,* since ensuring the sustainability of earth systems depends on incorporating justice and fairness in all institutions governing the global economy (Kashwan et al., 2020). The concept of planetary justice expands traditional notions of global, environmental or ecological justice, with global justice focusing more on purely socioeconomic inequalities, environmental justice more on injustices from local environmental conflicts, and ecological justice more on ecological inclusiveness (Agyeman et al., 2016). Planetary justice, instead, is a broader and more holistic framework for justice in the Anthropocene (Biermann & Kalfagianni, 2020; Gupta et al., 2021). It aims to include the notions of global, environmental and ecological justice while adding a novel understanding of justice that deals with the entire human and non-human world.

This chapter expands on these notions with three main goals: first, we discuss how the global economic system affects the allocation of environmental benefits and burdens among people and countries around the world. We focus on trade and investment as important elements of today's global economic system and of the relationship between the global economic system and the environment (see also Berensmann & Volz, Chapter 10 in this volume). Second, we analyse varying approaches to earth system governance and their distinctive proposals for an effective and just earth system governance. We conclude by laying out our policy proposals for earth system governance in this field, focusing on redistribution in a pro-poor manner. Pro-poor redistribution in earth system governance acknowledges how individuals from different classes and communities are disproportionately affected by environmental and socioeconomic injustices. It emphasises that the poorer and marginalised should not be further disadvantaged, but rather their circumstances must improve through policy decisions. Additionally, it emphasises the importance of recognising them as legitimate participants in decisions regarding earth system governance.

THE ARCHITECTURE OF EARTH SYSTEM GOVERNANCE

We conceptualise earth system governance as 'the interrelated and increasingly integrated system of formal and informal rules, rule-making systems and actor-networks at all levels of human society (from local to global) that are set up to steer societies towards preventing, mitigating and adapting to global and local environmental change and, in particular, earth system transformation, within the normative context of sustainable development' (Biermann, 2007). The architecture of earth system governance is then defined as 'the interlocking web of widely shared principles, institutions and practices that shape decisions at all levels in a given area of earth system governance' (Biermann, 2014).

One key element of this architecture is the network of more than 3000 international environmental agreements (Mitchell, 2003). Despite the growing number of treaties, standards and protocols, there are reasons to doubt whether these approaches can tackle the environmental challenges the world is facing. For instance, international environmental agreements seek to make progress based on consensus which tends to lead to a lack of ambitious targets or voluntaristic approaches, such as the Nationally Determined Contributions under the Paris Agreement, that often fail to address the most pressing challenges. Moreover, global environmental governance is weakened by a lack of enforcement mechanisms, which can undermine implementation and lead to free-riding.

Next to international agreements, earth system governance also includes an increasing number of private transnational initiatives by non-state or private actors. Grassroots movements have become prominent as well, challenging environmentally harmful policies of governments and ecologically destructive activities of governments and private companies (Martínez-Alier et al., 2016). They enlighten conflicting values over the environment and unsustainable resource uses affecting people and the planet (Scheidel et al., 2018). Global grassroots environmentalism may have evolved into a promising force for sustainability and economic transformation. For example, by calling for increased action on climate change, the Fridays for Future movement has gained momentum around the world and become through strikes highly visible in more than 150 countries.

Because strategies to improve planetary justice are shaped by how one sees global economic governance affecting the earth system governance, we continue by first discussing the impact of global economic governance on the distribution of environmental benefits and burdens. Then we assess other dominant approaches to earth system governance and their views on the impacts of economic governance on earth system governance. Finally, we propose our redistributive solutions prioritising the poorer classes in the socioeconomic strata.

GLOBAL ECONOMIC GOVERNANCE AND ENVIRONMENTAL BENEFITS AND BURDENS

Drawing on Gönenç et al. (2020) we now discuss the impact of the global economic system mainly of trade and investment on the distribution of environmental benefits and burdens in three channels: the direct impact of trade and investment; the impact of economic empowerment through trade and investment on participation in decision-making for earth system governance; and the impact of international environmental agreements on earth system governance through these agreements' impact on trade and investment.

Direct Impact of Trade and Investment on Environmental Benefits and Burdens

Trade and investment systems, including the rules and processes set by the governing institutions, shape the allocation of environmental benefits and burdens (Gönenç et al., 2020). In many cases, they also directly affect the ability of individuals and social groups to access the environmental resources required to meet their cultural, economic and environmental needs (Ceddia, 2019). This is especially true for countries with high economic inequalities and poorly functioning democratic institutions, where it leads to corporate capture of land, water and other types of commons (Kashwan et al., 2021).

In the realm of international trade, scholars have different views on how economic liberalisation influences the distribution of environmental resources. Some argue that the expansion of free trade has adverse effects on the environment. For instance, around one-third of deforestation-related emissions are driven by international trade, mainly in beef and oilseeds like palm oil (Pendrill et al., 2019).

Others argue that trade helps resolve environmental problems. Some contend that trade efficiently allocates resources, resulting in less depletion of those resources and facilitating environmental protection. Moreover, by promoting economic growth and hence enabling greater investments in clean energy technologies, diffusion of environmental standards and environmentally friendly technologies, trade could be a tool to conserve the environment (Evenett & Whalley, 2009).

A third group of scholars argue that the environmental impacts of trade depend on the design of global economic governance (Brandi & Morin, 2023). For example, the preferential treatment of certain production processes, such as the use of clean technology or trade in certain goods (Brandi et al., 2020) can reduce pollution and combat climate change. However, the potential of environmentally motivated restrictions in international trade forcing countries to change their production processes and product designs can push exporting countries to adopt the environmental standards of the other trading partners (Biermann, 2014).

Impact of Trade and Investment on Participation in Environmental Decision-Making

In addition, it is imperative to not only study the implications of trade and investment from a direct outcome-based perspective but also understand the governance processes that lead to these outcomes. Notably, the governance of trade and investment may affect environmental benefits and burdens through their impact on participation, for example, of vulnerable groups and communities in environmental decision-making processes and legal justice systems (Gönenç et al., 2020).

First, international trade and investment agreements have traditionally remained isolated from public participation and access to justice in the context of investor-state dispute settlement procedures (Tienhaara, 2006; see also Bergert et al. and Banai, Chapters 2 and 3 in this volume). These agreements have frequently been perceived as eroding the capacity of local communities to express their concerns and safeguard their land and natural resource rights (Gönenç et al., 2020). The Columbia Centre on Sustainable Investment and the UN Working Group on Business and Human Rights (2018) have shown that numerous indigenous communities affected by mining ventures in South America have raised grievances about their exclusion from foreign investment procedures that posed a direct threat to the environmental resources essential to their livelihoods.

Secondly, global trade and investment trends can undermine the autonomy of marginalised communities and entrench or amplify socioeconomic disparities even in systems that provide procedural rights (Gönenç et al., 2020). To illustrate, efforts at improving participation in the Codex Alimentarius Commission's standard-setting processes have led to an enhanced capacity for influential economic entities to demand accountability from the Commission. However, this improvement has not been accompanied by a corresponding increase in the engagement of concerned constituencies in developing nations (Spagnuolo, 2011).

Impact of Environmental Governance on Allocation through Trade and Investment

While international environmental agreements directly impact environmental protection, they also have a secondary impact on the allocation of environmental resources by influencing trade and investment (Gönenç et al., 2020). Beyond the specific regulations outlined in environmental treaties, many such agreements can also shape the distribution of environmental advantages and disadvantages by either facilitating or constraining trade and investment in environmental resources. For example, the Ramsar Convention on Wetlands from 1971 has led to increased investments in the tourism sector on Malaysia's Pulau Kukup Island, resulting in socioeconomic benefits. However, this influx of tourists has harmed the island's ecological integrity over the long term (Barau & Strigner, 2015).

PROMINENT APPROACHES TO EARTH SYSTEM GOVERNANCE

How then should the global economic structure, particularly about global trade and investments, be altered to improve earth system governance? The relationship between the environment and the economy can be conceptualised in many ways (Adaman & Özkaynak, 2002). Different understandings about planetary stewardship inform different political–economic visions and lead to different policy proposals to improve earth system governance. In this section, we build on Kashwan et al. (2020) to discuss five different dominant approaches to earth system governance, how each proposes to improve planetary stewardship and the interlinkages with global economic governance. Importantly, we scrutinise these approaches through a planetary justice lens.

To begin with, a *market liberal approach*, grounded in neoclassical economics and the premise of rational individual behaviour, posits that economic growth and higher incomes are crucial for effective earth system governance.

Advocates of this perspective argue for limited government involvement and market-based interventions as a primary tool for global environmental protection. Hence, they welcome the promotion of free trade policies and foreign direct investment for an effective and appropriate earth system governance. They also assert that environmental degradation decreases as the national income goes up, chiefly because more investment can promote clean technologies. Their concept of justice often relies on aggregate social welfare as a benchmark for policy decisions, occasionally considering hypothetical scenarios of redistribution, although such possibilities are seldom explored in practice. According to this viewpoint, achieving justice through market mechanisms depends on the idea of trickle-down economics, which suggests that unrestricted market operations will eventually benefit everyone, including the global poor. However, critics argue that these theoretical assumptions fail to produce the anticipated outcomes. There is at best mixed evidence about the accuracy of trickle-down economics (Akinci, 2018) and the environmental Kuznet's curve (Kashwan, 2017b).

Second, a *bio-environmentalist perspective* emphasises the limitations imposed by the planet's carrying capacity. According to this approach, environmental degradation is primarily caused by population pressure and excessive consumption of natural resources. Informed by Neo-Malthusian and Hardin's tragedy of the commons theories, bio-environmentalists advocate for policy choices that address these issues. They propose controlling global population growth and establishing strictly protected nature reserves (Alberro, 2020). Since trade and foreign investment are tools to boost economic growth and consumption, they also favour introducing limits to these types of consumption-fuelling economic policies. However, it is increasingly acknowledged that these approaches may infringe upon human rights (Vidal, 2016). The bio-environmentalist worldview is not well-equipped to address the multifaceted causes of the global crisis, such as socioeconomic inequality, social injustice and environmental protection together (Kashwan et al., 2020).

The *ecomodernist perspective* emphasises instead harnessing human ingenuity and creativity to address global challenges like climate change (Nisbet, 2014). They propose solutions such as utilising modern technologies like carbon capture, genetically modified organisms and geoengineering (Keith & Irvine, 2016). Some ecomodernists argue that geoengineering can be seen as an act of climate justice, particularly because climate change disproportionately affects marginalised communities (Preston, 2016). They promote free trade and foreign direct investments, in general, mainly because such policies boost economic growth and enable resources to invest in geoengineering technologies. Additionally, they eagerly embrace trade and investment in green technologies since they view them as the ultimate remedy for the environmental crisis. However, ecomodernism often fails to acknowledge the lived realities and struggles of the poor, who bear the brunt of global change and seek to have their voices heard. For example, the widely referenced 'Ecomodernist Manifesto' overlooks the issue of overconsumption and rejects the potential contribution of social protest to environmental protection (Asafu-Adjaye et al., 2015). In essence, while ecomodernism aspires to include the global poor in their vision of a 'good Anthropocene', it is doubtful that global technocracy can genuinely improve the well-being of marginalised communities. Instead, it is more likely to exacerbate systemic risks and disempowerment that they face.

The fourth perspective, known as an *institutionalist approach,* aims to promote cooperation between countries to address the global responsibility of protecting the planet. This approach relies on international environmental agreements, intergovernmental organisations and cooperative rules to tackle specific sustainability issues. Institutional interventions are considered the primary strategy to counter the social and environmental consequences of unregulated capitalism. By establishing global institutions based on multilateral agreements and active participation from countries in the Global South, it becomes possible to safeguard the rights of the poor and advocate for their interests (Kotzé, 2019). An example of this is the principle of Common but Differentiated Responsibilities and Respective Capabilities in the 1992 UN Climate Convention, which reflects the idea of international justice. Such a planetary stewardship would not necessarily imply any particular political economic stance on global environmental degradation and would leave the political economic policy decisions to the international negotiations or institutions. However, social justice considerations often lack the same legal and political weight as market-based institutional arrangements in many global environmental regimes (Kashwan, 2017a). Hence, the root causes of environmental degradation arising out of global political economic policies are often disregarded or not dealt with in international environmental regimes. Furthermore, many institutionalist research programmes remain focused on the goal of effective protection of the global environment and not on increasing justice at the same time. That said, in times of a global capitalist economy, growing nationalism and populism, and the rise of a multipolar order with multiple conflicting centres of power, global institutions still seem indispensable in a progressive agenda to promote the twin goals of protecting the environment and providing social justice together (Biermann, 2014).

A fifth perspective, the *social green approach,* views the deterioration of the environment as closely tied to social, economic and political inequalities. This approach attributes both environmental degradation and poverty to the impacts of large-scale industrialism, corporate dominance over the economy and the pervasive influence of capitalism and consumerism through globalised ideologies. Within this approach, justice considerations play a significant role. Such an approach supports limitations on free trade and foreign direct investment for the sake of environmental protection and calls for a transformation of global economic governance in line with socio-ecological priorities. For example, there is a focus on safeguarding and supporting local economies, which can be achieved through fair trade initiatives and targeted funding. Another crucial aspect is the restoration of land and resource rights for indigenous peoples and other rural communities, as emphasised in the United Nations Declaration on the Rights of Peasants and Other People Working in Rural Areas (UNDROP, 2018). The goal is to pursue justice for impoverished and marginalised communities that rely on environmental resources. While a social green view points out the required transformations for planetary justice more completely compared to other approaches, the poor and marginalised groups may face significant challenges, such as exclusionary practices that hinder their participation in decentralised environmental governance due to prevailing socioeconomic inequalities (Ostrom, 2010).

In sum, although these five approaches underline important aspects of various transformative changes for global environmental protection, none of these five approaches entirely address the required changes for the pursuit of planetary justice (Kashwan et al., 2020). In the last section, we conclude by suggesting some solutions based on redistributive policies in a pro-poor way.

CONCLUSION: GLOBAL GOVERNANCE WITH A FOCUS ON PLANETARY JUSTICE

This chapter has shown how the global economic system has profound implications for the distribution of environmental benefits and burdens and is closely linked to various aspects of earth system governance. To address this challenge, we put a spotlight on planetary justice with a focus on prioritising redistributive policies, particularly favouring the interests of the poor people within planetary stewardship. We argue that there is an urgent need for better theoretical approaches and empirical studies that prioritise the needs of the poorer classes in the socioeconomic strata when analysing and advocating for effective governance responses to planetary ecological crises. Our proposals chiefly comprise shortened and updated discussions of the entry points for reform proposed by Kashwan et al. (2020).

We recognise the structural analysis of capitalism as the primary framework for examining the main drivers of the earth system crisis (Albert, 2020) and propose that redistribution, favouring the poorer classes in the socioeconomic strata, is required. Therefore, acknowledging the political–economic roots of the earth system crisis and the power relations fuelling this crisis is essential to achieving planetary justice. A vision of earth system governance that subordinates market mechanisms to democratic economic planning at multiple scales, empowering the whole society without excluding the poorer and marginalised classes, seems vital (Graham, 2023). Societies need to have a say in determining which production lines will be privileged and how resources will be invested, without leaving such decisions only to market mechanisms.

We hence propose a planetary justice strategy calling for robust international institutional transformation that explicitly focuses on the redistribution and needs of poorer communities. Material redistribution, as well as the redistribution of representative capacities, are among our propositions. Institutional reform, especially at the global level, requires careful and systematic scrutiny of how it affects the situation of the poorest classes and communities. For the twin goals of social justice and environmental protection, rapid decarbonisation, just energy transitions, curbing profligate consumption, and degrowth in certain sectors are necessary. Some forms of production need to be substantially reduced, and capacity and resources in their production need to be shifted to different lines of development in a pro-poor manner, such as public transportation, agroecological farming and the care economy (Löwy et al., 2022). Investing in key sectors that are central to securing the basic dignity of the world's poor and marginalised majorities needs to be prioritised. This includes investments in critical sectors such as food, water, energy and infrastructure. Especially the characteristics of global food production illustrate the challenges of radical transformations in these sectors: here, a few multinational corporations control nearly all the global food business and consume 75 per cent of the energy requirements of the entire food sector, but they feed a much smaller proportion of the global population (GRAIN & IATP, 2018). On the other hand, smallholders with less than 5 ha of agricultural land per farming household use only about 30 per cent of the farmland to produce more than 70 per cent of the total food calories in eighty-three countries in Latin America, sub-Saharan Africa, and South and East Asia (Samberg et al., 2016). Scaling up agroecological food systems would require the protection of the rights of these smallholders. Furthermore, pro-poor policies are also crucial for securing the integrity of local socio-ecological systems. Here, innovations developed by indigenous people and peasants often offer some of the best tools in today's climate-changed world. Examples are systems of controlled fire interventions, ethics of landscape conservation and agroecological systems of food production (Perfecto & Vandermeer, 2010). Innovative models of multi-use agroecology promoted by transnational movements such as *La Via Campesina* can point the way forward. Even though it is not easy to replicate agroecological approaches in industrialised countries, many of the challenges here are rooted in the structure of current regimes that can be adjusted and not in the feasibility of transitioning to an agroecological regime (Levidow, 2015).

Finally, to achieve pro-poor planetary justice and curb excessive consumption, it is crucial to form broad social alliances, including the middle class. For example, making behavioural changes in key areas such as food, agriculture, transportation and energy could lead to emission reductions of 19 per cent to 38 per cent compared to projected emissions from 2020–2050 (Williamson et al., 2018). However, it is also important to structurally reform the economy to avoid unfairly burdening the poor and ensure that the necessary changes in consumption patterns and practices are supported. All this comes down to an increasing call for more effective and egalitarian planetary stewardship and transformative change towards stronger earth system governance, from local to global levels.

REFERENCES

Adaman, F., & Özkaynak, B. (2002). The Economics-Environment Relationship: Neoclassical, Institutional, and Marxist Approaches. *Studies in Political Economy, 69*(1), 109–35.

Agyeman, J., Schlosberg, D., Craven, L., & Matthews, C. (2016). Trends and Directions in Environmental Justice: From Inequity to Everyday Life, Community, and Just Sustainabilities. *Annual Review of Environment and Resources, 41*, 321–40.

Akinci, M. (2018). Inequality and Economic Growth: Trickle-down Effect Revisited. *Development Policy Review, 36*, O1–O24.

Alberro, H. (2020). Why We Should Be Wary of Blaming 'Overpopulation' for the Climate Crisis. *The Conversation, 28*.

Albert, M. J. (2020). Capitalism and Earth System Governance: An Ecological Marxist Approach. *Global Environmental Politics, 20*(2), 37–56.

Asafu-Adjaye, J., Blomquist, L., Brand, S., Brook, B., DeFries, R., Ellis, E., & Teague, P. (2015). *An Ecomodernist Manifesto*.

Barau, A. S., & Stringer, L. C. (2015). Access to and Allocation of Ecosystem Services in Malaysia's Pulau Kukup Ramsar Site. *Ecosystem Services, 16*, 167–73.

Biermann, F. (2007). 'Earth System Governance' as a Crosscutting Theme of Global Change Research. *Global Environmental Change, 17*(3-4), 326–37.

Biermann, F. (2014). *Earth System Governance: World Politics in the Anthropocene*. MIT Press.

Biermann, F., & Kalfagianni, A. (2020). Planetary Justice: A Research Framework. *Earth System Governance, 6*, 100049.

Brandi, C., & Morin, J.-F. (2023). *Trade and the Environment: Drivers and Effects of Environmental Provisions in Trade Agreements*. Cambridge University Press.

Brandi, C., Schwab, J., Berger, A., & Morin, J.-F. (2020). Do Environmental Provisions in Trade Agreements Make Exports from Developing Countries Greener? *World Development, 129*, 104899.

Ceddia, M. G. (2019). The Impact of Income, Land, and Wealth Inequality on Agricultural Expansion in Latin America. *Proceedings of the National Academy of Sciences, 116*(7), 2527–32.

Columbia Centre on Sustainable Investment and UN Working Group on Business and Human Rights. (2018). *Impacts of the International Investment Regime on Access to Justice*.

Evenett, S. J., & Whalley, J. (2009). The G20 and Green Protectionism: Will We Pay the Price at Copenhagen? *The Centre for International Governance Innovation, Policy Brief, 14*.

Gönenç, D., Piselli, D., & Sun, Y. (2020). The Global Economic System and Access and Allocation in Earth System Governance. *International Environmental Agreements: Politics, Law and Economics, 20*, 223–38.

Graham, N. (2023). Planning and the Ecosocialist Mode of Cooperation. *Monthly Review 75 (3)*.

GRAIN & IATP (Institute for Agriculture and Trade Policy). (2018). Emissions Impossible: How Big Meat and Dairy Are Heating up the Planet. *GRAIN and IATP*.

Gupta, J., Liverman, D., Bai, X., Gordon, C., Hurlbert, M., Inoue, C. Y. A., & Ciobanu, D. (2021). Reconciling Safe Planetary Targets and Planetary Justice: Why Should Social Scientists Engage with Planetary Targets? *Earth System Governance, 10*(3), 100122.

Kashwan, P. (2017a). *Democracy in the Woods: Environmental Conservation and Social Justice in India, Tanzania, and Mexico*. Oxford University Press.

Kashwan, P. (2017b). Inequality, Democracy, and the Environment: A Cross-National Analysis. *Ecological Economics, 131*, 139–51.

Kashwan, P., Biermann, F., Gupta, A., & Okereke, C. (2020). Planetary Justice: Prioritizing the Poor in Earth System Governance. *Earth System Governance, 6*, 100075.

Kashwan, P., Mudaliar, P., Foster, S. R., & Clement, F. (2021). Reimagining and Governing the Commons in an Unequal World: A Critical Engagement. *Current Research in Environmental Sustainability, 3*, 100102.

Keith, D. W., & Irvine, P. J. (2016). Solar Geoengineering Could Substantially Reduce Climate Risks A Research Hypothesis for the Next Decade. *Earth's Future, 4(11)*, 549–59.

Kotzé, L. J. (2019). The Anthropocene, Earth System Vulnerability and Socio-ecological Injustice in an Age of Human Rights. *Journal of Human Rights and the Environment, 10(1)*, 62–85.

Levidow, L. (2015). European Transitions towards a Corporate-Environmental Food Regime: Agroecological Incorporation or Contestation? *Journal of Rural Studies, 40*, 76–89.

Löwy, M., Akbulut, B., Fernandes, S., & Kallis, G. (2022). For an Ecosocialist Degrowth. *Monthly Review: An Independent Socialist Magazine, 73(11)*, 56–8.

Martínez-Alier, J., Temper, L., Del Bene, D., & Scheidel, A. (2016). Is There a Global Environmental Justice Movement? *The Journal of Peasant Studies, 43(3)*, 731–55.

Mitchell, R. B. (2003). International Environmental Agreements: A Survey of Their Features, Formation, and Effects. *Annual Review of Environment and Resources, 28(1)*, 429–61.

Nisbet, M. C. (2014). Disruptive Ideas: Public Intellectuals and Their Arguments for Action on Climate Change. *Wiley Interdisciplinary Reviews: Climate Change, 5*(6), 809–23.

Ostrom, E. (2010). Beyond Markets and States: Polycentric Governance of Complex Economic Systems. *American Economic Review, 100*(3), 641–72.

Pendrill, F., Persson, U. M., Godar, J., Kastner, T., Moran, D., Schmidt, S., & Wood, R. (2019). Agricultural and Forestry Trade Drives a Large Share of Tropical Deforestation Emissions. *Global Environmental Change, 56*, 1–10.

Perfecto, I., & Vandermeer, J. (2010). The Agroecological Matrix as an Alternative to the Land-Sparing/Agriculture Intensification Model. *Proceedings of the National Academy of Sciences, 107*(13), 5786–91.

Preston, C. J. (ed.). (2016). *Climate Justice and Geoengineering: Ethics and Policy in the Atmospheric Anthropocene*. Rowman & Littlefield.

Samberg, L. H., Gerber, J. S., Ramankutty, N., Herrero, M., & West, P. C. (2016). Subnational Distribution of Average Farm Size and Smallholder Contributions to Global Food Production. *Environmental Research Letters, 11(12)*, 124010.

Scheidel, A., Temper, L., Demaria, F., & Martínez-Alier, J. (2018). Ecological Distribution Conflicts as Forces for Sustainability: An Overview and Conceptual Framework. *Sustainability Science, 13*, 585–98.

Spagnuolo, F. (2011). Diversity and Pluralism in Earth System Governance: Contemplating the Role for Global Administrative Law. *Ecological Economics, 70(11)*, 1875–81.

Tienhaara, K. (2006). What You Don't Know Can Hurt You: Investor-State Disputes and the Protection of the Environment in Developing Countries. *Global Environmental Politics, 6(4)*, 73–100.

UNDROP (United Nations Declaration on the Rights of Peasants). (2018). United Nations Declaration on the Rights of Peasants and Other People Working in Rural Areas. *UN Human Rights Council.*

Vidal, J. (2016). The Tribes Paying the Brutal Price of Conservation. *The Guardian*, 28.

Williamson, K., Satre-Meloy, A., Velasco, K., & Green, K. (2018). Climate Change Needs Behavior Change: Making the Case for Behavioral Solutions to Reduce Global Warming. *Rare.*

Chapter 21

NATURAL RESOURCES AND GLOBAL ECONOMIC GOVERNANCE

Chris Armstrong

INTRODUCTION

Under international law, individual states enjoy 'permanent sovereignty' over the natural resources found within their borders (Schrijver, 1997). Although there are some constraints on their freedom (flowing, for instance, from duties to avoid serious transboundary environmental harms), by and large, this means that states are permitted to preserve or destroy resources at their discretion, and to retain the proceeds if they do decide to exploit them. Like the practice of hard borders, permanent sovereignty is a highly consequential legal–political feature of our world. Whereas hard borders allow states to lock people out, permanent sovereignty allows them to lock an important set of benefits in. The burdens that can arise from natural resources also tend to fall on local states (Mancilla, 2015). So too do the costs of conserving resources, even if they turn out to play key roles in global ecosystems.

Outside of state borders, by contrast, we can identify a patchwork of different resource regimes. The 1982 Convention on the Law of the Sea permitted coastal states to extend resource sovereignty over two-fifths of the planet's ocean, and an even larger portion of the seabed. In the ocean column beyond state jurisdiction – that is, on the 'High Seas' – resources have until now largely been available freely, to whoever is willing and able to exploit them. The new Agreement on Biodiversity beyond National Jurisdiction will change that scenario to some extent, although perhaps not dramatically. Underneath the High Seas, by contrast, lies the stretch of deep seabed known in international law as 'The Area.' The Area is governed by the International Seabed Authority, and functions as a distinctive common property regime. In principle, this means that the proceeds of any eventual exploitation of deep-sea minerals should be shared internationally (though whether significant funds emerge for redistribution remains to be seen). Blanketing our world, meanwhile, the atmosphere functions largely as an open-access resource, although there are some (largely voluntary) constraints on our ability to consume its sink capacity by emitting greenhouse gases, and some constraints too on our ability to emit destructive compounds such as CFCs.

It is an open question whether this patchwork of resource governance serves us or our planet well. In this chapter, I will raise a series of worries about it. I will show that it leaves much to be desired from the point of view of political, socioeconomic and intergenerational justice. I will also point the way towards some reforms that should promote the values of political inclusion and distributive equality more effectively, both within and between generations. Taken together, they suggest that a just and inclusive form of resource governance would be very different from the one that characterises contemporary global politics.

POLITICAL JUSTICE IN NATURAL RESOURCE GOVERNANCE

States appear to be firmly attached to both the principle and the practice of permanent sovereignty, and highly reluctant to qualify the privileges it grants them. Achieving resource sovereignty was a key objective of societies emerging from colonial rule during the 1950s and thereafter, and advocates of a 'New International Economic Order' believed that this sovereignty would help bring about a more egalitarian world order. Profound changes to the global economy would also be required (Getachew, 2019), to prevent the Global North from trapping Southern countries in their role as exporters of cheap natural resources, with most market value captured elsewhere. Against that altered background, newly independent countries could dramatically improve their position within the global economic hierarchy. That vision has never entirely materialised, however (Salomon, 2013). In the absence of broader reforms to the global economy, the resource sovereignty of developing countries has often been constrained by the rights of investor states and foreign corporations, and resource-rich countries still regularly find themselves in an unenviable position within the global economy, selling raw materials for very modest rewards.

Resource sovereignty *has* led to rapid economic growth in some countries – most prominently in the Arabian Gulf, where, boosted by enormous oil and gas exports, several countries progressed into the top centile of states arranged according to GDP per capita. But, as scholars of the so-called 'resource curse' have observed, dependence on resource exports (and especially oil exports) has also frequently been associated with a range of political and economic maladies (Ross, 2012). In 'resource-cursed' countries, citizens are typically shut out of the benefits accruing from oil sales, which serve only to entrench unrepresentative elites. The idea of popular resource sovereignty (the idea, that is, that resources belong to 'the people' rather than their rulers) may be a powerful norm across the world, but it is often honoured only in the breach, and it is questionable whether the norm is enshrined within key instruments of international law, which when it comes to resources appear to remain largely focused on the prerogatives of states, rather than their citizens (Armstrong, 2017, chapter 6; cf. Wenar, 2016).

Although permanent sovereignty was a major goal of independence movements – on the assumption that it would place control over resources in local hands, rather than the hands of foreign corporations – it is important to recognise that it has also acted as a barrier to political justice. Internally, indigenous communities have often found themselves prevented from accessing resources to which they are deeply attached, and their pleas for inclusion in resource policy-making have met with intransigence, and sometimes brutality, from state elites. Several states have continued a fundamentally 'extractivist' model of development reminiscent of the colonial era, with elites still monopolising the proceeds from resource exploitation, and even spiriting them away overseas much as colonisers did (Veltmeyer, 2012). Though familiar from Latin America, this process has reached its apotheosis in the Arabian Gulf, where ruling families treat domestic resources as their private property. In these circumstances, the battle for control over local resources on which people may be dependent, or to which they may be deeply attached, continues to face major obstacles even in an age of national resource sovereignty.

Externally, individual states' monopoly on decision-making about domestic resources can expose those who are *not* part of the state's *demos* to significant vulnerability. One community's exploitation of natural resources will often have profound implications for the interests of outsiders. However, constraints on their ability to set back outsiders' interests are relatively weak. International environmental law certainly forbids the imposition of significant harm on outsiders. But if outsiders' rights are to be adequately protected, negative externalities arising from resource exploitation may need to be much more heavily restricted than that (Shue, 2014, chapter 7). This is likely to mean a prohibition on degrading or destroying some natural resources, including those we could plausibly call 'key ecosystem resources' because they play a vital role in underpinning the conditions of life on our planet. Notably, even some erstwhile defenders of communal resource control argue for limits to that control in the case of 'global systemic resources' which play important ecosystem roles (Stilz, 2019, pp. 238–9).

It is also important to recognise that many resource pools are transboundary, and this raises the question of whether sovereignty over them should also be pooled across borders (see for example Espejo, 2020). Others still are fugacious or migratory in nature. The global water cycle, for instance, is no respecter of boundaries. If we are prepared to call living organisms natural resources, we confront a world of massive regular movements and complex transboundary interdependencies (Mancilla, 2016). On the assumption that decisions should be made by those whose interests will be significantly affected by them (the so-called all affected principle; see Goodin, 2007), we can plausibly make good arguments, in many cases of transboundary or migratory natural resources, for compulsory transnational forms of resource governance.

The all-affected principle also plausibly requires mechanisms to ensure the fair and effective international governance of many resource pools existing *entirely* beyond state borders. Such mechanisms are generally rather rudimentary, however, and are typically intergovernmental rather than genuinely global in form. Consider, for instance, ocean politics. The 1982 Convention on the Law of the Sea provided a pathbreaking new settlement for the blue seven-tenths of our planet. Most notably, it effected an enormous expansion of states' resource sovereignty over two-fifths of the entire ocean (Armstrong, 2022, chapter 3). Beyond each state's marine territory (that is, on the High Seas), by contrast, the constraints it places upon individual states' (or private actors') exploitation of oceanic resources have until now been for the most part weak and consensus-based. It is to be hoped that the new Agreement on Biodiversity beyond National Jurisdiction will enable greater progress in establishing vital marine reserves on the High Seas, alongside other conservation measures. Antarctica, meanwhile, has its distinctive form of shared international resource governance, but it is an imperfect one, which continues to bear the traces of colonial adventure, and in which the distribution of decision-making power is improperly connected to factors such as scientific capacity (Mancilla, 2018).

Progress in advancing political justice, then, appears to require at least four reforms to the status quo (in which states retain enormous power over most natural resources). First, we should seek greater participation for local communities dependent upon (sustainable) interaction with resource pools, but who are currently locked out of decision-making over those resources. Indigenous communities living in close, possibly interdependent, relationships with specific resources, but which face threats from extractivist elites, would be a key example. Second, we should explore mechanisms capable of respecting the interests that outsiders have in the fate of key ecosystem resources within states; in practice, this is likely to mean the development of a more robust version of the prohibition on significant transboundary environmental harms. Third, we should seek mechanisms to more adequately accommodate the interests of diverse stakeholders in the sustainability of transboundary and migratory resources. Fourth, we should seek more inclusive and participatory governing institutions for resources falling entirely outside of national jurisdiction, such as the resources of Antarctica and the High Seas.

SOCIOECONOMIC JUSTICE

Over time, state control over resources has become a more, rather than less pronounced feature of global economic governance. The Law of the Sea

Convention, for instance, ushered in a massive wave of resource enclosure, with at least 85 per cent of the world's fish stocks now being the property of individual states (Gagern & Van den Bergh, 2013), as well as two-thirds of the petrochemical supplies which have been newly tapped this century. Viewed from the angle of socioeconomic justice, the consequences of this enclosure have been highly inequitable. One reason is that claims of resource sovereignty at sea are determined by coastal geography and by the vestiges of colonialism. The countries with the largest Exclusive Economic Zones are Russia, the United States, the United Kingdom, France, New Zealand and Australia. Apart from Russia (which simply has an enormous coastline), the other members of the 'big six' coastal states have seen their holdings swell enormously because of overseas possessions captured during the colonial period. The Pitcairn Island group, for instance – a British Overseas Territory in the Pacific Ocean – has a population of less than seventy people, but provides an EEZ of 836,000 km^2. This is similar to the total size of China's EEZ, which must serve a population of well over a billion (Nolan, 2013). The statist enclosure of the ocean has, however, been accompanied by only very weak benefit-sharing mechanisms. In an era of shrinking sea ice, Northern states may soon divide up the resource spoils of much of the Arctic region.

Back on dry land, meanwhile, states have largely succeeded in resisting any obligation to share the benefits that domestic natural resources can bring in tow. The 1992 Convention on Biological Diversity, for instance, emphasised the need for effective conservation efforts but also reiterated state sovereignty over natural resources. Although it did discuss the issue of fair access to genetic resources, it did not mandate robust benefit-sharing mechanisms at the international level.

In the absence of powerful benefit-sharing mechanisms, permanent sovereignty therefore acts as an obstacle to socioeconomic justice. Some scholars of global justice have suggested that resource endowments make little difference to development, and hence should not trouble us from the normative point of view. Rawls, for instance, argued that most states do at least possess the means of subsistence, whereas beyond that resources appear not to matter a good deal (Rawls, 1999). There are two reasons for doubting that conclusion. First, it attempts to prove too much based on empirical findings which are much less clear than this suggests. Resources often matter to development, whether directly or indirectly (Armstrong 2023). Second, it diverts our attention from pressing questions about the sharing of resources. In a globalised world, the idea of resource autarky is increasingly a mirage. The planet's burgeoning population depends upon a massive trade in foodstuffs, as well as a much less widely recognised 'virtual' trade in water, without which many states' populations would be seriously imperilled (Hoekstra & Chapagain, 2011). Such resource independence as states do possess will itself come to be more and more threatened in light of climate change and other large-scale environmental problems. At the most dramatic, some small island states will become uninhabitable, and in many places, there will be widespread threats to stable water supply and agricultural productivity. These threats will inevitably force questions about access to scarce resources including water and fertile land up the political agenda, and will also increase migration pressure.

Even in cases where everyone's basic rights are secure, it would be problematic if permanent sovereignty enriched some countries while leaving others with more modest opportunities. Again, some scholars of global justice have doubted whether this is empirically true (Nili, 2016). It is certainly the case, as the resource curse literature has shown us, that there can be serious difficulties in converting resource wealth into broad-based development, and that the interaction between growth, institutions and resource wealth is complex. But on closer inspection, the so-called resource curse applies mainly to oil (Ross, 2012), whereas access to scarce resources such as water and fertile land can be highly consequential to development. As such, we should resist the easy conclusion that unequal resource endowments are of little concern from the point of view of global justice. While they are certainly not the only things that matter, they will often make a difference in people's access to well-being worldwide.

As well as inequalities in access to the benefits flowing from resources, we can also observe massive inequities in the allocation of *burdens*, including conservation burdens. We will frequently have reason to conserve particular natural resources, perhaps because they perform important ecosystem roles, because they may be important to future generations or members of other species, or simply because they have value in their own right. But conserving resources – which can involve refraining from exploiting them, taking concrete actions to protect them from threats, or restoring them – will often be costly. In a context of great inequality – and widespread severe poverty – to leave local communities to carry these costs alone will often compound injustice. Instead of leaving conservation costs where they happen to fall, justice will often demand that these costs are pooled, in line with principles such as the ability to pay and contribution to the problem (Armstrong, 2019).

Priorities of socioeconomic justice, then, include the need to ensure more equal access to the benefits flowing from natural resources, especially in a time of population growth and climate-induced pressure on inhabitable land and water resources. They also include the need to ensure a fairer distribution of the burdens of conserving key ecosystem resources on which we all depend, but which are often unfairly placed upon the shoulders of local communities. Finally, socioeconomic justice requires us to rethink access to resources outside of state sovereignty, such as the resources of the High Seas or the deep seabed. In these latter cases, the principle of first-come-first-served should be resisted. Distributive equity, as well as environmental sustainability, speaks in favour of the international management of such resource domains as the genuinely common international spaces they are (Armstrong, 2022).

INTERGENERATIONAL JUSTICE

Our interaction with the world's natural resources also prompts important questions about intergenerational justice. Are we obliged to leave our world's pools of natural resources in place for future generations more or less intact? Or can we deplete them, so long as we leave future people with access to some other means of fuelling their well-being?

People committed to 'weak' and 'strong' conceptions of sustainability are said to give opposed answers to that question. Advocates of so-called weak sustainability believe that the various goods that fuel our well-being (or which drive economic growth) are in practice likely to be more or less interchangeable. If so, it seems that we can permissibly exhaust natural resources, so long as we leave in their place something equally as effective in advancing the well-being (or economic growth) of our descendants. Advocates of so-called strong sustainability provide a series of reasons for resisting that conclusion. For instance, they point out that some natural resources may need to be preserved because they play key ecosystem roles, without which human and/or non-human life would be endangered. They might also claim that they ought to be preserved because of their intrinsic value. Alternatively, perhaps they should be preserved because the ability to interact with 'nature' is a key element of human well-being, or simply because future people should have the choice whether to interact with natural resources or not. In practice, neither perfectly strong nor perfectly weak forms of sustainability are at all plausible (the perfectly strong version because it would never allow us to exploit resources, and the perfectly weak version because it always will). The weak–strong contrast is better thought of as representing a continuum rather than a hard choice, with those who are persuaded by the kind of reason above favouring a *relatively* strong form of sustainability. Plausibly, our account will also be somewhat fine-grained, with stronger reasons to preserve some kinds of resources rather than others (Armstrong, 2021).

To what extent do the mechanisms of global economic governance promote natural resource sustainability? Ever since the influential *Limits to Growth* report of 1972 (Meadows et al., 1972), the idea that there *are* ecological constraints on growth has gained currency. It is increasingly recognised that the earth's ecosystems have been put under serious strain by resource-intensive development and that overconsumption has contributed to massive global problems such as climate change, ocean acidification, long-term pollution challenges, as well as biodiversity and habitat loss. We recognise too that future people will be seriously affected by these processes. But that understanding has not yet translated into serious constraints on action at the global level. The Convention on Biological Diversity reaffirms states' resource sovereignty, and as such would not prohibit the destruction of key ecosystem resources such as rainforests, or limit the extraction of fossil fuels (Vanderheiden, 2020, p. 198). Some global environmental problems have been dealt with quite effectively (with the CFC-induced hole in the ozone layer being a leading example). But on the whole, state decision-making has often been short-term in nature. Even when states do possess the motivation to engage with global environmental problems, they face an assurance problem insofar as the efforts of *other* states cannot be presumed.

As we have seen, for the most part, national sovereignty over resources is constrained only by relatively limited duties towards outsiders. The same can be said with regards to duties towards both future people, and the wider environment. At present, international law only substantially interferes with resource use when that use generates clear and significant transboundary harms. Paying due heed to the importance of sustainability may mandate a much more demanding set of rules, involving clear prohibitions on the destruction of key ecosystem resources that are likely to be important to the interests or projects of future people, and, plausibly, to members of other species too.

REFORMS

With the melting of the Arctic and the improvement of deep-sea mining technologies, the 'resource frontier' pushes ever onward. Struggles to control resources far from the borders of nation-states are only likely to intensify. Within states, meanwhile, the practice of resource sovereignty has locked in advantage and locked outsiders out of engagement in some very consequential decisions about resource use. I have suggested in this chapter that a concern for political, socioeconomic and intergenerational justice speaks in favour of reforms to our frequently inegalitarian and exclusionary brands of resource politics. Such reforms would aim to promote more equitable and inclusive forms of resource governance. I will close by sketching some key options that those concerned with resource justice might support. They fall into four broad categories.

First, we should explore policies that would promote a more equitable sharing of the benefits from resource exploitation, both within and between countries. Within states, it is notable that even states that describe themselves as welfare democracies typically govern natural resources in highly inegalitarian ways. Giving large corporations cheap and easy access to precious resources has too often been the norm. Those who endorse arguments for national ownership of natural resources, as well as those who are sceptical about them, can agree that a wider sharing of the benefits from resource exploitation is highly desirable. But how might the revenues from exploitation be shared more widely? Some states have established Sovereign Wealth Funds that invest resource revenues on global markets, and these could (at least in principle) be used to pursue long-term projects of social justice (Widerquist & Howard, 2016), or to smooth the transition away from fossil fuels, for example. Indeed, there may be good arguments that resource-rich states should use at least some of the revenues to pursue projects of global justice (Armstrong, 2013). At the global level, there are good arguments for taxing the use or consumption of at least some natural resources, such as the ocean and atmosphere's carbon-absorptive capacity. If global carbon taxes came into being, one appropriate destination for tax receipts would be countries in the Global South whose citizens will be especially vulnerable to the effects of climate change.

It is also important to explore what principles should regulate the sharing of any proceeds arising from the sustainable exploitation of the ocean's many resources, including in the High Seas beyond state jurisdiction. Debates about what would constitute fair benefit-sharing continue to play out within international legal circles (they are a key issue, for example, within the new Agreement on Biodiversity beyond National Jurisdiction). Should corporations which exploit the genetic diversity of the High Seas, for example, share some of the proceeds with the Global South? Or is sharing the knowledge gained enough? Political theorists can make an important contribution to thinking through these live political issues.

Second, political justice demands that those who will be significantly affected by a decision are able to play some role in making it. Within states, local and/or indigenous communities which live in a close connection with specific resources ought to be empowered to participate in decision-making. But there are also wider implications. More inclusive mechanisms for representing those touched by the exploitation of transboundary resources are desirable, as explored by Espejo (2020). On a truly global scale, it is regrettable that ocean politics is dominated by legal and political elites, with precious little participation by ordinary citizens. A new ocean politics would open up decision-making to all of those affected by ocean governance (in a time of climate emergency, this means all of us), and indeed seek ways of representing those who cannot actively participate in those decisions. Non-human animals, for instance, may have a right to representation even if they are not able to participate in political decisions (Cochrane, 2019). There are also good grounds for exploring ways of mainstreaming a concern for future people in our political institutions (Caney, 2016).

Third, socioeconomic justice demands greater limits on states' resource sovereignty. Respect for our physical security rights may mean we need to strengthen or broaden existing constraints on transboundary environmental harms. Arguably, the rule in international law that states should avoid causing serious cross-border harm when they exploit domestic resources is too permissive. Some resources might be worthy of protection in their own right, whether their exploitation harms outsiders or not. And some might be key to the interest of future generations in living in a diverse and healthy natural environment. There is no doubt that further restrictions on states' resource sovereignty will be strongly resisted. However, the radical threats posed to the stability of key ecosystems suggest that modest, incremental reforms to resource sovereignty are not likely to be sufficient. Provocatively, Robyn Eckersley has suggested that the international community must be prepared to countenance 'ecological intervention' in cases where vital natural resources are endangered by state action, just as it has shown itself willing to countenance humanitarian intervention when basic human rights are at stake (Eckersley, 2007). More recently, Catriona McKinnon has suggested that some forms of environmental destruction are so threatening to the future well-being of humans and other species that they ought to be considered a form of 'postericide' (McKinnon, 2017). Prosecuting such a crime might involve recourse to a new institution along the lines of an International Court for the Environment (Schuppert, 2014).

Fourth, such moves would have to be accompanied by robust and fair burden-sharing mechanisms at the international level (Armstrong, 2024). A prohibition on exploiting key ecosystem resources must not lock some into poverty. Frameworks such as the United Nations REDD+ scheme – under which states are paid to preserve vital ecosystem resources such as rainforests – have been controversial in practice. They have often seen state elites extending control over ecosystems, and monopolising the benefits, to the detriment of indigenous populations who may have led sustainable lifestyles within those ecosystems for generations (Reed, 2011). But much as this framework leaves to be desired, we surely need *some* way of ensuring that the costs of conservation – including its opportunity costs – are shared internationally, instead of falling on the shoulders of those who can least afford to bear them. We would proceed on more secure ground, I would argue, if we stopped conceiving of such mechanisms as a way of paying countries for ecosystem services, and instead thought about them as ways of ensuring that the allocation of the *costs* of conservation – including the opportunity costs – does not jeopardise the legitimate and sustainable development aspirations of those who find themselves at the receiving end of global inequalities (Armstrong, 2017). Any transfers to countries which agree to protect rich and diverse ecosystems should be conditional on both fair benefit-sharing and political inclusion for local communities – including indigenous groups – which are currently dependent on those ecosystems. If they are not, they will not have succeeded in dissolving the tension between environmental protection and the desire to escape poverty.

REFERENCES

Armstrong, C. (2013). Sovereign Wealth Funds and Global Justice. *Ethics & International Affairs, 27*(4), 413–28.

Armstrong, C. (2017). *Justice and Natural Resources: An Egalitarian Theory*. Oxford University Press.

Armstrong, C. (2019). Sharing Conservation Burdens Fairly. *Conservation Biology, 33*(3), 554–60.

Armstrong, C. (2021). Natural Resources, Sustainability, and Intergenerational Justice. In Gardiner, S. M. (ed.), *The Oxford Handbook of Intergenerational Ethics*. Oxford University Press.

Armstrong, C. (2022). *A Blue New Deal: Why We Need a New Politics for the Ocean*. Yale University Press.

Armstrong, C. (2023). Domestic Institutions, Growth and Global Justice. *European Journal of Political Theory*, 22(1), 4–25.

Armstrong, C. (2024). *Global Justice and the Biodiversity Crisis: Conservation in a World of Inequality.* Oxford University Press.

Caney, S. (2016). Political Institutions for the Future: A Five-Fold Package. In González-Ricoy, I., & Gosseries, A. (eds.), *Designing Institutions for Future Generations*, 135–55. Institutions for Future Generations.

Cochrane, A. (2019). Should Animals Have Political Rights? *Polity.*

Eckersley, R. (2007). Ecological Intervention: Prospects and Limits. *Ethics & International Affairs, 21*(3), 293–316.

Espejo, O. P. (2020). *On Borders*. Oxford University Press.

Gagern, A., & van den Bergh, J. (2013). A Critical Review of Fishing Agreements with Tropical Developing Countries. *Marine Policy, 38*, 375–86.

Getachew, A. (2019). *Worldmaking after Empire: The Rise and Fall of Self-Determination.* Princeton University Press.

Goodin, R. E. (2007). Enfranchising All Affected Interests, and Its Alternatives. *Philosophy & Public Affairs, 35(1)*, 40–68.

Hoekstra, A.Y., & Chapagain, A. K. (2011). *Globalization of Water: Sharing the Planet's Freshwater Resources*. John Wiley & Sons.

Mancilla, A. (2015). The Volcanic Asymmetry or the Question of Permanent Sovereignty over Natural Disasters. *Journal of Political Philosophy, 23*(2), 192–212.

Mancilla, A. (2016). Shared Sovereignty over Migratory Natural Resources. *Res Publica,* 22(1), 21–35.

Mancilla, A. (2018). The Moral Limits of Territorial Claims in Antarctica. *Ethics & International Affairs, 32*(3), 339–60.

McKinnon, C. (2017). Endangering Humanity: An International Crime? *Canadian Journal of Philosophy, 47*(2–3), 395–415.

Meadows, D. H., Meadows, D. L., Randers, J., & Behrens, W. W. (1972). *The Limits to Growth,* Universal Books.

Nili, S. (2016). Liberal Global Justice and Social Science. *Review of International Studies,* 42 (1), 136–55.

Nolan, P. (2013). Imperial Archipelagos. *New Left Review,* 80, 77–95.

Rawls, J. (1999). *The Law of Peoples*. Harvard University Press.

Reed, P. (2011). REDD+ and the Indigenous Question: A Case Study from Ecuador. *Forests,* 2(2), 525–49.

Ross, M. L. (2012). *The Oil Curse: How Petroleum Wealth Shapes the Development of Nations.* Princeton University Press.

Salomon, M. E. (2013). From NIEO to Now and the Unfinishable Story of Economic Justice. *International & Comparative Law Quarterly*, *62*(1), 31–54.

Schrijver, N. (1997). *Sovereignty over Natural Resources: Balancing Rights and Duties* (Vol. 36). Cambridge University Press.

Schuppert, F. (2014). Beyond the National Resource Privilege: Towards an International Court of the Environment. *International Theory*, *6*(1), 68–97.

Shue, H. (2014). *Climate Justice: Vulnerability and Protection*. Oxford University Press.

Stilz, A. (2019). *Territorial Sovereignty: A Philosophical Exploration*. Oxford University Press.

Vanderheiden, S. (2020). *Environmental Political Theory*. John Wiley & Sons.

Veltmeyer, H. (2012). The Natural Resource Dynamics of Post-neoliberalism in Latin America: New Developmentalism or Extractivist Imperialism? *Studies in Political Economy*, *90*(1), 57–85.

Wenar, L. (2016). *Blood Oil: Tyrants, Violence, and the Rulers That Run the World*. Oxford University Press.

Widerquist, K., & Howard, M. (eds.). (2016). *Exporting the Alaska Model: Adapting the Permanent Fund Dividend for Reform around the World*. Springer.

Chapter 22

GLOBAL INEQUALITY AND GLOBAL GOVERNANCE

Armando Barrientos and Daniele Malerba

INTRODUCTION

By now, inequality has assumed centre stage in many international debates. For example, whilst the headline focus of the MDGs until 2015 was on halving extreme poverty, the 2030 Agenda for Sustainable Development added an SDG on inequality reduction. This shift in policy focus has implications for global governance. This chapter discusses key measures and trends of global inequality, investigates the importance of inequality for other important aspects of the global economy, and sketches some of the implications for global governance. For space limitations, we focus on global *income* inequality.

Why is inequality now prominently featured in global policy dialogues? One reason is that focusing on extreme absolute poverty measures like the 'dollar a day' oversimplifies the task of global governance to that of promoting economic growth. This is problematic, especially in the context of climate change, which questions the sustainability of unlimited economic growth. In addition, the focus on the poorest left out a large share of the world's population in moderate poverty or vulnerable to falling into poverty. Moreover, societies with high inequality often score poorly in many other social and economic indicators. Inequality is thus not just related to socioeconomic issues but also to political and intergenerational injustices and other important moral objectives (see also Tan, Chapter 23 in this volume). Income inequality sustains asymmetric power and lowers political participation. Inequality reinforces the accumulation of wealth and spurs intergenerational injustice.

This chapter discusses inequality measures and trends in income inequality and wealth. It also distinguishes national and global inequality. The chapter covers income and wealth and their respective trends before sketching out key implications for global governance.

GLOBAL INCOME INEQUALITY

An effective measure of global inequality (i.e. inequality between all persons across the world) combines two dimensions: inequality across countries, usually referred to as international inequality or between-country inequality; and inequality within countries. These two distinct dimensions of global inequality reflect connected but separate inequality-generating structures. Within-country income inequality is the outcome of the workings of a particular economy, society and polity. Between-country inequality, conversely, reflects the working of the international economic order.

Income inequality is conventionally measured as a single number representing the extent of inequality. Several indicators are available in the literature, and their relative effectiveness in capturing inequality is contested. In this chapter, we focus on the Gini coefficient. The Gini measures the absolute mean difference of income across pairs of income units, divided by average income. It is a number between 0 denoting no inequality and 1 denoting complete inequality. One weakness is that different distributions of income in a population could produce the same Gini coefficient. It also emphasises the middle of the income distribution and takes less account of the tails of the distribution. Household surveys usually provide the data on which the Gini is calculated, raising issues about the coverage, regularity, precision and consistency of the available Gini estimates. Where data on the Gini is not available, we show available estimates on other inequality measures, such as the share of income or wealth held by the top 1 per cent or bottom 50 per cent; compared to the Gini index, these measures focus on the tail rather than on the middle of the distribution. The choice of indicator is not value-neutral and can have substantive policy implications. For example, the use of the 'shared prosperity' approach in the SDGs has been criticised as pushing for the narrative of economic growth rather than redistribution as it focuses on the income growth of the bottom 40 per cent, without a focus on the upper tail of the distribution (Fukuda-Parr, 2019).

Figure 22.1 shows estimates of global Gini income inequality, and its main components of between- and within-country income inequalities. The left-hand side panel focuses on global 'relative' income inequality. It is the main inequality concept used in policy and research. It is referred to as 'relative' because it assumes that the summary measure of income remains unchanged with equiproportional changes in income: a 10 per cent increase in income across the population should not affect the measured Gini coefficient. The right-side panel of Figure 22.1 shows the global 'absolute' income inequality measure; in this case, inequality is measured in the dollar income amounts, remaining unchanged in the event of a $10 USD increase across the population. The absolute Gini coefficient can be obtained by multiplying the relative index by the average income of the population of interest. The use of 'relative' and 'absolute' reflects alternative conceptual and normative views on inequality.

The left-hand side of the figure shows that global relative income inequality is high, estimated to be equal to 60.6; indeed, this value is higher than that of any individual country (Niño-Zarazúa et al., 2017). South Africa's

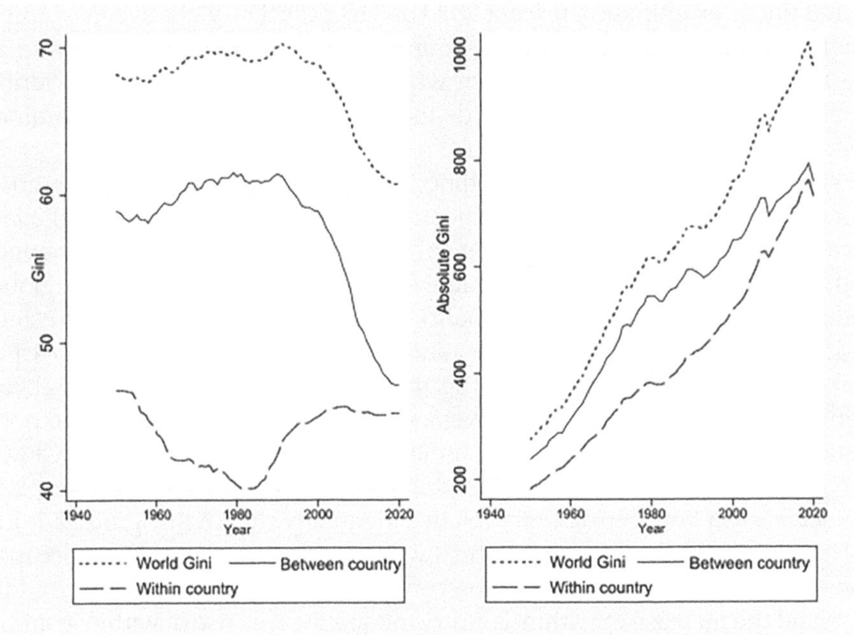

Figure 22.1 Trends in relative and absolute inequality, by component.
Source: Own estimations based on the World Income Inequality Database (UNU-WIDER, 2022).

Gini is the single country that comes close to the global Gini. A more positive finding is that, while remaining in the high 60s during the second half of the twentieth century, global income inequality has finally begun to decline in the twenty-first century (Bourguignon & Scott-Railton, 2015). The Gini index of global income inequality fell from 69 in 1988 to 62 in 2013, trending markedly down since 2008.

Figure 22.1 also shows diverging trends for the between- and the within-country global income inequality components. The former (shown by the continuous line) is the largest, and therefore dominant, component of global income inequality (Milanovic, 2024). It declines in significance towards the end of the period with a pronounced decline in the new century. The within-country component declines up to the 1980s, rises to the mid-2000s, and then stabilises. By the late 2020s, the two components of global income inequality come closer together. One main message is that the within-country component is becoming more important in terms of its contribution to global income inequality. While Figure 22.1 uses the Gini index, the rising importance of within-country inequality has also been noted when alternative measures of inequality are used (Chancel et al., 2022).

Compared to the 'relative' Gini, global income inequalities measured in 'absolute' terms (right part of Figure 22.1) show a rising trend through the period under examination (except 2020 due to COVID-19). Between-country inequality rises faster than within-country inequality from the 1950s up to the 1990s, but the relative rate of growth declines afterward. Within-country global inequality catches up towards the end of the period under examination, reflecting the trend seen also for relative inequality.

What can explain the trends outlined above? Milanovic (2024) has argued that changes in the distribution of income across global percentiles in the last decades resemble the picture of an elephant facing rightwards. These changes in the distribution reflect relative gains for the global poor and for the global middle class (the body of the elephant), but relative declines for the Western middle classes (the drooping trunk) and large gains for the global top 1 per cent up until the financial crisis. The main driver of these trends has been identified as the strong growth in average incomes in relatively poor and populous countries such as China and India coupled with the growth slowdown in rich countries in the wake of the global financial crisis. This could explain the decrease in between-country relative inequality shown in Figure 22.1. Job polarisation in high-income countries with a contraction in routine occupations could help explain the income contraction among the Western middle class and the increase in within-country inequality. This rise of within-country inequality since 1980 is a feature in many large countries including China, Russia and India, except Latin America.

While in the last ten years, there has been a stop in the increase of incomes of the global 1 per cent and the poorest part of the global population experienced higher growth (the elephant curve became a downward shape curve; Milanovic, 2024), the future is still uncertain. For example, Hellebrandt and Mauro (2015) predicted the main growth in global incomes will happen at the higher end rather than the middle of the global distribution. This implies that global inequality may start to increase again.

GLOBAL WEALTH INEQUALITY

While income can be defined as a flow, wealth is the stock of economic resources or property rights of economic agents. Why should we also care about wealth inequality? First, incomes are drawn from wealth owned by people, meaning that inequality in wealth affects income inequality. This can operate through several channels including interest, dividends, capital gains and rents coming from the ownership of houses or financial assets. Second, wealth inequality has become more prominent due to the shift of reported income from labour to capital, with the implication that incomes from capital are larger than wages leading to rising capital accumulation and economic rents. Finally, wealth also affects the political power of the richest (Zucman, 2019).

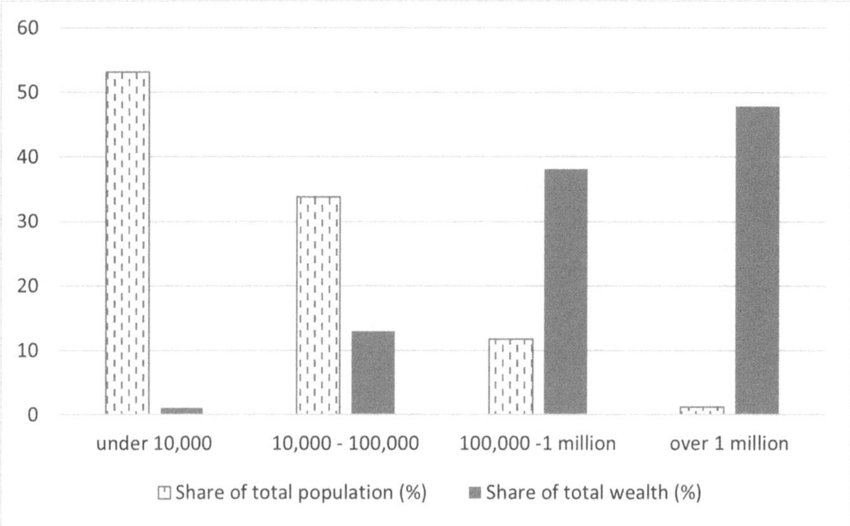

Figure 22.2 Distribution of wealth and population, by wealth categories.
Source: Own estimations based on Credit Suisse (2022).

The standard global approach measures wealth as financial and non-financial assets 'over which households can enforce ownership rights and that provide economic benefits to their owners, net of any debts' (Zucman, 2019, p. 112). Wealth data is scarce, even among high-income countries, and its distribution is difficult to estimate. Figure 22.2 shows an estimate of the distribution of financial and non-financial wealth among adults in the world in 2022 provided by Credit Suisse (2022). The figure shows that around 1 per cent of adults in the world own almost half of global wealth whereas 53 per cent of the population own 1.1 per cent of global wealth. Based on similar data, Davies et al. estimate the global Gini coefficient of adult wealth at 92.2 (Davies, Lluberas, & Shorrocks, 2017). Therefore, wealth inequality is higher than income inequality.

Data restrictions make it hard to assess (longer-term) trends in wealth inequality. The World Inequality Database (Alvaredo et al., 2021) provides estimates for a small number of countries since the 1970s and finds a gentle decline in the share of wealth held by the bottom 50 per cent of the populations of the USA and France and a steeper decline for China. It also documents a significant rise in the share of wealth of the top 10 per cent. These estimates suggest increasing within-country wealth inequality. A recent report also estimated that the richest 1 per cent have appropriated more than half of the new wealth created in the last decade (Oxfam, 2023). Even if time series data on wealth is patchy, especially at the global level, recent estimates from 1995 onwards indicate that wealth per adult has grown between 3 and 4 per cent for the bottom 40, middle 50, and top 10 per cent. The group that saw their wealth rise the most is the end of the distribution (the top 0.01 per cent and richer) (Chancel et al., 2022).

A final point concerns the rise in the share of private wealth, which mirrors a fall in the share of public/government wealth in advanced economies. Blanchard and Rodrik (2021) report that while public wealth-to-income ratios have decreased, private wealth-to-income ratios have nearly doubled in the last decades in four major European countries plus the USA and Japan.

ECONOMIC INEQUALITY INSTRUMENTAL FOR OTHER MORAL OBJECTIVES

The previous sections have underlined how income and wealth inequality negatively affect political outcomes and political fairness since economic inequality gives political power to the richest. Empirically, it has been found that economic inequality tends to increase political inequality through different mechanisms: widening the gap in policy preferences across income groups, reducing participation and depressing support for democracy. Although a link between economic inequality and political participation is contested, studies have established that high levels of inequality discourage political participation and political interest (Schäfer & Schwander, 2019). This is consistent with relative power theory, which holds that greater inequality enables wealthier citizens to more fully reshape the political landscape to their advantage.

A second effect of inequality is related to poverty. The literature on the poverty-growth-inequality triangle has shown that inequality reduction is critical (even more than economic growth) for poverty reduction as lower inequality usually means lower poverty (Malerba, 2020). This holds for both changes in national (within country) and international (between country) inequality.

Finally, income inequality is linked to inequality in greenhouse gas emissions. Since 1990, the global Gini of emissions has decreased from 0.64 to 0.61; as for income inequality, this reduction is to be attributed to reductions in between-country inequality, despite increases in within-country inequalities (Chancel, 2022). The bottom 50 per cent of the world population has been responsible for only 16 per cent of all emissions growth, whereas the top 1 per cent has been responsible for 23 per cent of the total. While per capita emissions of the global top 1 per cent increased since 1990, emissions from low- and middle-income groups within rich countries declined. Contrary to the situation in 1990, 63 per cent of the global inequality in individual emissions is now due to a gap between low and high emitters within countries rather than between countries.

A more equal world is thus better for the climate for at least two reasons. First, emissions of the rich affect the entire global population while low-income households have lower adaptive capacity, and the global poor are located in areas vulnerable to climate change. Second, to mitigate climate change, we need to change the sharing of existing resources and the remaining carbon budgets. Income is the main driver of emissions, and global income inequality shapes inequalities of energy consumption and the quantity and composition of overall energy demand (Oswald et al., 2021). Reducing global income inequality is therefore essential to tackle climate change and address intergenerational justice.

IMPLICATIONS FOR GLOBAL GOVERNANCE

The shift in focus from extreme poverty to inequality in the SDGs raises important issues for global governance. Consensus on the normative, conceptual and policy underpinnings of inequality as applied on a global scale is sorely lacking. This is evident when set against the earlier focus on extreme poverty.

In terms of conceptualising inequality, informed consensus is needed to select adequate inequality measures at the international level. The main SDG target and indicator on inequality (10.1) focuses on improvements among the bottom 40 per cent of the population (shared prosperity). This indicator relates more closely to the 'leave no one behind' agenda for inclusion as opposed to that of reducing inequalities (Fukuda-Parr, 2019). The bottom 40 per cent indicator was pushed by the World Bank, as it reflected its political agenda and minimised adjustments to comply with the SDG inequality goal (van Driel et al., 2023).

In terms of policy, the literature underlines the primary role played by national governments, especially through fiscal policies. This is highly relevant to the trend of increasing within-country inequality. It is also relevant to debates on the policies that governments can adopt to address inequality, including the groups to prioritise (lower, middle or upper part of the distribution) (Blanchard & Rodrik, 2021). Different policies focus on reducing inequality during pre-production, production or post-production stages. For example, social assistance transfers in developing countries can reduce market-based inequalities whilst increasing human capital for future productivity (Barrientos & Malerba, 2020).

Alongside national policies, inequalities are shaped by the international order. Global economic governance can shape national and global inequalities through different channels (e.g. regulatory constraints) and different sets of rules (trade, capital flows, intellectual property rights, taxation, investment agreements) (Ocampo, 2019).

As globalisation has given a more significant role to the market over states, international rules need to be strengthened, especially in policy areas critical for inequality where they are currently weak. As discussed in this volume (Ronzoni, Chapter 13; von Haldenwang & Laudage Teles, Chapter 12), taxation is an essential case in point, where cooperation rather than competition needs to be enhanced. On a positive note, a broad-based international agreement on a global minimum tax rate at 15 per cent was reached in 2021 by the OECD's Inclusive Framework on Base Erosion and Profit Shifting (BEPS) (Lassourd, 2022).

Finally, global institutions need to be reformed and made more inclusive: this includes power relations in multilateral institutions, the composition and voting rights in the United Nations Security Council, and the boards of the Bretton Woods system. The introduction of inequality-increasing consumption taxes has been particularly prominent in the poorest countries, where the IMF has played an important role in promoting them as the main tool to yield revenues (Reinsberg, Stubbs, & Kentikelenis, 2020). Piketty (2020), in this sense, underlines how inequality is more political and ideological rather than economic and technological.

REFERENCES

Alvaredo, F., Chancel, L., Piketty, T., Saez, E., & Zucman, G. (2021). World Inequality Database.

Barrientos, A., & Malerba, D. (2020). Social Assistance and Inclusive Growth. *International Social Security Review, 73*(3), 33–53.

Blanchard, O., & Rodrik, D. (2021). *Combating Inequality: Rethinking Government's Role*: MIT Press.

Bourguignon, F., & Scott-Railton, T. (2015). *The Globalization of Inequality*: Princeton University Press.

Chancel, L. (2022). Global Carbon Inequality over 1990–2019. *Nature Sustainability, 5*(11), 931–8.

Chancel, L., Piketty, T., Saez, E., & Zucman, G. (2022). *World Inequality Report 2022*: Harvard University Press.

Credit Suisse. (2022). The Global Wealth Report 2022. *Switzerland: Research Institute*.

Davies, J. B., Lluberas, R., & Shorrocks, A. F. (2017). Estimating the Level and Distribution of Global Wealth, 2000–2014. *Review of Income and Wealth, 63*(4), 731–59.

Fukuda-Parr, S. (2019). Keeping out Extreme Inequality from the SDG Agenda: The Politics of Indicators. *Global Policy, 10*(S1), 61–9.

Hellebrandt, T., & Mauro, P. (2015). The Future of Worldwide Income Distribution. *Peterson Institute for International Economics working paper* (15-7).

Lassourd, T. (2022). What Does the Global Minimum Tax Deal Mean for Developing Countries? https://www.iisd.org/articles/global-minimum-tax-deal.

Malerba, D., 2020. The Trade-off between Poverty Reduction and Carbon Emissions, and the Role of Economic Growth and Inequality: An Empirical Cross-Country Analysis Using a Novel Indicator. *Social Indicators Research, 150*(2), 587–615.

Milanovic, B. (2024). The Three Eras of Global Inequality, 1820–2020 with the Focus on the Past Thirty Years. *World Development*, 177, 106516.

Niño-Zarazúa, M., Roope, L., & Tarp, F. (2017). Global Inequality: Relatively Lower, Absolutely Higher. *Review of Income and Wealth, 63*(4).

Ocampo, J. A. (2019). *International Policy Rules and Inequality: Implications for Global Economic Governance*: Columbia University Press.

Oswald, Y., Steinberger, J. K., Ivanova, D., & Millward-Hopkins, J. (2021). Global Redistribution of Income and Household Energy Footprints: A Computational Thought Experiment. *Global Sustainability, 4*, e4.

OXFAM. (2023). *Survival of the Richest: How We Must Tax the Super-Rich Now to Fight Inequality.*

Piketty, T. (2020). *Capital and Ideology*: Harvard University Press.

Reinsberg, B., Stubbs, T., & Kentikelenis, A. (2020). Taxing the People, Not Trade: The International Monetary Fund and the Structure of Taxation in Developing Countries. *Studies in Comparative International Development, 55*(3), 278–304. doi:10.1007/s12116-020-09307-4.

Schäfer, A. and Schwander, H. (2019). 'Don't Play If You Can't Win': Does Economic Inequality Undermine Political Equality? *European Political Science Review, 11*(3), 395–413.

UNU-WIDER, World Income Inequality Database (WIID) Companion dataset (wiidcountry and/or wiidglobal). Version 30 June 2022.

van Driel, M., Biermann, F., Vijge, M. J., & Kim, R. E. (2023). How the World Bank Engages with the Sustainable Development Goal on Reducing Inequalities: A Case of Organizational Jiu-Jitsu. *Global Studies Quarterly*, 3(3).

Zucman, G. (2019). Global Wealth Inequality. *Annual Review of Economics, 11*, 109–138.

Chapter 23

GLOBAL ECONOMIC EQUALITY

Kok-Chor Tan

INTRODUCTION

Why does global economic inequality matter?[1] One view is that global economic inequality itself is an injustice (unless otherwise justified). Another view holds that economic inequality (henceforth 'equality') is not unjust in itself, but is a problem of justice when it impairs other important values. On this last, equality matters indirectly; we should care about inequality because we care about other values.

I begin by surveying some early arguments in favour of global egalitarianism. I then turn to indirect considerations for egalitarianism and examine how these considerations apply globally. In addressing indirect arguments for global egalitarianism, empirical facts about the world, particularly the causal links between inequality and other values that matter (such as eliminating poverty, social respect and global political fairness) are relevant. In this respect, philosophical debates about global egalitarianism must attend to the empirical research on the impact and consequences of economic inequality on other important global values.

GLOBAL EGALITARIANISM

We will start by clarifying the normative terrain of global egalitarianism. A commitment to global equality is distinct from a commitment to eradicating or mitigating poverty. Concerns about poverty can be described as 'sufficientarian'. That is, the goal of poverty elimination is to bring people up to some defined level of attainment or satisfaction of needs. This defined level may be set robustly, for example in terms of some demanding criterion of human flourishing. For instance, on one possible demanding conception, a person

[1] This chapter draws on previously published writing, including Tan (2019) and (2010). Many thanks to Axel Berger, Clara Brandi and Eszter Kollar for their helpful comments.

passes the sufficiency threshold when she is not only able to meet her basic subsistence needs, but also enjoys access to good health care, education, a clean environment and a functional social system. Or the threshold can be set relatively modestly, as in the World Bank's $2/day definition, in which case a person lacking access to good public education, decent health and a clean environment need not necessarily be in poverty. Either way, these different views illustrate a fundamental threshold concept. Some standard of sufficiency (subject to revision depending on social conditions) is defined, and the goal is to meet that standard. The sufficient rain *form* remains whether we define the poverty threshold robustly or weakly.

In contrast, egalitarianism is a comparative concept as opposed to a threshold one. Even when everyone is above a defined sufficiency threshold, it is still possible that significant economic inequality exists among people. For an egalitarian, inequalities that linger can present a possible problem of justice. They will ask: are these inequalities justifiable? For the egalitarian, it is not only important that people meet some defined absolute standard of attainment, but also how they stand in relation to each other. In this respect, egalitarianism is fundamentally of a different form than sufficientarianism. It is concerned with people's relative standing rather than just their standing concerning an absolute standard. While egalitarianism is compatible with sufficientarianism, it goes beyond that. It remains operative beyond the target threshold.

Global egalitarianism, therefore, is distinct from the global problem of poverty. The values are different in character – relative or comparative as opposed to absolute; and these values issue different demands, with egalitarianism being more demanding than sufficientarianism. But while these are distinct values, they are not separate. That is, unchecked inequality can result in the impoverishment of the disadvantaged. We will examine this connection below. The point for now is to recognise that these are conceptually distinct values.

Next, a commitment to economic *equality* does not entail a commitment to equal economic *outcomes*. That is, it does not mean that everyone must have the same amount of resources (or whatever economic goods the egalitarian might favour) when the dust of redistribution has settled. A few egalitarians do argue for equality of outcome in this sense (e.g. Nielsen, 1979). But many egalitarians reject radical egalitarianism of this kind. They are egalitarians in that they believe economic inequality ought to be regulated or limited by an appropriate principle of distribution. An egalitarian distributive principle takes an equal distribution of some economic goods to be the benchmark and specifies the conditions under which departures from the benchmark of equality are acceptable. Different egalitarian theories thus offer different explanations for why equal distribution is the default and propose different justifications for admissible deviations from the egalitarian default.

Also, economic equality among persons is distinct from the question of the equal moral worth of persons. Indeed, the more interesting dispute in the literature on economic equality begins from the basic principle that all persons have equal moral worth and are entitled to equal respect. Where the disagreement concerning economic equality lies is in how we are to understand the value of moral equality or equal respect. Does the ideal of equal respect for persons require economic equality among persons? Not all commentators think so. For example, libertarians would hold that all persons are moral equals. But precisely because they are moral equals, libertarians go on to argue, that economic equality is unacceptable since its realisation will violate the equal liberty of persons in their property, which libertarians take to be basic. Indeed, the interesting arguments against global economic equality do not deny, but affirm, the ideal of global moral equality of persons. What these arguments deny is that the moral equality of persons *entails* some commitment to global economic equality. For clarity, following one standard usage, one may use the term 'egalitarianism' to refer to the specific ideal of economic equality, and proponents of global economic equality will be referred to as 'global egalitarians'. But for the present, by equality, I mean specifically economic equality. Moral equality is simply assumed here as a background value too basic to need reaffirmation.

Finally, egalitarian distributive obligations can arise independently of facts about past injustices (e.g., colonialism). Mitigating inequality can be something we owe to each other as a direct moral concern, or it can be an obligation that arises because of living under common arrangements. Repairing past injustices can entail redistribution (by way of compensation) from perpetrators to injured parties, but this is a distinct concern. This is not to deny the importance of reparation or corrective justice. On the contrary, one might argue that this is even more urgent or basic than distributive justice. But egalitarian justice and reparations constitute dimensions of justice. From an egalitarian justice perspective, even in a world with no past injustices, there is still the duty to mitigate economic inequality.

In summary, the discourse on global egalitarianism is not about our moral duty to respond to poverty or other forms of absolute deprivation; it is not about the moral equality of persons (which is taken for granted); and it is not about whether we should aim at the distributive equal outcome as an ideal. The concern is the extent to which unequal distribution ought to be allowed. What the debate engages is the question of whether global justice includes some principle for regulating or controlling economic inequality in the world.

ARGUING FOR GLOBAL DISTRIBUTIVE JUSTICE

So how does one make the case for global egalitarianism? First, global egalitarians typically do not reinvent the egalitarian wheel. Rather, they begin from some widely accepted or influential theory of egalitarian justice (conceived for domestic society), and from this starting point, attempt to show that the favoured egalitarian theory logically extends to the global domain.

In this respect, Charles Beitz's *Political Theory and International Relations* (1979) published over thirty years ago, has paved the way. To simplify, Beitz takes Rawls's theory of justice as his starting point and seeks to demonstrate that there is no good reason to limit Rawls's basic commitments and methodology to the state domain. To the contrary, Beitz argues, consistency in reasoning and methodology would require extending Rawls's conclusions to the global domain as well. That is, we must arrive at a globalised version of Rawls's two principles of justice, including his egalitarian distributive principle.

The details of Rawls's theory of justice and Beitz's interpretation of it need not detain us at the moment. What I want to draw attention to is the form of the argument that we can call 'the argument by extension'. The extension argument seeks to show that a favoured set of arguments for egalitarian justice for the domestic state ought not to be confined to the context of the state, but should extend outwards to the global arena. The normative core of the extension argument is that state and national borders are morally irrelevant and therefore ought not to obstruct the logical outward flow of arguments for egalitarianism to the world as a whole.

The way an extension argument unfolds will depend on the egalitarian theory it begins with. In general, in the contemporary egalitarianism literature, there are two basic approaches to defending egalitarianism. One approach takes it that egalitarian obligations exist between individuals as such given their status as equal moral agents. The other takes egalitarian obligations to apply not between moral agents as such but only between persons who enjoy or ought to enjoy some kind of associational relationship or tie. We can label the former the moral approach to egalitarianism, and the latter the relational approach.

The moral approach can take a variety of forms. 'Luck egalitarianism' is just one version of the moral approach to egalitarianism but it is an illustrative example (Lippert-Rasmussen, 2015). Luck egalitarianism, briefly, is the idea that economic inequality among persons due to their misfortunes and bad luck is the common fate of society to be shared by all and not by the unfortunate alone. Therefore, justice would require some distributive mechanism to mitigate inequality among persons as a result of their luck. Globalising this approach, since the place of one's birth or one's country of residence is, in general, a matter of luck rather than personal choice, there must be some global egalitarian distributive principles to counteract the unequalising effects of state borders and citizenships on persons' opportunities (Caney, 2005).

The relational approach likewise can take different forms. However, one account holds that the relationship that is necessary for generating egalitarian commitments is that of fair social cooperation. That is, egalitarian duties are activated only when the relevant actors are also participating (or ought to be participating) under some shared cooperative arrangement. Some global egalitarians, adopting this cooperative ideal of egalitarianism, accordingly try to make the case that the global order is a cooperative arrangement of the sort that should trigger global egalitarian commitments (e.g., Beitz 1979). They point to features of the world order, such as trade relations and regulations, and international law and legal norms, as evidence of a global cooperative institutional order, and conclude that if the ideal of social cooperation entails egalitarianism in the domestic context, there is a case as well for global egalitarianism. Global egalitarians need not, however, be necessarily committed to the view that global egalitarian principles are just domestic egalitarian principles writ large. What makes a position egalitarian is the presumption of an egalitarian default and the commitment to control deviations from this default. Thus, a global egalitarian does not forfeit her egalitarian stripes if she holds that domestic egalitarian principles and global principles can differ in their content. Thus, a difference can be noted between the pattern of distribution (that is, whether a distribution should be egalitarian or not) and the content of the principle of distribution (for example, the form of the egalitarian principle itself). A global egalitarian, therefore, can easily allow global principles to have different content from domestic egalitarian principles since the set of practices and institutions that global principles are meant to regulate are quite different from domestic ones. Some have argued, for example, that the economic practices and institutions that global distributive principles are meant to guide are limited to trade laws, practices and agreements, unlike in the domestic case where economic institutions are more encompassing and determine production and ownership rights at a more fundamental level (James, 2012; see also James, Chapter 5 in this volume). So a more holistic principle of distribution, like Rawls's second principle that regulates the basic structure of a society as a whole may not be appropriate as a principle of distribution if the institutional target is a narrower one, like international intellectual property rights regimes, or trade relations.

THE PATRIOTIC CHALLENGE

In response to this extension argument, challenges emerged. Among the early waves of objections are the arguments that global egalitarian demands are in tension with more local and special commitments that persons ordinarily have. In particular, as a member of a nation-state, a person has special concerns and commitments to fellow members that one need not have towards strangers, and global egalitarianism risks riding roughshod over these national or patriotic commitments. Nationalist theorists like David Miller (2007) argue that when there is a conflict between different domains or spheres of justice, it is not straightforwardly the case that one domain should dominate the other. When the demands of global justice compete with the demands of national justice, one cannot assume that the default is to grant primacy to global demands. On the contrary, there are good special reasons, reasons having to do with the idea of the nation-state, for giving preference to national demands.

It is important to appreciate the form of the challenge here. The patriotic challenge does not deny that there are valid global distributive principles. That is, it does not take issue with the extension project of the first stage. What it puts forward is what we may call a limitation or 'limiting' argument, namely, that while there could be good reasons for global distributive obligations, there are also good (if not more important) reasons for other kinds of obligations that conflict with the global ones (Jones, 1999). The challenge aims to show that at the very least global distributive commitments have to be limited if not generally overridden by patriotic commitments.

Understanding properly this specific form of the challenge is important because it also shows the form of a possible response. Faced with the patriotic challenge (read as a limitation argument), the cosmopolitan need not provide another independent argument for global egalitarianism. That such a commitment could be independently valid is accepted by the patriotic challenge. All the cosmopolitan needs to do, rather, is to show that in cases where there are competing principles or commitments between global and patriotic ones, global commitments take priority. That is, what is at stake is the *priority* rather than the *validity* of global justice. Thus presented, some might think that the patriotic challenge is rather weak since it has already conceded the validity of global justice, or worse yet that I have presented a straw-person version of the argument. But as mentioned, the patriotic challenge as described is an instance of a deep and recurring quest in moral philosophy, that of reconciling valid but competing moral claims. Rather than representing a weak challenge that can be ignored, the patriotic challenge is one expression of an abiding problem of moral philosophy and poses a serious philosophical and normative challenge that globalists cannot ignore.

In response, global egalitarians argue that national and patriotic commitments cannot be *justly* discharged unless the obligations of global justice are met. Just as justice constrains the range of personal pursuits and activities, either individually or in associations, in the domestic context, so too global justice should limit the demands of patriotism and other national demands rather than the other way around. Special cooperative and interest groups within a domestic society may have their local distributive concerns, but these groups will not know what they are justly entitled to with which to distribute among their members without reference to what distributive justice for society at large requires of them. A cooperative may have its internal distributive ideals, but if its internal distribution is to be just, the cooperative must first honour the rightful demands of other cooperatives and non-members generally. In other words, claims of justice regulating external relations *among* groups have priority over claims of justice *within* groups, for members of a group cannot know otherwise if their internal organisation is valid concerning what is owed to non-members. We can call the former 'external justice' and the latter 'internal justice', and hold as a norm that external justice takes precedence over internal justice. Thus, the demands of global justice have priority over the demands of patriotism. Global justice sets the bounds of acceptable patriotic concern, as justice in the domestic setting provides the parameters for acceptable personal pursuits.

To illustrate the above, consider this question: may a relatively well-off nation devote some of its resources to further improving its already very good healthcare system, or should it direct these resources to support healthcare efforts in poorer countries? Suppose this nation decides that as a matter of justice, its priority is to provide even better care for its citizens. The argument above suggests that if the well-off nation is not entitled to these resources, then its priority claim is invalid. Before we can determine whether this nation may use these resources to promote the ends of its members or to serve the cause of domestic justice, we need to ask: from the standpoint of global justice, is that nation entitled to these resources? Yes, if these are resources that it has left over after it has discharged its duties of global distributive justice. No, if these are resources it can retain precisely because it has ignored its duties of global distributive justice. Global justice has priority in this sense: it determines the bounds of permissible national pursuits (Brock, 2009).

GLOBAL EGALITARIANISM AND SELF-DETERMINATION

As mentioned, some global egalitarians take themselves to be extending Rawls's theory of justice to its logical end, whereas some anti-global egalitarians take such an extension to be a misapplication of Rawls's method and arguments. In particular, the critics say, the extension project fails to see the sense in which equality is an indirect concern. To lay the stage for this, we can turn to Rawls himself.

In *The Law of Peoples*, Rawls (1999) explicitly opposes the global extension of his egalitarian principles. Instead, he argues that a global duty of assistance – to ensure that all societies are able to meet the basic needs of their citizens and have the means to support well-ordered institutions of their own – is sufficient for international economic justice.

One line of response that Rawls makes against global egalitarianism can be described as an argument for national self-determination. One might say here that this is where political justice – in the form of collective self-determination – is in tension with economic justice, or egalitarian distributive justice in this case. Rawls invites us to imagine two societies starting equally well-off, with an equal amount of resources, comparable population size, human capital and the like. But one society invests in its economy in such a way that, over time, it becomes twice as well-off as the other (Rawls, 1999). A global egalitarian principle will require some redistribution of resources from the better-off society to the less well-off one, but Rawls says that this would be 'unacceptable'. Presumably, the reason why it would be unacceptable is that we would be requiring a society to subsidise another that is less well-off because of its choices. Indeed, this amounts to our penalising the better-off society for its superior decisions and hard choices.

But it seems that Rawls's self-determination argument works only if we already presume that there is no prior global egalitarian obligation. After all, if there is an antecedent obligation of egalitarian justice, then it is not the case that complying with it undermines self-determination. For example, we cannot say that even though paying our domestic taxes is an obligation of justice, this obligation violates individual self-determination. This is because, as seems most plausible, the admissible space for self-determination is defined in terms of what we owe to others, not the other way around.

In other words, following the discussion on the patriotic challenge above, the value of self-determination does not limit the requirements of egalitarianism. The exercise of self-determination has to be constrained by the demands of egalitarian justice, not the other way around. If Rawls's 'two societies' objection is to have traction, he has to have some independent reason that global equality is not a requirement of global justice. Rawls's 'two societies' arguments are preceded by a different line of objections against global egalitarianism. These objections invoke the view that inequalities are an indirect concern. If inequalities are unjust, it is because of their 'unjust effects on the basic structure of the Society of Peoples' (Rawls, 1999, p. 113).

INDIRECT REASONS FOR EQUALITY AND GLOBAL EGALITARIANISM

Indirect reasons for egalitarianism take egalitarianism to matter because it serves or is tied to some other important values. For Rawls, these indirect reasons show why equality matters domestically, but but also why it does not matter globally.

Rawls argues that the first indirect reason why we care about economic inequality in the domestic context is that we want to prevent persons from falling into poverty. However, since there is a global duty of assistance within Rawls's *Law of Peoples*, the problem of poverty within the global arena is addressed without the need for economic equality.

Why does a concern for poverty in the domestic setting translate into some requirement to regulate inequality, whereas the same does not hold in the global context? Rawls' idea here seems to be that in a more closely entwined market, unmitigated inequality can result in the impoverishment of some. This is, of course, a very plausible point – in a given market where people compete for the same goods, the more another has, the easier it is for her to outbid me in the competition for goods, and I can become impoverished when necessities become out of my reach in this way.

But is it the case that the global marketplace is not one where inequality can matter in this way? Do people not compete for similar goods or resources? Global demands for cash crops like coffee, compete for and claim scarce arable land that could otherwise be used to cultivate food crops. Thus, differences in global purchasing power can contribute to the actual impoverishment of some communities. These are all matters to be settled not by philosophical arguments but by empirical analysis of the relationship between global economic inequality and poverty (Malerba & Barrientos, Chapter 22 in this volume).

A second indirect reason that Rawls discusses is that unregulated inequalities between persons within a state can result in the social stigmatisation of the less well-off and, consequently, the corrosion of their basis of self-respect. Yet, Rawls believes, that economic inequality between persons across state boundaries need not have such effects. The presumption here seems also to be that more tightly economically entangled social orders constitute significant comparison or reference groups for individuals that would make economic inequality a salient factor. To construct a simple example, the idea is that Americans may care about how they fare about other Americans, and Mexicans to other Mexicans. But, for Rawls as it seems, Mexicans do not compare themselves in this way with Americans.

Contra Rawls, one might suggest that telecommunication, the internet, the global reach of the arts and culture (such as films and television shows), etc. make it more likely that inter-state or cross-border comparisons will matter more and more to persons. We will need more empirical socio-psychological research to settle this argument. But it does not appear implausible that people's comparison groups cut across state boundaries, pace Rawls.

Rawls's third reason why economic inequality matters within the state is that it can undermine the fairness of political processes. It is commonplace among observers that economic inequality within a society threatens democracy. Candidates for public offices with greater financial power are better able to win attention and garner votes, and affluent lobbyists and other interest groups can influence the political agenda. Thus, to help maintain political fairness in domestic society, Rawls believes we must limit inequality among persons. But there are no analogous political processes in the global domain that would be corrupted by economic inequality, the argument implies.

Again, the interesting question this argument raises is highly complex and will require more empirical research into how international organisations work in practice. For example, consider the fact that the number of votes a country has within the International Monetary Fund depends on its financial contribution to the organisation, which in turn, of course, depends on its wealth. Is this or is it not an instance of unfairness in political processes in the international arena?

So, even if the reason for worrying about inequality is because of its possible impact on political fairness, it does not seem implausible that global inequality can compromise global political fairness. Rawls's view that the fairness of international political justice does not necessitate a principle of global economic equality is inconclusive. Even though there is no democratic world government whose fairness can be directly impaired by global economic inequality, there are institutions of global governance for which the ideal of political justice seems relevant. While the institutions and bodies of global governance do not directly exercise coercive political authority over persons, they do impact people's lives in significant ways, as noted in several chapters in this volume. International labour laws, global environmental regulations, international trade laws, etc. are not fixed facts but the outcome of international bargaining, agreements and negotiations. Differences in countries' economic capacities surely have an impact here (e.g. see Berensmann, Chapter 14 in this volume).

In addition to the indirect reasons for egalitarianism having to do with the problems of poverty, stigmatisation and political fairness, Rawls also hinted at another, namely the ideal of reciprocity. Rawls says that the gap between the rich and poor in domestic society cannot be 'wider than the criterion of reciprocity allows' (Rawls, 1999, p. 114). But this invites the question: why does domestic reciprocity, in particular reciprocity between democratic citizens, require the limiting of economic inequality among individuals, but international or global reciprocity does not? That is, what is so special about the state such that the ideal of reciprocity uniquely generates an egalitarian obligation among its people?

One influential account of the special status of the state is that the state is inherently a coercive institution. It is coercive in that it necessarily restricts the autonomy of individuals subject to its powers (Blake, 2001). The fact of the coercive state thus raises an issue of legitimacy: under what conditions is the exercise of the state's coercive powers acceptable in the eyes of those subject to its authority? On this view, a necessary pathway towards legitimising the coercive state is through institutional egalitarian justice. Accordingly, this special character of the state explains why the ideal of reciprocity among members of a democratic state entails egalitarianism within the state. But since, the argument would continue, there is no coercive global state, the criterion of reciprocity does not require that the gap between rich and poor globally be regulated.

This argument for egalitarianism from coercion can be seen as another form of indirect reasoning for equality: the idea here is that equality matters because it matters for state legitimacy. The argument raises interesting philosophical questions about the instrumental relationship between equality and state legitimacy. But in the context of the global justice debate, it also raises interesting points about the distinctive character of international relations, that it is not coercive, at least not coercive in the relevant legitimacy-threatening sense. The debate will turn significantly on how we conceptualise 'coercion'.

For example, with respect to the autonomy conception of coercion, the claim that the global arena – with its complex institutions, norms, laws and the territorial rights of states – does not threaten individual autonomy is too hasty.

On the contrary, trade conventions, international norms and laws restrict individual and state conduct globally, and such restrictions are often backed by global sanctions of varying kinds, such as trade retaliation, withdrawal of cooperation, imposition of embargoes and even military intervention in cases of extreme transgressions. As a vivid example, states' immigration policies have coercive implications for individuals at large. Borders keep people out and are protected by well-armed guards. Immigration policies are indeed domestic, and so one might retort that this tells us nothing about *global* coercion as such. But one has to note that it is the international 'state system' that sanctions the bounded territorial state and grants states the power of self-determination including the authority to control movement. Individual states have standing to exercise coercion over immigration thanks to the presence of the constructed state system (Brock, 2020). State-level coercion in this regard is made possible because of a coercive global order that we have put in place. It might very well be true that there is no viable alternative to the state system. But this is precisely why it is all the more important that this unavoidable coercive arrangement has to pass the legitimacy test (that is, by undertaking global distributive commitments).

CONCLUSION

The philosophical debate over global egalitarianism is in the first instance normative and conceptual. What is equality, and why and how does it matter? Is equality a value in itself or only in relation to other values? However, the philosophical debate can also run into disputes over more factual matters, such as the causal connection between equality and the other values that it is supposed to support (see Malerba & Barrientos, Chapter 22 in this volume). The need to attend to the empirics of the world is clearest in discussions about possible indirect considerations for global equality. The arguments – by Rawls for instance – that there are no indirect reasons for worrying about global equality on grounds of poverty, social stigmatisation and global political fairness, are too quick. On the contrary, the state of the world suggests that these indirect reasons do motivate the case for global egalitarianism. But ultimately these are empirical disagreements to be resolved by a better socio-scientific understanding of the world.

If global equality is a requirement of justice, what are its implications for global governance? Global taxation, such as a global resource tax, whereby countries are taxed on the market value of the natural resources they extract from their territories is one possibility (Pogge, 2002). More generally, it will require an attitude shift and the adoption of new global norms. For instance, intellectual property rights, trade rules, technology transfer and so on, could be guided by the principle of prioritising the interests of the disadvantaged. A more globally egalitarian approach to environmental conservation will also formalise the transfer of funds from wealthy countries to poor ones to offset the protection, restoration and opportunity costs of environmental conservation (Armstrong, 2023). These proposals for new forms of global governance will face the tough challenge of mustering the necessary political will. But this does not mean that they are infeasible or unrealistic (for example, in the sense of being contrary to human nature).

REFERENCES

Armstrong, C. (2023). Global Justice and the Opportunity Costs of Conservation. *Conservation Biology, 37*(2).

Beitz, C. (1979). *Political Theory and International Relations*. Princeton University Press.

Blake, M. (2001). Distributive Justice, State Coercion, and Autonomy. *Philosophy and Public Affairs, 30*(3), 257–96.

Brock, G. (2009). *Global Justice: A Cosmopolitan Account*. Cambridge University Press.

Brock, G. (2020). *Justice for People on the Move*. Cambridge University Press.

Caney, S. (2005). *Justice beyond Borders*. Oxford University Press.

James, A. (2012). *Fairness in Practice*. Oxford: Oxford University Press.

Jones, C. (1999). *Global Justice*. Oxford University Press.

Lippert-Rasmussen, K. (2015). *Luck Egalitarianism*. Bloomsbury Publishing.

Miller, D. (2007). *National Responsibility and Global Justice*. Oxford University Press.

Nielsen, K. (1979). Radical Egalitarian Justice: Justice as Equality. *Social Theory and Practice, 5*(2), 209–26.

Pogge, T. (2002). *World Poverty and Human Rights*. Polity Press.

Rawls, J. (1999). *The Law of Peoples*. Harvard University Press.

Tan, K. C. (2010). Poverty and Distributive Justice. In D. Bell (ed.), *Ethics and World Politics*, 256–73. Oxford University Press.

Tan, K. C. (2019). Global Egalitarianism. In J. Gordon et al. (eds.), *Ethics in International Relations*. Routledge.

EPILOGUE

This book set out to address a significant gap in the literature by providing a comprehensive analysis of justice in global economic governance from both normative and empirical perspectives. By bringing together leading scholars from political philosophy, law, economics and political science, we present a multifaceted understanding of how global economic governance can and should be reformed to promote justice.

Through the assessment of key areas such as trade, investment, finance, labour, taxes, intellectual property rights, digitalisation and natural resources, this volume has demonstrated the interdependencies and multidimensional nature of global economic governance. Each chapter, whether focusing on empirical data or normative theory, has contributed to a better understanding of the current state and future possibilities for more just global governance arrangements. By integrating insights from multiple disciplines and domains, we offer a richer and more comprehensive understanding of the challenges and potential solutions and the possibility of learning and integrating insights across the various governance domains. Our book thereby underscores the importance of interdisciplinary collaboration in tackling the complex issues of global economic governance.

As the world continues to grapple with the challenges of globalisation and de-globalisation, the need for just and effective global economic governance becomes ever more pressing. We hope that the insights and proposals presented in this book will contribute to ongoing debates and inspire further research and policy action aimed at creating a more just and equitable global economic order.

In conclusion, this book provides a pioneering step towards a systematic and integrated analysis of justice in global economic governance. It calls for continued efforts to bridge normative and empirical reflections on global economic governance and encourages the development of governance structures that are fair, inclusive and sustainable for current and future generations.

INDEX

Note: Word by word order. Page numbers in **bold** refer to figures.

EU Authorised Representative:
Easy Access System Europe Mustamäe tee 50, 10621 Tallinn, Estonia
gpsr.requests@easproject.com

Printed and bound by CPI Group (UK) Ltd, Croydon, CR0 4YY
31/01/2026
02045716-0001